THE MORTAL SEA

THE

MORTAL SEA

FISHING THE ATLANTIC

IN THE AGE OF SAIL

———

W. JEFFREY BOLSTER

The Belknap Press of Harvard University Press

Cambridge, Massachusetts, and London, England

First Harvard University Press paperback edition, 2014

Library of Congress Cataloging-in-Publication Data
Bolster, W. Jeffrey
The mortal sea : fishing the Atlantic in the Age of Sail / W. Jeffrey Bolster.
p.   cm.
Includes bibliographical references and index.
ISBN 978-0-674-04765-5 (cloth : alk. paper)
ISBN 978-0-674-28396-1 (pbk.)
1. Fisheries—North Atlantic Ocean—History.   2. Fishers—North
Atlantic Ocean—History.   3. Atlantic Coast (New England)—History.
4. Atlantic Coast (Canada)—History.   I. Title.   II. Title: Fishing
the Atlantic in the Age of Sail.
SH213.5.B65 2012
639.209163'1—dc23   2012010747

CONTENTS

PREFACE

I'm not a fisherman, though I know something of the craft and the sea after thousands of days and nights underway in the North Atlantic. For years I savored the thrill of the hunt and the kill, and fed off the anticipation that always accompanied hauling back, when we never really knew what was on the end of the line. My first fish was a tautog, a "blackfish" as Dad called it, landed around 1960 from his skiff, the *Irish Rover,* in Connecticut's Norwalk Islands. Flounder followed, and eels, and snapper blues in my youth. Later my old shipmate and fishing master, Doug Hardy, had us jigging squid in Maine's Muscongus Bay, gill-netting spiny dogfish in Delaware Bay, and trolling the slippery edges of the Gulf Stream. During the late 1970s I jigged on Brown's Bank one notable summer day until we were knee-deep in cod, arms numb from landing fish on three-pound stainless-steel jigs that were lethal, even without bait, in the mysterious crosscurrents below.

Back then, before I understood the plight of the living ocean—or knew that thoughtful fishermen from generations past had realized they were hitting it too hard—I enthusiastically long-lined swordfish on the northeast peak of Georges Bank, east of Cape Cod. As skipper aboard the schooner *Harvey Gamage,* during the 1980s, I once fished fifty miles seaward of Cape Hatteras in a run of tuna that would not stop hitting yellow-feather lures despite an intensifying fall gale; and as mate aboard *R/V Westward* tagged sharks one summer, for scientists, in the North Atlantic fog. Throughout the years, I've continued to talk fish with high-liners in Brigus, Newfoundland; Lunenburg, Nova Scotia; Boothbay, Maine; and Gloucester, Massachusetts. But I'll never be in the inner circle. I don't think like a fish. And my satisfaction at watching noble animals such as sharks and blue marlin shake the hook and flee lingers still. One doesn't easily forget the tenacious glint of life in their eyes. Sometimes I think I know too much now about changes in the sea to fish anymore, but the question is really one of scale. How many fish should one catch?

Scale is one of the unsung quandaries of historical writing, too. Historians always begin by gazing back at a vast and virtually limitless past from which they intend to reconstruct telling moments and trends. We uncover a bit here, and illuminate a bit there, knowing, of course, that most of that past will remain shrouded in darkness. The rub comes in deciding what is sufficiently large to be meaningful but not so large as to be unfathomable. Engineers, for whom precision is everything, routinely mark drafts and plans "N.T.S." (not to scale), reserving their official stamp for a final product whose precision is guaranteed. Sometimes I envy them. Historical writing works differently. Each of us selects a scale that seems appropriate, and applies it as best we can to the challenge at hand. This seemed especially daunting as I looked back at the ocean, which I wanted to write into history, but which covers 71 percent of the surface of our Earth and seems older than time.

As a historian of early America trained in the conventions of my craft, but convinced that the time had come for historians to take the living ocean seriously, and to include its stories in our work, I wanted to reconstruct a vivid and immediate history peopled by flesh-and-blood individuals making what, they hoped, were the best decisions in the circumstances they faced. But I also wanted to tell a story sufficiently large to show dramatic changes in the sea over time, a story that would peel back shadowy layers from a supposedly "traditional" past. So the book in your hands is not about the Seven Seas—only the North Atlantic. It ranges across more than a thousand years, back to the Viking Age, though it covers intensively only the four centuries from 1520 to 1920, the long transition to industrialized fishing in which the western Atlantic—my old stomping grounds—had center stage. Beginning the story well before industrialization emphasizes the longevity of people's short-sighted impact on the ocean, and emphasizes, as well, how modern technology was not necessary to affect the balance of nature. With its deep roots, this tale is probably the longest history possible of Euro-Americans' interaction with any aspect of their natural environment, a story of unrealistic hopes, frequently articulated concerns, destruction, and denial.

Until rather recently, mere decades actually, the combined heft of tradition, literature, and science insisted the sea was immortal—despite centuries of evidence to the contrary. My generation may have been the last to come of age influenced by those flawed assumptions. Uncovering long-lost evidence about human impact on the sea and asking why that evidence had been ignored so long seemed like a worthwhile challenge for someone who had spent so much time at sea, but knew less of it than he imagined.

I owe a great deal to the environmental historians and historical marine ecologists who preceded me, although I confess that my greatest inspiration remains that of Joseph Conrad, the Victorian seaman and novelist who threw down the gauntlet when he wrote: "My task which I am trying to achieve is, by the power of the written word to make you hear, to make you feel—it is, before all, to make you *see*. That—and no more, and it is everything."

This is a big story. I hope I have got the scale right. If nothing else, this book may explain why my fishing days are behind me, and why—without genuinely historical perspectives on changes in the sea—we can have no idea of the magnitude of the restoration challenges we face.

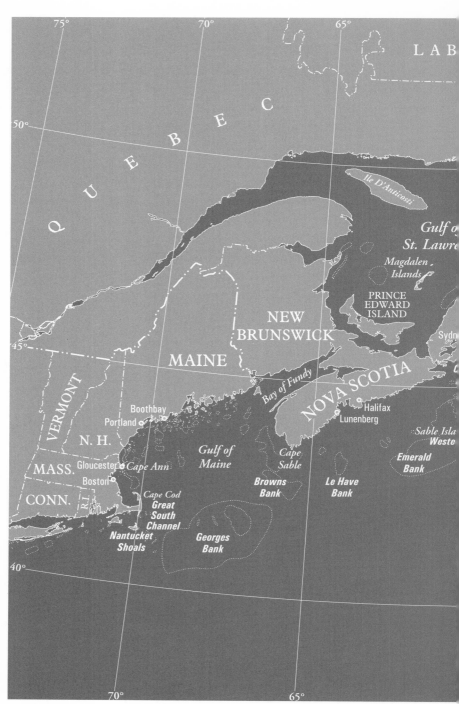

Major fishing grounds in the Northwest Atlantic—Cape Cod to the Grand Banks of Newfoundland

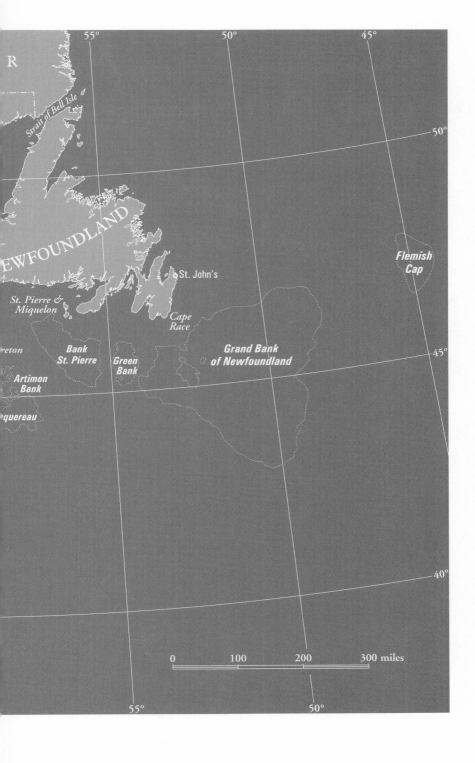

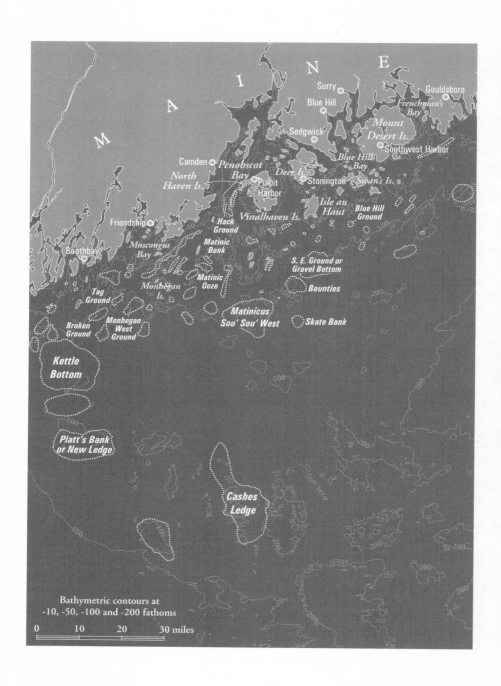

MAINE

Surry
Blue Hill
Gouldsboro
Frenchman's Bay
Sedgwick
Mount Desert Is.
Southwest Harbor
Camden
Penobscot Bay
Blue Hill Bay
North Haven Is.
Deer Is.
Pulpit Harbor
Stonington
Swans Is.
Friendship
Hack Ground
Vinalhaven Is.
Isle au Haut
Blue Hill Ground
Matinic Bank
Boothbay
Muscongus Bay
S. E. Ground or Gravel Bottom
Matinic Ooze
Monhegan Is.
Bounties
Tag Ground
Matinicus Sou' Sou' West
Skate Bank
Broken Ground
Monhegan West Ground

Kettle Bottom

Platt's Bank or New Ledge

Cashes Ledge

Bathymetric contours at
-10, -50, -100 and -200 fathoms

0   10   20   30 miles

Coastal Maine, from Boothbay to Schoodic Point

PROLOGUE

The Historic Ocean

———

He [mankind] cannot control or change the ocean as, in his brief tenancy of earth, he has subdued and plundered the continents.

—Rachel Carson, *The Sea Around Us* (1951)

On clear, dry days in the age of sail, with fish coming over the rail, the coast of northern New England and Atlantic Canada could charm the most hardened fisherman. Green-capped islands and barren dark rocks, each girt round by waterline stripes of living white barnacles and fringed with mustard-hued bladder wrack, protruded from waters teeming with life. Offshore, dainty petrels skimmed the surface plucking tiny invertebrates from the sea, while white gannets with six-foot wingspans plunged into the schools of baitfish on which cod thrived. Vast armies of porpoises, the horsemen of the sea, arced across the surface like cavalry rolling across a plain. And every cod yanked unceremoniously from the hook had, as fishermen said, a coin in its mouth. Still, when the wind veered to the northeast and the sky closed with the sea, the stunning productivity of that ecosystem came with a price.

Half-tide ledges lurked for the unwary in those fish-rich seas. In that fickle environment, where a rapidly falling barometer brought gale-force winds and ship-killing waves, fog could reduce a skipper's world within minutes to a hazy circle only three waves wide. Hercules Hunking, a Cornish immigrant to New England, knew that gray sea in its moods during the 1650s as he hand-lined near New Hampshire's Isles of Shoals from a stoutly planked shallop. The captains of graceful Fredonia schooners, such as the *Effie M. Morrissey*, who dory-trawled for cod on the offshore banks around 1900, and unloaded their salted fares at Boston's T Wharf, knew it intimately as well. For centuries the constancy of the threats meant that time-tested routines guided those who dared to wrest a living from the tempestuous North Atlantic. Tradition deter-mined the appropriate beam for a boat of a certain length. Tradition influ-enced how a man set his gear, and which jigs he picked for handlining on a given bank in a specific season. Sometimes those traditions kept fishermen alive in their dangerous calling.

Tradition wore other faces along the coast. For centuries, from Cape Cod to Newfoundland the return of fish, birds, and marine mammals—each in their season—sparked quiet rejoicing in fishing towns and outport villages. Many of those communities had few economic alternatives to harvesting the sea, and fishing folk chose to believe that the sea would provide forever. That belief dovetailed with the attitude of naturalists and scientists, who often in-sisted, at least until the mid-twentieth century, that the sea was eternal and unchanging, even though almost every generation of harvesters noted evidence to the contrary and raised disturbing questions about the perpetuity of the stocks on which they relied. Beginning in the nineteenth century, however, fishermen's hard-won knowledge all too often disappeared as new technologies increased catches. Bumper catches obliterated memories of how the same num-ber of men, with the same gear, fishing in the same place, had been catching fewer fish as time passed—an indicator that stocks were diminishing. Shore-side naturalists' insistence that the sea was eternal and fishermen's periodic loss of vernacular knowledge that stocks were declining reinforced each other. Combined, they camouflaged one of the northwest Atlantic's great untold sea stories, a true tale of changes in the sea.

An irony sharp as a sculpin's spines pervades that story. No profession has ever placed more emphasis on avoiding disaster than seafaring. Mariners in-stinctively anticipated danger, maintained a sharp lookout, and constantly scanned their surroundings for indication of the slightest problem. To relax vigilance was to court catastrophe. Yet disaster struck for both fish and fisher-men, periodically in the seventeenth, eighteenth, and nineteenth centuries, then universally at the end of the twentieth century, in part because neither fishers nor scientists nor policymakers chose to believe that what they were seeing was happening. The sea was not immortal.

Now, at the beginning of a new millennium, reams of evidence document the living ocean's deep predicament and the implications for the rest of our planet. Following publication in the journal *Nature* of an essay estimating that large predatory fish had declined worldwide by 90 percent, *Newsweek*'s cover story on July 14, 2003, asked, "Are the oceans dying?" In its Global Environmental Outlook released in 2007, the United Nations Environmental Programme noted that the number of fish stocks classified as "collapsed" had doubled over the past twenty years, to 30 percent, and it warned of a global collapse of all fished species by 2050 if fishing around the world continued at its current pace. The speed with which this crisis got the attention of ecologists, fisheries managers, and conservationists is head-turning. As Tony J. Pitcher, a respected scientist, noted in 2005, "Ten years ago most fisheries scientists would have reacted to news of a global crisis in fisheries with disbelief. Today few dispute the matter."[1]

A historical approach puts this crisis in perspective. How might our understanding of the past change if the North Atlantic, rather than simply serving the narrative purpose of separating the Old World from the New, was enlisted instead as a player in the historical drama, one that influenced people and was influenced by them? Such an approach would require a new geography of the early modern world to include oceanic regions, a rereading of mariners' canonical narratives, a commitment to marine biology as an essential component of Atlantic history, and a view of the ocean and its harvesters over the *longue durée*. It would be a sea story on a heretofore unimaginable scale.

During the Age of the Ocean, circa 1500 to 1800, Europeans not only crossed oceans, and used them to stitch together empires of commerce and meaning, but relied on ocean products and services as never before. The salient connections were not only *across* oceans, but *between* people and the sea. It has long been known that western Europeans' adaptation to the late medieval and early modern commercial revolution included searches for distant sources of whale oil and merchantable fish.[2] Other relationships between people and the sea have received far less attention. Tides in the Thames River and elsewhere, for instance, were harnessed to make possible enclosed docks for ships. That riparian engineering affected not only the flow and siltation of estuarine rivers, but their tidal range, biological productivity, and ultimately the magnitude of flooding endured by coastal residents. At about the same time, the seaside was recast psychologically (at least for people in the western tradition), from the terrifying edge of the abyss to a sublime and inviting space. The impact on European and colonial littoral resources was immediate and profound as human populations oriented themselves to the shore.[3]

During the seventeenth century, as naturalists began to study the ocean systematically for the first time, coastal lands were being reclaimed from the sea in the Low Countries, in Acadia, and in South Carolina and Georgia. Meanwhile colonists and slaves were diving for pearls in Latin American waters, hunting monk seals and sea turtles in the Caribbean, and fishing in the Chesapeake and other corners of the Atlantic world. Europeans' imperial and colonial expansion was not simply a maritime phenomenon limited to the surface of the sea, but a marine phenomenon whose long reach was refashioning the supposedly eternal ocean. Nowhere was this more apparent than in the lush marine ecosystem of the northwest Atlantic.[4]

Despite the recent flowering of Atlantic history, the story of environmental consequences associated with the formation of the Atlantic world remains veiled, as do the ways in which a changing natural world affected Europeans, colonists, and Natives. Retelling the story of North American discovery and colonization with close attention to the coastal ocean—at once a workplace, treasure house, complicated ecological system, and source of unending mystery—shifts the essence of the narrative considerably. This new story centers upon "changes in the sea," a deeply historical process well under way in the Mediterranean during the Roman Empire, a process already notable in northern European estuaries and coastal seas by the late Middle Ages. The process accelerated with the evolution of an integrated Atlantic economy, and was both cause and effect of European voyages to America. Those changes were neither simply natural phenomena nor localized depletions caused by humans, but a complicated dynamic between natural events and human impacts on the marine environment.

Telling that tale, with its consequences for people, requires a much deeper look into the European past than is often the norm in American histories, for the scale of this tale, like the sea changes it reveals, is immense. But the payoffs are palpable. Connecting ocean time scales to human time scales and writing the ocean into history is not the least of those rewards. Preposterous as it seems, the perspectives of the first generation of explorers in coastal North

America have never been fully understood because their accounts have not been presented in light of what was "normal" in European coastal seas during the sixteenth century. This dimension of the transatlantic sea story and its implications may ultimately be as consequential for human history as the European settlement of North America and the creation of nations there. Yet it is just coming into view.

Proceeding from medieval Europe, this book focuses most intensively on the territory between Cape Cod and Newfoundland, which in the sixteenth and seventeenth centuries became an Atlantic crossroads, a critical site of interactions among Natives, itinerant Europeans, and settlers in search of marine resources. Known for some time by oceanographers as the northeast continental shelf large marine ecosystem (LME), this underwater region and its adjacent shore supported the most storied fisheries in North America.[5] That continental shelf and its adjoining coastline is an ideal place to examine how humans interacted with the marine environment in the preindustrial age, which for most northwest Atlantic fisheries lasted until the early twentieth century. Documented in detail by legions of explorers, settlers, and fishermen during the sixteenth and seventeenth centuries, when it was virtually a pristine ecosystem; then settled by literate, commercial people who kept illuminating records of their activities; and later prominent as one of the birthplaces of modern marine science, the northwest Atlantic has the experience and the evidence that allow us to write the ocean into history.

The story recounted here begins before itinerant European fishermen arrived in the northwest Atlantic, and runs to the era of World War I, when the advent of steam- and gasoline-powered draggers made it clear that large-scale industrialization had come to the fisheries. Long before late-twentieth-century factory trawlers with polyester nets and fish-finding sonar transformed fish-killing from a handliner's art into an efficient industrial enterprise, human hands were remaking the sea. Focusing on the era of "iron men and wooden ships" (a premechanized age characterized by sails, oars, hooks, and handheld harpoons), this history reveals the hidden origins of today's unnatural ocean.[6] Scale matters a great deal in this tale, in both time and space. Each chapter intentionally covers a shorter span of time, from a millennium in the first, to several centuries in the second, to just twenty years in the final one. Yet the pace of ecological change accelerates as the time scale contracts.

For centuries along the coast from Cape Cod to Newfoundland, fishing communities occasionally found themselves in disarray because of changes in the ecosystem. As early as 1720 the *Boston News-Letter* reported: "We hear from the towns on the Cape that the Whale Fishery among them has failed much this Winter, as it has done for several winters past." In 1754 Selectman John Hallet petitioned the province to excuse the town of Yarmouth (on Cape Cod) from sending a representative to the legislature because of that ongoing failure.[7] When the Gulf of Maine menhaden fishery collapsed in 1879, as one resident of Swans Island remembered, "Many of our townsmen lost heavily by this failure . . . and others never recovered from these losses." A decade later, when the mackerel fisheries collapsed after numerous towns had invested considerable capital in sleek mackerel schooners, the town of Pulpit Harbor collapsed too. An island community on North Haven, Maine, the town literally disappeared after discouraged fishermen sold their land to summer rusticators, who removed buildings, wharves, and fish stages to suit their own aesthetic sensibilities.[8]

Towns were not the only communities in disarray along the coast. Marine ecologists use the term *community* to refer to a group of populations of different species that live in the same area: the benthic (seafloor) community in the Gulf of Maine, for instance, includes seaweeds, mollusks, polychaete worms (including the segmented sandworms often used for anglers' bait), scallops, sculpins (a family of small, spiny, omnivorous bottom-dwelling fish with no commercial value), and lobsters, in addition to mobile predators such as cod and halibut that cruise the bottom foraging for prey. Throughout the five centuries that Europeans and their descendants have fished the northwest Atlantic, human maritime communities always have relied on the vitality and productivity of these marine biological communities. It is not just coincidence that right whales were hunted in coastal waters during the seventeenth century, halibut during the nineteenth century, and bluefin tuna during the twentieth; or that lobstering accounts for the lion's share of fishermen's effort in the early twenty-first century. Although market whims and changing technology were partly responsible for those shifts, a greater truth is that each human generation's chances existed in light of what the ecosystem could produce, which, in turn, was contingent upon natural factors and the impacts of previous harvesters.[9]

The interactions of human maritime communities with marine biological communities have remained largely uninvestigated because of the enduring assumption that the ocean exists outside of history. Relegated to the role of sublime scene or means of conveyance, and shorn of its genuine mysteries and capacity for change, the ocean appears in most histories as a two-dimensional, air-sea interface—a zone for vessel operations and a means of cultural interactions. Even though familiarity with the ocean and the changing nature of its resources was at the heart of indigenous peoples' and settlers' success, it has remained beyond serious scrutiny. Sentiments of the sort expressed by Henry David Thoreau in the 1850s, during a visit to Cape Cod, have prevailed in the face of facts. "We do not associate the idea of antiquity with the ocean, nor wonder how it looked a thousand years ago," noted Thoreau, "for it was equally wild and unfathomable always."[10] Actually, it wasn't.

With its laden dory cresting a gray North Atlantic wave and its lone fisherman glancing to windward at the ominous fog, Winslow Homer's striking oil painting *The Fog Warning* has often been seen as a master narrative of traditional fisheries. Painted in 1885 at Prout's Neck, Maine, when a vast fleet of American schooners still fished the offshore banks, Homer's traditional fishing scene reassured viewers that despite the flux and uncertainty of their Gilded Age lives, heroic Down East fishermen were still at work on the eternal sea. In fact Homer's halibut fisherman tub-trawling from a dory in 1885 was anything but traditional; New England fishermen had first deployed dories from schooners a scant thirty years earlier. By the middle of the nineteenth century, as catches decreased, men had begun to leave their schooners to set longlines from dories, increasing the area in which they fished and the number of hooks they deployed. Tub-trawling (as contemporaries called long lining, because the lines were coiled in tubs) increased fishermen's catching power from 4 hooks to 400 or more. Despite its expansion of risk for fishermen, dory-fishing with tub-trawls became accepted as a way to compensate for declining catches of halibut, cod, and other bottom fish. Atlantic halibut, the dead fish in the painting, were the largest member of the flounder family, mere "trash fish" in fishermen's eyes until the 1830s, when merchants created markets for halibut. But this large, slow-growing fish, late to mature and reproduce, was extraordinarily vulnerable to fishing pressure. The species had already been seriously overfished in New England and Atlantic Canada by 1885; the previous year one expert noted that "halibut are very scarce . . . and vessels have to hunt for new grounds and fish in deep water." Some Yankee skippers were already ranging as far afield as Iceland, on the northern fringes of Europe, to fill their holds.[11]

Seen in this light, Homer's *Fog Warning* depicts a specific historical and ecological moment rather than a timeless fishing scene. Technologically, it represented the brief era of tub-trawling, which ran from the 1850s to the 1920s. Ecologically, it was the tail end of a relatively brief halibut bonanza, which extirpated one of the northwest Atlantic's largest apex predators. Historically, it was a little-known moment between the two well-known bookends that define the Euro-American experience in the northwest Atlantic coastal ecosystem: the incredible abundance of marine organisms encountered by explorers like Jacques Cartier and Captain John Smith, and the impoverished remnant of the ocean ecosystem with which we live today.

About the time that Homer released *The Fog Warning* to great acclaim, Joseph Nudd was lobstering from a dory each summer off Great Boar's Head, a promontory jutting seaward from Hampton, New Hampshire. Nudd tended his traps as the weather allowed; his wife and sister, capitalizing on summer boarders' attraction to tourist rooming houses along the beach, boiled and served the lobster. His great-grandson Bob, standing on a wharf near Hampton in the fall of 2007, had the easy assurance of a man who had been fishing for thirty-five years, a man who had seen it all, and who could fix anything. Anything, that is, except the coastal ecosystem in which he had worked and defined himself for decades, and the managers who controlled it. "It's a tragedy that the fisheries have come to this," he said, his voice cracking with emotion, as we talked about his career and fishing heritage. "I'm a very bitter person when it comes to the way the fisheries were regulated. They took my right to fish away. My family came to Hampton in 1643. To the best of my knowledge there has been at least one person in every generation fishing or in the coastal trade. Very simply, I am the last Nudd that will ever participate in the fisheries after 360 years or so. I'm the end of a tradition that began in 1643."[12]

Bob had started on an inshore dragger out of Rye Harbor one winter in the 1970s, but he was a lobsterman now, and an excellent one, fishing 1,200 traps from his 35-foot Bruno & Stillman, the *Sheila Anne*. Until 1991, when groundfish stocks in the Gulf of Maine collapsed, he gillnetted cod, pollock, and haddock each winter and spring, and lobstered the rest of the year, interspersed with trips to Stellwagen Bank or other grounds where he caught tuna for the Tokyo market. As he put it, with satisfaction, "I'd handline bluefin any day instead of take a vacation." His words came with the same evident satisfaction and involuntary smile that animated his other stories of past abundance, of finding "all the haddock you wanted" only "seven or eight miles offshore"; or how "in the '70s, when I first started, we always had a baitnet on the boat. Could fill the net with mackerel. Set it right on the beach." Or how "during that time when I was growing up the river always had herring, mackerel, and pollock. All the lobstermen torched herring," that is, attracted them with torches or spotlights. "Two of us could supply the whole harbor [with bait] in one night." From the perspective of this thoughtful and quietly competent man, born in 1947 and rooted in one place in a way that few Americans can imagine, a massive sea change had occurred in his own lifetime. "A person in the fishery now," he emphasized, "even one making money and being satisfied, has no idea what it was like when it was good."[13]

In order to make sense of the changes that occurred in the sea in Bob Nudd's lifetime, it is necessary to return to the era of *The Fog Warning* and long before, to the moment of Europeans' encounter with the pristine ecosystem of coastal North America. Bob Nudd's was not the first generation of fishermen to yearn for the days "when it was good." Changes in the sea had been occurring since the end of the seventeenth century. The warning signs existed in virtually every generation, and in many instances fishermen were the ones who drew attention to them. After the middle of the nineteenth century change occurred so rapidly as to make the notion of "traditional fisheries" obsolete, comforting though it remained to influential writers such as Sarah Orne Jewett, whose *Country of the Pointed Firs,* published in 1896, conveyed the self-reliance and timelessness of Down East fishing towns.[14]

The earliest explorers and fishermen arriving in North America brought with them their perspectives on the late medieval and early modern European ecosystems that they knew firsthand, ecosystems quite similar to those of the New World except that they had already been fished hard for centuries. Explorers' narratives of abundance were thus framed by Europe's depleted estuaries and coastal ocean. By the inauguration of George Washington, the large marine ecosystem between Cape Cod and Newfoundland had been reshaped by localized depletions, range contractions, and near extinctions. Human-induced ecological change affected oceanic and estuarine structure and function. Those changes, in turn, shaped the possibilities open to coastal people. Financial loss, technological innovation, geographic exploration, and refashioning of social identities followed changes in the sea.

Concerns about overfishing are hardly new. By the nineteenth century at least, in certain times and places, it was common knowledge that when the same number of men, using the same gear, fished on the same ground for a set time, catches were smaller. Marine environmental history illuminates what ecologist Daniel Pauly has called the "shifting baseline syndrome." Each generation imagined that what it saw first was normal, and that subsequent declines were aberrant. But no generation imagined how profound the changes had been prior to their own careers. The halibut fisherman in Homer's painting and lobsterman Bob Nudd each experienced declining catches. That they were by no means the first is the single most compelling finding of five hundred years of fisheries history.[15]

Schooner crews from Massachusetts fishing off Nova Scotia, for instance, watched their seasonal landings of cod decrease by more than 50 percent from 1852 to 1859. It is still not clear to what extent natural fluctuations, or overfishing, or some combination, contributed to the decline of cod. Fishermen at the time, however, blamed overfishing by large French factory ships, each of which set longlines with thousands of hooks. Astute handliners, fearing the ruthless efficiency of new longline technology, petitioned the Massachusetts legislature during the 1850s to outlaw longlines, arguing that without such a ban haddock and other bottom fish soon would become "scarce as salmon." But by the 1860s most New Englanders were setting longlines themselves, losing sight of their own guild's knowledge that catches were decreasing because of overfishing. By the turn of the century, New Englanders lamented the commercial extinction of Atlantic halibut, the disappearance of menhaden north of Cape Cod, the crash of mackerel and lobster populations in the Gulf of Maine, and the depletion of bottom fish on inshore grounds. Some men insisted on their God-given or supposedly constitutional right to fish and to dig clams as they always had; while others pointed out that circumstances had changed, and that limitless harvesting was pushing to the brink the resources on which they relied.[16]

Meanwhile, turn-of-the-century scientists promoted intensification of commercial fisheries even as nature's production appeared unable to keep up with increasing demands. Then, around World War I, steam-, gasoline-, and diesel-powered draggers began to replace hookfishing from schooners. Catches rose exponentially. An avalanche of cheap fish silenced the concerns of conservation-minded fishermen. Between 1900 and 1920 fishermen regularly adopted technologies that their parents and grandparents had protested because of their ruthless efficiency and because they sensed there were fewer fish in the sea. My attempt to lay a foundation for a new generation of sea stories ends there. It is a tale of ecological transformation in the coastal sea before mechanized harvesting, a tale that unfolds in light of village economies, sea-food corporations, law, and art in coastal New England and Atlantic Canada. It is the tale of a sea of ghosts.

Humans have long been captivated by the ocean's mysteries, its moods and fogs, its diurnal tidal pulse, its extraordinary creatures, and its effects on people's imaginations and communities. Rarely though, have we understood that we share with the ocean a common destiny—that oyster reefs, bluefin tuna, and invasive periwinkles are the stuff of history. It's not just that the ocean, covering 71 percent of our blue planet, is, as one scientist recently observed, the Earth's heart and lungs, the great climate driver and stabilizer that makes our planet livable. That geophysical perspective, for all its profundity, is based on ahistorical deep time. By shifting time scales to the realm of history, and by concentrating on documentable and remembered phenomena, the living ocean, in all its vastness and vulnerability, becomes connected to human societies in intimate and time-specific ways. That seems like a story worth telling, a sea story with the ocean included. Perhaps it will contribute to the restoration of marine ecosystems. In the time-honored words of Newfoundland fishermen, "We must live in hopes."[17]

One

DEPLETED EUROPEAN SEAS
AND THE DISCOVERY OF AMERICA

The Native Staple of each Country is the Riches of the
Country, and is perpetual and never to be consumed;
Beasts of the Earth, Fowls of the Air, and Fishes of the
Sea, Naturally Increase.

—Nicholas Barbon, *A Discourse of Trade*, 1690

Renaissance seafarers and cartographers confronted the "great and marvelous things of the Ocean Sea" in astonishing ways after 1522, when the remnant
of Ferdinand Magellan's tattered fleet arrived in Seville following their unprecedented circumnavigation. Within a few years Antonio Pigafetta, the most
literary of the survivors, produced a memorable account of that Ocean Sea's
immensity and exotic variety, a tantalizing tale of "contrary winds, calms,
and rains" in the equatorial doldrums, "large fish with fearsome teeth called
tiburoni" in the South Atlantic, and incomprehensibly gigantic shellfish near
Borneo—"the flesh of one which weighed twenty-six pounds and the other
forty-four." As similar reports by other explorers trickled back to Europe along
far-flung sea routes from the West Indies to the Straits of Magellan and Asian
archipelagos, the ocean frontier and its web of life appeared ever more mysterious and provocative.[1]

Meanwhile Basque, Breton, Portuguese, and English West Country fishermen quietly crossed the Atlantic each spring to fish near Newfoundland and

in the Gulf of St. Lawrence. There they encountered a familiar marine ecosystem that was "new" only in the sense that it had not been systematically harvested for centuries by fishermen using sophisticated technologies to catch,
preserve, and market sea fish. This was distinct from the Philippine Seas, where
Magellan's men had seen "large sea snails, beautiful in appearance," probably
chambered nautilus *(Nautilus pompilius);* or from the American tropics, where
oysters improbably grew on mangrove trees, and where crystal-clear waters
prompted European newcomers such as Christopher Columbus to startle readers with depictions of fish "so unlike ours that it is amazing," fish "of the brightest colors in the world—blue, yellow, red, multi-colored, colored in a thousand
ways." Gonzalo Fernández de Oviedo's *Natural History of the West Indies,*
available in London in English translation as early as 1555, reinforced the Caribbean's bizarre allure. It introduced English readers to an ecosystem populated by "manatee and murene and many other fishes which have no names in
our language." The experience of Magellan, Columbus, and Oviedo could
not have been more different from that of the Englishman Anthony Parkhurst,
who found himself in the midst of a reassuringly familiar sea near Newfoundland in 1578. "As touching the kindes of Fish beside Cod," he wrote," there are
Herrings, Salmons, Thorneback [skates], Plase, or rather wee should call
them Flounders, Dog fish . . . Oisters, and Muskles." Customers of English
fishmongers would not flinch from such fare or need to cultivate a taste for
the exotic. The living ocean along the northeast coast of America mirrored
Englishmen's coastal ecosystem at home.[2]

Riveted to a land-centered geography, modern people have difficulty imagining the meaningful oceanic areas that were second nature for experienced
mariners at the birth of the Atlantic world, or how areas of the coastal ocean
had already been changed by human influences. Sixteenth-century voyages
such as Sir Humphrey Gilbert's reconnoitering of Newfoundland in 1583 have
almost always been presented as a passage from the Old World to the New
World rather than as an episode occurring in a single oceanic region. But the
experienced men aboard Gilbert's small ship saw it both ways: what English
sailors called the "New-found-land" was surrounded by a familiar sort of sea,
albeit one swarming with fish.[3]

A pamphlet published by Robert Hitchcock in 1580 suggests how contemporaries understood the fishing banks of Newfoundland as something like an
extension of the Irish Sea. Lobbying his countrymen to build 400 "fishyng
Shippes: after manner of Flemmish Busses," as Dutch herring boats were then

known, Hitchcock, a military strategist, veteran of wars on the Continent, and fisheries promoter, envisioned that in "March, having victuals for five months, with hooks, lines, and salt," each town's fleet could "set out to fish for Cod and Ling where . . . the Town liketh best; or else to Newfoundland." Hitchcock's Elizabethan rendering of the North Atlantic crossing as commonplace not only puts fishermen back into the story of American beginnings where they belong, but, more importantly, illuminates the boreal North Atlantic as a single eco- system linking the coast of Lancashire with the banks of Newfoundland—a system being affected by human activities at different rates in different places.[4]

When Hitchcock and his contemporaries advocated expanding England's fisheries, they did not imagine an "Atlantic Ocean" separating Europe from America. The sailors working in what we call the northwest Atlantic, whether English, Basque, French, Spanish, or Portuguese, understood that they were fishing on the periphery of a body of water called variously the "Western Ocean," "Mar Del Nort," or "Great Ocean Sea." During the 1520s, when the colonization and importance of North America still lay far in the future, ocean basins were neither named nor conceptualized in the constant ways that seem natural today. The term *Atlantic,* for instance, did not become commonplace until the seventeenth century; it was not used consistently until the eighteenth century. By then, of course, the Atlantick Sea (or Atlantic Ocean) was under- stood to separate Europe from America. During the sixteenth century, how- ever, when whale oil from the Gulf of St. Lawrence illuminated European lamps and lubricated primitive European bearings, when dried cod from the coasts of Newfoundland filled the bellies of European soldiers, artisans, and town-dwellers, and when thousands of transient European mariners frequented those distant shores each year, the North American mainland remained vague at best beyond the distance of a harquebus shot from the shore. The outline of Newfoundland itself was not even accurately mapped until 1612, when Samuel de Champlain turned his considerable cartographic skills to the challenge. And for a century beforehand, Renaissance seafarers saw the real action as neither in "America" nor in the "Atlantic Ocean," but on the shallow extremi- ties of the "Great Ocean Sea."[5]

From the standpoint of those sixteenth-century European fishermen more familiar with tarred hemp rope and leather fishing aprons than with charts of the world, and more comfortable talking about seasonal baits and favorable bottom conditions than about global geography, the cold, gray waters lapping the coast of Newfoundland were rather routine. Every time fishermen working the waters of the North Sea or the English Channel had hauled a net, responded to a tug on their lines, or examined the stomach contents of a recently caught fish to see what it had been eating, they studied the sea's creatures. By the time some of those fishermen began to harvest the waters around Newfoundland and in the Gulf of St. Lawrence during the early sixteenth century, the similarities with home waters were striking. Whether in the Irish Sea or on the Grand Banks of Newfoundland, fishermen watched fulmars wheeling overhead, eager for bits of "gurry," the entrails and bits of flesh discarded when cleaning fish. At night, when conditions were right for dinoflagellates and other bioluminescent organisms, disturbances in the water lingered as a ghostly green trace, whether prompted by the splash of a lead line or by a dolphin's sinuous track. Shoals of silvery herring rose to the surface after sunset. Cod took bait by day; hake, by night. Most of the starfish, anemones, lobsters, and whelks looked the same. So did toothless, filter-feeding basking sharks as they plowed slowly through nutrient-rich waters with their oversized mouths agape. Some of those sharks were longer than the stoutly planked shallops from which men fished. Other sea monsters, such as the ninety-footer that washed ashore at Tynemouth in 1532 (probably a blue whale) or "the piercing serpent . . . that is in the sea" (referred to in the book of Isaiah), were regarded as portents or supernatural prodigies—glimpses of the inexplicable that struck fishermen with fear and reinforced the skimpiness of their understanding of the world beneath their keels.[6] As they cleared kelp from their anchors and peered over the side at the fish on their lines, fishermen could not help but see the northwest Atlantic ecosystem as biologically and geologically akin to the northeast Atlantic they had left behind.

Oceanographers refer to that great arc of ocean stretching westward from the British Isles to Newfoundland as the North Atlantic boreal region. It includes the North Sea, the Irish Sea, the English Channel, the Norwegian Sea, the waters south of Iceland and Greenland, and the large marine ecosystem from the north coast of Cape Cod to Newfoundland and southern Labrador. With its eastern and western edges sculpted by the Pleistocene glaciations; its similarities in ocean temperature, productivity, food supplies, and predator-prey relationships; and its relatively uniform populations of boreal fish, including herring, cod, and salmon, the historic North Atlantic boreal region was characterized by defining unities; in fact the European and American boreal coasts share many identical animals and plants, and many others that are very similar.

Biogeography, or the correspondence of organisms to place, is the basis for contemporary oceanographers' division of the oceans into natural regions. Seawater temperature is the single most important factor in defining those regions. Sixteenth- and seventeenth-century seamen understood the basic relationship between ocean temperature and resident species. They understood in an elemental way that the Mediterranean was a separate biogeographical region from the North Atlantic boreal region, and that each was separate from the Arctic Sea. The warm, saline Gulf Stream served as the southern boundary to the entire North Atlantic boreal region; icy subarctic waters created its northern boundary. While some species such as bluefin tuna, swordfish, and humpback whales migrated from one distinct oceanic region to another, most species thrived within a certain range of water temperatures. A sixteenth-century mariner leaving the English Channel for the Bay of Biscay would have confronted albacore, anchovy, pilchards, and conger eel. Sailing north through the Celtic Sea toward the Faroe Islands, he would have found ling, herring, and harbor seals. Temperature mattered. "Greenland" was the *"slaughtering house"* of the world, according to Daniel Pell in 1659, because of its vast population of "the great and warlike *Horses* of the Sea," now known as walrus, a temperature-sensitive marine mammal. Walrus, like most other creatures, congregated in specific regions of the sea. Sixteenth- and seventeenth-century voyages to Newfoundland from northern France and the British Isles sometimes took place entirely within the North Atlantic boreal region. More commonly, outbound shipmasters encountering prevailing westerlies on a starboard tack were forced to the southwest into warmer waters, where "the strange fish which we there saw," according to Christopher Levett in 1623, included "some with wings flying above the water." Flying fish, along with the blunt-headed and multihued dorado, denizens of the tropics and temperate Atlantic drift current, were strangers to boreal seas.[7]

European fishermen's complacent familiarity with the northwest Atlantic's marine ecosystem during the sixteenth century has not fitted well with the dominant narrative of America as a New World. Romantic national histories of the sort that flowered during the nineteenth century, and which still have many readers in their grip, had a desperate need for colonial beginnings, such as the voyage of the *Mayflower* or the settlement of Quebec. Nationalist historians regarded the ocean as a non-place, an apparently eternal source of fish and whales, an inscrutable testing ground, and a dangerous, if necessary, means of conveyance. The eventual colonization of North America by Europeans, and the subsequent creation of nations there, however, overshadowed the fact that for more than a century the familiar coastal marine ecosystem was the only part of North America of consistent interest to Europeans. Sixteenth- and early-seventeenth-century maps of what are now Atlantic Canada and New England delineated the sea from the shore with a single line, revealing little detail of the interior landmass, but highlighting the shoals, islands, ocean basins, and river mouths in which European mariners encountered right whales, haddock, mackerel, and herring. For more than a century before permanent settlements took root, transient fishermen were amphibious denizens of the North American coastal environment, fully at home neither on the inhospitable shore nor on its off-lying fishing grounds. Long after European colonization of the region commenced, ocean harvesting remained central to coastal people's economic development and cultural elaboration.

ECOSYSTEMS IN TIME

European fishermen familiar with the North Sea, the English Channel, and the Irish Sea had learned their trade in one of the world's most productive fishing grounds, a set of ecosystems in which humans had been players to varying degrees for millennia. Ecosystems can be imagined as functional units consisting of all of their organisms (including humans) interacting with one another and their physical environment through time. Ecosystems are natural, but never timeless. In both terrestrial and marine ecosystems, "natural" does not equate with "static," and the complicated functioning of an ecosystem, in which fluctuations are inherent, can be shifted significantly by nonhuman natural events, such as storms or climate change, or by intensive human pressure, such as overharvesting or habitat alteration. A schematic presentation of ecosystems' functioning can all too easily convey the impression of consistency, but attention to timescales and changes over time are especially germane when one is examining the living ocean.

The ocean is an extraordinarily changeable environment, much more so than many terrestrial ones. Seasonal and annual variations exist, as on shore, along with cyclical variations and gradual trends in species composition, ecosystem productivity, and other characteristics. The sea itself is sharply divided in places by thermoclines, layers of water that separate areas differing in temperature. It is anything but immutable. The ocean changes daily, seasonally, and historically, as well as over evolutionary and geological time.[8]

Ecological timescales in the sea vary from those on land. The primary producers at the base of the marine food chain are phytoplankton, microscopic plants that live only for days. The primary producers on land, by contrast, include perennial grasses and trees with life spans measurable in decades or centuries. Marine systems are thus much more responsive than terrestrial ones to modest climate changes. Rising or falling atmospheric temperatures can influence ocean waters in a specific locale, affecting the distribution of phytoplankton, zooplankton (microscopic animals), and ichthyoplankton (larval fish and eggs), which in turn can lead to shifts in the fish communities sought by humans.

For people interested in historical ecosystems and the way humans have affected them, determining some sort of baseline from which to chart change is necessary. However, this is a challenge: research increasingly shows that there has never been an absolute steady baseline marine community—a pristine or natural system. Fluctuations are the norm, and temporary alternative stable states are possible. Human impacts on the system must be assessed against constantly occurring natural change in which, as one biologist puts it, virtually "imperceptible environmental fluctuations may be associated with biological changes of great economic impact."[9] Likewise, economic impacts, such as overfishing or habitat destruction, can lead to substantive biological changes, which may push a coastal ecosystem into an alternative stable state.

Distinguishing between human and nonhuman causes of change in marine ecosystems requires some understanding of the role of environmental variability, including long-term climate change and periodic fluctuations. The North Atlantic Oscillation (NAO) has been one of the primary weathermakers in Europe for millennia, a phenomenon that affected when armies could march, when ships could sail, and whether a given winter would be bearable. Relative differences in atmospheric pressure between Iceland and the Azores create the NAO. Strong westerly winds and relatively mild winters in Europe lead to a high NAO index. Conversely, a low NAO index corresponds to weak westerlies, which allow colder Siberian air to dominate coastal Europe, creating more severe winter weather conditions.

Those oscillations determined more than which harbors would freeze or how many baskets of faggots and turf were needed to withstand a winter. They influenced the availability of herring, that staff of life in Christian Europe on the numerous meatless days of the Roman Catholic liturgical calendar. Herring was the most widely eaten fish in medieval Europe. Smoked, salted, or pickled, it appeared at meal after meal for both people of means and the common sort. Observant Catholics were not the only consumers of herring. After the Reformation, Protestants from England to Scandinavia sustained their appetite for the silvery little fish. But herring were not universally available. Periods of robust herring landings in the English Channel, the Bay of Biscay, and waters east of Sweden corresponded, it turns out, with severe winter conditions in western Europe, intense sea ice off Iceland, and relatively weak westerly winds. Conversely, long stretches of mild European winters were associated with modest herring catches. This pattern was not entirely understood until 1997, when a study demonstrated correlations between climate fluctuations and herring catches over six centuries, from 1340 to 1978. The important point is that natural cycles, such as the North Atlantic Oscillation, over which humans have little or no influence, provide the background "noise" against which we must look for "signals" indicating human impacts on coastal systems.[10]

Marine environments are so complex that differentiating the signals from the noise is not always straightforward. The significant historical shifts between populations of herring and pilchards (a sardine-like fish) in the western English Channel make the point. Since the Middle Ages fishermen in Cornwall and Brittany have lived by harvesting herring and pilchards, but they understood not only that flush herring years could alternate with lean herring years, but that herring might be replaced by pilchards, or vice versa, sometimes for extended periods. These regime shifts in the western English Channel have occurred for centuries, with real consequences for harvesters and their communities. Herring predominates when one of its favorite foods, a certain species of arrow worm, exists in large numbers. When environmental conditions change so that the zooplankton are dominated by a different species of arrow worm, which pilchards eat, pilchards outnumber herring.[11]

While humans have affected fish populations for centuries, even for millennia in some coastal seas, it is clear that multiyear and decadal fluctuations are "normal" in many marine populations—including ones that humans like to hunt. That is a complicating factor looming in the background of the new field of marine environmental history, in which interdisciplinary study of maritime communities and marine environments must pay attention to linked phenomena occurring on widely varying timescales. The critical challenge is to avoid the false dichotomy that changes in marine systems are caused *either* by human factors (such as overfishing, pollution, or habitat destruction) *or* by natural environmental effects. The impact of fishing occurs in the context of environmental effects, and vice versa. If, for instance, environmental conditions become less favorable for pilchards, continued fishing for pilchards will exacerbate those poor environmental conditions, making it less likely that the pilchard stock will be able to withstand the downturn. The sea is a variable environment that does not provide endlessly or produce eternally. The fact that it changes, both naturally and as a result of human influences, means that it has a history. The fact that people rely on it, and create some of the changes, means that the ocean's history and human histories are entwined.

Seawater is the most deceiving of mediums. Appearing uniform from the surface, or to an observer without instrumentation, the water in most areas of the ocean actually is naturally stratified into layers of different densities, the result of variations in temperature and salinity. Scientists conceptualize those layers as the "water column." Its distinctions are as telling as zoning regulations in a city ashore. The photic zone, or layer through which sunlight penetrates and in which plants can grow, lies on the surface. Meanwhile dense, nutrient-rich water, fertilized with creatures' excrement and the decomposing bodies of dead organisms, settles to the depths. Unmixed seawater remains relatively lifeless; life in the ocean depends on plants, and those microscopic plants can grow only in the presence of *both* light and nutrients. The crucial nutrients include carbon, nitrogen, phosphorous, and silica. If nutrients remain in the depths and the light is limited to the surface, the ocean remains a virtual desert. That is typically the case throughout the seven seas. In certain parts of the world, however, including the eastern and western edges of the North Atlantic boreal region, currents colliding over relatively shallow banks stir seawater in the presence of light. Such mixing is the incubator of life. For instance, nutrient-rich polar water flowing southward toward the British Isles mixes with the eastern extremity of the Gulf Stream on a multitude of historic fishing grounds such as Ballynahinch Bank, Fastnet Ground, and the Patch. In the western Atlantic, the cold, nutrient-laden Labrador Current flows southward and mixes with warm Gulf Stream waters on the storied Grand Banks and Georges Bank, as well as on lesser fishing grounds, some of which receive additional nutrients carried by rivers' runoff. Rotary tidal currents further affect the water column above each of those banks as the twice-daily ebb and flood swirls the sea. The resultant mixing and upwelling provide ideal conditions for free-floating phytoplankton, the microscopic plants at the base of the marine food pyramid.

The productivity in which fishermen were interested (and which was so notable around the British Isles, on the Norwegian coast, in the western Baltic Sea, and along the western Atlantic shore between Cape Cod and Newfoundland) depended on what oceanographers call primary production—the ability of photosynthesizing plants and microalgae to convert nutrients into energy-rich organic compounds in the presence of light.[12] In 1583, when Edward Hayes observed "Abundance of Whales" near Placentia and Grand Bay, Newfoundland, and simultaneously noted silvery schools of "Herring, the largest that have bene heard of, and exceeding the Malstrond herring of Norway," he was sailing through a savory soup chock-full of protein, carbohydrates, and lipids, the phytoplankton and zooplankton of the summer bloom.[13]

Primary productivity in the sea is based on phytoplankton abundance. The microscopic algae known as phytoplankton are either single-celled organisms or short chains of identical cells. With a life span measurable in days, phytoplankton are nevertheless the most important plants in the sea. A single bucket of seawater can hold millions. Diatoms and dinoflagellates, some of which have prickly shapes reminiscent of snowflakes, dominate the boreal phytoplankton. Drifting freely in the surface layer of the sea, these tiny plants harvest sunlight and carbon dioxide while producing both oxygen and the carbohydrates on which large and small herbivores rely. Phytoplankton reproduce by dividing in half, then growing again. During the winter, with low temperatures and light levels, they have little energy for reproduction. When light, temperature, and available nutrients create conducive conditions in the spring, however, phytoplankton reproduce explosively, blooming into vast oceanic pastures. Satellites carrying spectrometers to detect chlorophyll in the sea have revealed phytoplankton pastures in the North Atlantic of 60,000 square kilometers, and occasionally 3 million square kilometers. But the richest concentrations are often above fishing banks, such as those in the Gulf of Maine or the North Sea.[14]

Luxuriant meadows of phytoplankton nourish tiny, filter-feeding animals known collectively as zooplankton. Larval fish (ichthyoplankton) and invertebrates are among the zooplankton; so, too, are creatures such as arrow worms. The most abundant animals in the world are found in zooplankton. Called copepods, these tiny crustaceans are the size of a grain of rice. From the perspective of fishermen, copepods vie with euphausiid shrimp, a one-inch-long omnivore that eats both phytoplankton and zooplankton, as the first-among-equals in zooplankton. Copepods graze in sunlit surface waters. One cope-pod, *Calanus finmarchius,* is a favorite food of herring, shad, menhaden, mack-erel, baleen whales, and other commercially valuable species. A mature right whale, which uses baleen plates to filter the water in its mouth, can eat as much as one ton of zooplankton daily, much of it copepods. Like right whales, Atlan-tic herring are also filter-feeders: they strain zooplankton from the water column with their gill rakers. For centuries fishermen were baffled about what herring ate. The naked eye simply cannot identify the contents in the gut of a herring, which are primarily zooplankton, and as late as the 1550s, when the declining Skånor herring fishery persisted in the straits between Sweden and Denmark, a Swedish observer noted that "This fish has virtually no intestine, or at any rate a meager one, so that nothing is found in its stomach." It took develop-ment of the microscope and plankton nets to determine that wherever herring are found, the sea is swarming with copepods. Euphausiid shrimp, also a fa-vorite food of pelagic fish and baleen whales, generally live in the same waters. (Pelagic fish live on the surface or in the water column, not on the bottom or on reefs.) For centuries fishermen called euphausiids "red feed" for the crim-son flash on their transparent bodies; since the early twentieth century, eu-phausiid shrimp have been known by their Norwegian name, krill.[15]

Like grass in a New England hayfield, phytoplankton generally blooms twice a year in the North Atlantic boreal region, once in late winter or early spring, followed by a lesser bloom in late summer. This multiplying phytoplankton nourishes the entire food web: the tiny herbivorous zooplankton, including co-pepods and larval fish; benthic invertebrates such as polychaete worms and brittle stars; filter-feeders such as basking sharks and right whales; vast schools of bottom-dwelling hake, plaice, and cod; pelagic fish such as herring and mack-erel; and crustaceans such as clams and mussels.

As in New England and the Canadian Atlantic provinces, the European littoral was rife with estuaries and a complex suite of intertidal habitats. Flowing into the coastal ocean were rivers rich in fish, ranging from Scottish salmon streams like the Spey to the mighty Rhine. These aquatic and marine micro-environments contributed to the remarkable overall productivity of Europe's Atlantic coastal fisheries from the Bay of Biscay to Scandinavia. In fact mea-surements of primary productivity, which ecologists express as milligrams of carbon per square meter, are remarkably similar along northern Europe's coast-line and that of northern New England and the Canadian Atlantic provinces.

The primary productivity in the southern part of the North Sea, for instance, also known as the Wadden Sea, is virtually identical with that of the southern Gulf of St. Lawrence. In other words, the ability of the coastal ocean to produce biomass, ranging from plankton to whales, was not appreciably greater in the New World than in the Old. Yet during the 1500s fishermen agreed that codfish were larger and more numerous in American waters, and that big fish existed closer to shore. The abundance and productivity of the western Atlantic's boreal ecosystem appeared dramatically higher than that of the eastern Atlantic. What explained the discrepancy?[16]

DEPLETED EUROPEAN SEAS

Relying primarily on traditional excavation techniques, including painstaking sieving to retrieve bones and other faunal remains, as well as on stable carbon and nitrogen isotope analysis of human skeletal remains, archaeologists have been able to reconstruct when various human communities in Europe began to consume significantly increasing amounts of seafood. After the Mesolithic period (10,000–5,000 radiocarbon years B.P. [before present]), seafood consumption in regions around the North Sea basin declined significantly, not to resume again in a major way until about 1000 A.D. Western Europeans' new orientation to sea fish at that time marked a dramatic turning point in their relationship with the sea.[17]

Evidence indicates that until about 1000 A.D. most fish consumed in Western Europe were locally available freshwater species such as pike, perch, bream, tench, and trout, in addition to anadromous and catadromous species. Anadromous fish such as salmon, sturgeon, and shad are born in freshwater rivers or streams, but migrate to the ocean, where they spend most of their lives, before returning to rivers to spawn. Eels, something of a biological mystery, also were eaten regularly in ancient and medieval Europe. Eels are catadromous fish. Born in the Sargasso Sea, they ascend rivers as tiny, translucent "elvers" (juveniles) to spend their entire lives in fresh or brackish water, until it is time to return to the sea for their once-a-lifetime spawning. Anadromous and catadromous species all shared a moment in their life cycles during which they could be trapped easily by people fishing from the safety of river banks, an apparently providential dispensation of food from the deep-sea sea to the dooryard. Ancient and early-medieval inhabitants of the British Isles and the Continent concentrated their efforts on freshwater and anadromous fish, essentially ignoring plentiful schools of sea fish in close proximity to their shores.[18]

Archaeological excavations from the Low Countries confirm this story. Excavated prehistoric and protohistoric sites in Belgium contain the bones of freshwater fish, but not sea fish. Until the middle of the tenth century some marine mollusks, but no marine fish, were consumed in Ghent, one of the major medieval cities in Belgium. From the middle of the tenth to the end of the twelfth century, however, sea fish rose in importance in householders' diets. In fact archaeological excavations reveal that flatfish such as flounder and plaice were the first marine fish to be regularly consumed, followed by cod, and finally by herring. Flatfish are more easily caught than cod or herring because they spend considerable time in shallow estuaries, such as those flanking the coasts of the Low Countries. Capturing flatfish requires less sophisticated technology than that necessary for herring or cod; they can be speared in shallow water. Around the turn of the millennium Flemish fishermen, like those in England, began to expand their efforts into coastal waters in the southern North Sea. Marine fish were first traded inland from coastal regions, initially to growing urban populations along the Schelde River, and several centuries later along the Meuse. By about 1300 almost all fish eaten in major cities such as Ghent or Antwerp were sea fish.[19]

Of course Roman soldiers and administrators had brought their appetite for oysters, fish, and the zesty fish sauce known as *garum* when they conquered Gaul and Britain at the beginning of the Christian era (50 B.C. to 50 A.D.), along with barbed hooks and net-sinkers of lead or fired clay. Mussels, cockles, limpets, whelks, and oysters appear to have been a considerable part of the Romans' diet at the villa of Llantwit Major. But those were exceptions to the rule. Seafood generally was not harvested in western Europe on a large scale throughout the era of the Roman conquest and the first millennium of the Christian era. Most people in Britain and on the Continent, including those who lived near the sea, ate protein originating primarily from terrestrial creatures or freshwater fish. Even on Orkney and Shetland, the northern isles off Scotland, where one might expect sea-girt residents to turn to the sea, fish and marine mammals were not exploited very intensively before the ninth or tenth century. Fish bones that remain in kitchen middens are from small inshore species, the sort that could be caught with simple gear and without much risk to the fisher. Moreover, note a team of archaeologists, "Stable isotope analysis of human bone collagen also indicates that marine protein was a negligible component of the Northern Isles diet at this time."[20]

Viking invaders, those seafarers nonpareil from the pagan north, became fishmongers to Britain and the Continent, providing technology and expertise that made deep-sea fishing possible. As early as the eighth century Scandinavians were catching, drying, and distributing codfish from the Norwegian Sea in a precommercial "web of obligation and exchange." That would have been air-dried cod preserved without salt, known as stockfish. It kept for years. Stockfish became the staple of Viking civilizations and the food source supporting their notoriously long voyages. And it was the first sea fish traded over extended distances in northern Europe, predating the Hanseatic League's herring business. By the twelfth century, Norse chieftains had inaugurated a genuine commerce in stockfish. By then Viking economic notions—once predicated on honor and power—were being recast in terms of accumulating wealth. This transformation was accelerated by an emerging international system centering upon banking and credit, and by the Viking diaspora that saw Scandinavian settlement in the Faroes, Shetlands, Orkneys, Hebrides, Ireland, Iceland, and Greenland, in addition to their conquest and colonization of parts of England and France, where "Northmen" became the "Normans" of Normandy. Dried cod, once the ration of choice for marauding pagan warriors, insinuated itself into the menu of everyday people during the Middle Ages. Catholic Europeans observing days of abstinence increasingly relied on dried cod and clamored for more.[21]

After the arrival of Viking settlers in the Orkneys, which occurred circa 850–950 A.D., sea-fishing and consumption of sea fish increased noticeably. In York, England, sea-fishing began circa 975–1050; in Norwich, between the late tenth and late eleventh centuries. Increased consumption of seafood began in Eynsham Abbey, in Oxfordshire, between the late eleventh and early twelfth centuries. While a Scots herring fishery existed in the mid-900s, exporting herring to the Netherlands, the beginning of relatively large-scale sea fishing in England and the Low Countries, notably for herring and gadoids (cod, haddock, hake, etc.) began in earnest only around 1000 A.D. It is significant that the Anglo-Saxon language of pre-Norman England did not even have a word for cod.[22]

Viking mariners left their mark on Europe and the North Atlantic islands in notorious fashion; the mark they left on the living ocean is less well known.

Norse colonists involved in settlement of fragile island ecosystems were responsible for significant localized depletions on or near some of those islands, affecting the baseline of what came to be considered normal. Settlers disembarking from Viking ships in Iceland during the ninth century apparently exterminated the local population of walrus quite rapidly. Vikings later moved on to harvest considerable numbers of walrus from the Greenland herds, and maintained pressure on herds in northern Norway. The abundance and geographic distribution of walrus had shrunk by the end of the Viking Age. Kitchen remains from Norse settlements in Iceland and the Faroe Islands indicate substantial harvests of seabirds, which came ashore to nest on the rocks and cliffs. As two archaeologists note, "The two early Icelandic sites appear to reflect the drawdown of the massive natural capital represented by the previously unharvested bird colonies of the south coast at a time when the small herds and flocks of imported domesticates could not yet fully provision the first colonists." The birds hunted were primarily Alcidae, members of the auk family. The birds may have been harvested sustainably in the sense that their populations did not crash, like those of the walrus, but it is likely that continued human hunting (and egg collecting) reduced populations from what they had been before the arrival of human predators. At the Junkarinsfløtti Viking site in the Faroes, 30 percent of the faunal remains were from birds, primarily puffins. Faroese islanders continued to harvest puffins well into the Middle Ages and beyond, an indication that the birds were being hunted somewhat sustainably, although their numbers were probably diminished from what they had been. With birds and walrus, and perhaps with seals in some locations, Viking hunters shifted the baseline of what was considered normal.[23]

Viking voyagers to Vinland left a different sort of biological signature. The common European periwinkle, which arrived as an invasive species in Nova Scotia during the nineteenth century, and which is now the most abundant snail along the rocky shores of New England and Nova Scotia, first crossed the Atlantic as a hitchhiker on a Viking longship. Archaeologists excavated the first American periwinkles from the Viking settlement at L'Anse aux Meadows, in northern Newfoundland. Traveling west across the Atlantic with Leif Ericson and his crew, probably on ballast stones, those periwinkles made the voyage but failed to reproduce successfully—a stillborn invasion. Nevertheless, that invasion indicates how biological changes to the sea were under way as early as the Middle Ages. Another invertebrate apparently transported by Vikings eastward across the Atlantic began to compete successfully with indigenous species in coastal European ecosystems. The softshell clam, *Mya arenaria,* traveled from North America to the North Sea and Baltic, where it had become established by the 1200s. Radiocarbon dating of softshell clam shells from Denmark indicates "without doubt" that those clams predate Columbus' voyage in 1492. Unlike the movement of periwinkles, this transplant appears to have been arranged intentionally by humans. Long before the "Columbian exchange" led to the two-directional biological transfer of terrestrial plants, animals, and microbes between the Old World and the New, ships carrying marine organisms on long voyages were beginning to reshape local coastal ecosystems. After arriving in the Baltic and North Seas, softshell clams began to compete with other mollusks, such as the common edible cockle. They also became available to local harvesters. But those biological invasions, undeniably intriguing, were very much a sideshow in the interrelated histories of humans and the sea during the Middle Ages. The real action was on the fishing banks and in the fish markets of western Europe.[24]

For medieval Europeans life without fish would have been unimaginable, and by the end of the eleventh century that fish increasingly originated in the sea. Dried, smoked, salted, or fresh, fish was the staff of life in Roman Catholic societies. "Abstinence, atonement, fasting and penance lay at the core of Christian belief," as Brian Fagan has explained, and "from the earliest times fish had a special association with such practices." On Christendom's holy days, including all Fridays and Saturdays, the six weeks of Lent, and the vigils of important festivals such as Christmas Eve, abstinence and fasting were required, supposedly dampening believers' carnal lust, heightening their spirituality, and helping to purify their souls. Meatless days of atonement and penitence were *de rigueur.* The flesh of fish, however (loosely defined to include seals, whales, seabirds, and even beaver, since Pliny's *Natural History,* a definitive work in medieval Europe, explained that "the beaver has a fish's tail"), was appropriate for fast days. Beaver in England were an early ecological casualty: penitent folk searching out lawful meat for fish days extirpated them. Seabirds suffered as well. As a British food historian explains, "roasted puffins were part of the fish feast held for the enthronement of the Archbishop of Canterbury in March 1504/5." Such exceptions, or loose definitions of fish, however, were not typical. For the most part, actual fish and eels were the protein of choice on fast days, especially for those in aristocratic or monastic households, and for the middling sort.[25]

By the late Middle Ages, crudely salted herring was the preeminent table fish in Europe, accessible even to common people. Herring were consumed as ubiquitously in medieval England as hamburgers are in modern America. An extensive herring fishery existed in the straits between what are now Denmark and southern Sweden, controlled by merchants of the Hanseatic League. Herring fairs on the east coast of England, such as those at Whitby and Yarmouth, were established in the twelfth century. Timed to correspond with the arrival of shoals of spawning herring, the largest of those fairs attracted thousands of transient fishers, traders, and processors. In 1086 the monks of Ely collected 24,000 herring in rent from the town of Dunwich; the king received 68,000 herring from the same town. Barrels of salted "white" herring and smoked "red" herring sat in cellars, and traveled far inland. Cod, haddock, hake, whiting, and pollock (all members of the gadoid family of white-fleshed fishes) were also regularly eaten during the late medieval period, along with skates, rays, salmon, mackerel, and mullet.[26]

Large-scale sea-fishing began not only because of the advent of Viking technology, but also because freshwater fisheries were declining in western Europe and Britain. During the late Middle Ages growing human populations exerted pressure on fish stocks in lakes, streams, and rivers. Deforestation, dams, and disposal into watercourses of sewage, domestic animal waste, and industrial effluent combined to degrade freshwater fish habitats. Milldams stopped migratory fish and slowed running water. As agricultural silt settled and waters warmed, streams became unsuitable for some species' spawning. Yet fishing pressure continued. King Philip IV of France lamented in 1289 that "every river and waterside of our realm, large and small, yields nothing due to the evil of the fishers and the devices of [their] contriving." Unable to consume meat during approximately one-third of each year, medieval Catholics turned to sea fish after freshwater fish had been depleted by overfishing and habitat degradation.[27]

Extensive fixed-gear fisheries existed in the rivers that marked manorial boundaries. Typically the boundary line ran down the center of the river. To accommodate proper allocation of resources, and to permit vessel traffic, fish weirs usually were built from the shore only to the center of the stream. "Frequently long stretches of major rivers would contain a succession of contemporary fisheries belonging to different manors," notes one medievalist.

Weirs consisting of stakes and nets predominated, though there were brush weirs as well, along with basket weirs, and variations known as kiddles. Some of the "engines," as contemporaries referred to permanent fishing structures, were massive. Constructed of heavy timbers, to which nets were secured, such engines littered the waterways.[28]

By the early thirteenth century they had become the target of punitive legislation. In 1224–25 Parliament ordered that "wears shall be utterly put down . . . through all England, except by the sea-coast." In 1285, during the reign of Edward I, the "Salmon Preservation Act" imposed penalties for taking young salmon with nets or mill-engines from the "midst of April unto the Nativity of S. John the Baptist." In a reflection of ongoing concerns about salmon stocks' sustainability, the act was reconfirmed in 1389 and 1393. The 1389 act specifically banned the use of the "stalker," a fine-meshed net that captured juvenile salmon and lampreys. An "Act Remedying Annoyances in the Four Great Rivers of England, Thames, Severn, Ouse, and Trent," passed in 1346–47, targeted permanently installed fisheries apparatus that impeded vessels' free passage. Five years later it was followed by an order that all "Wears, Mills, Stanks, Stakes, and Kiddles" that disturbed ships and boats in the great rivers of England should be "utterly pulled down" and not replaced. This act was reiterated frequently for more than a century following 1370, a clear reflection that it was ineffective and generally unenforced. The image that remains is one of narrow rivers, once highways to spawning grounds for salmon, sturgeon, shad, lampreys, eels, and sea trout, choked and clogged by fish traps. The devices well upstream generally took freshwater species such as perch, pike, roach, and bream, but for much of the length of the rivers anadromous species were removed in great numbers. Near the mouths of the great rivers, in their estuaries, weirs routinely trapped porpoise, flounders, herring, skates, smelt, and other marine fish.[29]

In addition to those in rivers, primitive corral-shaped weirs, constructed of brushwood fences or stone walls, had been built in estuaries and on beaches in England since at least the tenth century. As the tide receded, fish were trapped in the enclosures. Between the years 956 and 1060, Bath Abbey possessed a large estate at Tidenham, in Gloucestershire, which included at least 104 fish weirs, most of them on the Severn. Consisting of stakes driven into the sand or mud, with nets stretched between them, these kiddles could be hundreds of feet long, creating an effective barrier in a river or along a beach. By the thirteenth century these foreshore weirs were particularly common off the coast of Essex and in the Exe estuary, where plaice, dab, sole, and flounder were targeted.[30]

The Essex and North Kent estuaries also supported productive oyster fisheries. The Colne estuary had provided oysters particularly prized by the Romans. By the thirteenth century Colchester was asserting its rights to the Colne estuary oyster fishery. Oysters, cockles, and mussels appear in medieval accounts from the tenth century, when Aelfric, Abbott of Cerne (Dorset), noted them among fishermen's catches, to the fifteenth century, when Fountains Abbey purchased oysters at York, Hull, and Scarborough. Oysters were also an important natural feature of the Fal estuary, the location of Falmouth, one of Britain's finest harbors, and a center for trade and fishing in Cornwall from medieval times.[31]

Commercial oyster fisheries also existed during the twelfth and thirteenth centuries in the Wadden Sea, the coastal area of the southern North Sea stretching from the Netherlands through Germany to Denmark; and along places on the French coast, too. Oysters are easily gathered in shallows. As far back as the era of Roman domination of the Mediterranean, oysters were one of the first estuarine species depleted by humans. The impact on the environment was serious because oyster reefs provide habitat for other organisms, as well as erosion control. Even more importantly, oysters filter the water column. Each oyster pumps water across its body with thousands or hundreds of thousands of pulsing, hairlike cilia, extracting phytoplankton, bacteria, and debris. Oysters eat the edible part and deposit the inorganic sediment nearby, removing it from active suspension in the water column. A single oyster can filter ten to twenty gallons of water per day. A large oyster reef, covering acres, is able to filter a huge volume of water, contributing to light penetration and estuarine productivity. Sponges, mussels, barnacles, and other filter-feeders do similar work, but oysters are more effective. Removing large numbers of oysters from an estuary degrades those estuarine waters.[32]

Commercial sea fisheries expanded rapidly in Europe after the turn of the millennium, led by refinements in the herring fleet. By 1300, England's east coast fisheries "constituted a complex and widely dispersed business activity, the scale of which was immense by medieval standards." Marine fishing in southwestern England intensified considerably during the late fourteenth century. By the fifteenth century fish exports from the ports of Devon and Cornwall surpassed those of every other English region. This newly energized southwestern fishery employed multiple technologies and targeted numerous species, overshadowing herring as the dominant food fish. During the early fourteenth century, 99 percent of the fish shipments arriving by sea at Exeter were herring; a century and a half later, herring accounted for only 29 percent of fish imports, and twenty-two varieties of fish were arriving in Exeter. Meanwhile, as commercial fisheries drove the engine of economic expansion in southwestern England during the fourteenth and fifteenth centuries, the Dutch herring fishery developed exponentially, built on new techniques that allowed herring to be processed and barreled aboard fishing ships. Without the need to return to shore for salting or pickling their catch, Dutch busses, as they were called, could remain at sea for weeks or even months at a stretch, following the shoals of migrating North Sea herring.[33]

By 1630, eighty-three species of fish were available in Devon markets, and well-capitalized West Country men were routinely fishing all around the British Isles, and ranging as far afield as Norway, Iceland, Newfoundland, and the Gulf of Maine. By then, when Renaissance seamen and naturalists such as Anthony Parkhurst, Captain John Smith, and James Rosier were describing lush boreal estuaries on the American shore, the assault on European boreal estuaries, rivers, and coastal seas had persisted for centuries. During the early 1630s, when William Wood wrote glowingly about marine productivity in Massachusetts Bay, Edward Sharpe referred to "pernitious *Trinker-men*," who worked from small boats to "destroye the River of Thames, by killing the Fry and small Fish there, even all that comes to the Net, before it bee eyther meate or Marketable."[34]

Some European species were being fished sustainably. During the early seventeenth century the total annual production of the North Sea herring fishery typically ranged from 60,000 to 80,000 metric tons, but it never surpassed 95,000 tons. While the Dutch were responsible for about 80 percent of these herring landings, Danish, Scottish, and Norwegian fishermen also contributed. When assessed in light of estimates of North Sea herring's spawning stock biomass made in 2005, the seventeenth-century landings should have been well within the limits of a sustainable fishery.[35]

Other species and the system as a whole were not faring so well. Despite spotty evidence, certain indicators exist regarding the state of sixteenth-century ecosystems in the North Sea, the English Channel, and the Bay of Biscay, the points of origin for most voyages to America. The size of the flocks of migratory waterfowl, the magnitude of oyster reefs, the extent of springtime spawning runs of anadromous fish, the presence or absence of great whales in inshore waters, and the effort necessary for a hook-and-line fisherman to land cod or haddock: these were the unspoken baselines assumed as natural by chroniclers departing for the western periphery of the boreal North Atlantic. While precise measurements of those late medieval and early modern systems are lacking, the overall patterns are clear.

Biologists know that the coastal waters of Europe are appropriate habitat for several species of whales. The North Sea, with its high productivity, is especially hospitable: it undoubtedly had a dense population of whales at one time. Roman residents of the British Isles were quite familiar with the "Britannic whale," so named by the Roman poet Juvenal. That familiarity could only have existed for a species commonly seen near the shore, and one different from whales in the Mediterranean—possibly the right whale. By the medieval period, Basque, Flemish, and Norman whalers were pursuing whales from shore-based operations. Basques had been killing whales in the Bay of Biscay since the eleventh century, and possibly longer. At one point the right whale *(Eubalanena glacialis)* was known as the "Biscayan whale"; later hunted in the far north, it was also called the "nordcaper." Perceptions that stocks were decreasing caused King Alfonso XI of Castile to reduce his tax on Lekeitio whalers in 1334, though evidence suggests that the Basques were still pursuing right whales in the English Channel up to the sixteenth century. Norman and Flemish whalers hunted right whales and/or gray whales in the English Channel and the North Sea, and whale meat appeared regularly in medieval markets in the towns of Boulogne, Nieuwpoort, Damme, and Calais, among others. A survey of English fisheries compiled in 1580, however, suggests that by then the right whale stock had been much reduced. The survey made no mention of local whales, but indicated that Englishmen routinely traveled "to the coast of Rushe towards Muskovie and St. nycolas" for summer whaling. The International Whaling Commission has reported that by "the first half of the 17th century . . . the local [European] population of *E. glacialis* was already severely affected." This circumstance explains why the Reverend Richard Mather, approaching the New England coast in 1635, delighted in "the multitude of great whales, which now was grown ordinary and usual to behold." Travelers like Mather and experienced mariners noted that the ecosystem in the western Atlantic was organized differently because of the presence of great whales.[36]

Harbor seals and gray seals were once common in the North Sea and around the British Isles. Gray seals *(Halichoerus grypus)* are much larger than harbor seals; bulls can exceed eight feet and weigh over 600 pounds. After birth, gray seal pups stay on shore for several weeks, where they are vulnerable to hunters. In the Netherlands and Germany subfossil remains of gray seals are more common than those of harbor seals. Archaeologists have excavated gray seal remains from at least eight sites in the Netherlands alone, ranging in date from about 2000 B.C. to the early Middle Ages. The scarcity of reports on the presence of gray seals in the southeastern North Sea, off the Low Countries, since 1500 suggests that the population was virtually wiped out through hunting pressure by the end of the Middle Ages, even though a small breeding population remained in the Faroe Islands. Europeans subsequently encountering vast herds of gray seals and harbor seals in boreal North American waters were flabbergasted by their numbers.[37]

Eider ducks *(Somateria mollisima),* another boreal species once common in both the eastern and western Atlantic, may have bred throughout a large part of northern Europe until the Middle Ages. Eiders are the largest and most common sea duck in Europe, and a resource prized for meat, eggs, and their unsurpassed eider down. As early as the seventh century, Bishop Cuthbert and his monks attempted to protect eiders nesting on Lindisfarne, off the northeast coast of England. Eiders are particularly vulnerable to human predation. Most seabirds shed their feathers one at a time, replacing worn ones in rotation. Eiders molt all at once, and thus are rendered flightless for several weeks in August, during which time they raft in vast numbers. Hunters in boats can capitalize on eiders' flightlessness during the molt by herding the defenseless ducks toward choice spots on the beach for killing. Narrow ravines and funnel-shaped gullies were ideal, but even open beaches could be made to serve. Evidence suggests that human pressure on eiders eradicated the species from much of the North Sea by the end of the Middle Ages. While eiders were especially valued, other coastal birds, especially colonially breeding seabirds, were likewise exploited for feathers, down, meat, and eggs for millennia. Never extirpated, they nevertheless existed in a diminished state.[38]

The clearest evidence by far about the degraded state of late medieval European estuaries and rivers concerns anadromous fish—the European sea sturgeon, the shads, the whitefish family, and the closely related salmon and sea trout families. Sturgeon bones recovered by the thousands from archaeological excavations in the southern Baltic reveal that between the tenth and the thirteenth centuries the average size of sturgeon landed decreased considerably—indicating a population in which fish were being caught before growing to their full size. Other records show that sturgeon landings in the Low Countries likewise decreased in average size from the eleventh to the fourteenth centuries. In lower Normandy the number of salmon landed from small rivers decreased significantly between 1100 and 1300. Plow agriculture, siltation, milldams, warming waters, and overfishing all took a toll on salmon, which, like trout, sturgeon, shad, and whitefish, thrive in clear, well-oxygenated, cold, rapidly moving streams. As one historian has noted, "Even in wealthy Parisian households and prosperous Flemish monasteries, consumption of once-favored sturgeon, salmon, trout, and whitefish shrank to nothing by around 1500."[39]

Late medieval and early modern fisheries clearly were depleting estuarine and river systems like the Rhine and the Thames, even as they were fishing herring sustainably. The more open-ended question concerns northern European fisheries' impact on stocks of cod, ling, hake, and other sea fish. Reliable quantitative data simply do not exist for most late medieval and early modern fisheries. However, biologists today understand that, among many stocks subject to fishing, the largest fish are caught first. Continued fishing reduces the average size and age of individuals, and the fish respond by maturing earlier. Younger, smaller fish begin to spawn. It is axiomatic that among fish, larger females produce more eggs, often exponentially more eggs. So a reduction in spawning size can impede reproduction. While it is impossible to state with any certainty whether or not most European sea fish stocks were being affected, it is clear that the system as a whole had been significantly degraded by 1500, as measured by the depletion of whales, seals, seabirds, and anadromous fish. Five hundred years of fishing had changed the nature of coastal European ecosystems, and affected the baselines for what contemporaries assumed to be normal.[40]

ASSESSING ABUNDANCE

When in August 1527 the Englishman John Rut trimmed the sheets on his baggy flax sails and steered through the narrow mouth of St. John's harbor in Newfoundland to find "eleven sail of Normans, one Breton, and two Portugal barks, and all fishing," he confronted the westernmost outpost of a network of European fishermen, fishmongers, and fish markets that stretched from the Norwegian Arctic Circle to the Mediterranean Sea, from inland cities near the

Alps to island outposts such as the Faroes, from fishing grounds in the expansive shallows seaward of the Low Countries to those surrounding Newfoundland, that great rock rising out of the western Atlantic. Just thirty years before, a Venetian named Zoane Caboto, better known to Englishmen as John Cabot, and a crew of about eighteen men had reached Newfoundland aboard the ship *Matthew*, owned by Bristol merchants. Except for the voyages that had resulted in a brief Scandinavian settlement in L'Anse aux Meadows, Newfoundland, subsequently abandoned around the year 1000, Cabot's voyage in 1497 is the earliest known connection between the east and west sides of the North Atlantic boreal region. Shortly after the *Matthew* returned to England, an Italian envoy to the English court wrote a letter about the voyage to the duke of Milan. "This Messer Zoane, as a foreigner, and a poor man, would not have obtained credence, had it not been that his companions, who are practically all English and from Bristol, testified that he spoke the truth. . . . They assert that the sea there is swarming with fish, which can be taken not only with the net, but in baskets let down with a stone. . . . These same English, his companions, say they could bring so many fish that this kingdom would have no further need of Iceland, from which place there comes a very great quantity of the fish called stockfish."[41]

During the fourteenth and fifteenth centuries the heraldic symbol of the powerful Hanseatic League prominently displayed images of stockfish. With the Viking ascendancy long past by then, Hanse merchants monopolized stockfish distribution in what are now Germany, Poland, the Low Countries, France, and England. But interlopers were eager for a share of the action. So when John Cabot and his crew reconnoitered western Atlantic waters in 1497, they saw its ecosystem in terms of the international fish market. Here, indeed, was a store of fish that would make Iceland irrelevant.

Similar in most ways to northern Europe's coastal ecosystem, though clearly better stocked with cod, the northwest Atlantic nevertheless had its distinguishing wonders. Jacques Cartier was among the first to delineate those differences. As comfortable with a quill pen in his hand as with a pine deck under his feet, Cartier had the sensibilities of a man simultaneously active and meditative. No one of his generation had lived more intimately with the sea or studied it more devoutly. Born in 1491 in St. Malo, an ancient Breton town walled off from the threatening ocean on which it depended, Cartier knew that the sea kept its secrets. By the time the two ships of "sixty tons burden each, manned in all with sixty-one men" that he commanded slipped through the narrow sea gate of St. Malo, heading for Newfoundland and the Gulf of St. Lawrence in 1534, Cartier had thousands of ocean miles under his belt, including—it appears—previous crossings to Brazil and Newfoundland, as well as innumerable coasting and fishing voyages in Europe.

No one was better suited to report on seabird colonies in the Gulf of St. Lawrence, where he found "a great number of tinkers [razorbills, a smaller relative of the great auk] and puffins which have red beaks and feet and make their nests in holes under the earth like rabbits"; on "the best fishing possible for big cod" along the west coast of Newfoundland; or on the "large quantity of mackerel they [Mi'kmaq people] had caught near the shore with nets." Keen observer and well-prepared mariner that he was, Cartier nevertheless held no illusions that he could determine the outcome of his voyage, or guarantee his return. His fatalism was tinged by his sense that a man then "could neither rationally comprehend nor actively control the world in which he lived." Renaissance Europeans' relations with the nonhuman natural world were conditioned by this sensibility, by this notion that nature was infinite and overwhelming, and that humankind's attempts to tame or improve it were likely to be futile.[42]

During September 1535 in the St. Lawrence River, as Cartier explained, his men "discovered a species of fish, which none of us had ever seen or heard of. This fish is as large as a porpoise but has no fin. It is very similar to a greyhound about the body and head and is as white as snow. . . . The people of the country call them *Adhothuys* and told us they are very good to eat." Breton mariners from St. Malo knew the sea and its life, but the beluga, often called the white whale—a marine mammal from twelve to sixteen feet in length and distinctive for its lack of a dorsal fin—was primarily an Arctic species and rarely seen in the waters of Western Europe. It seemed worthy of comment, a distinguishing hallmark of the western Atlantic.[43]

Also unknown in European waters was the ungainly horseshoe crab, an invertebrate common along the beaches and in the shallows of the Gulf of Maine. In 1605 Samuel de Champlain, the most fastidious observer of New France and the American coast, marveled at them. Champlain encountered hundreds of species of birds, fish, mammals, and invertebrates on his voyages between Cape Cod and the St. Lawrence River, including the Bay of Fundy. He rarely bothered with detailed descriptions of boreal creatures well known in France. The horseshoe crab's outlandishness caught his imagination. It was "a fish with a shell on its back like a tortoise," he wrote, with intense curiosity, "yet different; for it has along the median line a row of little prickles coloured like a dead leaf, as is the rest of this fish. At the end of this shell is another, which is smaller and bordered by very sharp points. The length of the tail varies accordingly as the fish is large or small, and with the end of it these people [Natives] tip their arrows. . . . The largest I saw was a foot in breadth and a foot and a half long."[44]

Champlain found them in great abundance along the Maine coast, where horseshoe crab eggs and larvae were an important seasonal food for other invertebrates, birds, and fish. Shorebirds such as dowitchers, sanderlings, and sandpipers gorged on horseshoe crab eggs in the spring, as did several crab species and some gastropods, including whelks. Striped bass, eels, various flounders, and other sea fish frequenting estuaries in the spring also consumed prodigious quantities of horseshoe crab eggs and larvae. Though the French explorer did not know it, this strange "fish with a shell on its back like a tortoise" contributed greatly to the signature productivity of the Gulf of Maine.[45]

The "Morses or Sea oxen," as another sailor referred to walruses in 1591, likewise needed explanation. Except for occasional stragglers they had not been seen for centuries in Europe: overhunting had reduced their range, squeezing them to the far north in Norway and the Svalbard archipelago. During the sixteenth century Basque, French, and English sailors encountered vast herds of walrus in the Gulf of St. Lawrence. Estimates are that the gulf herd numbered 250,000 animals when Europeans arrived, while the Sable Island (Nova Scotia) and Newfoundland herd numbered 125,000. If these estimates are accurate, the combined live weight (biomass) of the region's walrus herds was 450,000 tons. Each of the 375,000 individual animals consumed on average ninety-nine pounds of food per day, primarily benthic invertebrates such as clams, oysters, scallops, starfish, and sea squirts.[46]

The Gulf of St. Lawrence is a huge estuary, providing a smorgasbord for creatures such as walrus. Its major oceanographic feature is the outflow of freshwater from the Great Lakes and the St. Lawrence River, which moves eastward along the north coast of the Gaspé Peninsula at ten to twenty nautical miles per day, accelerating during the ebb tide and slowing during the flood tide. Subsurface upwelling of ocean water that enters the gulf through the Straits of Belle Isle and the Cabot Strait contributes significantly to sustaining the current. The upwelling and constant movement guarantee that nutrients are well dispersed throughout a relatively shallow water column readily penetrated by sunlight—perfect conditions for plankton reproduction. Many marine invertebrates are filter-feeders. Much of the Gulf of St. Lawrence provided a vast pantry for such creatures, similar to the Gironde estuary in southwestern France, or the smaller estuaries fringing the south Brittany coast with which Cartier and Champlain were familiar. Quahogs, scallops, oysters, soft-shell clams, razor clams, cockles, whelks, and other mollusks thrived, providing food for bottom-dwelling predatory fish such as cod, haddock, and halibut, and also for walrus. A mature male walrus can weigh 2,600 pounds and measure twelve feet in length. Such an animal does not have many enemies in the sea, but it needs to consume more than 6 percent of its body weight each day, meaning that each of the "great beasts" that Cartier saw at Brion Island could need to eat as many as 7,000 shellfish per day.[47]

Walrus were a striking component of the northwest Atlantic ecosystem for Europeans, and were immediately recognized as a profitable source of oil, leather, and ivory. They were also novel. By the sixteenth century walrus had largely disappeared from the collective consciousness of European mariners, though centuries before, at the height of the Viking Age (ca. 750–1050 A.D.), walrus ivory and inch-thick walrus hides had been prestigious trade goods throughout maritime Europe. A walrus could be skinned by starting near the tail and peeling the hide from the animal in a continuous strip about one inch wide, resulting in a one-inch-thick leather rope of great length, and stronger than any fiber rope known at the time. Hide ropes had been crucial for rigging Viking ships.[48]

Sailors wondered aloud whether these cumbersome and frightening beasts were oxen, horses, lions, or fish. Cartier described them as "fish in appearance like horses which go on land at night but in daytime remain in the water." Edward Hayes, who accompanied Sir Humphrey Gilbert to Newfoundland in 1583, tried desperately to capture the essence of a walrus, drawing on the comparisons at his disposal. He wrote, with wonder and considerable accuracy, of "a very lion to our seeming, in shape, hair and colour, not swimming after the maner of a beast by mooving of his feete, but rather sliding upon the water with his whole body (excepting the legs) in sight, neither yet diving under, and againe rising above the water, as the manner is, of Whales, Dolphins, Tunise [tunas], Porposes, and all other fish: but confidently shewing himself above water without hiding."[49]

Sixteen years later at a small archipelago in the Gulf of St. Lawrence, another Englishman observed walrus, which he called "Sea Oxen . . . a sleepe upon the rockes: but when we approached nere unto them with our boate they cast themselves into the sea and pursued us with such furie as that we were glad to flee from them." Accounts published between 1591 and 1600 in French and English revealed that walrus from the Gulf of St. Lawrence, known "in Latin as Boves Marini," were "very big: and hath two great teeth: and the skinne of them is like Buffes leather." When butchered and rendered they produced "very sweet" oil, and their tusks could be "sold in England to the combe & knife makers" for twice the price of ivory. Moreover, those tusks, when powdered, according to a "skilful Phisition" from Bristol, were "as soveraigne against poison as any Unicornes horne."[50]

For the most part, however, neither the novelty nor the magical qualities of marine organisms from the northwest Atlantic captivated European mariners so much as their familiarity and sheer abundance. On back-to-back summer days in 1597, for instance, the veteran sea captain Charles Leigh sailed into a marine cornucopia in the Gulf of St. Lawrence the likes of which he could barely conceive. "In little more than an hour we caught with four hooks two hundred and fifty" cod, he wrote—a rate slightly better than one cod per minute per hook. At the Bird Islands Leigh saw "such abundance of Birds as is almost incredible to report." The gannets, murres, razorbills, puffins, and others sat "there as thick as stones lie in a paved street." Near what is now Sydney, Nova Scotia, he encountered "the greatest multitude of lobsters that we ever heard of; for we caught at one haul with a little draw net above one hundred and forty." Account after account reiterated the same wide-eyed sense of wonder at the boreal ocean's productivity. John Brereton noted that in "five or six hours" on a single May day in 1602, under the lee of Cape Cod, "we had pestered our ship so with Cod fish, that we threw numbers of them ouer-boord againe." Shellfish abounded, too: "Scalops, Muscles, Cockles, Lobster, Crabs, Oisters, and Wilks, exceeding good and very great." Brereton was almost apologetic. "But not to cloy you with particular rehearsal of such things as God & nature hath bestowed on these places," he wrote, "in comparison whereof, the most fertil part of al England is (of its selfe) but barren."[51]

Sixteenth- and seventeenth-century accounts of the northwest Atlantic's coastal seas by men such as Anthony Parkhurst, Samuel de Champlain, and Captain John Smith described a boreal marine ecosystem that seemed *very* different in certain ways from the one in Europe, despite the similarity of species.

After 1578 barely a decade went by without some commentary detailing the abundance and distribution of species in the northwest Atlantic, the seasons in which those species appeared in or departed from coastal waters, the nature of predator-prey relationships, the size of average and extreme organisms, the system's overall biological productivity, and the behavior of fish, seabirds, marine mammals, and invertebrates. There seemed to be fewer perturbations to the system, and more buffers. If coastal European boreal seas had once looked like those off the coast of North America, then the human impact on long-lived creatures in European waters, such as mammals, birds, and large fish, were immediately discernible. The explorers' accounts provide not only a description of the environment that fishermen and settlers encountered, but as thorough an assessment as will ever exist of an almost unperturbed boreal North Atlantic marine ecosystem.

These descriptions, which have sometimes been dismissed as extravagant propaganda, are numerous, and they corroborate one another, though written by different authors, in different languages, with different agendas, over more than a century.[52] All speak to the extraordinary bounty of undisturbed seas in the northwest Atlantic. Charles Leigh observed in the Gulf of St. Lawrence in 1597 that "the sea yeeldeth great abundance of fish of divers sorts."[53] John Brereton wrote from the Gulf of Maine in 1602 of "fish, namely Cods, which as we encline more unto the South, are more large and vendible for England and France, than the Newland [Newfoundland] fish." During one of the first recorded voyages into the Gulf of Maine Brereton put his finger on what fishermen for centuries to come would consider one of the region's distinguishing hallmarks, that cod got larger as one moved south from Labrador to Massachusetts. He also noted "Whales and Seales in great abundances," and pointedly observed that "Oiles of them are rich commodities for England, whereof we now make Soape, besides many other uses." In addition to cod and marine mammals, Brereton noticed "Salmons, Lobsters, Oisters having Pearle, and infinit other sorts of fish, which are more plentifull upon those Northwest coasts of America, than in any parts of the knowen world." Recounting Captain Bartholomew Gosnold's voyage to the Gulf of Maine in 1602, Gabriel Archer remembered: "Neare this Cape we came to anchor in fifteene fadome, where we took great store of Cod-fish, for which we altered the name, and called it Cape Cod. Here wee saw sculs of Herrings, Mackerels and other small fish in great abundance."[54] Captain John Smith summed up the delights of the Maine coast with an implicit comparison to home waters, and prophetic words: "He is a very bad fisher, [who] cannot kill in one day with his hooke and line, one, two, three hundred Cods: . . . may not both the servant, the master, and the merchant, be well content with this gaine?"[55]

When it came to quantifying stocks of prosaic species regularly encountered in European coastal waters, including cod, mackerel, oysters, right whales, seals, and seabirds, men such as Leigh, Brereton, and Smith implicitly fell back on the baselines of abundance that they had developed during years of voyaging in European boreal waters. Veteran seafarers knew what to expect of the living ocean. Men for whom vigilance and observation were second nature paid close attention to their surroundings, and wrote copiously about them, without realizing that American abundance reflected European depletion.

During these early voyages it was not just the size of individual fish that struck Europeans as noteworthy, or the overall amount that could be seen or caught in one place, but also their quality. In 1605 James Rosier, a gentleman in George Waymouth's crew, wrote that while anchored off Monhegan Island on the midcoast of Maine, the sailors "with a few hooks got above thirtie great Cods and Hadocks, which gave us a taste of the great plenty of fish which we found afterward wheresoever we went upon the coast. . . . And toward night we drew with a small net of twenty fathoms very nigh the shore: we got about thirty very good and great Lobsters, many Rockfish, some Plaise, and other small fishes called Lumpes, verie pleasant to the taste: and we generally observed, that all of the fish, of what kind soever we tooke, were well fed, fat, and sweet in taste." Rosier, probably the best naturalist among the first generations of English observers, sensed that the ecosystem was not producing one species at the expense of another, but that invertebrates, baitfish, benthic food fish, seabirds, and marine mammals were all flourishing.[56]

The repetition and insistence of these accounts—some in English and others in French, some by clergy and others by laity, some by experienced seamen, others by landsmen, some in the sixteenth century and others in the seventeenth century—create a reinforcing pattern of veracity. Time after time observers compared the compromised European boreal ecosystem that they knew with the fresh one in the western Atlantic. "The sturgeons and salmon ascend the Dauphin River at the said Port Royal in such quantities that they carried away the nets which we had set for them," wrote Marc Lescarbot of spring in Nova Scotia in 1612. "Fish abound there in like manner everywhere, such is the fertility of this country."[57]

Fish bone analyses from a variety of Native American middens spanning the period from 5,000 years B.P. to 400 years B.P. reveal that that prehistoric people routinely caught cod of 1 to 1.5 meters in length in inshore waters. During the seventeenth and eighteenth centuries, and possibly earlier, French fish-mongers had four categories for New World cod, sorted by size. The first two, "gaffe cod" and "officer's cod," were for fish 1–2 meters in length. Size is an indication of age in fish such as cod. Native fishers, and then newcomers such as French fishermen, were routinely catching cod three to five feet long in inshore waters—an indication of a stock in a virtually pristine state. Over pre-ceding centuries Europeans had already skimmed the cream from their home waters. So the northwest Atlantic's boreal marine ecosystem struck the first few generations of Europeans to arrive as incomprehensible in its abundance. Of all the riches encountered in Newfoundland, wrote John Mason in 1620, "the most admirable is the Sea, so diversified with several sorts of Fishes abounding therein, the consideration whereof is readie to swallow up and drown my senses not being able to comprehend or express the riches thereof."[58]

Mason's turn of phrase, like those of other early writers, needs to be regarded in the context in which he wrote it, and not necessarily as an exaggeration. Most men of his generation and previous ones, even educated men, had limited computational skills. Systematic procedures had not yet been established for estimating very large magnitudes. In 1520 or 1620, however, such estimates were hardly necessary. Counting and measurement were largely geared toward trade at that time. Unless a commodity was transported over some distance for sale, it was unlikely to be measured or counted with precision. Standardized mea-surements existed for commodities such as foodstuffs and cloth, but units varied for each. The volume of a wine barrel, for instance, differed from that of a barrel of olive oil or pickled fish. Moreover, standardized measurements, par-ticularly for liquids, varied from nation to nation.[59] As late as 1643 the Plymouth Colony decided to standardize its "bushel" to conform to that of the Massachu-setts Bay Colony for ease of trade. Until then, these two English outposts, only half a day's walk apart, measured in bushels that were not the same size. Mea-surement and valuation, along with accurate counting and computation, were specialized professional skills uncommon among even literate people until well into the eighteenth century.[60]

Without standardization, the head-spinning array of measures, units, dis-tances, and containers confounded systematic quantitative comparisons in the late Renaissance and early modern periods. However, a practical arithmetic developed around comparative empirical units with which everyone was famil-iar, and for which no special tools were necessary. When distance was measured by pacing, distances in feet could be easily reproduced within acceptable certainty. A very small unit of length, the barleycorn, was readily available in all English farming villages. Even the innumerate could measure conventional things in units like feet and barleycorns. For unusual circumstances, including those such as were found in the New World, observers typically reverted to a system of analogy. This mode of representation was as conventional among early modern naturalists and men of letters as precise measurements are among scientists today. Mason, an educated royal official, simply admitted that no analogy at hand conveyed the magnitude of Newfoundland's marine resources.

Captain John Smith or John Mason would not have thought to stretch a net across a specific bay on a specific day and instruct their men to count or weigh all the fish landed. Without a market nearby, it is unlikely that scales would have been available. Counting would have left scores of hash marks on peeled sticks. Contemporaries of Smith and Mason did not expect such specificity or consider it all that useful—otherwise promoters such as Smith would have weighed and counted. When the baseline accounts of the northwest Atlantic ecosystem were recorded, between the middle of the sixteenth century and the middle of the seventeenth century, metaphor was the normative means of conveying large magnitudes. Charles Leigh assessed sea bird populations on islands in the Gulf of St. Lawrence as "thicke as stones lie in a paved street." Metaphor, however, did not necessarily mean hyperbole; though seventeenth-century explorers did not value precise quantification, their observations are not without merit.

The presence of so many men with firsthand experience in American waters acted as a check on hyperbole. Had the accounts of American coastal ecosystems been wildly exaggerated or inaccurate, plenty of experienced mariners were on hand to set the record straight. Before permanent European settlements took root at Jamestown, Quebec, or Plymouth, thousands of European fishing vessels made the roundtrip voyage to Newfoundland, the Gulf of St. Lawrence, and the Gulf of Maine. The exact number will never be known, because of scattered and incomplete data, but the patterns are clear: tens of thousands of European mariners had firsthand experience in the northwest Atlantic before 1600. For most of the sixteenth century the English secured only a small fraction of what Richard Hakluyt called "the manifold gaine which the French, Britaynes, Baskes, and Biskaines do yerely return." Basques concentrated on whaling and, to a lesser extent, cod fishing in the Straits of Belle Isle, the narrows between the northwest tip of Newfoundland and the Labrador shore. By the second half of the sixteenth century as many as 2,000 Basque whalemen and fishermen congregated there annually during the season, though none intended to colonize or settle permanently on that distant shore. Concrete evidence also indicates a robust French New World fishery. During 1559, according to notarial records, at least 150 ships for Newfoundland were outfitted in the three ports of Bordeaux, La Rochelle, and Rouen. In 1565 those three ports dispatched at least 156 ships. Actual numbers were much higher: records no longer exist for many important fishing ports. European fishermen strayed far from home because European ecosystems seemed unable to produce enough fish and whales to satisfy demand. In the summer of 1578 alone, when the English were still minor players in the transatlantic fishery, the Englishman Anthony Parkhurst tallied about 350 vessels in Newfoundland and the Gulf of St. Lawrence, including French, Spanish, Basque, Portuguese, and English ones. Most were fishing for cod, although twenty to thirty Basque ships were whaling. When Silvester Wyet of Bristol sailed the *Grace* to the Gulf of St. Lawrence and Newfoundland in 1594, he encountered "two and twentie sayles of Englishmen" and "threescore and odd sayles" of "fishermen of Saint John de Luz and of Sibiburo and of Biskay"—a total of about 85 ships in just two harbors. These admittedly incomplete figures, whether drawn from notarial records or from firsthand observations, indicate that during the sixteenth century, "far from being an area on the fringe worked by only a few fishermen, the northern part of the Americas was one of the great seafaring destinations in the New World." Every crew shared the same inspiration for their dangerous voyage, and the same ambition: to cram living resources from that undepleted coastal ocean into their cargo holds. Counting fish species, much less individual fish, was not a concern of a high order, but it is noteworthy that not a single account accusing other explorers of hyperbole was ever published by any of the tens of thousands of European fishermen with firsthand knowledge of the northwest Atlantic marine ecosystem in this era.[61]

Landsmen wrote some accounts of the western Atlantic's abundance, but many were the work of seamen with considerable experience in European marine systems.[62] These men had come of age knowing that "the fishing for cod upon the coasts of Lanchshire begenithe at East[er] and contyneth til mydsommer," that hake were found "in the deeps betwixt Wales and Ireland," and that the best fishing for herring "beginith at Bartholomewe tyde at Scarborough and so preadithe along the coast until they come to Thames mouth conteynewinge very good until hollentyde." George Waymouth, who made a "most prosperous voyage" to the midcoast of Maine in 1605, was from a family that had fished for several generations in his home parish of Cockington, as well as in Ireland and Newfoundland. Confronting a familiar suite of fish, seabirds, and marine mammals in the northwest Atlantic, men like Waymouth framed New World abundance in light of the shopworn European marine systems they knew firsthand.[63] Without knowing it, Hayes, Brereton, Leigh, Smith, and other early observers in the northwest Atlantic were privy not only to a vision of American waters' abundance prior to systematic commercial exploitation, but also to how European estuaries and coastal seas in the North Atlantic boreal region may have looked thousands of years earlier, when Neolithic people made the transition from hunting and gathering to settled agricultural villages on the coast of Europe. The explorers' voyages were thus journeys in space and journeys through time—ecological time; their accounts reflected not just American abundance, but the depletion of European coastal ecosystems that had occurred by the end of the medieval period. Nothing else explains the astonishment of John Cabot, Jacques Cartier, and other Renaissance seafarers who sailed into the western extremity of the North Atlantic boreal region. The baselines they had taken for granted no longer made sense.[64]

The first generation of European observers to document American waters wrote from their assumptions of normalcy. Father Pierre Biard, later the head of the first Jesuit mission in Nova Scotia, had been born in 1567 in southeastern France. An educated man and keen observer, before his departure for Acadia Biard spent years in Lyons, a city at the confluence of the Rhone and Saône Rivers, and lived for at least a year or two in Bordeaux, a city upstream from the Gironde estuary, the largest in France. He undoubtedly knew that lamprey, salmon, sturgeon, sea trout, and shad could be found in the Rhone, and probably was aware that sand smelt lived downstream, in the Rhone River delta. Fishmongers and chefs dealt in all those species, with the possible exception of sturgeon, already severely depleted in many French rivers. Yet Biard's account of the spring spawning runs in Nova Scotia—notable for its explicit comparison of some species in France with those of North America—was not that of a man who had seen anything similar before. "In the middle of March," he wrote, after moving to Nova Scotia in 1611, "fish begin to spawn, and to come up from the sea into certain streams, often so abundantly that everything swarms with them. Anyone who has not seen it could scarcely believe it. You cannot put your hand into the water, without encountering them. Among these fish the smelt is the first; this smelt is two and three times as large as that in our rivers; after the smelt comes the herring at the end of April. . . . At the same time come the sturgeon, and salmon, and the great search through the Islets for eggs, as the waterfowl, which are there in great numbers, lay their eggs then, and often cover the Islets with their nests."[65]

Biard's sense of wonder was matched by that of men who sailed from other Old World estuaries. Martin Pring departed on his voyage to New England in 1603 from the mouth of the Avon River, which was the roadstead of Bristol and located within the Severn estuary. The Severn is one of England's largest rivers, navigable for much of its length and notorious for its extraordinary tides and tidal bore. Pring had sailed from one of the larger boreal estuaries in Britain, yet he marveled at the biological productivity he encountered in Massachusetts. In June there were "Seales to make Oile withal, Mullets, Turbuts, Mackerels, Herrings, Crabs, Lobsters, Creuises, and Muscles with ragged Pearles in them," he wrote, awed by the "great abundance of excellent fish" and by the "great store of other River and Sea-Fowles."[66]

Samuel de Champlain, who would become the best American naturalist and cartographer of his generation, grew up on the edge of a marine ecosystem where rivers, marshes, and sea converged, and where locals specialized in harvesting marine resources. Champlain was born about 1580 in Brouage, a small town on the Bay of Biscay just north of the Gironde estuary. Notorious for its saltworks, and a magnet for ships from Scotland, Flanders, Germany, and England, Brouage nestled in the marshes fringing the Gulf of Saintonge, a bay fronted by the Isle d'Oléron and the Isle d'Aix. Its people were seafarers, and both Champlain's father and uncle were captains. By the time he departed on his first overseas voyage, probably to the West Indies with his uncle, Champlain knew those local environs well.[67] And yet he had nothing but awe for the abundance and productivity of coastal ecosystems in North America. Other chroniclers of the western North Atlantic's boreal region had similar stories, whether Leigh or Rosier, departing from the mighty Thames River; Archer or Brereton, departing from Falmouth in the Fal estuary; or Edward Hayes, whose voyage west with Sir Humphrey Gilbert began near Plymouth in the Tamar estuary. All of them knew what to expect of the boreal North Atlantic in terms of sturgeon, salmon, seabirds, right whales, seals, flatfish, cod, and herring; yet all were astonished at the productivity of the western Atlantic.

The European-dominated Atlantic world originated, to no small degree, from insatiable demands placed upon marine ecosystems in the Bay of Biscay, the English Channel, and the North Sea. Like every ecosystem, those were constantly being reshaped by natural changes. "Fluctuations," as contemporary ecologists point out, are "the very essence of ecosystems," and the populations of many species sought by humans, including mackerel, herring, and pilchards, fluctuate dramatically. The Devon pilchard catch, for example, was poor in 1587, low again in 1593, and virtually nonexistent in 1594. Irish herring were scarce in 1592. Faroe Islands cod fisheries collapsed in 1625 and again in 1629. Perceived "shortages" like these—in other words, the inability of the ecosystem to produce the volume desired by harvesters—prompted fishing merchants to seek other stocks. Cooling temperatures may have contributed to the geographic expansion of the late medieval fishery. Scientists now know that seawater below a certain temperature inhibits cod's ability to reproduce. As formerly reliable fishing grounds off Norway failed during the 1400s, at the outset of the Little Ice Age, well-capitalized English fishermen began to sail west instead of north, first to Iceland, then to Newfoundland and Maine. Whether northern Europe's once abundant waters were being depleted by "the long continuance of fishing and some abuse in the taking," as one sixteenth-century document attested, or whether the ecosystem could no longer produce enough to satisfy heightened demand, perhaps because of climate change associated with the onset of the Little Ice Age, is not clear. It is clear, however, that European fishermen wanted more fish than they could catch in home waters.[68]

Whalers and fishermen became shock troops pushing west, inspiring chroniclers such as Richard Hakluyt to promote overseas expansion. As Europeans established outposts around the Atlantic rim, ecological changes followed. Commodities harvested from American ecosystems routinely were transported from New World centers of production to Old World sites of consumption. The rapid intensification of long-distance bulk trading in organic products, notably foodstuffs, timber, tobacco, and whale oil, constituted barely recognized ecological revolutions. By the seventeenth century, for instance, as many as 200,000 metric tons of cod per year (live weight) were leaving Newfoundland for Europe. Around the turn of the twentieth century, when Rudyard Kipling immortalized the fleet in his novel *Captains Courageous,* landings were not even twice that amount.[69]

During the century before the American Revolution striking improvements in shipping efficiency reduced the cost per ton/mile required to transport bulk goods. The story typically has been told as one of accounts payable, commodities transported, and fortunes made and lost. Silenced in that telling, however, is an account of biomass and energy being transferred from one ecosystem to another. Vast numbers of European consumers were then eating, as Richard Hoffmann puts it, "beyond the bounds of natural local ecosystems" and, as a result, refashioning distant environments. The ocean was not immune. Pressured by commercial capitalism and cornucopian fantasies, the northwestern Atlantic's coastal ocean rapidly became an extension of Europe's diminished seas, a sea change comprehensible only in transatlantic perspective.[70]

Two

PLUCKING THE
LOW-HANGING FRUIT

———

No sea but what is vexed by their fisheries.
—Edmund Burke, "Speech on Conciliation with America," 1774

No sixteenth- or seventeenth-century European community relied on the sea as much as the Mi'kmaq and Malecite hunter-gatherers of what are now eastern Maine, New Brunswick, and Nova Scotia. The sea nourished their bodies and souls. Seal hunters, seabird egg collectors, scavengers of drift whales, weir builders, hook fishers, and harpooners, Mi'kmaqs and Malecites studied the tides and remained alert for ecological signals from the neighboring sea. As much as 90 percent of their annual caloric intake came from marine resources. Not only did they know the sea; they felt it. Imagining themselves as descended from animal ancestors, including marine creatures such as eels, Mi'kmaqs and Malecites along the Bay of Fundy and the coast of Nova Scotia inhabited a totemic universe in which humans participated in the natural world without considering themselves separated from it. Likewise, in southern Maine and along Massachusetts Bay, Abenaki agriculturalists were also expert fishermen "experienced in the knowledge of all baits" and "when to fish rivers and when at rocks, when in bays, and when at seas." Before Abenakis acquired iron hooks and manufactured lines from the English, one visitor noted, "they made them of their own hemp more curiously wrought of stronger materials than ours, hooked with bone hooks."[1]

Accomplished Native harvesters understood the ocean differently from European newcomers, but both knew that, like the land, it was biologically productive only in specific places and in its seasons. Natives, however, assumed that the fish, whales, and birds were inextricable from the place; that its signature productivity would endure in perpetuity. Some English mariners knew otherwise. The weirs that had fished so effectively on the Thames, the Severn, and the Ouse had already depleted anadromous fish there, and hook fishers apparently had removed the largest of the cod, ling, and hake from coastal European ecosystems by the time permanent settlement began in New England.

The calamity facing fishermen, noted Christopher Levett, who sailed Maine's southern coast in 1623 and 1624, was that their "trade is decayed in England." Fish stocks in English waters certainly had not been destroyed. Yet with the simple gear at their disposal English fishermen could not work intensively enough to sustain robust landings in areas traditionally fished. In a pattern that would be repeated throughout the centuries, harvesters confronting that problem saw two alternatives. They could develop better gear to fish familiar grounds more intensively, or fish more extensively by searching for virgin stocks on unknown grounds. Both actions masked the depletion that had already occurred: both shifted downward the baseline of what was considered "normal." Captain John Smith concurred with Levett's assessment. He contrasted the western Atlantic's freshness with exhausted European fisheries. "And whereas it is said, the Hollanders serve the Easterlings themselves, and other parts that want, with Herring, Ling, and wet Cod; the Easterlings a great part of Europe, with Sturgion and Caviare; Cape-blanke, Spaine, Portugale, and the Levant, with Mullet . . . yet all is so overlaide with fishers, as the fishing decayeth, and many are constrained to return with a small fraught." The sea off New England was different, according to Smith, "her treasures having yet never beene opened, nor her originals wasted, consumed, nor abused."[2]

Francis Higginson, a clergyman from Leicestershire, and one of the first-generation settlers in Massachusetts, testified to that freshness immediately after his arrival. "The abundance of sea fish are almost beyond believing," he wrote home in 1629, with the conviction of a man accustomed to being heard, "and sure I should scarce have believed it except I had seen it with mine own eyes. I saw great store of whales and grampus and such abundance of mackerels that it would astonish one to behold, likewise codfish. . . . And besides bass we take plenty of skate and thorneback and abundance of lobsters, that the least boy in the plantation may both catch and eat what he will of them."[3]

Almost without knowing it, staid newcomers of the middling sort who had been landsmen in England, such as Higginson, were forced into the arms of the sea. Once in New England they imitated Native ways, studying the tides to capitalize on the seasonal presence of fish, seabirds, and marine mammals. Missing the orchards, taverns, and roads that defined the reassuring English landscape, the first generation of settlers reoriented themselves to New England's realities. To begin with, the charter generation selected place-names acknowledging the creatures that defined their new world. Within the first decade of the Plymouth Colony religious separatists there named the Smelt River, Eel River, Blue Fish River, First Herring Brook, and "ye creeke called ye Eagls-Nest." Settlers in Salem initially called what is now Beverly the "Bass River." Pioneers on the Piscataqua from the 1620s to the 1640s named that river's tributaries the Lamprey River, Oyster River, Salmon Falls River, and Sturgeon Creek. Newcomers in every locale made powerful associations between the places in which their lives had begun anew and the mind-boggling density of useful organisms found there.

Important decision-making, including selection of town sites, followed from the presence or absence of marine resources. William Wood noted in 1634 that new towns on the bay "reap a greater benefit from the sea in regard of the plenty both of fish and fowl . . . so that they live more comfortably and at less charges than those . . . in the inland plantations." At Chelsea, he explained, "The land affordeth the inhabitants as many rarities as any place else, and the sea more." His list of benefits included smelt, frost fish, bass, cod, mackerel, and, at low tides, "flats for two miles together, upon which is great store of mus-cle banks and clam banks, and lobsters among the rocks and grassy holes."[4] Both Dorchester and Salem, Wood continued, lacked an "alewife river, which is a great inconvenience." Unknown in Europe, alewives were the passenger pigeons of the sea in colonial America. "Experience hath taught them at New Plymouth," wrote one eyewitness, "that in April there is a fish much like a her-ring that comes up into the small brooks to spawn, and when the water is not knee deep they will presse up through your hands, yea, thow you beat at them with cudgels, and in such abundance as is incredible." Roxbury, on the other hand, according to Wood, had a "clear and fresh brook running through the town," which, while it lacked alewives, featured "great store of smelts." Smelt are a slender, pale green fish with a silver belly and a broad silvery band along its sides. Smaller than alewives, only six to nine inches long, smelt wintered in brackish estuaries and then—driven by an ancient biological clock—ascended rivers to spawn in the spring. Like alewives they could be seined in vast numbers, or trapped with weirs; like alewives, too, they could be panfried or roasted for immediate consumption, salted or smoked for the future, or used to fertilize fields. Unlike alewives, smelt were well known in Europe.[5]

Promoters' stories had prepared colonists for abundance, but not for the ways in which they would reorient to the sea, or affect it. By 1628, when fewer than 200 men, women, and children lived in Plymouth, settlers there had already built an ingenious trap on a rapid but shallow freshwater river. Reminiscent of the kiddles so effective in English rivers throughout the Middle Ages, their trap caught the eye of a Dutch visitor. In "April and the beginning of May," he wrote, "there come so many shad from the sea which want to ascend that river, that it is quite surprising. This river the English have shut in with planks, and in the middle with a little door, which slides up and down, and at the sides with trellice work, through which the water has its course, but which they can also close with slides . . . between the two [dams] there is a square pool, into which the fish aforesaid come swimming in such shoals, in order to get up above, where they deposit their spawn, that at one tide there are 10,000 to 12,000 fish in it, which they shut off in the rear at the ebb, and close up the trellices above, so that no more water comes in; then the water runs out through the lower trellices, and they draw out the fish with baskets, each according to the land he cultivates, and carry them to it, depositing in each hill three or four fishes, and in these they plant their maize."[6] Fertilized by fish, even the corn that sustained those colonists had roots to the sea.

Within a generation, in addition to building such clever traps, settlers constructed weirs across virtually every negotiable river on the coast. They stop-seined creeks full of striped bass, gathered seabird eggs from rocky islet rookeries, pursued right whales swimming lazily off the beaches of Cape Cod, built fleets of shallops for the cod fishery, and collected oysters, clams, and lobsters wherever possible. The Puritan historian Edward Johnson regarded among New England's providential wonders the fact that a "remote, rocky, barren, bushy, wild-woody wilderness, a receptacle for Lions, Wolves, Bears, Foxes, [and] Rockoones" had been transformed within a generation into "a second England for fertilness."[7] Colonists celebrated God's bounty and their own "improvements," but by the inauguration of George Washington marine ecosystems from Cape Cod to Newfoundland had been reshaped by localized depletions, range contraction, extinctions and near extinctions, and diminished estuarine productivity. Some colonists understood that fishing and fowling could have deleterious consequences, even in a sea of plenty. What is most striking about settlers and the sea in seventeenth-century New England is that, although the ocean around them teemed with life, the first two generations of magistrates imposed conservation restrictions on sea fisheries in the midst of that marine dreamscape.

REGULATIONS IN A SEA OF PLENTY

From the perspective of seventeenth-century fishermen the familiar continental shelf on which they plied their trade extended north-northeast from Cape Cod toward Newfoundland as a maze of shallow banks, named basins, submerged ledges, and deep gullies, the jumbled signature of a retreating glacier. The physical features of this underwater landscape were not unlike those ashore, a place at once dangerous and tempting, a place, as the scriptures said, that in its seasons revealed "the blessings of the deep that lieth under."[8] Within a few decades of settlement coastal villagers who had never walked inland a full day in their lives were nonetheless intimately familiar with distant parts of that 100,000 square miles of underwater terrain.

From the middle of the twentieth until early in the twenty-first century oceanographers called this watery territory, which overlaps parts of New England and Atlantic Canada, the Northeast Shelf large marine ecosystem (LME). LMEs are coastal zones extending from the shore to the outer edge of continental shelves or, in some cases, to the outer margins of major coastal currents. Oceanographers characterize LMEs by distinctive "bathymetry, hydrography, and productivity, within which marine populations have adapted reproductive, growth, and feeding strategies," a technical way of saying that the topography of the seafloor, its water circulation patterns, its normal range of temperatures, and its level of productivity influence the types of organisms found there, along with who eats whom. Scientists, of course, do not assume that the boundaries of such systems are precise. By 2002, after decades of study and as part of a global initiative to isolate coastal ecosystems for research and management, the region between Cape Cod and Newfoundland was redefined into three LMEs—the Northeast U.S. Shelf, the Scotian Shelf, and the Newfoundland-Labrador Shelf. However, from a perspective simultaneously historic and ecological, it makes more sense to imagine the region between Cape Cod and southern Newfoundland as a unified area, as scientists did until 2002, and as Captain John Smith did in 1616, when he wrote of the fishery there "in the deepes, and by the shore" that "stretcheth along the coast from Cape Cod to Newfound-land, which is seaven or eight hundred miles at the least." Throughout the seventeenth century and much of the eighteenth century, that area was crucial to New England's export economy and economic survival.[9]

The first generation of laws in New Plymouth and Massachusetts Bay, like laws and regulations everywhere, were laden with values, assumptions, and inferences about the future. Those early regulations reflected actions taken and stories told. They concerned, among other things, public safety, nuisances, fraud, untimely deaths, idleness, the consolidation of wealth, thefts, wages, fornication, and "the many & extraordinary mercyes wch the Lord hath beene pleased to vouchsafe." They also spoke to the allocation, harvest, and conservation of natural resources. In keeping with seventeenth-century assumptions that the plants and animals of God's creation existed for humans' sake, one of the first laws passed by the freemen and magistrates of Plymouth Colony assured "that fowling, fishing and Hunting be free" to all the inhabitants. A decade later they reaffirmed the principle of free access, but qualified it by reserving to the industrious the fruit of their own labor. The revised law stated that "if any man desire to improve a place and stocke it with fish of any kind for his private use, it shalbe lawful for the court to make such grant, and forbid all others to make use of it." In 1633, shortly after the great migration of Puritans to Massachusetts Bay, Plymouth's magistrates passed a law to reserve local alewives to "such as doe or shall inhabit the town of Plymouth." Relying on those fish for "the setting of corne," and convinced that stocks were not inexhaustible, they were determined to prevent outsiders from pirating spring spawning runs.[10]

Conserving striped bass stocks was also a concern in seventeenth-century Massachusetts. Bass had providential associations for the first generation of settlers. But for God feeding "them out of the sea," as Governor William Bradford wrote, the Pilgrims would not have survived their starving time. "The best dish they could present" that first year, he noted, "was a lobster or a piece of fish without bread or anything else but a cup of fair spring water." Compared to the bread, beef, and beer dear to the English, the fishy menu seemed hopelessly bleak. Bradford forever associated striped bass with starvation rations. He didn't share the enthusiasm of William Wood, a contemporary who described striped bass admiringly as "a delicate, fine, fat, fast fish . . . though men are soon wearied with other fish, yet are they never with bass."[11]

Striped bass spawn in brackish water at the heads of estuaries or in freshwater close to the sea. Like all river fish, their propensity to congregate seasonally in rivers and streams made them an easy target. Plentiful in their summer season from Cape Cod to southern Maine, striped bass were less numerous from mid-Maine eastward. According to Wood, "the English at the top of an high water do cross the creeks with long seines or bass nets which stop in the fish." As John Smith had noted farther south in 1622, "there hath beene taken a thousand Bayses [bass] at a draught," that is, in one set of a net.[12]

Striped bass can weigh more than 100 pounds. As Wood observed in 1634, "some be three and some four foot long, some bigger, some lesser." Bigger fish are more solitary. Those that school are typically up to 10 pounds, but sometimes 20 or 25 pounds. Even if the average bass landed in a single set of the net weighed just 10 pounds, the catches were impressive. Small bands of gaunt Pilgrims, such as the ones Wood watched, were landing up to 10,000 pounds of stripers in one haul. The Pilgrims later shipped barrels of pickled bass to Spain, but found no buyers. Bass, when available, was consumed locally.[13]

Such robust landings spelled trouble, even for a Chosen People to whom God had given "dominion over the fish of the sea." By 1639, less than twenty years after the arrival of the *Mayflower,* when the entire area from Connecticut to southern Maine was inhabited by only 20,000 English settlers, and when silvery shoals of mackerel, menhaden, bass, and cod boggled the minds of observers such as Francis Higginson and William Wood, the gentlemen-magistrates in Massachusetts Bay outlawed using cod or bass as manure in the fields. In what appears to be the first fishery regulation in New England aimed specifically at conservation, the magistrates recognized the specter of waste and the threat of local depletion. No minutes remain from the discussion preceding passage of the law, but the inference is that the gentlemen did not believe that local marine resources were infinite, even when harvested by a tiny human population.[14]

Controversies about the state of bass stocks persisted for decades. During the 1640s the General Court of New Plymouth had granted a lease for bass fishing at Cape Cod to John Stone, of Hull, in the Massachusetts Bay Colony. With his lease Stone was allowed to use "lands, creeks, timber, &c upon the Cape." Stone sailed across Cape Cod Bay from Hull each spring with his assistants, and set up temporary fishing camps along the streams in which bass were known to spawn. The goal would have been to catch, clean, and pack as many bass as they could handle during the spawning runs. Bass, unlike cod, were not air-dried, but were packed in barrels with salt. A successful bass fishery required barrel staves and other cooperage supplies, seine nets or weirs, sufficient salt for the season, a shallop or other vessel for freighting, and provisions for the fishermen. In October 1650, when the total population of the Plymouth Colony numbered only 2,000, the General Court revoked John Stone's lease. Members of the court said explicitly that they wanted to return bass fishing rights to men from towns in their own colony. Yet they did not throw open the fishery to all: far from it. "Wee are informed," they wrote, "yᵗ two companies, with nett, boats, and other craft, is as much as the place can beare." The records do not indicate who informed the court that Cape Cod's rivers and creeks could accommodate only two companies of bass fishers, but it seems reasonable that the court would have been swayed only by individuals conversant with the fishery. In their opinion, at least by 1650, the state of bass stocks did not warrant an open fishery, although numerous rivers in which bass might have spawned emptied into Cape Cod Bay from the Cape's upland drainage, including Herring River, Blackfish Creek, Fresh Brook, Herring Brook, Bass Creek, Mill Creek, Marasapin Creek, and Scorton Creek. In view of the possibility of overfishing, the court adopted a precautionary approach.[15]

Conservation laws such as the one from 1639 forbidding bass as fertilizer, and the one passed in 1647 requiring that all weirs "be opened from noon of the last day of the week until morning of the second day," reflected not only the magistrates' sense that a well-ordered society was a well-regulated society, but also their appreciation that the marine resources that overwhelmed their senses were finite, and too valuable to squander. Opening weirs over the long sabbath reduced fishing pressure substantially, increasing the likelihood of fish in the future. Another recognition of the seashore's prominent place in their fledgling colony came in 1636, when "Water baylies" (or water bailiffs) were appointed in Boston "to see that noe annoying things eyther by fish, Wood, or stone or other such like things, be left or layd about the sea shore."[16]

Conservation measures notwithstanding, settlers were quick to build permanent weirs, such as those that littered the waterways of Old England. Massachusetts Bay settlers built their first weir within two years of their arrival. Wood reported that there was "a fall of fresh waters which convey themselves into the ocean through the Charles River. A little below this fall of waters the inhabitants of Watertown have built a weir to catch fish, wherein they take great store of shads and alewives. In two tides they have gotten one hundred thousand of those fishes." By the fall of 1632 the Court of Assistants approved construction of another weir in Saugus, and two years after that granted Mr. Israell Stoughton "liberty" to "builde a myll, a ware, & a bridge over the

Naponsett Ryver," which flowed into Massachusetts Bay on the southern end of Boston, and "to sell the alewyves hee takes there att 5ˢ the thousand." Roxbury residents had already built a weir without the General Court's permission. The inhabitants of New Town received liberty to erect a weir on the Winotomy River in 1634, and the next year Messrs. Dummer and Spencer petitioned successfully for permission to build a mill and weir at the falls on the river in Newbury. In 1639 Plymouth Colony granted rights for weirs "to take fish at Mortons Hole, Eagles Nest, and Blewfish River," along with a herring weir at Jones River. Several weirs already existed in New Plymouth. Individual farmers and fishermen rapidly came to expect the presence of vast numbers of fish to use as they saw fit. Refereeing a squabble over rights to alewives in the town of Sandwich, the New Plymouth Court determined in 1655 that "Thomas Burgis shall haue anually ten thousand herrings."[17]

By the 1640s weirs with considerable catching power latticed many of the rivers in the southern third of the Gulf of Maine, an area ranging from Cape Cod to Kittery, Maine. The rash of newly built weirs and milldams inevitably reduced the number of fish seeking to spawn, though precise percentages are unknowable. Native inhabitants, itinerant explorers, and first-generation settlers had all lauded those rivers' spawning runs of shad, alewives, smelt, salmon, sturgeon, bass, and other fish. Such anadromous species formed one piece of the gulf's signature productivity. It is not clear when those fish began to spawn in the Gulf of Maine watershed. We do know that the gulf is one of the youngest arms of the world's oceans. Formed by retreating glaciers some 13,000 years ago, by a landmass that rebounded after being depressed by the weight of that ice, and by rising sea level as a result of glacial melting, its functional age, or time in which its characteristic tidal regime has been similar to that of today, is only several thousand years—"less than the duration of recorded human history," as a team of scientists has written, "and more recent than the arrival of early man in the area we now call the Gulf of Maine watershed." Far from being part of an eternal sea, the gulf's geography, hydrology, and biological productivity were all quite recent when the Vikings arrived in North America. No impact on anadromous fish in the gulf during the preceding 3,000 years had been equivalent to that of the weirs erected between 1621 and the 1640s.[18]

Providentialism and abundance provided foundations for the written history of seventeenth-century New England. As the chroniclers saw it, tracts of unimproved land, virgin forests of pine and hardwoods, and incomprehensibly bountiful fish stocks transformed a hardworking, God-fearing population into a people of plenty in a temperate New World Eden. During the seventeenth and eighteenth centuries Britain's thirteen North American mainland colonies had a rate of economic growth nearly double that of Great Britain itself. By the outbreak of the American Revolution, per-capita gross domestic product in the provinces that would become the United States was substantially higher than that of every other country in the world, and higher than it would be for the foreseeable future. Such unparalleled prosperity rested on the abundance of natural resources in British North America, and on colonists' work ethic and willingness to exploit both land and dependent laborers.[19]

Yet the dominant narrative of abundance, so valid in many ways, has eclipsed an important back-story. Emigrants carried knowledge of resource depletion in their baggage to the New World. Early settlers were concerned about preserving resources. First-generation emigrants' knowledge of coastal and estuarine overfishing in England and continental Europe became an incentive to conserve resources in America. For several generations, settlers articulated the need for a precautionary approach to their sea fisheries, seeking to balance short-term needs against long-term costs, even as they harvested marine resources with the fervor of men on the make and squabbled over rights of access.

Perpetuating stocks of alewives, which farmers regarded as vital for fertilizer, was always a concern. In May 1664 "the whole town of Taunton," led by Joseph Gray, Samuell Linkhorne, and George Watson, "complained of great wrong" when the owner of the sawmill straddling the herring river in Taunton refused "to leave a sufficient passage for the herrings or alewives." Blocking the river with a milldam prevented access to the fish by upstream farmers, and prevented the fish from reaching their spawning grounds. Everyone understood the implications. By May 1664 much of the spawning season was over and the damage had been done, though the court immediately instructed James Walker, owner of the mill, "to speedily take course that a free passage bee left for the goeing up of the alewives . . . whiles yet some pte of the season remains." The court also ordered that before the next spawning season the owners of the mill make "a free, full, and sufficient passage" for the fish; otherwise "the said town . . . is in danger to suffer much damage." Towns took seriously residents' access to marine resources in other ways, as well. In 1659 the towns of Barnstable and Yarmouth, both in the Plymouth Colony, agreed that henceforth their shared town boundary would extend "into the sea one mile," a far-sighted means of preventing disputes over both shellfish and finfish.[20]

Yet officials' concerns regarding depletion extended well beyond anadromous fish such as striped bass and alewives. While striped bass was not indigenous to the boreal region of the eastern Atlantic, emigrants to New England knew all too well that any anadromous fish stock could be reduced by overfishing. Whether by outlawing its use as fertilizer or limiting the numbers of bass fishers, the magistrates' determination to preserve striped bass made sense in light of their Old World experience.

One of the most striking expressions of concern for the preservation of fish, however, focused on mackerel, literally one of the most numerous fish in the sea. In fact Massachusetts' seventeenth-century fishery regulations were much more concerned with sea fish than with anadromous species. In 1660 the Commissioners of the United Colonies of New England took it upon themselves to prevent the destruction of New England's mackerel stocks. An act that year stated:

> Fforasmuch as diuers of the most experienced ffishermen in seuerall ptes of the Countrey haue complained that the early fishing for Mackerell before they haue spawned doth extreamly wast consume and destroye them; and that the goeing out of some to meet them farr into the sea doth alsoe beat them of the coast; The Comissioners considering that the fish is the most staple commoditie in this Countrey and might bee much more benificiall then yet it hath bine if wisly managed; they doe therefore Recommend vnto the Courts of the seuerall Jurisdictions that they prohibit fishing for Mackerell vntil the fifteenth day of July yearly that soe fish may increase and bee continued.

The United Colonies of New England had been established in 1643 as a "Consociation amongst ourselves for mutual help and strength in all our future concernments." The league of friendship, in which each colony sent two delegates who then elected a president from among themselves, linked Massachusetts Bay, New Plymouth, New Haven, and Connecticut, then centered at Hartford. (Conspicuously missing was Rhode Island, which the others considered theologically schismatic.) The Articles of Confederation specified that the commissioners would not meddle with the government of any of the independent jurisdictions, but would concern themselves only with issues of consequence to their collective security and friendship. The United Colonies' greatest successes came in the realm of common defense through diplomacy (and threats) directed at regional Natives, the French, and the Dutch, but the commissioners also occasionally directed their attention to other matters, including economic development. Their act in 1660 regarding management of the mackerel fishery is significant not only because it was rooted in the complaints of experienced fishermen, but also because it had support across much of New England. It reflected the concerns of fragile societies dependent on the sea.[21]

The Atlantic mackerel is a sleek, fast-swimming fish. Ivory colored on the belly, mackerel are distinguished by an iridescent greenish-blue back, marked transversely with wavy tiger stripes. Individual fish are generally twelve to eighteen inches long when mature, and weigh between one and two pounds. With rather oily flesh, similar to that of herring and bluefish, mackerel are flavorful and were much sought after. They can be smoked, salted, pickled, or eaten fresh. But the oiliness that makes fresh mackerel so succulent keeps them from preserving as well as white-fleshed fish, such as cod. A staple in Europe from the Bay of Biscay to the Norwegian coast since the Roman era, mackerel were well known to seamen and fishmongers alike, though every winter they disappeared. Fisheries scientists now know that mackerel winter in deeper water offshore. For fishing communities, the mackerel's return provided a welcome sign of spring. But mackerel were fickle, irregular in their migrations, and always restless. Requiring considerable oxygen, they move constantly to increase water flow across their gills. Following the zooplankton, squid, and small fish that they eat, mackerel generally move diurnally, receding into the depths during the day and surfacing at night, although schools also appeared at the surface in daylight. Vast surface-flitting schools were seen routinely by seventeenth-century mariners. A keen-eyed man at the masthead, with the sun behind him, could see schools of mackerel eight to ten fathoms below the surface on a calm summer day. At night submerged schools betrayed themselves by "firing" the water, disturbing bioluminescent microorganisms. On overcast or moonless nights, the eerie bluish trace of bioluminescence enchanted observers, magically revealing shoals of sleek fish darting and pirouetting in the forbidding depths. During spring and summer mackerel more conveniently closed with the shore. As William Wood noted at Chelsea in 1634, "shoals of bass have driven up shoals of mackerel from one end of the sandy beach to another, which the inhabitants have gathered up in wheelbarrows."[22]

Those shoals were just the tip of the iceberg. Ecologists studying schooling behavior of fish during the late twentieth century reported individual schools of overwintering North Atlantic mackerel that measured five nautical miles long by one-and-a-half nautical miles wide, and twelve meters thick, containing approximately 750 million individual fish. Scientists now know that herring, mackerel, and menhaden are the most numerous species in the North Atlantic. So how could a few seventeenth-century fishermen from New Haven, New London, Duxbury, and Boston, equipped with modest seines and hooks, and sailing in heavy shallops, imagine that they could "consume and destroy" what Francis Higginson had referred to in 1629 as "such abundance of mackerels as it would astonish one to behold"?[23]

The point is that they did. By 1660 enough regional fishermen were concerned about the future of mackerel stocks to convince their elected officials that the fish would "increase and bee continued" only "if wisly managed." They may have felt that mackerel's abundance in 1660 compared poorly with abundance in decades past. They may have observed several seasons of poor year-classes, when recruitment of juveniles to adults lagged the norm. The late 1650s may have been years when mackerel did not come inshore to the extent that had been normal. We don't know exactly what prompted their concern, though it is clear that they believed human activity could affect mackerel stocks.[24]

Fishing continued, however, as did stories about fishing. Ten years later, in October 1670, the General Court of Massachusetts took action after "being informed that the taking of mackerel at vnseasonable times doe greatly diminish their increase, & will, in the issue, tend to the spoyle of the trade thereof." They ordered that "henceforth no mackerel shall be caught, except for spending while fresh"—that is, for immediate consumption—"before the first of July, annually." And the next year, when residents of Hull, in Massachusetts Bay, petitioned the colony of New Plymouth "to haue libertie to employ some boates and theire companies for the takeing of mackerel with netts, at the season thereof, att Cape Cod," the court granted "libertie only for two boats." Whether the residents of Hull had requested permits for more than two boats ("some boates") is not known. The court may have been simply exercising its prerogative to grant licenses and to collect revenue "due to the collonie from forraigners," rather than acting to preserve fish stocks. At a time when much about nature was unfathomable, especially the mysteries of the sea, New Englanders nevertheless saw the world in certain ways and operated on those assumptions. And by 1670 Massachusetts fishermen and gentlemen were convinced that the seine technology at their disposal had the capacity to affect schooling fish such as mackerel.[25]

In 1684, for instance, an experienced fisherman named William Clarke convinced the General Court at Plymouth to take seriously "the great damage that this collonie and our naighbours is likely to sustaine by the catching of mackerel with netts and saines at Cape Cod, or else where near any shore in this collonie, to the great destruction of fish, and the discurragement of severall fishermen." Clarke put his money where his mouth was. He offered the treasurer of the colony thirty pounds "in currant New England money" for each of the next seven years for the rights to the bass fishing at Cape Cod, provided that the court prohibit mackerel seining. Clark believed that without bountiful supplies of mackerel for forage, striped bass would not frequent inshore waters near Cape Cod, and he was convinced that seining mackerel would deplete them.[26]

From 1660 to 1702 various regulatory bodies of the United Colonies of New England, Massachusetts Bay, and, to a lesser extent, New Plymouth, expressed concerns about the future of mackerel stocks and the possibility of overfishing them. While the words on the tips of fishermen's tongues are lost to time, it is fair to say that the preservationist language of the commissioners and the General Court distilled the essence of numerous conversations by "the most experienced ffishermen," as they put it, conversations about how catching mackerel before they spawned each year could "destroye them," conversations about fishing pressure affecting mackerel's migratory path, and conversations about the importance of beneficial commodities being "wisly managed." By the 1660s some of those fishermen and merchants had been born in the colonies, but there were also still fishermen such as "Robert Willie, allias Willis, sometimes of Milbrooke in the countey of Cornwall, and sence belonging to Winter Harboure, at Saco, in New England," who was part of the crew of a mackerel fishing trip near Plymouth in 1652. Men like Willie, with firsthand comparisons of coastal ecosystems in Old England and New England, had reason for concern about overfishing.[27]

Massachusetts's most dramatic precautionary restrictions on New England's embryonic commercial fisheries came in 1668. Real earnings from fisheries, as everyone knew, would come not from mackerel, bass, or herring, but from cod. Dried cod became the cornerstone of colonial New England's export economy by the middle of the seventeenth century. Yet with the exception of the settlement at Pemaquid, Maine, attempts to organize a New England-based commercial fishery during the 1620s and 1630s faltered, despite legislative incentives and land grants. While it was common knowledge that the marine ecosystem east-northeast of Cape Cod furnished among the best fishing grounds in the world, few of the Puritan migrants from the south and east of England had the skills or commercial contacts to make the fishery succeed. Rough men from the West Country, who understood the fishery, were not readily welcomed by "the saints," as Puritans called their covenanted communities. And hiring fishing servants for a fixed seasonal wage, as had been the system in Newfoundland for more than a century, generally did not work in Massachusetts or southern Maine, where alternative opportunities abounded. Servant fishermen simply disappeared to seek their own fortunes.[28]

Despite these problems cod-fishing operations commenced in the western section of Massachusetts Bay, immediately adjacent to Boston, during the height of the Puritans' great migration. In 1632 Reverend Thomas Welde optimistically wrote to his former parishioners in England that "The plantation is now set upon fishing for a staple commodity . . . shallops [are] made and tackling provided to catch it withal and to send it into other countries to fetch in all other commodities." A fishing station at Scituate commenced that year. At Dorchester, Henry Way had two shallops fishing by 1631, one locally and one in waters to the east. By 1634 Matthew Craddock, an absentee capitalist, had a fleet of eight shallops fishing from Marblehead manned by servants under the management of Isaac Allerton, who had been the deputy governor and commercial agent at New Plymouth before parting ways with other Pilgrim fathers. For a variety of reasons, Allerton's servant fishery never thrived. These false starts and small-scale operations prompted the Massachusetts Bay government to give several gentlemen "power to consulte, advise, & take order for the setting forwards & after manageing of a fisheing trade," and appropriated public money for the task. In 1639, the same year they forbade using cod or bass for manure, the magistrates ordered that a "fishing plantation shalbee begun at Cape Anne," assigning Mr. Morrice Tomson to take charge.[29]

Unlike a seasonal river fishery for striped bass, which could be worked by farmers with nets, or a weir fishery for alewives, which required only the simplest of boats, commercial cod fishing was daunting. It involved arranging substantial credit to procure supplies, as well as catching, processing, storing, shipping, and marketing large volumes of dried fish. As Daniel Vickers, the preeminent historian of the fisheries, explains, "Competing with the highly skilled and well-capitalized fisheries of Western Europe for markets and with the developing rural economy of the Bay Colony itself for labor and capital was not going to be easy."[30]

The English civil war (1642–1651) gave colonial merchants the break they needed. The number of West Country fishing boats working on the coast of Newfoundland fell from 340 in 1634, before the war, to fewer than 200 by 1652. The West Country vessels that had worked the coast of New England disappeared entirely. These disruptions to production, followed by a dwindling supply, elevated the price of cod in southern Europe. All of this provided New England merchants with the incentive to try fishing again, and during the next several decades New England's output of dried cod steadily rose. Initially carried to Spain, Portugal, and the Atlantic islands in English ships, cod was soon being exported in prodigious amounts in American bottoms to Catholic markets in southern Europe and to the Caribbean plantation islands, where an increasingly large population of enslaved workers needed to be fed. Exports of dried, salted cod were on their way to becoming the lynchpin in the New England economy, spurring the shipbuilding and shipping services at the heart of New England's remarkable economic development. Between 1645 and 1675 New England's total output of cod rose between 5 and 6 percent each year, increasing from about 12,000 to 60,000 quintals (one quintal was 112 pounds of dried cod).[31]

In the midst of this remarkable expansion of the fisheries, in October 1668, the General Court halted open access to stocks of gadoids, ordering "that no man shall henceforth kill any codfish, hake, hadduck, or pollucke, to be drjed up for sale, in the month of December or January, because of their spawning tjme."[32] Why would development-minded authorities limit the cod season, closing the fishery for two months each year?

Northwest Atlantic cod catches—originally in Newfoundland, but later in Nova Scotia and New England—fluctuated significantly throughout the sixteenth, seventeenth, and eighteenth centuries. The year 1592 was an especially poor one for fishermen in Newfoundland, one that "coincided with scarcity in the Cornish and Irish fisheries." And 1621 was a lean year, too. The Dorchester Company failed to develop the fisheries near Cape Ann, Massachusetts, during the 1620s, partly because of a perceived lack of fish. As Christopher Levett wrote in 1624, "the Shippes which fished there this yeare, their boats went twenty miles to take their Fish, and yet they were in great feare of making their Voyages, as one of the Masters confessed unto me who was at my house." At Boston in June 1651 Captain John Leveret was unable to deliver 308 quintals of fish to his assignee, William Stratton. As Leveret explained, Stratton "knoweth that fish hath not been to be pcured for money." One Mrs. Norton stated in her husband's absence that "if her husband could have procured fish he would have done it to his utmost." But fish were scarce near Boston that year. Fishermen could never predict seasonal catches with certainty. And it was more than a matter of luck.[33]

Scientists today attribute fluctuations in historic landings to climate change and other natural factors that influenced the annual size of cod stocks, along with fishing pressure. Female cod laid millions of eggs each year, but the number that hatched, much less lived to become juvenile fish, was quite small. Poor year-classes seem to have affected Newfoundland's southern shore fishery in 1723–1725, and again in 1753–1755. Townsmen in Eastham on Cape Cod complained in 1748 that the "fishery in a great measure has failed of late." Nantucket fishermen lamented in 1751 "that the codfishery round the Island has failed yearly insomuch that there have not been half enough caught . . . for the Inhabitants to eat fresh, and the fishery on the shoals so fails that it is now entirely neglected." Natural deviations such as these, which occurred in some years of each century, had real consequences for fishermen.[34]

Assessed over the *longue durée,* from the middle of the seventeenth century to the middle of the nineteenth century, the northwest Atlantic ecosystem seemed able to produce the approximately 150,000 to 250,000 tons per year that fishermen extracted from it. Significant fluctuations year-to-year were common, and are best explained by climate change. Abnormally cold spells, such as the period from about 1660 to 1683, saw marked reductions in cod landings. That overall sustainability, however, may have masked an emerging pattern of localized depletions. As early as the middle of the eighteenth century Newfoundlanders began to shift their fishing effort from areas of declining catch to unexploited places. Resident Newfoundlanders from the southern and southeastern parts of that great island, who were accustomed to fishing from shore in small boats, began to fish eastern Labrador, a distant and inhospitable place that required seasonal migrations. By late in the eighteenth century they increasingly fished Notre Dame and White Bays on the north shore of Newfoundland, which also required a seasonal trek to establish shore-based fishing operations in a wilderness area. While the evidence is far from conclusive, the declining catch rates that Newfoundlanders lamented among certain inshore stocks may have reflected overfished and locally depleted cod populations.[35]

In this light, the decision of the Massachusetts General Court in 1668 to close the commercial cod fishery during December and January of each year may indicate that the court perceived problems with the Massachusetts Bay cod fishery as early as 1668. The historical record is too thin for an absolutely conclusive answer, but examination of the process of farm-building, town-building, and fishing in light of local regions' ecological productivity reveals that as early as the 1660s cod fishing between Cape Ann and Cape Cod, within the confines of Massachusetts Bay, was already on a different path from cod fishing east of Cape Ann, where territories ranged from Essex County, Massachusetts, to the wilds of Maine.

Cod stocks in Massachusetts Bay had a somewhat more fragile foundation for their food chain than did cod stocks east of Cape Ann, a result of the underwater topography of the Gulf of Maine, and the gulf's characteristic distribution of plankton by its dominant counterclockwise currents. Biologically the Gulf of Maine is a garden, one of the most productive coastal ecosystems in the world. Geologically the gulf is a semienclosed inland sea, a factor that contributes to its productivity. Georges Bank and Brown's Bank, vast shallows that provide a significant barrier to the rest of the Atlantic, prevent the gulf's colder and less saline water from mixing freely with the Atlantic. Cold, well-oxygenated freshwater flows from numerous rivers into the gulf, where it mixes with nutrient-enriched seawater in the presence of sunlight, providing perfect conditions for phytoplankton reproduction. The virtually enclosed topography of the gulf, however, means that its currents circulate in a counterclockwise gyre, with a major current flowing from northeast to southwest along the shore of New Brunswick, Maine, and New Hampshire. Scientists now refer to that current as the Gulf of Maine coastal plume. It carries plankton down the coast as far west as Ipswich Bay, a prime cod spawning area, but is then deflected by Cape Ann so that its plankton-rich waters flow over Georges Bank, but not into Boston harbor or into the inner reaches of Massachusetts Bay from Salem to Plymouth. "Because the deflected Plume bypasses the northwestern bight of Massachusetts Bay in most weather, pelagic plankton feeders, such as herring and menhaden that attract larger predators such as cod, were not drawn in large numbers into that area. But salt marshes and estuaries around the littoral west of Cape Ann were productive enough before

European contact to maintain anadromous fish in quantities that supported large local cod populations. In short, Cape Ann ensured that for the demersal fish in Broad and Salem sounds, there was one principal menu: anadromous fish."[36]

By the latter part of the seventeenth century, about the time that the Massachusetts General Court forbade catching cod during their spawning season, two sorts of cod fisheries existed in New England. East of Cape Ann to the midcoast of Maine, shore-based fishermen in relatively small craft pursued cod on inshore grounds, as would their descendents until well into the nineteenth century. West of Cape Ann, however, Marblehead, and then Gloucester and Boston, became home to deep-sea fisheries. Men from those communities did not pursue a mixed fishing, farming, timbering, and coasting economy, but became full-time fishermen earning a living on distant offshore banks. Cod stocks in coastal waters from Cape Ann to Cape Cod were insufficiently robust to support intensive shore-based fisheries, especially as the process of town-building and farm creation disrupted the habitats necessary to support anadromous fish, such as alewives, shad, and smelt.

Weirs erected across the short rivers that fed Massachusetts Bay compounded the habitat destruction created by siltation from plow agriculture and marsh drainage. Within forty or fifty years of settlement, the Puritans had degraded the forage base for predatory fish such as cod and haddock. While those species continued to thrive farther down east, the small-boat fishery atrophied in Boston harbor and Massachusetts Bay to a large extent, with the exception of trips to Middle Bank (now known as Stellwagen Bank), between Provincetown and Gloucester.

It has long been taken for granted that fishing communities eastward of Cape Ann developed differently from those on Cape Ann and westward, because of sociological factors. Human impacts on the coastal marine environment as early as the 1660s, however, may have influenced the future shape of fishing communities. By the late seventeenth century fishermen based in Massachusetts Bay were sailing to the banks on Nova Scotia's continental shelf in search of cod, because trips made close to home simply were not worthwhile. Simultaneously, fishermen in New Hampshire and Maine continued to find productive grounds on nearshore banks watered by the plankton-rich Gulf of Maine Coastal Plume.

The state of cod stocks in Massachusetts Bay by the late seventeenth century was probably analogous to that of cod stocks in the Irish Sea and the

North Sea by the end of the Renaissance. By no means had cod been eradicated. Fishing pressure, however, had already removed the largest fish, which were the most productive spawners. With the simple gear at their disposal, essentially unchanged from the medieval period, fishermen found it more profitable to seek out new grounds than to persist in fishing locally once the cream had been skimmed. Fishing never stopped in the North Sea or the Irish Sea, but many English fishermen took the trouble and risk to sail to Iceland as early as the fifteenth century because catches were better. By the sixteenth century English fishermen, along with those from Spain, France, and Portugal, were sailing to Newfoundland. Likewise, by the final third of seventeenth century, fishermen based in towns along the shore of Massachusetts Bay preferred to sail hundreds of miles to the east, and fish off Nova Scotia, rather than fish in the bight of Cape Cod—waters whose productivity had astonished early explorers only sixty years before. Settler societies were making an impact on New England's coastal ecosystems.

A few men lamented the deleterious effect of consistent fishing in one place, such as the Englishman who wrote from coastal Newfoundland in 1703 that "the fish grows less, the old store being consumed by our continual fishing." His practical concerns flew in the face of what natural philosophers then assumed about the eternal sea. In the first half of the eighteenth century, for instance, Baron du Montesquieu asserted that oceanic fish were limitless. Such sentiments often prevailed, contradicting fears that sea fish could be depleted by overfishing.[37]

Some New Englanders went a step further. Borrowing the dominant trope of "improvement" as applied to terrestrial ecosystems, whereby a forest wilderness could be "improved" through clear-cutting and the arrangement of orderly fields, or a wetland could be "improved" if drained and transformed into a meadow, coastal New Englanders entertained the notion that they could "improve" the ocean by fishing. This ran counter to the idea that purposeful action might create problems. In 1680 William Hubbard noted, "The first improvement that was ever made to this coast" was that of "the marriner and fisher man." The notion of people improving the sea by fishing it persisted as settler societies picked the coastal ocean's low-hanging fruit. Explaining the calamities that had befallen them during the Revolutionary War, petitioners from New Castle, New Hampshire, a small town that supported itself "almost Intirely" by its cod fishery, wrote to the General Court in 1786 that "they again to hope to improve the Ocean, the only source of their riches," by resuming their fishing. As late as 1832 Lorenzo Sabine reiterated the notion that fisheries could be "improved." By the middle of the eighteenth century such conventions, privileging hard work and the transformation of wild places into orderly zones of civilized production, worked against the likelihood that New Englanders would imagine that their maritime enterprise might be undermining the resources on which it was based.[38]

THE FIRST PERTURBATION

The *Mayflower* anchored at Provincetown, in the bight of Cape Cod, on November 11, 1620. "Every day we saw Whales playing hard by us," observed one of the Pilgrims, "of which in that place, if we had instruments & meanes to take them, we might have made a very rich returne. . . . Our master and his mate, and others experienced in fishing, professed we might have made three or four thousand pounds worth of Oyle."[39] A few days later a scouting party from the *Mayflower* came across "ten or twelve Indians very busy about something" on the beach. As William Bradford related it, they had been "cutting up a great fish like a grampus," also known as a blackfish or pilot whale. The Pilgrims "found two more of these fishes dead on the sands," according to Bradford, "a thing usual after storms in that place." Blackfish provided welcome meat and oil.[40]

Whales were everywhere, unlike in coastal Europe. There were apparently tens of thousands of great whales in the Gulf of Maine for much of the year at the beginning of the seventeenth century.[41] Even landsmen such as Bradford noticed the difference. Experienced fishermen could not help but observe that the ecosystem in the western Atlantic was structured differently because of the presence of great whales, even if they did not push their conclusions to acknowledge that the paucity of whales in home waters was the result of overharvesting.[42]

Natives from Cape Cod to the Gulf of St. Lawrence may have occasionally hunted large whales during the precontact period, but the archaeological evidence is inconclusive, as are the early ethnographies. Nevertheless, Natives treasured whales. Mi'kmaqs' "greatest liking," according to Nicolas Denys, a fisherman and early settler in Acadia, was "grease [which] they eat . . . as one does bread." According to Denys, Mi'kmaqs in Acadia relished the blubber from whales "which frequently came ashore on the coast." Along with hunting pilot whales and porpoise, all Native people from Nantucket eastward routinely availed themselves of drift whales—stranded live whales or dead whales that washed up on the beach. Along certain sections of the coast "drift whales were so numerous that no need had arisen to go to sea to kill them."[43] The fact that Natives rarely or never hunted great whales suggests that whale populations along the coast of New England were virtually unexploited at the time of European contact. Robust whale stocks and relatively low aboriginal population densities meant that Natives' opportunistic reliance on drift whales sufficed for their needs.

Following permanent English settlement, Natives' right to appropriate drift whales was lost rather quickly on Martha's Vineyard and Long Island. On Nantucket, however, that right was codified into law in 1673. "The Court do order that . . . all the whal fish or Other drift fish belong to the Indian sachems." Purchasing shore frontage from Nantucket sachems in a series of transactions between 1684 and 1701, English buyers always agreed to the caveat, "except drift whales." And on Nantucket and eastern Long Island, at least, because "Indian ownership of drift whales pre-empted the crown's rights . . . whale oil from Indian drift whales may have been exported tax-free." The exact steps by which settlers proceeded from scavenging beached whales to pursuing whales from the beach are lost to time, but whales' significance is not. In 1635 Governor John Winthrop noted that "Some of our people went to Cape Cod, and made some oil of a whale which was cast on shore." The Plymouth Colony began to tax the enterprise in 1652. Reverend Cotton Mather called whale oil "a staple commodity of the colony."[44] Shore whaling began in Massachusetts during the 1650s or 1660s, but very few human generations were required to deplete the abundant stock of nearshore whales. As early as 1720 the *Boston News-Letter* reported that "We hear from the towns on the Cape that the Whale Fishery among them has failed much this Winter, as it has done for several winters past." Contemporaries claimed that the nearshore whaling grounds had been "fished out" by 1740. The economic consequences were dire: capital equipment sat idle, and expected earnings did not materialize. Minor political consequences followed, too. In 1754 Selectman John Hallet petitioned the province to excuse the town of Yarmouth from sending a representative to the legislature because of the failure of inshore whaling.[45]

According to one conservative study, colonists killed a minimum of 2,459 to 3,025 right whales between 1696 and 1734 in the coastal area between Delaware Bay and Maine, in addition to numerous pilot whales and occasional other great whales. Other informed estimates suggest a much larger harvest.

In 1794 the Reverend John Mellen of Barnstable, Massachusetts, noted, "Seventy or eighty years ago the whale bay fishery was carried on in boats from shore, to great advantage. This business employed nearly two hundred men for three months of the year, the fall and the beginning of winter. But few whales now come into the bay, and this kind of fishery has for a long time (by this town at least) been given up."[46] The killing of northwest Atlantic whales had begun in earnest about a century before the *Mayflower* sailed. Basque whalers killed tens of thousands of right whales and bowheads in the Straits of Belle Isle, between Labrador and Newfoundland, from 1530 to 1620. Then, while coastal New Englanders were exploiting local stocks, Dutch and Basque whalers in the western Arctic harpooned 35,000 to 40,000 whales between 1660 and 1701, reducing stocks considerably and affecting the whales' migratory patterns.[47]

Once inshore stocks were depleted along the Massachusetts coast, sachems' possession of drift whales became a rather hollow "right." Lookout masts, whalemen's taverns, and try yards (the boiling facilities where whale blubber was rendered) were abandoned on Cape Cod and Nantucket. Merchants in towns on the north shore of Massachusetts Bay, such as Ipswich, that formerly had dabbled in shore whaling turned their attention entirely to fishing and sea trading. This transition took time. Whalemen did not give up all at once. But by the early eighteenth century, the number of whales being killed, getting stranded, or washing up dead was decreasing dramatically. By midcentury, shore whaling was no longer a source of reliable seasonal income. An air of desolation hung over facilities that not long before had been bustling and profitable, such as the whalers' tavern on Wellfleet's Great Island, abandoned about 1740 during the denouement of shore whaling. Once inshore stocks of whales had been depleted, whalemen had no call to rest or recuperate in a tavern at Wellfleet. By the 1750s, well-capitalized Cape Cod vessels were voyaging to Labrador and Newfoundland, almost 1,000 miles eastward, to hunt for whales. Meanwhile, as the biomass of the coastal ecosystem shifted to include fewer whales, Nantucket's remnant Indian population sailed as "men before the mast" aboard whaling vessels. Long gone were the days when they could scavenge whales from the beach.[48]

The consequences of shore whaling were not limited to the geographic expansion of deep-sea whaling, much less to the depletion of town coffers, the abandonment of once-productive whaling installations, or the redefinition of Native life on Nantucket and Long Island. Killing large numbers of whales in a relatively short time removed their qualitative contribution to ecosystem stability. Baleen whales are not apex predators. As large, long-lived creatures, however, whales embody vast biomass in stable form. Mature blue whales routinely weigh 125 metric tons; large ones are often 170 tons. An individual right whale can weigh 100 tons. Before commercial harvesting began, naturally occurring populations of whales concentrated hundreds of thousands of tons of biomass in continental shelf ecosystems. Each animal effectively "locked up" the biological matter of which it consisted throughout its long life. This incorporation of vast biomass in numerous long-lived animals imposed constraints on biological variability in the system, and helped maintain a natural equilibrium. Overharvesting baleen whales liberated considerable prey from capture, and thus may have allowed prey populations to oscillate more dramatically than previously.[49]

Colonial New Englanders referred to one species of North Atlantic whales as "scrags," a name now anachronistic. Obed Macy's *History of Nantucket* claims that the first whale killed in Nantucket was a "scragg." Paul Dudley, a Massachusetts resident who published an essay on the natural history of whales in 1725 in the *Philosophical Transactions of the Royal Society of London,* explained that "The Scrag whale is near-a-kin to the Fin-back, but instead of a Fin on his Back, the Ridge of the After-part of his Back is scragged with a half Dozen Knobs or Knuckes; he is nearest the right Whale in Figure and for Quantity of Oil." A commission from the Muscovy Merchants to Thomas Edge in 1611 referred to a whale called the "otta sotta," whose description—like Dudley's "scrag whale"—corresponds to that of an Atlantic gray whale. Subfossil specimens of gray whales have been found along European shores, and from Florida to eastern Long Island. Radiocarbon dating has established that this species disappeared around 1675. Evidence suggests that a population of Atlantic gray whales lived on both sides of the Atlantic; that those whales, like others, were hunted; and that the population became extinct during the late seventeenth or early eighteenth century. Whether human hunters caused this extinction, accelerated it, or had nothing to do with it is unknowable. Given the rate at which whales were being killed then, however, it appears likely that this extinction of a North Atlantic marine mammal—the first of the post-Pleistocene era—resulted from the intensified whaling associated with the exploitation of western Atlantic waters and the creation of the Atlantic world.[50]

All marine mammals had value, though whales and walruses were hunted much more regularly than seals and porpoises before the nineteenth century.

Walrus hides, ivory, and oil had been a considerable attraction to sixteenth-century European adventurers in the Gulf of St. Lawrence. When killed and rendered each walrus provided one to two barrels of oil. Walruses were historically abundant from Sable Island northward to the Gulf of St. Lawrence and the coast of Labrador. They are gregarious creatures, and despite their great size and unwieldiness 7,000 or 8,000 animals could congregate together at a single terrestrial haul-out, called an "echourie" by fishermen. Echouries were generally at least 80 to 100 yards wide and, whether sand or rock, sloped gradually from the sea to a place sufficiently large for vast assemblies of walruses. Those haul-outs were located in the greater Gulf of St. Lawrence region at the Isle Madame Islands, the Magdalen Islands, the Ramea Islands, and at Miscou Island, among others. The southernmost was at Sable Island, east of Nova Scotia, a treacherous graveyard for ships on account of its constantly shifting sands. Walrus typically spent considerable time on shore during the calving season, between April and June, and when thousands hauled out together, individual animals could go for several weeks without food or water.[51]

Walruses have few predators, but their tendency to cluster together made them vulnerable to humans. The hunters, explained an eighteenth-century writer, "take the advantage of a sea wind, or a breeze blowing rather obliquely on the shore, to prevent the smelling of these animals (who have that sense in great perfection, contributing to their safety), and with the assistance of very good dogs, endeavour in the night time to separate those that are the farthest advanced from those next the water, driving them different ways. This they call making a cut." Once some had been driven up the slope of the echourie, they could be "killed at leisure," sometimes by the hundreds. The crew of one European ship killed 1,500 walruses during the 1591 season at Sable Island. Later, once the art of "cutting" had been perfected, hundreds of walruses were killed at a time.[52]

During the summer of 1641 Boston merchants sent a vessel with twelve men to Sable Island, off Nova Scotia, to hunt walruses. As John Winthrop explained, they "brought home 400 pair of sea horse teeth [walrus tusks], which were esteemed worth £300," leaving some of the crew and "12 ton of oil and many skins" on the island. Prior to commercial exploitation the largest herds in the world apparently lived near the Magdalen Islands in the Gulf of Saint Lawrence, an archipelago surrounded by shellfish beds, and well supplied with the conveniently sloping haul-outs. The last large-scale walrus hunts of the eighteenth century took place at the Magdalen Islands during the era of the American Revolution. The scale of the slaughter was not sustainable. By the late eighteenth century the great, gregarious herds that had once hauled out on islands and beaches from Sable Island to Labrador had been extirpated. Walruses were not extinct, but they suffered the most dramatic range contraction of any marine animal in the age of sail. By the early nineteenth century that range had been reduced in the western Atlantic to northern Labrador, southeastern Baffin Island, and Hudson Strait and Hudson Bay—in other words to the Arctic and immediate subarctic.[53]

During the eighteenth century seal hunting and porpoise fishing in the Gulf of Maine were occasional pursuits. Porpoises competed with Eastham men for cod and mackerel. During the 1730s the town of Eastham, on Cape Cod, declared porpoises a pest and offered a bounty on porpoise tails. The most successful bounty hunter, Elisha Young, presented about 500 tails between 1740 and 1742. In addition to this sporadic bounty hunting of marine mammals, fishermen killed harbor seals and gray seals as opportunities presented themselves, eradicating competitors and profiting from the oil and skins. In the Gulf of St. Lawrence, however, and along the southern coast of Labrador, eighteenth-century fishermen and market hunters netted seals, including harp seals, in a large-scale commercial operation. Men who fished in the spring and summer turned to sealing during the early winter. Pelts were shipped to furriers in England. And the fat from a single seal could produce anywhere from a few gallons to ten gallons or more of oil, depending on the species and the size. The price of seal oil varied according to the international oil market, determined by the annual success or failure of global whaling fleets.[54]

"There are two modes of catching the seals," explained Edward Chappell, a visiting Royal Navy officer: "the one is, by mooring strong nets at the bottom of the sea; and the other, by constructing what is called a *'frame of nets'* near the shore of some small bay." The typical net used in the first method was forty fathoms long and two deep. It worked on the same principle as a gill net for fish, though with stronger twine. Sealers anchored the foot rope "on a shallop's old rode," as the veteran hunter George Cartwright noted, and moored it with "a couple of killicks" (primitive anchors). The foot of the net was thus kept close to the bottom, while corks on the headrope made it stand perpendicularly. "As the seals dive along near the bottom to fish," explained Cartwright, "they strike into the net and are entangled." The other system was more complicated and required considerably longer nets, more anchors, and capstans ashore to raise and lower specific sides of the pound. Such frames were semipermanent, erected by sealers along shores where seals were known to congregate, often near narrow slots, called "tickles," that helped funnel the seals into the pound.

In December 1770 Cartwright heard with "pleasure" that "Guy and his people had killed near eight hundred seals." A year later, "we have killed nine hundred and seventy-two seals, which is the most I ever heard of." In January 1775 he noted that a "man belonging to Captain Darby came here today; and informed me that one of his master's crews had killed seven hundred seals; the other two, thirty each." The sealing posts were few and far between, and as these relatively modest tallies reveal, the eighteenth-century seal fishery was rather limited. Sealers relied not only on seals coming to them but also on advantageous weather conditions. As Cartwright wrote on December 8, 1775, "The mildness of the weather still keeps the seals back. I do not expect them until hard weather sets in; and as the season is so far advanced, it will freeze so severely that . . . our nets will all be frozen over." Contrasting with the very limited scale of these passive operations was that of the Newfoundland seal fishery that began in 1795, an active hunt in which schooners carrying from fifteen to forty men each sailed to the ice on which seals were whelping, and moored there as the men fanned out over the ice to club and shoot the listless seals. In those conditions a single crew could kill 3,500 seals in a single week. After 1795 the seal slaughter increased annually by orders of magnitude.[55]

The rapid removal of large numbers of whales and walruses, and some seals and porpoises, affected those populations, their prey populations, and the mariners, too. Shortly before the outbreak of the American Revolution, products from marine mammals—primarily whales—constituted 15 percent of the value of New England's exports.[56] The whale fishery was big business, and, though prosecuted far from home, it was still Atlantic-based: not until the mid-1780s would Yankee whalers round the great capes to kill whales, seals, and sea elephants in high southern latitudes and throughout the Pacific. But the size of Atlantic whale populations, their geographic distribution, their role in stabilizing marine ecosystems, and the nature of New England whaling had all changed significantly during the previous half-century. New Englanders' relatively short-term accumulation of wealth; their knowledge of whales' seasonal migration and feeding habits; and their development of technologies appropriate for pursuing, killing, rendering, and marketing whales all came at the cost of downward trends in biocomplexity and ecosystem resiliency.

RIVER FISH FROM THE SEA

As he sailed up the Kennebec River in 1607 Captain Robert Davies noted "aboundance of great fyshe in ytt Leaping aboue the Watter on eatch Syd of vs," characteristic behavior of sturgeon as they ascend rivers to spawn in freshwater during May, June, and July. Sturgeon were head-turners. Giant, toothless, and armored with rows of bony shields along their sides and back, bottom-feeding Atlantic sturgeon—with peculiar little barbells under their snouts—could be mistaken for no other fish. Archaeological evidence indicates that prehistoric Native inhabitants relied on Atlantic sturgeon in their seasonal eating strategy. Each year as the ice broke, and the annual springtime bloom of phytoplankton turned coastal waters murky brown, the return of spawning fish such as sturgeon, salmon, and alewives signaled Natives' season of plenty. Malecites and Mi'kmaqs relied so much on anadromous fish that they named several months for their return. One Englishman observed that Natives made "very strong sturgeon nets" of "their own hemp." As early as the 1630s, according to William Hammond, Indians were capturing "great store of sturgeon" in the Merrimack River for English buyers. "The sturgeons be all over the country," noted William Wood, "but the best catching of them is upon the shoals of Cape Cod and in the river of Merrimac, where much is taken, pickled, and brought for England. Some of these be twelve, fourteen, eighteen foot long." A twelve-foot sturgeon could weigh 600 pounds.[57]

John Josselyn, who lived on the midcoast of Maine in 1638–39, and from 1663 to 1671, depicted the Pechipscut River (now the Androscoggin) as "famous for multitudes of mighty large *Sturgeon*." Settlers in the Piscataqua estuary named one of its tributaries Sturgeon Creek. Few settlers had ever seen sturgeon in Old England, where an 800-year fishing spree had almost eradicated them. Every Englishman, however, shared Thomas Morton's understanding of sturgeon as a "regal fish." In France and England, sturgeon was king's fare. But in New England, as Morton pointed out in 1632, every man "may catch what hee will, there are multitudes of them."[58]

During the mid-seventeenth century, sturgeon linked resourceful Native fishers, colonial settlers, London fishmongers, and highbrow English consumers because of the degraded state of European aquatic ecosystems. By the fourteenth century, chefs in France and England had a recipe "to 'make sturgeon' from veal, a distinct mark of the prestige and favor still attached to an almost extinct food fish."[59] So New England's early settlers knew they would find a seller's market for sturgeon. Captain John Smith noted during the 1620s that one ship returning to England from the Pilgrim settlement at Plymouth carried "fourscore kegs of sturgeon." Samuel Maverick bemoaned the lack of a substantial sturgeon fishery in 1660. The Merrimack River, he noted, "in the Sumer abounds with Sturgeon, Salmon, and other ffresh water fish. Had we the art of takeing and saveing the Sturgeon it would prove a very great advantage, the Country affording Vinager, and all other Materialls to do it withal."[60]

Sturgeon were low-hanging fruit in the arbor of marine resources, and they were plucked quite quickly in all of northern New England's major rivers. They could be trapped in weirs, netted, or lanced—all by part-time shore-based fishermen. Englishmen learned successful techniques from Natives. As Josselyn explained: "in dark evenings when they are upon the fishing grounds near a Bar of Sand (where the *Sturgeon* feeds upon small fishes . . .) the *Indian* lights a piece of dry *Birch-Bark* which breaks out into flame & holds it over the side of his *Canow,* the *Sturgeon* seeing this glaring light mounts to the Surface of the water where he is slain and taken with a fis[h]gig."[61]

By 1673, less than fifty years after Morton had written that "every man in New England may catch what hee will," men from the Merrimack River towns determined that insufficient sturgeon existed for an open fishery. William Thomas, of Newbury, then seventy-four years old, petitioned the General Court to prohibit pickling or preserving sturgeon for transport (that is, other than for personal consumption) by anyone "except by such lawful authoritie shall be licensed thereto." Thomas successfully arranged a partial monopoly: henceforth the Merrimack River sturgeon fishery was limited to those "able and fit persons" whom the General Court licensed for "the art of boyling and pickling of sturgeon." Inspectors (each of whom was dubbed a "searcher and sealer of sturgeon") were employed to maintain quality. Licensed townsmen in Newbury and Salisbury then conducted an extensive sturgeon-packing business. An act passed in Boston in 1687 mandated that "all sorts of Greene Dry Salted or Pickled ffish Sturgeon fflesh or Butter That shall be put up for Transportac'on to a fforaigne Market shall be searched and Surveyed." A similar regulation for "Preventing Deceit in Packing," which specifically mentioned sturgeon, passed in New Hampshire in 1719. At that point, when permanent English settlement had existed in New Hampshire and Massachusetts for approximately a century, and when the total population of the two provinces was only about 100,000, roughly the same size as the precontact Native population, the ancient sturgeon stock was headed for trouble. On July 6,

1761, when Matthew Patten caught a six-footer at the Merrimack's Amoskeag Falls, it created a stir. An accomplished fisherman and diarist, Patten had neither caught a sturgeon nor noted anyone else catching one during the previous six years. By then sturgeon were relatively rare in the Merrimack, the Piscataqua, and the other rivers of northern New England, even though as late as 1774 the Merrimac River was labeled the "Merrimak or Sturgeon R." on Thomas Jeffery's "Map of the most inhabited part of New England."[62]

Atlantic sturgeon must grow about four feet long to reach sexual maturity. Their survival as a species was predicated on their longevity: as large armored fish with few natural enemies, they could afford the luxury of low reproductive rates. Throughout the first century and a half of English settlement in New England, nearly every river and creek was flanked each spring by eager fishermen with weirs, seines, and spears. Towns sold rights for the best places or for annual hauls, and seining companies pooled capital for rope, twine, lead, and boats, betting that they would more than recoup the cost of shares. Immature sturgeon packed and sold as well as older fish, and all were captured indiscriminately. Neither regulation nor custom impeded colonial fishermen from taking all they could. By the end of the eighteenth century the combination of overfishing and sturgeon's naturally low reproductive rate had essentially doomed this "regal fish" in the estuaries of northern New England. In 1793, for instance, when the Massachusetts General Court passed an act "to enable the town of Newbury to regulate and order the taking of Fish called Shad, Bass, and Alewives in the River Parker," sturgeon were already a distant memory, not even mentioned.[63]

Sturgeon would not be virtually exterminated in Chesapeake and Delaware Bays nor in the Hudson River until the caviar craze between 1870 and 1900. But in northern New England, where competitiveness in the emerging Atlantic economy depended on fishing and trade, only two centuries were necessary to accomplish what had taken a millennium in Europe—the severe reduction of a huge fish that in a natural state was likely to die of old age. Ecologically speaking, we do not know the exact qualities or contributions of sturgeon, or how the presence of many year-classes, with individuals of different sizes and ages, functioned in the ecosystem. Yet clearly the ecosystem had been perturbed by sturgeon removal. As the eminent biologist E. O. Wilson reminds us, "The power of living Nature lies in sustainability through complexity." Each reduction in complexity contributes to degradation. It makes the overall system qualitatively different, and less sustainable. As long-living, large animals, sturgeons, like whales, had contributed stability to coastal eco-systems in North America where they were prominent bottom-feeders. More-over, they had contributed to the cultural and aesthetic values through which Natives and the first generations of English knew themselves and the region. For Natives, the abundance of sturgeon and other marine species affirmed their traditional consciousness of themselves as descendents from the totemic creatures on whom they depended, and with whom they coexisted. For English settlers, the presence of sturgeon conveyed security, prosperity, and upward mobility. By the outbreak of the American Revolution, sturgeon's contribution to resident identity and ecosystem stability was largely gone in New England, as was the once-thriving fishing and packing industry in old towns like Newbury.[64]

Like sturgeon, striped bass spawned in freshwater beyond the tide. William Hubbard's seventeenth-century *General History of New England* explained that the starving Pilgrims netted "a multitude of bass, which was their liveli-hood all that [first] summer. It is a fish not inferior to a salmon, that comes upon the coast every summer pressing into most of the great creeks every tide. . . . Sometimes 1500 of them have been stopped in a creek." Despite the 1639 Mas-sachusetts Bay law forbidding use of bass for fertilizing fields, the pressure on that fine, fat fish persisted. Josselyn noted that settlers in southern Maine were still taking bass "in Rivers where they spawn" and that he had seen "3000 Bass taken" with one set of the net.[65]

Unlike cod or whale oil, the cornerstones of New England's long-distance commerce, bass became part of the local exchange economy. Part-time fisher-men put up bass for their own families, exchanged fresh-caught or barreled bass to square their debts, and sold the fish when they could. As town popula-tions swelled in places like Boston and Portsmouth, part-time fishermen ped-dled fish directly or vended it to consumers through fishmongers. When nets strained to the breaking point, surplus striped bass ended up as "manure" in tilled fields. In the heart of New England, overfishing threatened householders' livelihoods. On the periphery it threatened the peace. During the 1680s Cotton Mather attributed rising tensions between settlers and Abenakis in southern Maine to the newcomers' use of nets that prevented anadromous fish in the Saco River from reaching Native fishers.[66]

By 1770, according to the government of New Hampshire, fishing "hath Almost extirpated the bass and blue fish" in the Piscataqua River. Reverend Jeremy Belknap elaborated during the 1790s: "The bass was formerly taken in great plenty in the river Pascataqua; but by the injudicious use of nets . . . this fishery was almost destroyed." So, too, in Massachusetts: in 1771 petitioners from Newbury lamented the decline of striped bass in the Parker River, and implored the Massachusetts General Court to preserve them. The court obliged with regulations, but they were ignored or unenforceable, and stocks did not rebound. In 1793 town fathers in Newbury outlawed putting "a seine, hedge, weir or drag into the river Parker at any season" for "catching Bass." The regulations were too little, too late. By then the providentially abundant fish that had saved William Bradford and the Pilgrims during their starving time teetered on the verge of commercial extinction between Cape Cod and southern Maine. Residents lamented the loss. "Formerly large fish such as salmon, bass and shad came up the river in plenty," wrote Judge Benjamin Chadbourne from South Berwick, Maine, about 1797, "but they have forsook it and now there remains only Tom Cods, or what we call Frost fish which come in the month of December, smelts in the month of April, alewives in the months of June and July, and eels in about all seasons of the year."[67]

Chadbourne revealed how fishing had altered the composition of fish species and, thus, the structure of his estuarine ecosystem. River fish were a crucial piece in most families' livelihoods, too valuable to be stewarded effectively. Striving to secure a "competence," which they defined as financial independence and security for themselves and their dependents, householders targeted spawning runs each spring. Chadbourne ignored sturgeon, which he had never known, even though Sturgeon Creek (named before 1649) was just a few miles south of his home. He personally witnessed the disappearance of salmon, shad, and bass—long-lived, valuable fish—and his plaintive assessment reflected the diminishment of an estuary by human population pressure and ineffectual regulation since its insertion into the Atlantic economy. Both the nature of the place and people's relationship to it had changed significantly.[68]

Chadbourne's lament fingered the ineffectiveness of river fishery regulations during the eighteenth century. Beginning with Massachusetts (1710), and followed by Connecticut (1715) and Rhode Island (1735), most New England provinces passed legislation against "obstructing the passage of fish in rivers." Although New Hampshire never passed such laws in the colonial period, various petitioners approached the governor, council, and assembly in favor of it. The precautionary approach to the regulation of *sea* fisheries had run its course in New England by the first decade of the eighteenth century. Prohibitions on catching mackerel before the first of July, or with seines or nets at any time, had been repealed in 1692, but then briefly reinstated in 1702. By the early eighteenth century legislators' attention had been redirected to the plight of anadromous fish, notably salmon, shad, and alewives. Massachusetts' first law stipulated that "no wears, hedges, fish-garths, stakes, kiddles, or other disturbance . . . shall be set . . . across any river, to the stopping . . . of fish, in their seasons, or spring of the year" without permission from the general sessions of the justices of the peace in the given county. Subsequent acts noted ongoing depletion, pointing out that "Whereas the river Merrimack hath heretofore abounded with plenty of fish, which hath been of great advantage to the inhabitants of the several towns near the river," excessive fishing led valuable fish to forsake the river. Laws required passageways for the fish to get through dams, and often prohibited seines and dragnets, while allowing low-tech dip nets or scoopnets. Nevertheless, fishermen were convinced that the numbers of alewives, shad, and salmon were decreasing, and that the fish had been diverted from their natural routes. Massachusetts' legislation in 1767 regarding the decay of the Merrimack River fisheries echoed that of 1710.[69]

The Merrimack, like the Connecticut River, flowed through several provinces. Massachusetts controlled the lower portions of the Merrimack through which the fish passed, but New Hampshire controlled the ponds and gravelly streams in which they spawned. People with local knowledge were quite clear about what was happening. "The Shad and Salmon fishery in Merrimack river within this province," explained eighty-two New Hampshire petitioners in 1773, "has in years past been very much decreased by the needless and extravagant methods people have practiced by building dams, fixing weares and drawing long nets or seines, etc. in said river whereby the fish have been so harassed, catched, and destroyed . . . that we have great reason to fear that the river fishery will be wholly destroyed unless some proper methods are taken to prevent or remove those impediments." A few years later John Goffe of Derryfield, New Hampshire, held out hope of restoration. "For neare twenty years there was not a fish that went up" Cohass Brook, a tributary of the Merrimack River, he explained, "and I thought they had left the Brook intirely but upon a Sabbath day two years ago great numbers appeared." Goffe pulled his dam down, and got his upstream neighbors to do the same, and was gratified the next year when the fish "Increased Abundantly." As he saw it, however, other shortsighted men then fished too hard. "I think that if all fishing were prohibited for at least one year it would be a means of Great Increase, for it is a free passage that encourages them." Of course Goffe was a miller, and while he was all for fish, he did not want the assembly to require that all dams be pulled down, for then "there can be no grinding."[70]

Goffe's vision and his self-interest encapsulate the issue. The problem was palpable. Enough people commented on it as the eighteenth century progressed that little doubt exists: schools of alewives, shad, and salmon were getting smaller. Most interested parties, however, were in favor of regulating others. Dam owners would prohibit fishing, or dipnet and scoopnet men would come down hard on seiners or weir tenders. While a consensus existed that fish were valuable, that stocks were being depleted, and that a reduction in fishing effort could turn the problem around, insufficient political will existed to impose a workable solution. The bottom line was that river fish were too precious in the short run to be allowed to live. They could be eaten immediately, put up in barrels for the future, sold, traded, and used for fertilizer. Male heads of households not only enjoyed the camaraderie of catching fish during the spring spawning runs, but also depended on river fish from the sea as one piece of their annual livelihood, a way to settle accounts or set up their children. New England's anadromous fisheries were not being conducted sustainably throughout the eighteenth century, certainly not by the end of that century, and river dwellers knew it. Ultimately they were content, however, to push the day of reckoning further into the future.

SEABIRDS IN THE COLONIAL ECONOMY

The cod fishery affected seabird populations quite early, and their depletion triggered ripples throughout human and nonhuman natural communities. At least eighty-five species of birds were likely to have been seen on salt water between Newfoundland and Cape Cod, including wading shorebirds (such as sandpipers); sea ducks (such as eiders); dabbling ducks, geese, and swans (such as teal); and genuine seabirds (such as puffins), which lived on land each year only long enough to nest. Marine birds exhibited a wide variety of ranges, migration patterns, and reproductive strategies. Some, including double-crested cormorants, bred locally and roosted each night on sandbars, rocks, or trees. Others, including fishermen's favorite avian bait source, the greater shearwater, nested in the remote South Atlantic and appeared on northwest Atlantic waters only during the summer, staying offshore and foraging for squid and fish. Seabirds ranged in size from the northern gannet, a magnificent white plunge-diver with a six-foot wingspan, to the diminutive Wilson's storm petrel, smaller than a robin. Fundamental to the large marine ecosystem of which they were a part, seabirds were not particularly susceptible to its vagaries. Their relatively stable populations consisted of long-lived individuals relying on food supplies that were generally sufficient for reproduction, even in lean years.[71]

Although Natives had long relied on birds for eggs, meat, and feathers, the sheer numbers of birds, especially on offshore island rookeries, flabbergasted the first generations of European seamen. In 1535 Jacques Cartier noted that Newfoundland's Funk Island was "so exceeding full of birds that all the ships of France might load a cargo of them without any one perceiving that any had been removed." This abundance augured well for commercial fisheries. Cod were not fastidious about what they ate, and along with capelin and herring, birds made fine bait. All of the Alcidae family of web-footed diving seabirds, such as guillemots, murres, puffins, razorbills, and auks, nested in vast colonies on remote rocky islands. Those numerous Bird Islands and Egg Rocks between Cape Cod and Newfoundland had been outposts of safety in a cold, dark sea. With the rise of commercial fishing, island sanctuaries became slaughterhouses. Prized for eggs, feathers, oil, and flesh, seabirds were decimated by fishermen and their dependents. From the late 1500s on, most crews fishing in the northwest Atlantic killed vast numbers of birds for bait during at least part of the season. A veteran noted in 1620 that "the Fishermen doe bait their hooks with the quarters of Sea-fowle."[72]

No bird had become better suited to fishermen's needs through 30 million years of evolution than the great auk, which early writers called "penguins." Standing two-and-a-half feet tall, with solid bones and stubby vestigial wings, auks had evolved into superb swimmers and divers. Great auks could not fly away from pursuers because, unlike every other North Atlantic bird species, they had sacrificed flying for underwater swimming as they evolved. They even migrated by paddling, traveling in vast rafts from Newfoundland to Cape Cod, and occasionally as far south as Carolina, before returning to the relative safety of rocky outposts near Newfoundland to nest. Like Antarctic penguins, auks laid but one egg a year. Anthony Parkhurst recounted in 1578 that sailors at Newfoundland's Funk Island drove "penguins" on "a planke into our ship as many as shall lade her."[73]

Seamen used the birds to navigate. J. Sellar's *English Pilot,* published in 1706, explained that on a westbound voyage sightings of the distinctive flightless bird meant the Grand Banks were not far, and that prudent seamen should take soundings. Mariners routinely noted the presence of auks in their log-books, as when Captain John Collings, on a voyage from Portsmouth, New Hampshire, to London in March 1733 wrote: "Saw Severall Pengwins & Other Birds at Six of the Clock in ye Evening. Dubell Reef Main Topsail."[74]

Great auks, like passenger pigeons, could thrive only in huge, gregarious groups. Flightless, colonial, and adapted to living in the midst of rich fishing grounds, they collided headlong with commercial fishermen. As late as 1833, John James Audubon was assured by fishermen in Labrador that great auks nested "on a low rocky island to the south-east of Newfoundland, where they [the fishermen] destroy great numbers of the young for bait." Those fishermen were wrong. By then great auks were nearly gone. By the end of the eighteenth century only occasional stragglers were seen in the western Atlantic. Extinction of the species came at Eldey, off Iceland, in 1844.[75]

Most seabirds breed in colonies. With their long wings, webbed feet set far back, and other adaptations for life in the marine environment, seabirds are clumsy on land, and vulnerable to predators. Small offshore islands uninhabited by terrestrial mammals are ideal rookeries if surrounding waters provide ample forage. Breeding birds on remote rocky islets confront avian predators such as eagles, gulls, and skuas. In defense, they tend to clump together in vast numbers. Seabirds that had adapted to incubating their eggs relatively free from molestation on remote islands were nevertheless susceptible to bait-seeking fishermen, who invaded nesting colonies with clubs and sacks. Cliff-nesters like northern gannets were not immune: ladders and lines provided access to hunters who relished the sport, whether seeking eggs or birds. Even birds like the tiny Wilson's storm petrel, which nested in the subantarctic, were not safe from bait-hunters. Fishermen made whips from lengths of stiff codline. As a fisherman remembered, the petrels were attracted with codfish liver: "when they had gathered in a dense mass, swish went the thongs of the whip cutting their way through the crowded flock and killing or maiming a score or more at a single sweep." Moreover, each spring coastal folk in communities from Massachusetts to Newfoundland sought eggs in the wild. Colossal quantities were gathered: four men from Halifax one year collected nearly 40,000 eggs, and scores of crews were at work. By the 1830s eggers were sailing to Labrador, in part because rookeries between Cape Cod and Newfoundland had already been significantly depleted. John James Audubon then observed, "This war of extermination cannot last many more years. The eggers themselves will be the first to repent the entire disappearance of the myriads of birds."[76]

Gunning probably wreaked less havoc on waterfowl and seabirds before 1800 than baiting and egging, but it also depleted flocks whose numbers had stunned early visitors. Swans, noted Thomas Morton in 1632, could be found in "greate store at the seasons of the yeare." Geese "of three sortes" existed in "great abundance": "I have often had 1000 before the mouth of my gun." Ducks, teals, widgeons, cranes, sanderlings—all were available. As Wood observed of shorebirds, "one may drive them on a heap like so many sheep, and seeing a fit time shoot them." As early as 1710, Massachusetts legislators observed that populations of shorebirds were diminishing as a result of gunners using canoes or floats "disguised with hay, sedge, seaweed" and the like "to shoot them . . . upon the flatts and feeding ground." An act that year outlawed such methods, but no evidence suggests it was effective.[77]

Natural characteristics made some bird species particularly vulnerable. Eider ducks in the northwest Atlantic, like those in European coastal waters, molt all at once. They typically rafted in great flightless flocks in August while new feathers grew in. Samuel Penhallow reported that in 1717 at Arrowsic, Maine, Abenakis in canoes drove eider ducks "like a flock of sheep before them into the creeks." "Without powder or shot they killed at one time four thousand six hundred," Penhallow noted. Killing eiders with paddles and sticks, Abenakis sold "a great number of them to the English for a penny a dozen, which is their practice yearly." Maine island residents capitalized on this as long as eiders lasted. Each August a flotilla assembled to drive the ducks into previously selected killing grounds. Duck Harbor, on the southwest side of Isle au Haut, was a choice spot. Its narrow mouth and steep walls trapped the birds. According to naturalist Philip Conkling, "A single drive on Vinalhaven took 2,100 birds, which may have been half the nesting population of eiders for the west [Penobscot] bay that year. After the 1790s, the drives became less and less successful as the eider population declined."[78]

As early as 1770 George Cartwright clearly sensed the pressure imposed on the coastal ecosystem. Cartwright spent years fishing for cod, trapping seals, and hunting birds and game in Newfoundland and southern Labrador. In 1770 he observed that the Native people would be "totally extinct in a few years." As he put it, with "the fishing trade continually increasing, almost every river and brook which receives salmon is already occupied by our people, and the bird islands are so continually robbed, that the poor Indians must now find it much more difficult than before to procure provisions." When Reverend Jonathan Cogswell published his history of coastal Freeport in 1816, he observed "that birds of no kind abound in Maine." The maritime economy had virtually extirpated seabirds and shorebirds in the Gulf of Maine, and had made serious inroads into their populations all the way to Newfoundland.[79]

True seabirds, such as shearwaters, petrels, and gannets, which had baited the cod hooks of several empires, actually share many similarities with marine mammals. As one ecologist explains, both have "long lives, late maturity, low reproductive rates," and "well-developed social behavior." Both are "highly migratory," and neither is "at the top of the food chain." Moreover, the small fish on which birds and most whales prey have high reproductive rates, meaning that birds consume juveniles "surplus to the supply needed to maintain the populations." Seabirds thus may function in an ecosystem similarly to marine mammals, stabilizing it and dampening dramatic oscillations. If that is the case, "an abundance of seabirds could in fact contribute some stability to the fisheries."[80] Ecological interactions are much more complicated than linear cause and effect. The systematic seabird slaughter not only restructured the marine ecosystem by depleting populations of seabirds, but may have destabilized the fisheries that were the cornerstone of the northwest Atlantic economy, in addition to drastically reducing a resource that could have been eternally renewable. The reputations that coastal residents cultivated as skilled gunners or persistent eggers came at a cost, as did fishermen's opportunistic slaughter of seabirds for bait.

When Edmund Burke rose in the House of Commons in 1775 to salute the not inconsequential accomplishments of His Majesty's subjects in North America, he attested to American whalers' ingenuity and work ethic. As Burke put it, there exists "no sea but what is vexed by their fisheries."[81] It was an apt turn of phrase by a masterful orator. New Englanders not only harvested the sea, Burke suggested; they troubled it. It is unlikely that he intended a point about ecological change. His word choice, however, reveals the link between hard physical labor in extractive industries and the toll that such labor takes on the environment. In retrospect, it is obvious that marine ecosystems could not be assaulted systematically over centuries by people wielding harpoons, hooks, seines, weirs, pots, guns, oyster rakes, and eggers' baskets without consequences, both ecological and cultural.

The notion of "traditional fisheries," often shorthand for preindustrial activity, obscures historical changes in marine ecosystems. It plays to the indefensible but commonplace assumption that the ocean has existed outside of history. Yet just as early modern people modified the terrestrial environments in which they lived, so, too, did they modify the marine ecosystems on which they increasingly relied. An ecosystem is considerably more than a group of isolated units; nevertheless, stocks of marine mammals, anadromous fish, and seabirds, all of which declined precipitously before 1800, serve as indicators of a changing sea. Increasing intimacy with the marine environment during the seventeenth and eighteenth centuries promoted commercial opportunities, curiosity about nature, new cultural forms—and changed ecosystems.

By 1800 the northwest Atlantic was beginning to resemble European seas. Seventeenth-century impacts, in keeping with the small population, were modest. Ironically, seventeenth-century settlers imposed restrictions on sea fishing, turning to closed seasons and limited entry in an effort to perpetuate stocks of cod, mackerel, and striped bass. Even more ironically, restrictions were not imposed on the species that endured the heaviest harvesting pressure, such as whales, sturgeon, and seabirds. In their precautionary approach to mackerel, cod, and bass fisheries, however, seventeenth-century settlers revealed their beliefs that humans could affect populations of sea fish. During the eighteenth century, when the only restrictions were on harvesting anadromous fish, each human generation confronted fewer whales, walrus, bass, sturgeon, alewives, seabirds, and shellfish. With but few exceptions this diminished ecological capital became regarded as the norm. Ecologists call this the "shifting baseline syndrome"; it appears to have been well under way in the northwest Atlantic by 1800. Despite stories that clearly conveyed some species' localized depletion, and the shrinking range of other species, and despite repeated insistence that fish stocks were "a Great Benefit to the Publick," the pressure persisted. The few attempts to mitigate it failed.[82]

Three

THE SEA SERPENT
AND THE MACKEREL JIG

———

As the human race has extended over the surface of the earth, man has more or less modified the animal population of different regions, either by exterminating certain species, or introducing others.

—Louis Agassiz and Augustus M. Gould,
Principles of Zoölogy (1848)

Sometime around 1815 in a Cape Ann fishing station called Pigeon Cove—named for the abundant passenger pigeons that once roosted on nearby Pigeon Hill—Abraham Lurvey experimented casting molten lead and pewter around the shank of a mackerel hook. Decades later a few old-timers gave credit for the jig to others, but the actual inventor had considerably less significance than the invention itself. Mackerel hooks were relatively small. Being iron, they rusted. Lurvey sensed that a bit of dried sharkskin or other sandpaper could shine the pewter sleeve, attracting mackerel in lieu of bait. As far back as anyone could remember, fishermen had baited mackerel hooks with pieces of pork "as big as a four-pence ha'penny," or more typically with bait from the sea. But bait had costs, and baiting took time. Mackerel hit shiny jigs faster than they ever had baited hooks. And though Lurvey and the men with whom he fished tried to keep their jigs secret, word spread.[1]

Dexterous jiggers could twitch a mackerel from the sea into a barrel on deck, jerk it from the hook with a technique they called "slatting," then flick the jig back into the water without touching fish or hook: no baiting, no handling, no wasted motion. Ground chum dumped over the rail attracted the fish, and if they bit slowly the men stuck morsels of bait on their hooks for better results. But when the fish bit relentlessly, no need for baiting existed, and a skilled man could land several hundred pounds of mackerel an hour, considerably more than with the older methods. Quintessential Yankee tinkering, simple as it seemed, had produced gear with more fishing power. And nineteenth-century America's growing infatuation with mackerel, and later with menhaden and other species, would rely on increasingly efficient gear.[2]

Cast pewter mackerel jigs created quite a buzz on the waterfront during the next few summers, but nothing comparable to the sea stories coming out of nearby Gloucester in August 1817. The *Essex Register* on August 16 noted "an unusual fish or serpent . . . discovered by the fishermen" in Gloucester harbor, "quick in its motions," very long, and extremely evasive. According to the editor, "All attempts to take the fish had been ineffectual." Some people claimed to have seen two of the serpents, and a letter-writer to the newspaper worried openly that "our small craft are fearful of venturing out a fishing." One eyewitness explained that the serpent appeared "in joints like the wooden buoys on a net rope . . . like a string of gallon kegs 100 feet long." The "head of it, eight feet out of water, was as large as the head of a horse." Later that month a broadside published in Boston stoked the excitement with assertions that "A Monstrous Sea Serpent: The largest ever seen in America" hovered in the vicinity of Gloucester. Initially "believed to be a creature of the imagination," as the broadside's author put it, the monster "has since come within the harbor of Gloucester, and has been seen by hundreds of people." So many saw the serpent, including gentlemen whose probity was beyond dispute, that the Linnaean Society of New England retained an Essex County justice of the peace to depose witnesses under oath. Eager to be taken seriously by scientists elsewhere, society members knew that identifying a dramatic uncataloged genus, or possibly even a living fossil, would interest not just provincial naturalists but the savants of Europe. Fishermen, meanwhile, were determined to "take it," and they organized several crews to do just that.[3]

At the very least, sight of the serpent and the discussions in its wake pointed to how little was known with certainty about the world beneath the waves, despite desires to increase fishing pressure. Contemporary publications on nature, whether in Europe or in America, rarely included the oceans. Questions regarding abundance and distribution of marine organisms, even commercially valuable ones, played second fiddle to larger questions about the study of nature as a whole, and what each class of creatures revealed about the Creator's plan. While many agreed that details of his plan were yet to be understood by inquisitive humans, the plan itself was assumed to be "fully matured in the beginning, and invariably pursued; the work of a God infinitely wise, regulating Nature according to immutable laws," as two respected naturalists explained it. Put another way, early nineteenth-century people worked within a cosmos in which nature was imagined as fixed, even if it was not entirely comprehended. The concept that nature's dispensations could fluctuate radically seemed offensive to the idea of the harmony of God's handiwork. Observations when tallying the catch from year to year contradicted that idea, but the two notions coexisted uneasily.[4]

The serpent's appearance not only raised questions about what a Massachusetts naturalist would call "the unsurpassed, unrivalled workmanship of Nature's plastic hand," but queries about knowledge of the living ocean. Such questions had once been of little significance, but by 1817 they reflected on the viability of science and natural history in the new nation. Whose word could be trusted when discussing ocean resources? After farmers, mariners were the second-largest occupational group in the nation. Day-to-day encounters with sea creatures were much more commonplace among unrefined workingmen than among learned naturalists. As men of science intensified their systematic inquiry into the mysteries of nature, and increasingly exchanged their findings through publication and participation in learned societies, what role would callused fishermen with firsthand knowledge of the sea play?[5]

Scientific thinking, still in its infancy, honored accumulated bodies of printed knowledge, all of which were familiar to naturalists. Once something about nature had been written, it became part of the canon, an eclectic canon that included scripture, Pliny, Comte de Buffon, and travelers' accounts, among other sources. But because it was the canon, it had authority. Challenging the written word remained somewhat problematic; naturalists in the early modern era were more comfortable adding to knowledge than disputing the known. Since sea serpents had a long paper pedigree in 1817, questioning their existence on the basis of mere observation, much less mere skepticism, continued to be considered slightly unscientific.[6]

Sea serpents had been observed and recorded in New England before, but none had ever prompted a protracted scientific investigation, a heated international discussion, and a systematic pursuit. *Scoliophis atlanticus,* the name bestowed on the serpent by taxonomists (despite the unsettling fact that no specimen had been collected or examined close at hand), appeared intermit-tently during the late summer months of 1817, 1818, and 1819. It generated a vast paper trail. And despite accusations of fraud by certain wits and scientists, and alternative explanations by fishermen who pursued it, *Scoliophis atlanticus* still found a place in respectable texts decades later, such as the American edition of Robert Blakewell's *Introduction to Geology* (1833) and D. Humphreys Storer's *Reports on the Fishes, Reptiles and Birds of Massachusetts* (1839).

No marine environmental historian worth his or her salt can afford to ignore early-nineteenth-century sea serpents. Human understanding of nature is always constructed as much through emotion, imagination, and received wisdom as through empirical observation. The stories that people tell about nature matter; and in the early republic one of New England's most compel-ling sea stories featured the Gloucester serpent. Captivatingly ambiguous, that serpent nevertheless was taken seriously by serious people. For them, approach-ing the sea serpent scientifically seemed *de rigueur*, as sensible as the determi-nation of the era's modern, well-equipped fishermen to catch it. For us, dismiss-ing the serpent as a maddening anomaly or, worse yet, as hocus-pocus can compromise our understanding of changes in the sea and of why people acted as they did.

The serpent made manifest in 1817 how overwhelmingly large and unknown the deep ocean of antiquity remained, even as ambitious American tinkerers and navigators such as Abraham Lurvey and Nathaniel Bowditch (the mathe-matical wizard from nearby Salem who improved practical navigation) sought to master its mysteries. Seventeenth-century New Englanders had taken for granted that inexplicable serpents existed within marine fauna, even as they imposed regulations on human harvesting of what was assumed to be a finitely productive ocean. Mid-to-late-nineteenth-century New Englanders, on the other hand, would begin to dismiss belief in sea serpents and, with their new-found confidence, would decide that technology could compensate for waning catches.

Considered together, the rapid acceptance of the mackerel jig by commer-cial fishermen and the simultaneous scientific furor over the Gloucester sea serpent speak to the reassessment of the sea by coastal New Englanders during the first half of the nineteenth century.[7] That reassessment proceeded fitfully, shadowed at times by concerns about the ocean's ability to produce infinitely. During the eighteenth century declining populations of alewives, salmon, and bass had been noted, along with oyster bed depletion and the virtual eradication of coastal whales. As the nineteenth century unfolded, clams, lobster, herring, shad, eels, and mackerel were added to the list of commercially valuable species in decline, at least as some fishermen saw it. Others protested that such complaints were conjectural. Whose authority would count, and how would they know?

Against the excitement of cataloging new marine creatures, creating ichthyological displays in museum cabinets, targeting previously underutilized species, developing new markets for fish, refining fishing vessels and gear, and promoting efficiencies in transportation and packaging to bolster access to seafood, nagging concerns continued to surface in legislatures and learned publications about the depletion of coastal marine resources during the first half of the nineteenth century. Attention to fisheries science, fishermen's innovations, and changes in the sea during this era, when the sea serpent of antiquity and the modern mackerel jig shared the spotlight, reveals contemporaries' growing confidence in their ability to comprehend God's supposedly predictable creation, and their tragic failure to take a precautionary approach in the face of profound uncertainty.

WHOSE KNOWLEDGE?

Observation, imagination, collection (and missed opportunities for collection) had long fed an uncertain stream of information about the sea's living creatures. What might a fisherman make of a fifty-foot-long humpback whale, for instance, with its snout covered in crusty barnacles, its long pectoral fins appearing like wings, its knobby head spouting geysers of steam, and its habit of propelling itself skyward in mighty leaps before crashing back into the sea—what indeed might a startled sailor in the fog make of such a spectacle from an unwieldy little boat only thirty feet long? Or what news was likely to come ashore after talkative sailors had encountered the tailfin scythe of a thresher shark, or a basking shark's vast bulk, much less a hammerhead lurking near the rudderpost, distorted by the water's refraction? The unknown wore many guises. Unaided by technology for centuries, human senses rendered large marine animals doubly enigmatic. Before the development of diving bells and scuba masks no swimmer could view a whale completely in its natural element. And when seamen killed one, no ship had the capacity to hoist the sea's largest creatures on deck until the late nineteenth century, when naval architects and shipwrights began building monster iron ships, outfitted with steam winches and wire rope. Thus the dimensions and appearance of outlandishly large sea creatures remained wrapped in mystery. When a vast animal such as a fin whale or giant squid stranded itself, the absence of the sea's buoyancy and the effect of gravity rendered it bloblike, distorted beyond recognition. Early-nineteenth-century people responded to such encounters with nature through their own senses and stories. And in coastal communities, common sense said that startling creatures lived in the sea.[8]

When Captain Crabtree arrived in Portland, Maine, in the midsummer of 1793 on a voyage from the West Indies, he and his men gave an account of a sea serpent "of an enormous size" they had encountered about ten leagues from Mount Desert Island, prime mackerel habitat at that season of the year. Its head was "elevated about six or eight feet out of the water," and its body he "judged to be about the size of a barrel in circumference." According to Captain Crabtree, this was no fleeting observation. "I was within two hundred yards of it near an hour; during which time, as it discovered no inclination to molest us, myself and the whole crew observed it with the minutest attention; nor was its attention less fixed on us." Crabtree's observations smacked of some familiarity with natural science. He recorded length, circumference, shape of the head, and color of the eyes, while noting that he could "observe clearly that there were no fins or external appendages to the body," and that its "motion was like the writhing of the body, like other serpents." Most striking is that he did not hesitate for a moment about what he and his men had seen. Crabtree did not *believe* in sea serpents; as an experienced mariner and literate citizen of the new democratic republic, he *knew* what he was seeing. "There is no doubt but that this is one of two which have been seen in these parts," he said. "All accounts agree." He remembered that "Two of them (perhaps the same) were once seen on the shores of the Cranberry island," just south of Mount Desert Island. "These are the first ever seen in our seas," he thought, "tho' they have been seen on the coast of Norway."[9]

Crabtree's observations, firsthand and neither hysterical nor fanciful, were thus qualitatively different from the accounts of learned medieval scholars such as Olaus Magnus, the archbishop of Sweden, who published an exceptionally detailed map of Scandinavia in 1539 in which the Baltic and the Norwegian Sea were full of monsters; or of Sebastian Münster, a Renaissance scholar whose *Cosmographia*—one of the most popular sixteenth-century books in Europe—included a host of fanciful and threatening sea creatures. Crabtree, a captain-cum-naturalist in the early republic, was much more precise in his observations than had been John Josselyn in 1674, whose *Account of Two Voyages to New*

England reported "a sea-serpent or snake that lay coiled on a rock" at Cape Ann. Nor did Captain Crabtree revert to sensationalism, as did a London broadside published in 1699, *A True and Perfect Relation of the Taking and Destroying of a Sea-Monster,* which depicted in detail killing a seventy-foot-long and fifty-ton whale off the coast of Denmark, but embellished the tale with lurid imaginings. "The upper part Resembles a Man, from the middle downward he was a Fish, had Fins and a Forked Tail. His head was of great bulk, contain'd several hundreds of weight, and had a terrible aspect." By the 1790s American seamen who fancied themselves even part-time naturalists, such as Captain Crabtree, strove for dispassionate presentation of what they saw in the sea.[10]

This is not to say that they remained uninfluenced by accounts such as *A Description of Greenland,* which recounted Hans Egede's encounter with a "most dreadful monster" at 64° north latitude in 1734. Originally published in Danish in 1738, Egede's book was available in English translation by 1745. A Norwegian missionary who sought to reestablish contact with the lost Norse colony of Greenland, Egede was also a capable naturalist, whose writing depicted the plants and animals of the far north, along with Inuit life and Greenland's geography. The monster he described reached its head "as high as the masthead" (the level of the ship's lowest yard). "It had a long pointed snout and spouted like a whale fish; had great broad paws" and "very rugged and uneven skin." Moreover, its lower part was "shaped like an enormous huge serpent." Egede trusted his senses and powers of description, and his book capaciously included accurate accounts of narwhal, musk ox, ptarmigan, and the sea serpent, even as it relied on experts including Pliny, Heliodorus, and the book of Psalms. Captain Crabtree, who described the serpent he and his men had encountered off Mount Desert Island in 1793, had come of age in a post-Linnaean era in which naturalists took for granted that detailed observations were necessary to add to canonical knowledge of nature, but in which there was still a great deal of uncertainty about the abundance, distribution, and taxonomic niceties of the sea's creatures.[11]

Captain Crabtree lived contemporaneously with William Dandredge Peck, a respected botanist and entomologist whose earliest publications included pioneering work in ichthyology, prompted by the collecting of the Piscataqua River fishermen. From 1805 to 1822 Peck occupied the first chair in natural history at Harvard University. As Augustus A. Gould, an accomplished naturalist in the next generation, remembered of Peck's experience at Harvard,

"He gave such instruction as was demanded, which was very little." Under-graduates' lack of interest reflected the shaky status of natural history, then the preserve of gentlemen amateurs but not yet an established discipline. In Sep-tember 1794, just a year after Cartwright described the sea serpent off Mount Desert Island, Peck wrote "Description of Four Fishes, taken near the Pisca-taqua in New Hampshire," subsequently published in the *Memoirs of the Ameri-can Academy of Arts and Sciences.* Noting matter-of-factly that the Gulf of Maine "affords a considerable number of fishes, many of which are but little known," Peck described in detail "four fishes of different genera," situating them taxo-nomically as best he could in the Linnaean system.[12]

One specimen, brought to him by a boy who called it a "white eel," had been caught "in a muddy creek in the river Piscataqua." It was some sort of blenny, a small shore-hugging carnivorous fish, probably what is known today as the rock eel, *Pholis gunnellus.* Another, "called Sucker in the neighborhood of Boston" and "improperly named Barbel" in the District of Maine, as Peck wrote, had already been described by Dr. John Reinhold Forster in the *Trans-actions of the Royal Society.* Peck felt comfortable describing it, but had no need to name it. Another, known to local fishermen as the wolf or conger eel, was a large fish with impressive jaws and teeth, "taken on the haddock grounds, principally in the months of March and April." Still known as the wolf fish today, Peck believed that it appeared "to differ from all the Linnean Blennii," and he was "uncertain whether it had ever been described." The other subject of his paper, which he thought "probably a migratory fish," was not well known by fishermen: "There is no popular name for it," Peck wrote, though it turns out to be what is now known as a butterfish, a regular summer visitor to the Gulf of Maine that became a popular food fish late in the nineteenth cen-tury as fishermen responded to market demand by targeting more species. "I have given it a trivial name and defined it as a new species; and have been induced to this by being unable satisfactorily to apply to it either of the Lin-nean definitions." Ever the careful scientist, however, Peck qualified his con-clusions, insisting that "truth is the great object in inquiries of this kind," and conceding that if he had erred, he would be "indebted to any experienced naturalist who shall set me right." Peck relied on working fishermen for speci-mens and background knowledge, though he simultaneously dismissed them rather patronizingly as "inattentive" to any species not "fit for food."[13]

Dispassionate natural history in the early republic would rely increasingly, on "naming, classifying, and describing" the New World's "plants, animals, and minerals; studying its geological structure; determining the latitude and longitude of its towns and cities; researching and speculating about its aborigines and antiquities; founding botanical gardens, museums, herbaria, and scientific societies; and transplanting to America the theories, techniques and systems of classification and nomenclature of Western science." But at the turn of the century there were many competing influences, many variants on taxonomic systems, many vestigial reports; in short, a "vacuum of zoological authority."[14] And uncertainties about plants and animals on land were magnified in the sea.

Into that vacuum, in the summer of 1817, swam the infamous Gloucester sea serpent. When it appeared off Cape Ann the massive serpent triggered heated discussions among gentlemen, fishermen, naturalists, newspapermen, and other members of the public. At the heart of those discussions lay a question rarely posed, but always present. Whose authority mattered, and on what basis? "We have heard from Gloucester that a Norway Kraken had visited their harbour within ten pound Island," Reverend William Bentley noted on August 15. "We have had letter upon letter." Bentley, minister of the East Church in Salem, stood tall among learned men in the Boston area. A Harvard graduate and bookish prodigy with one of the largest personal libraries in the nation, he wrote copiously on politics and theology, and was known as a student of philosophy, linguistics, and science. Bentley observed in his diary that "his body when out of water looks like the buoys of a net, or a row of kegs, or a row of large casks. We see in Bomare much such a description given by a Danish Captain of the Navy in 1746, so much so that they would not probably have been more alike had they been copied from each other." Bomare was Jacques Christophe Valmont de Bomare, author of the mid-eighteenth-century *Dictionnaire raisonné universel d'histoire naturelle.* Bentley naturally relied on the published work of a European savant, one now associated with the eighteenth-century scientific revolution, to make sense of what his countrymen were seeing a few miles down the coast.[15]

The sea serpent appeared at a time when understandings of the natural world were being challenged and transformed, not only in the new United States but in other colonial regions and in Europe. While classification of fish and shells received some attention by members of the American Academy of Arts and Sciences and the Linnaean Society of New England, mammalogy, botany, ornithology, mineralogy, and entomology took precedence. For the most part, the ocean would be peripheral to the great though decentralized enterprise of describing, classifying, and naming nature. Nevertheless, with a challenge as tantalizing as a sea serpent in the dooryard, the Linnaean Society of New England called a special meeting on August 18, 1817, at which it appointed a committee to "collect evidence with regard to the existence and appearance of any such animal."[16]

Justice of the Peace Lonson Nash "deposed eight witnesses: three merchants, two ship-masters, a mariner, a ship-carpenter, and James Johnstone, Jr.," a seventeen-year-old. All were "men of fair and unblemished character." Extracts from the depositions presented to the Linnaean Society reveal that the serpent's head "appeared much like the head of a turtle . . . and larger than the head on any dog"; that it was "something like the head of a rattlesnake, but nearly as large as the head of a horse"; that it was "as large as a four-gallon keg"; and that it was only the size of "the crown of a hat." The serpent's manner of propulsion appeared less contradictory than the shape of its head, but a close reading of the testimony reveals the justice of the peace accommodating himself to the society's desires and, as one historian explains, "leading the witnesses or tampering with their statements." The Linnaean Society, only three years old, and as financially insecure as it was elitist, had been struggling despite its distinguished membership. The appearance of the serpent trumped all other "curious facts and ingenious observations" noted at society meetings, and in late September it prepared to issue a report whose findings might extend the promise of new life for both the Linnaean Society of New England and the elusive serpent.[17]

Linnaean Society members were not alone in their interest. As sightings became more numerous and conversations about the serpent multiplied during September, William Bentley situated them in light of previous encounters. "Capt. N. Brown of Newburyport tells of seeing one in lat. 60° N. & Long. 7 . . . which he had an opportunity to view an hour & half at one time & within 30 ft. of the vessel." Brown had "noticed marks at the neck which he conceived to be the opening of the gills. . . . He supposed it could raise its head from the surface of the water 15 feet, which must give it great length." In addition to Brown's observation, there was "the account from Mount Desert" (Captain Cartwright's) and "testimonies from Cape Cod & Plymouth." The "testimonies from Cape Cod are that they were given at the time but suppressed from fear of ridicule." Yet as the evidence poured in and was juxtaposed with previous accounts, Bentley noted apologetically that "we have rather been unobservant of facts." Despite the lack of success of a Marblehead boat "on the look out for the Cape

Ann fish," Bentley had become convinced of the serpent's existence. "His repeated appearance last week is not doubted."[18]

Discovery of an unusual snake on the beach at Cape Ann in late September
bolstered believers' enthusiasm. Regarded as "the progeny of the Sea Serpent,
which had been so much talked of, and which was said to have been seen near
the cove where this snake was killed," the specimen was collected and dis-
sected, and once again depositions were taken from those who had seen it. The
Linnaean Society halted publication of its report to await resolution of these
striking developments. Most compelling was this snake's movement. While it
appeared in some ways like a common blacksnake, "his motion was vertical."
All known reptiles moved in sinuous waves from side to side. The dissection
revealed peculiarities in "the curvature in the backbone," indicating "increase
of *flexibility* and an increase of *strength* in *vertical motion*." According to its
hastily revised report, the Linnaean Society considered "this serpent as a non-
descript, and as distinct from other genera of serpents in the flexuous structure
of its spine," and "deemed it necessary to constitute a new genus." Admitting
that a "more close examination of the great Serpent" seen in Gloucester harbor
would be necessary to connect it definitively with the small black snake caught
on the beach, they nevertheless crafted an argument by analogy, reinforced by
witnesses' testimony, that the two were one and the same.[19]

Scoliophis atlanticus thus found its way into the scientific literature. Early
1818 saw a London edition of the society's report, followed closely by various
testimonials from men of science supporting its taxonomic distinction. The
well-known naturalist Constantine Rafinesque published a "Dissertation on
Water Snakes, Sea Snakes and Sea Serpents." General David Humphreys, formerly on General Washington's staff, sent a series of letters to Sir Joseph Banks,
president of the Royal Society in London. From his chair as Massachusetts
Professor of Natural History at Harvard, William Dandredge Peck submitted a
paper to the *Memoirs of the American Academy of Arts and Sciences,* noting that
"the appearance in this vicinity the last summer of an enormous animal of the
serpentine order, is a fact . . . remarkable here, and . . . interesting to naturalists
every where." Certain men of science remained silent, at least publicly—notably
Sir Joseph Banks. Other writers scoffed. The Charleston playwright William
Crafts lampooned the "Gloucester Hoax" in a stinging satire.[20]

All that remained was to capture the beast, and Captain Rich of Gloucester
determined to do it. A systematic seaman, he knew that serpent sightings
always occurred during periods of high barometric pressure, with the sea flat

as a sheet of glass. To catch a serpent one must think like a serpent, and he positioned his boat on a flat-calm day where the serpent had been observed. Rich assembled a crew notable for "respectability and integrity," each of whom had seen the creature. "I hired such men," he said, "in order that I might not be deceived, should he make his appearance, having never seen him myself." As the subsequent account in the *Boston Weekly Messenger* explained, their preparations paid off. Poised in a whaleboat, with harpoons and oars at the ready, the "crew all agreed to a man, that what we then saw was the *supposed Serpent,* which had been seen at that place and at Gloucester Harbour." Rich later said that at that moment he would "have given testimony upon oath, that I had seen a Serpent not less than one hundred feet in length." Having seen it, they determined to harpoon it.[21]

"It was some time before we could discover the deception," Rich admitted, "but by following it up closely we have ascertained that the supposed Serpent is no other than the wake of a fish such as we have taken"—a thunny or horse mackerel, as he called it, now known as a bluefin tuna. Biologists today recognize bluefin tuna as the fastest fish in the ocean. They characteristically arc across the sea at high speed, alternately breaking the surface and submerging. "Moving with uncommon velocity" on a calm day, as Rich explained, a tuna would heave up "little waves the true colour of the ocean, that appear at a little distance like what has already been described"—the humps of a serpent's back. After five days of determined hunting Rich's men brought in a good-sized horse mackerel, wrapped in a sail in the bilge of their boat. He swore that everyone with whom he discussed the matter "agree in the opinion . . . that this fish has caused many of the opinions that have been given of the *supposed* Serpent." His crew concurred. And as Captain Rich pointed out, the serpent's supposed "existence on this coast" had "been in part, founded on testimony they have given."[22]

Harpooning the tuna was far from driving the final nail into the serpent's coffin. Despite Captain Rich's bloody evidence, Craft's satire, and the contempt of Henri de Blainville (a French savant who simply did not accept the Linnaean Society's new genus), most enlightened New Englanders "preferred to believe in their giant sea serpent." Sightings continued in the summer of 1819, sometimes by eminent gentlemen equipped with spyglasses. Their accounts echoed those of previous believers. Yet not everyone was convinced. In the summer of 1820 a columnist for the *Essex Register* stated matter-of-factly that "on the question whether the great serpent is of the same species as the small one, the committee have exceed themselves in absurdity." Simply put, he continued, "the witnesses actually saw nothing but a fish sporting in the water."[23]

Captain Rich's methodical approach to the question of the sea serpent revealed him to be level-headed and empirically minded, but as an ongoing shark controversy during the next decade revealed, New England fishermen could be just as misguided as naturalists when it came to sorting out the sea's largest creatures. In the summer of 1820 several sharks were harpooned on the North Shore of Massachusetts Bay, one "A large 'Man-eating' Shark upwards of 9 feet long," the other an even larger but placid filter-feeding basking shark. "A Shark—No Serpent," read one headline. "As usual, whenever any *'odd fish'* has appeared in our waters, this was pronounced to be the celebrated Sea Serpent." Had it not been taken, and identified as an inoffensive basking shark, the *Essex Register* continued caustically, it would have been more ammunition for "the existence of a monstrous *Sea Serpent* on our coast."[24] But simply distinguishing sharks by species (or even genus) was not always straightforward, as revealed by a tragedy in the summer of 1830 whose aftermath featured both Captain Rich and Captain Nathaniel Blanchard of Lynn, a skilled fisherman who helped Dr. D. Humphreys Storer during preparation of his landmark monograph on Massachusetts fish.

On July 12, 1830, Captain Blanchard sailed his small schooner from Lynn to the south on a day trip, anchoring east of Scituate. Three men accompanied him, one of whom—his father-in-law, Joseph Blaney—headed off alone in a dory about half a mile from the schooner. Several hours later Blaney screamed for help and waved his hat, but before anyone could render assistance they saw a huge fish lying across the dory, a flurry of foam, and then nothing as Blaney, the dory, and the fish all disappeared. Blanchard and the other men recovered the victim's hat, and when the dory resurfaced it appeared scratched, as if "by the rough skin of a shark." Scientists and fishermen now know that only the great white shark, a visitor to the Gulf of Maine, acts that way. A shaken and vengeful Blanchard returned to the area a day or two later in keen pursuit of the killer. Baiting massive hooks with whole mackerel, and using half-inch manila rope, he and his crew caught two great white sharks, one of which—sixteen feet long and approximately 2,500 to 3,000 pounds—was too large to hoist aboard. They landed the smaller one, which was "pronounced by old ship-masters to be the 'man-eater' of tropical climates." Curious spectators with 12½ cents could view it in Boston. Taxonomic confusion reigned, however, in the wake of the tragedy. And experienced fishermen contributed to it.[25]

"Captain Blanchard, who has been engaged in fishing business for fifteen years past," noted the *Boston Gazette,* "states that he has often seen in our bay, sharks of a different species from that taken, but he never before saw a basking shark." Of course it wasn't a basking shark; it was a great white shark. Basking sharks had once been common in Massachusetts Bay. Prized for the high-quality oil that could be rendered from their livers, large numbers had been harpooned off Cape Cod in the early eighteenth century. So many had been killed it is possible that neither Rich nor Blanchard remained familiar with the species a century later, though just ten years earlier local papers had profiled a basking shark, with descriptions by the eminent naturalist Samuel Mitchill, to demonstrate that it was *not* a serpent. "Captain Rich, who has followed the same business for twenty-seven years, makes a similar statement," as the *Boston Gazette* continued: "he informs us that till very recently he never saw a basking shark in our waters, but a few days since off Brant Point, near Marshfield, there were no less than twenty of these sharks." Again, those were great white sharks. The one caught by Blanchard and exhibited for the public had the rows of sharp serrated teeth characteristic of a great white shark. And as the newspaper solemnly explained, "Its mouth is large enough to take in a common sized man." Great white sharks were less common in the Gulf of Maine than mackerel sharks (also known as porbeagles), and less distinctive than hammerheads, or thresher sharks, whose scythelike tails gave them away. Nevertheless sharks of different types were frequently caught in the gulf—snared in seines, taken as by-catch, or harpooned. Mackerel jiggers frequently encountered blue sharks and others among schools of mackerel, and lanced and gaffed them with abandon. Taxonomic niceties were simply not a concern of most fishermen, however, sometimes even among men such as Rich and Blanchard who interacted with naturalists. This lack of precision and the attendant confusion contributed to the vacuum of authority regarding creatures in the sea.[26]

During the 1830s, as natural science publications proliferated in New England, Dr. Jerome V. C. Smith and Dr. D. Humphreys Storer each produced books on the fishes of Massachusetts. Though Storer roundly criticized Smith's work, which preceded his by several years, and though both Storer and Smith relied on the assistance and insight of fishermen and mariners, neither was entirely comfortable giving mariners their due, and neither abandoned belief in the serpent. As Smith tortuously put it, "The existence, however, of such a creature as the serpent has been described to be, by the most unobjectionable evidence, is proved as clearly and conclusively, as human testimony can establish any truth." Storer included the serpent in his book, as well. And dis-regarding Captain Rich's explanation that the Gloucester sea serpent—seen repeatedly—had been a tuna, Storer called the bluefin tuna "a very rare species in the waters of this State." Actually, by acting like a sea serpent, bluefin tuna had caused more commotion in coastal Massachusetts than any other fish in the history of the commonwealth. Intent as they were on the truth, gentlemen with education and standing could not concede that a practical fisherman like Captain Rich had trumped naturalists of their own station.[27]

By no means did the division between Captain Rich and the would-be savants of the Linnaean Society create a wholesale divide between fishermen and naturalists. Right from the moment of its appearance some fishermen had believed the serpent a part of the ecosystem, supposing that it had come into Gloucester harbor to feed upon "a very numerous shoal of herrings." Decades later—in 1833—its influence was still touted. "The sea-serpent, or something else," noted a writer in the *Barnstable Patriot*, "has driven on shore upon the cape [Cape Cod], at several places, a considerable number of blackfish."[28] As controversies over serpents and sharks revealed, no group in Massachusetts monopolized natural knowledge of the ocean during the antebellum years. So much remained unknown that it was easy for people to imagine the ocean as infinite and overwhelming. That vacuum allowed skeptics to deny that deple-tions were occurring, even as other fishermen pointed increasingly to worri-some changes in the sea.

THE MOST FICKLE FISH

Prior to the American Revolution, and long before the serpent's appearance near Cape Ann, New England's mackerel fishery had been of minor importance. Fishermen took mackerel with hooks, small seines, or "meshes," as gill nets were known. Common knowledge had it that "those by hook are the best; those by seines are worst, because in bulk they are bruised." Occasionally mackerel were eaten fresh, but most were used for bait, or when "split, salted, and bar-reled," were exported "for the negroes in the sugar islands," as William Dou-glass wrote in 1755. Towns on the south side of Massachusetts Bay conducted most of New England's limited mackerel fishery during the eighteenth century. Scituate reputedly had thirty vessels catching mackerel in 1770. Annual land-ings ranged between 5,000 and 20,000 barrels, equivalent to about one-tenth of the value of the region's cod fishery.[29]

The mackerel fishery remained a labor-intensive sideshow before the War of 1812. Early spring mackerel fetched a high price in Boston because of their novelty—six to eight cents apiece, and sometimes ten—but the amounts harvested were modest. Gloucester fishermen in 1802 reported using seines to catch mackerel, along with herring and striped bass, during the spring. Until 1821 virtually all mackerel caught by Gloucester-based boats was sold fresh. At that time a fleet of Chebacco boats, seven or eight from Gloucester and another seven or eight from the north side of Cape Ann, near Pigeon Cove, pursued mackerel with seines and drails during the summer for the Boston market. Chebacco boats had two masts but no jibs, just a mainsail and foresail. Some were decked; some open. Small and relatively inexpensive to build, they had been employed in the shore fishery during the late eighteenth and early nineteenth centuries as New Englanders tried to rebuild a fishing fleet devastated by the Revolutionary War. Most mackerel landed then were caught close to home on Stellwagen Bank, between Cape Ann and Cape Cod. Fishermen high-graded their catch. As one remembered, they "saved only the large bloaters, which we slat into the barrels; the small fish we slat into the lee scuppers and stamped them up with our boots for bait with which to toll the fish." To land the freshest fish possible they fished at night, dressed the mackerel as soon as they were landed, and immersed them in tubs full of seawater. The goal was to chill the fish as much as possible and market them in the cool of the early morning. As late as 1804–1809 Massachusetts fishermen were landing only between 7,000 and 9,000 barrels per year. A barrel held 200 pounds of fish. After the war the pace picked up. Mackerel fishers in Hingham, on the south shore of Massachusetts Bay, packed thousands of barrels themselves in 1815, and by the time of the serpent controversy entrepreneurs were expanding the business.[30]

Mackerel were seasonal fish. Naturalists argued that mackerel returned to New England each spring as a function of rising sea temperature. Warming waters triggered the lush spring plankton bloom, which drew the vast hordes of mackerel arriving on the coast in late April. Fishermen in Nova Scotia, New England, and New York expected the fish then, led by a vanguard of far-ranging scouts. As had been the case since the early colonial era, coastal dwellers took for granted that no "normal" existed regarding the magnitude of the mackerel migration. Lean years could be followed by bumper years, such as 1781 and 1813, when a New York naturalist recounted that "the bays, creeks, and coves were literally alive with them, and the markets full of them." Whether it was a particularly bounteous year for mackerel or not, early each spring the fish were scrawny and lean, almost fat-free, and ready to spawn. Fall mackerel, which had gorged themselves all summer on copepods, shrimp, larval fish, herring, and squid, appeared so different from spring mackerel that as late as 1815 one of the nation's most eminent ichthyologists, Samuel L. Mitchill, still regarded spring and fall mackerel as two distinct species, *Scomber vernalis* and *Scomber grex*. The question as a few fishermen saw it, however, was whether intensified fishing pressure would affect mackerel.[31]

During the late eighteenth and early nineteenth centuries, before jigging became the technique of choice, hookfishers pursuing mackerel had relied on an awkward trolling system, towing baited hooks from outrigger poles at slow speed. Those "drails," so-called, were cumbersome, and even when frenzied fish bit furiously it took time to get the fish off the hooks and rebait. Drailers looked "strangely," according to fishermen; some "had the appearance of a long-armed spider" with the poles bristling from the vessel's sides. The lines were so far from the boat that each fisherman had a bridle connected to the lines to feel the bites and to retrieve the fish. Nathaniel Atwood remembered not only the awkwardness of the system, but how vital it then appeared to have forward motion on the hooks. "My first experience in mackerel fishing took place when I was a little boy, about 1815," he recollected. When the boat did not sail fast enough Atwood and another were forced to row. With that system mackerel "would not bite unless the line was towed." On the other hand, as soon as the breeze came up, a mackerel boat under sail would make too much headway. Thus while drailing, remembered a Maine fisherman, "the sails were trimmed in such a manner that, when the helm was partly down, the vessel would jog along slowly, making a little leeward drift, so that the lines would trend off at a slight angle from the weather side." With its rats' nest of lines and need to maintain a specific speed, drailing for mackerel was anything but convenient. Through the 1810s, however, it was mackerel fishers' technique of choice. The first Cape Ann fisherman to chance an early spring southern mackerel voyage, hoping to intercept the migrating schools and command a premium price for the first fish of the season, used drails. That was in 1817.[32]

As word leaked out about shiny jigs' phenomenal success, fishermen abandoned drails straightaway. In Massachusetts Bay the transition occurred about 1820, during several years when mackerel appeared in great numbers. Substituting jigs for drails and seines, skippers began to set out specifically to salt their mackerel, realizing that longer trips producing a substantial volume of salted fish could be more profitable than day trips for fresh fish. This trend, in turn, led to the evolution of more packing establishments in Gloucester, Hingham, and Wellfleet, competing with those already established in Boston. A nineteenth-century Gloucester historian noted that around 1820 "the size of the Chebacco boats was increased; and it began to be common to furnish them with a bowsprit and call them 'jiggers.'" By the early 1820s purpose-built pinkey schooners were being constructed for the mackerel fishery. In 1821 Mr. Epes W. Merchant had built for the mackerel fishery *Volante,* a 37-ton pinkey, considered a large vessel at the time. Pinkeys were larger and more seaworthy than the Chebacco boats, though their accommodations were still quite primitive. Cooking occurred "in a brick fireplace" just aft of the foremast. A "wooden smokestack or funnel . . . was intended to carry off the smoke, but did not always do so."[33]

Mackerel left a signature trail on the surface, a ripple distinctive from that of herring or menhaden, and very different from the cat's-paws left by puffs of wind. Lookouts raised schools of mackerel from the masthead, sometimes on calm days as far as a mile away. Skippers also "tolled," as they called it, tossing bait overboard to attract the fish. During the early days of jigging weary fishermen chopped menhaden or other baitfish with hatchets for chum. Beginning around 1823 hand-cranked bait mills were replacing hatchets, "a godsend to the fishermen, who could now smoke and spin yarns while on watch," as Gideon L. Davis remembered, "instead of chopping bait."[34]

Mills were mounted on the rail. After a few years it became customary to mount them on the starboard side, from which all fishing was done. The man designated the grinder dumped menhaden, herring, or tiny mackerel into the mill and cranked away, producing a chunky fish slurry that spread to windward. Once into a school of fish the crew jigged from the weather rail as the vessel went off slowly to leeward.

Skippers soon made sure that molds and materials were aboard so that the men could make jigs underway. Each man put hooks in the iron or soapstone molds with about one-third of the shank and point projecting, and then poured a molten mixture of lead and pewter into the mold, passing it on to the next man once his jigs had cooled. At off times, as one green hand remembered, "all hands were seated around the deck, with files, rasps, sandpaper, and dog-fish skin, shaping, scraping, smoothing, and polishing the jigs, each one according to his fancy." During the early years of the jig fishery jigs were relatively heavy, and not that refined. As the years passed, men increasingly took pride in sleek, well-shaped jigs, and in having a variety of weights available for different weather conditions.[35]

The southern New England mackerel fishery reinvented itself during the 1820s, putting what may have been the first noticeable pressure on the western North Atlantic mackerel stock. Vessels got larger, and the fleet grew rapidly. The use of bait mills and jigs became almost universal, and the number of packinghouses ashore grew exponentially, as did the area of the ocean in which mackerel were sought. From a small-boat, fresh-fish venture of little consequence, mackereling grew within a decade into a serious commercial enterprise in which mackerel were pursued earlier and later into the season, and farther from home. Expansion of the industry naturally bolstered expectations about what the ecosystem could produce. And for a while the ecosystem cooperated. Despite lamentations in July 1828 by the *Gloucester Telegraph* advising dealers "to hold on to what they have, as there is likely to be a scarcity this season," total landings that year for the entire New England fleet were about 108.6 million pounds—the second-highest recorded mackerel landings ever. The next year was almost as good. Despite huge hauls close to home, and in a reflection of the expansionist mood of the surging industry, fishermen were ready to try for mackerel farther afield. In 1830 the first voyage to the Gulf of St. Lawrence by a Cape Ann mackerel boat caused a stir. Sailing almost 1,000 miles each way to find mackerel, a fish heretofore regarded as available in their dooryards, nevertheless paid off. As a fisherman remembered, Captain Charles P. Wood's *Mariner* was "absent but four weeks and came in full of large fat mackerel."[36]

During the 1820s mackerel landings began to climb, and they kept climbing, stratospherically. Before 1816 the fleet had never landed more than 8 million pounds of mackerel. By 1820 landings were almost 53 million pounds; by 1822, more than 73 million pounds; and by 1825, more than 116 million pounds. Then during the 1831 season, about sixteen years after Abraham Lurvey molded his first jigs, American mackerel fishers using handlines and shiny jigs, and fishing from small vessels (generally less than 50 tons), landed 175 million pounds of mackerel, a record amount that would not be equaled or bettered until 1884, by which time the science and technology of mackerel fishing had improved dramatically.[37]

Charting historical phenomena is often more straightforward than explaining them, especially when they occur at the intersection of human actions and natural cycles. In retrospect it appears that a perfect storm of human desire, fishing effort, and ecosystem productivity coincided during the 1820s and early 1830s. As New England fishermen were conducting the first-ever large-scale, systematic fishery for mackerel, they happened to find the fish in particularly abundant quantities. Fish populations fluctuate, and populations of mackerel—like those of herring and other small pelagic schooling fish—fluctuate much more dramatically than populations of large, long-lived predators such as halibut or tuna. Late-nineteenth-century scientists believed that mackerel were highly influenced by water temperature, an insight sustained by modern science. All fish stocks respond in some fashion to the North Atlantic Oscillation and other climate drivers that affect wind speed and direction, precipitation, air temperature, and the transfer of heat and moisture. In turn, each of those factors influences surface temperature, the depth and intensity of the thermocline (the boundary layer separating warm surface water from deeper, colder water), and water circulation and nutrient mixing. Those variables, in turn, in specific regions of the ocean, exert influence on phytoplankton and zooplankton production, the basis of the food chain on which predators such as mackerel rely.

Ecological conditions never remain stable, despite human desires, and despite assumptions then prevalent about God's regulation of nature according to immutable laws. Five years after the record landings in 1831, mackerel landings fell to about 50 percent of what they had been that year, and they remained precipitously low for much of the next decade. During the financial panic of 1837, when, as the *Barnstable Patriot* said, "'hard times' have become the universal topic of conversation throughout the Union," New Englanders' mackerel landings were lower than at any time in the last twelve years. Commenting glumly in August 1838 on the huge and unsatisfied market for mackerel in the American west, the *Newburyport Herald* observed that "the time is not distant when, if we are not compelled in a great manner to abandon the business, it will be prosecuted as an uncertain one, and by a greatly decreased number of vessels and men. There is of late not more than one successful season out of four."[38]

A closer correlation of landings as a function of fishing vessel tonnage or as a function of yield per effort reveals the intersection of ecology, economics, and desire. Following the record mackerel landings in 1830, significant tonnage was added to the fleet. Some vessels were purpose-built, and others were shifted from the cod fishery or other fisheries into mackereling. That move paid off handsomely in 1831, with a record mackerel catch. Fleet size changed very little

for the next two years, but then increased significantly. In an early manifesta-
tion of what would become the classic pattern of late-nineteenth-century and
twentieth-century fisheries, effort was expanded even as landings continued
to free-fall. This trend lasted until 1836. Then, following the panic of 1837, the
combination of poor fishing yield and insolvency led to a significant reduction
in tonnage. From 1838 until 1843, effort fell. Fewer vessels and fewer men pursued mackerel.

Landings began to climb after bottoming out in 1840. Stocks appear to have
rebounded during the later 1840s, and—not surprisingly—fishermen began to
register more boats for mackerel fishing. As the registered tonnage rose during
the late 1840s, signaling an intensified fishing effort, landings grew, too. But
after 1851 they declined significantly.

At this distance the data are far from conclusive. It appears that landings
plummeted after especially good years. In other words, when successful, the
fleet's success seems to have diminished the stock on which it relied. Unlike
in the seventeenth century, however, when Massachusetts magistrates and
fishermen took a precautionary approach, most of those interested in the mid-
nineteenth-century fishery pressed on, seeking ever larger harvests.

Ironically, during years of overall scarcity, mackerel sometimes appeared in
colossal numbers in inshore waters and harbors. Nearly 400 barrels were caught
daily for two or three days in a row in the harbor at Portsmouth, New Hampshire, in August 1837. Local men reported that mackerel had rarely come into
the harbor in that fashion. The appearance of the fish seemed to reaffirm their
fickle, unpredictable nature. Much of the discussion about mackerel during
the late 1830s, however, reflected fishermen's laments that the fish had decreased
in number, become more skittish, or migrated beyond their accustomed waters.
"The complaint of the fishermen," noted the *Barnstable Patriot* during the
summer of 1833, "is not so much that they cannot find mackerel, but that they
'won't bite' when they find them."[39]

An undercurrent of concern, however, laced these conversations, attribut-
ing depleted mackerel stocks to human interference. During 1836 and 1838 at
least three Massachusetts newspapers ran stories in which knowledgeable individuals protested "against the barbarous method of taking mackerel, called
'gigging.'" Editors insisted that the practice was shortsighted: "if this destructive method of fishing is generally continued a few years longer, it will break
up the fishery." Newspapermen were not the only ones to raise the alarm.
"Several of our most intelligent fishermen inform me," noted D. Humphreys

Storer, the Boston physician and naturalist, "that the difficulty of taking mackerel is yearly increasing, from the barbarous custom prevailing of gaffing them." Simultaneously, a committee appointed by Nova Scotia's House of Assembly to "enquire into the State of our Fisheries" gathered testimony from fishermen and fish merchants that "gaffing" was injurious to mackerel schools. Mackerel gaffs were iron rods about one-quarter inch in diameter, three and a half feet long, terminating in two sharp hooks recurved back parallel to the rod. The gaffs were fastened to long wooden handles. When mackerel schooled densely about the sides of a vessel but would not bite, the men abandoned their jigs and resorted to gaffs. "The gaff was thrust among the fish and rapidly drawn back," remembered one, "often impaling one and sometimes two mackerel at a time." Gaffs' peak of popularity spanned several decades before 1850, but shortly thereafter fishermen abandoned them. Critics of gaffing protested that it maimed more fish than it caught, and spooked those that remained. The critics insisted that human actions could affect the fish.[40]

An outspoken Marblehead fisherman went further in 1839, explicitly linking harvesting pressure to declining yields, and warning the fishing community to heed the consequences of its actions. "All the mackerel men who arrive report the scarcity of this fish," he complained, "and at the same time I notice an improvement in taking them with nets at Cape Cod and other places. If this speculation is allowed to go on without being checked or regulated by the government, will not these fish be as scarce on the coast as penguins are, which were so plenty before the Revolutionary war that our fishermen could take them with their gaffs?" His "penguins" were great auks, then extinct in the western Atlantic. The Marblehead fishermen knew why. "Mercenary and cruel individuals used to visit the islands on the eastern shore [Atlantic Canada] where were the haunts of these birds for breeding. . . . This proceeding finally destroyed the whole race."[41] Clearly, some experienced fishermen during the intensification of the mackerel craze were not convinced that the sea was impervious to harm or that its treasures were limitless, though its mysteries remained largely incomprehensible.

IMPROVING THE SEA

Within a few days of the sea serpent's first appearance off Gloucester in August 1817, a newspaper advertisement in nearby Salem notified the public "that a more palatable fish than a Sea-Serpent will make his appearance Monday next." John Remond, the advertiser—a man of mixed race, locally known for his catering skills—was opening an "Oyster Establishment" on Front Street. *"Let them be roasted, stewed, or fried; Or any other way beside; You'll be well served, or ill betide."* Salem no longer had a commercially viable supply of oysters, but Remond, a savvy businessman, apparently had contracted with men from Wellfleet, on Cape Cod, to provide them. For at least the last fifteen years a small fleet of Wellfleet vessels, about thirty tons each, had regularly carried oysters to towns including Boston, Newburyport, Portland, and Salem.[42]

By the turn of the nineteenth century oyster stalls and shops were commonplace in sizable coastal towns. Residents patronized oyster cellars in Philadelphia, New York, Boston, Salem, Portland, and Providence, among other places. Oyster beds had occurred naturally from Penobscot Bay to points south, and substantial beds once had been found in the Piscataqua estuary, in the Parker and Rowley Rivers of Essex County, and in Boston harbor. During the 1630s John Josselyn had reported a "great oyster bank" in Boston Bay, southwest of the Charles River, an area subsequently filled. A French refugee visiting Boston fifty years later noted the town's substantial trade, listing among cargoes exported "oysters salted in barrels, great quantities of which are taken here." By the eighteenth century, however, when many of the far-flung oyster beds had been depleted, urban dwellers were relegated to eating from more distant ecosystems. The shallow waters of Cape Cod Bay remained the great shellfish producer for the region—notably the towns of Wellfleet, Eastham, and Orleans in Barnstable County. The extensive flats there had been known for prodigious quantities of oysters, clams, and quahogs since the arrival of the Pilgrims.[43]

Concern regarding the destruction of those bountiful oysters surfaced in 1765. A law that year recounted that it had "been the practice for some years past for persons to come, with their vessels and boats, into the rivers and bays lying either in the towns of Wellfleet, Freetown, Swanzey, Dartmouth, Barnstable, Yarmouth . . . to rake the oyster-beds, [and] carry away from thence large quantities of oysters, by means whereof said beds are almost destroyed." The law went on to prohibit raking or sweeping oyster beds in any town without written permission from the selectmen, excepting only inhabitants who wished to take oysters "for their own eating, or for market in their own town." It was too little, too late. Disaster struck in 1770, when all the oysters died in Billingsgate Bay, bordering the towns of Wellfleet, Eastham, Orleans, and Brewster. At this distance it is impossible to know with certainty what killed the oysters. They are susceptible to bacterial toxins, such as those produced by the bacterium *Vibrio tubiashi*. Infectious diseases caused by parasitic protozoans such as *Haplosporidium nelsoni* can also kill oysters. That was the root of the great oyster die-off in Chesapeake Bay and Delaware Bay that began in 1957. Researchers also believe that some red-tide blooms produce toxins, possibly induced by a virus, that kill oysters. One thing is clear: the more stressed an ecosystem is, the less ability it has to resist disease. Systematic overfishing may have paved the way for the great die-off.[44]

Oystering provided the principal support for many of Wellfleet's inhabitants, in part because the shore-based whaling trade had collapsed decades earlier. Residents of the district petitioned the General Court to amend the earlier act in 1772, claiming it was insufficiently protective. Faced with calamity, they wanted a moratorium on oyster harvesting for the Boston market and a closed season in July and August on harvesting even for local consumption. In 1773 the town of Wellfleet ordered that "more stringent regulations are necessary to prevent their [the oysters'] destruction." Twelve years later, in another recognition of the importance of shellfishing to the area, the town of Eastham (from which Wellfleet had separated a generation earlier) prohibited people of other towns from digging clam bait within the town.[45]

What nature could not restore, local men determined to fix. The oyster population did not rebound quickly, so after the Revolutionary War Wellfleet men began transporting oysters from Buzzards Bay and Narragansett Bay to spread on their flats. The best beds for transplantation had three to six feet of water at low tide. Ultimately seamen brought tens of thousands of bushels each year. The imported oysters filtered the nutrient-rich and slightly brackish water of Billingsgate Bay. While some reproduced, reseeding the beds, most of the increase—as oystermen saw it—came through the growth of transplanted oysters. The tasty bivalves that John Remond served in 1817 had probably been born in southern New England, fattened off Wellfleet in shallow oyster farms, and then raked for shipment and sale in Salem, Boston, and elsewhere.[46]

Other ad hoc manipulations of coastal marine ecosystems followed, though none on such a large scale. According to New York's premier ichthyologist of the early nineteenth century, Samuel L. Mitchill, the tautog—commonly called blackfish—"was not originally known in Massachusetts bay; but within a few years [that is, sometime shortly before 1814] he has been carried beyond Cape

Cod, and has multiplied so abundantly, that the Boston market now has a full supply." Tautog hug the coast, where they feed on invertebrates in relatively shallow water. A stout, dark-colored, and delicious fish, averaging two to four pounds, tautog were highly regarded by consumers and often available in market stalls. Not all naturalists are convinced that human intervention extended the range of tautog. Despite Mitchill's statement, Henry B. Bigelow and William C. Schroeder, authors of the definitive *Fishes of the Gulf of Maine,* think it more likely that tautog had been plentiful in the region years earlier and had then reappeared after a period of scarcity. Attempts at stocking tautog may have been augmented by a natural increase.[47]

In any event, fishermen certainly introduced alewives to streams on Cape Ann, hoping to establish sustainable populations. And sometime around 1833, as mackerel landings were falling, the skipper of a well smack brought a load of live scup, also known as scapaug, from New Bedford to Boston. "A portion of them were purchased by subscription among the fishermen in the market," as D. Humphreys Storer explained, "and thrown into the harbor." Scup were eight to twelve inches long, and a favorite food fish in Buzzards Bay and Vineyard Sound. They were caught with hooks and, in the fall of the year, with spears and nets in coastal ponds. They did not seem to thrive naturally north of Cape Cod, where the water was colder, and the ambitious fishermen's experiment at the Boston market came to naught. The year after the scup were transplanted to Boston two were caught from Boston wharves, and in each of the next two years one was caught at Nahant, where it "was considered *a very strange fish.*" Those random fish were regarded as having been part of the initial batch, and everyone agreed that no reproducing stock had been generated. The point is that early-nineteenth-century fishermen ambitiously tried to reengineer the productivity of their coastal ecosystem by transplanting oysters and fish, even though systematic knowledge of natural history was still extremely limited as late as the 1830s.[48]

The Linnaean Society of New England, problems and enthusiasms notwithstanding, lasted for less than a decade. It suspended meetings in 1822, and by the next year its "extensive and valuable collection . . . had gone to ruin for want of care." In 1830 a new organization formed, the Boston Society of Natural History. At that time, an eminent naturalist later recalled, "there was not, I believe, in New England, an institution devoted to the study of natural history. . . . There was not within our borders a single museum of modern science, nor a single journal advocating exclusively its interests. . . . There was no one among us who had anything like a general knowledge of the birds which fly about us, the fishes which fill our waters, or the lower tribe of animals that swarm both in air and in sea." Members of the new society, including Dr. Jerome V. C. Smith and Dr. D. Humphreys Storer, hoped to fill that void, but average annual attendance at society meetings for the next twenty years was underwhelming at best, about fifteen men a year. Fishermen frequently knew more than naturalists about the living ocean, though the naturalists often had unwarranted confidence in their own knowledge.[49]

As harvesters pointed to troublesome depletions in coastal waters, questions arose about who had the right to interpret the ecosystem, and on what grounds. Gloucester fishermen complained in 1828 that carrying away too many lobsters from Gloucester harbor tended to "Destroy other bay fishing." They knew that predatory fish ate young lobsters. In 1839, the same year that the Marblehead fisherman worried openly that mackerel might go the way of great auks, a group of eighty-nine Barnstable fishermen lamented that seining "greatly disturbs the fish in their spawning grounds, and frightens them from our waters." Seines were relatively small, and still all handmade in New England at that time. The Barnstable men, however, sought passage of a law "preventing any person from seining fish" in town waters. They were convinced that their fisheries were "endangered," and they wanted the state to intercede. Imagining them as conservationists would be anachronistic. Nevertheless, their concerns about endangered fisheries were real, as was their anxiety about the future. Yet fifty-two other townsmen objected that the statements regarding "disturbing the fish in their spawning grounds . . . and of frightening them . . . are merely conjectural and totally unsusceptible of proof." Because of the lack of zoological authority, the debate operated through recrimination and self-interest. The pro-seine faction also noted that menhaden seiners occasionally took scup, which by-catch they supported wholeheartedly. "It would be a result greatly to be desired if their utter destruction could be fully consummated, for it is a well-known fact that they, the scup, feed on and destroy clams, a valuable shellfish, which previous to the appearance of scup in our harbour, some twenty-five or thirty years ago, were found on the shores of our harbours in the greatest abundance . . . whereas now they have become exceedingly scarce and are in danger of becoming totally extinct." Manipulating the ecosystem to remove unwanted predators seemed to make sense, even as it reaffirmed the belief that humans could have an impact on the living sea.[50]

Petitions flooded the Massachusetts legislature that year from Martha's Vineyard fishermen convinced "that the increasing scarcity of fish of every kind" demanded "Legislative interference," as did "the digging of Clams on the flats and shores . . . (which are become scarce and small and are needed by us for fishing bait)." Convinced that the decline was measurable, the petitioners hoped that restrictions on seines, along with tighter requirements for clam-digging permits and exclusion of outsiders, would stop the problem. Chatham fishermen wanted protection, too. They complained that they were "suffering under great inconvenience in their Harbour fisheries from smacks and boats" from elsewhere entering town waters and taking "Lobsters Menhaden Bass Shad and other kinds of fish greatly to the annoyance of the Inhabitants." Chatham not only sat at the outer elbow of Cape Cod, where each spring and fall vast schools of migrating fish turned the corner, but the town also controlled the inlet between the sea and a vast salt pond. From a fisherman's perspective, Chatham was well positioned.[51]

Fishermen from other Cape Cod towns resented Chatham's attempt to monopolize a resource that could be open to all, especially because there was "no place on the shores of Cape Cod" where menhaden "can be procured with more ease or certainty than the shores of Chatham." Menhaden was the bait of choice in the cod and mackerel fisheries. A sizable contingent from Barnstable County put it bluntly: "we believe that all such fisheries . . . are the common property of all the inhabitants of this commonwealth, and neither need, nor can receive protection from mortal man." Chatham men disagreed. So did Nantucket Islanders. A few years later a group from the island insisted that "by seining, eeling, clamming, &c." outsiders "have nearly annihilated our Bass and Eel beds and have so reduced our clams, that where once there was an abundance for our purposes there is now a scarcity." Their solution was simple: preserve local resources for local people.[52]

Blaming outsiders for depleting resources had a long history, and was a tactic that would extend well into the future. Controlling knowledge or mustering actual facts about fisheries was another matter, as the saga of the sea serpent had made all too clear. Take herring, for instance, a fishery whose significance had increased during the second third of the nineteenth century. Maine lawmakers had regulated the herring fishery as early as 1821, one year after attaining statehood. During the early 1840s, however, herring regulations were liberalized, and fishermen from Jonesport, an eastern Maine town near the New Brunswick border, feared the consequences. The old law, they said, "prevented our fishery from being destroyed by setting netts." The law that they requested "forbids setting netts but for bait only and admits of Torching Herring, which method of taking herring from our experience we know to be far less destructive to the Herring fishery than Netting." They went on to explain that the "Herring fishery has almost been entirely destroyed west of Washington County where it has always been lawful to sett netts." Jonesport was remote, and only recently settled. Families there relied on the herring fishery, which they prosecuted with weirs and with dip nets and torches, and they predicted financial ruin "if our Fisheries are destroyed, as we Verily believe it will be under the operation of the present law."[53]

The problem was that other experienced men disagreed about the effects of torching. In the fall of 1817, shortly after the sea serpent had been seen off Cape Ann for the last time that year, William Bentley noted in his diary that "Our Herring fishery still succeeds & great numbers are taken still near our shores." The herring that year had come into the bay off Ipswich "for the first time in the memory of this generation," and, as Bentley pointed out, fishermen "have been employed by torchlight in taking them & with great success." As with the men from Jonesport a generation later, no one worried that attracting herring with torches created problems. But during the 1830s Boston fishermen became convinced of the perniciousness of torching. "Upon some portions of our coast, *herring* have been limited in quantity for the last few years," D. Humphreys Storer wrote in 1839, "and during the years 1835–6 very few, comparatively speaking, were taken. Their scarcity has been attributed by the fishermen to *torching* them at night, by which the shoals are broken up and the fish frightened away." No one knew with certainty.[54]

Storer, the preeminent ichthyologist in antebellum Massachusetts, had relied to some extent on fishmongers and fishermen as he prepared his book on fishes of Massachusetts during the 1830s. He thanked Captain Nathaniel Blanchard of Lynn, whose father-in-law had been killed by the shark, for "constant and unwearied efforts" and "for many judicious remarks and valuable details," but it is clear from his text that Storer was much more comfortable with amateur naturalists who got their knowledge from books (many of whom were, like himself, medical doctors) than with fishermen. His discussion of the "Common Tunny," for instance, made no mention of Captain Rich's insistence that the sea serpent had been a tuna. And Storer, as we have seen, included *Scoliophis atlanticus* in his book in 1839, despite the controversy and Captain Rich's disavowal, noting "That this is a new and very curious animal, is acknowledged by distinguished foreign naturalists."[55]

By 1842, however, as he was working on revisions to his first edition, Storer sought the assistance of Captain Nathaniel Atwood, a veteran fisherman from Provincetown. Atwood had been ten years old when the sea serpent first appeared, and was then day-boat fishing with his father and other men from Race Point, the outer tip of Cape Cod. They had only what they called "five-handed boats," lapstrake boats a little smaller than a whaleboat, fitted with four oars and sometimes with a small sail on a twelve-foot mast. Without ability to sail far from shore, they relied on what the sea delivered in its seasons. Late winter and early spring meant handlining for cod. February was most productive, but brutal. Beginning about May 20, with the vanguard of mackerel, they set nets in the harbor for mackerel that would be sold fresh in Boston. After the mackerel season ended around the first of July quiet times followed, when they overhauled the boats and gear, until the middle of September, when "the dogfish struck in on their way south." They caught spiny dogfish—one of the smallest and certainly the most numerous shark in the Gulf of Maine—from the middle of September to the middle of November. That was the best fishing of the season, as dogfish oil was worth about ten dollars a barrel.[56]

By the time the dogfish disappeared winter had come, and it was back to handlining cod and the occasional haddock. As Atwood remembered, "We didn't have any haddock at that time. . . . For many years haddock were altogether higher [in value] than codfish, owing to their scarcity. This was in 1817." During the next twenty-five years he fished mackerel, halibut, cod, shad, and whiting, experimenting with various gears, and ranging as far afield as Long Island Sound, the Gulf of St. Lawrence, and the Azores. When he received Storer's request for help with his book on the fishes of Massachusetts, Atwood "supposed, having been a fisherman for so long, I knew a good deal." As he recollected, he "answered questions about thirty-two kinds of fish he sent me in his report. . . . I looked over it and found that I could do a good deal, and this was the beginning of my acquaintance with scientific men." Captain Atwood had a thirst for learning matched only by his capacious photographic memory.[57]

Within five years Atwood had joined (by invitation) the elitist Boston Society of Natural History. In 1848 the society acknowledged its indebtedness to him for providing "several fine specimens, two of which," Thomas Bouvé explained, "were of genera new to the waters of Massachusetts." Storer's trust in Captain Atwood became sufficiently strong that in the summer of 1849 he allowed two of his sons, Horatio and Frank, to accompany Atwood on a voyage to Labrador. Jeffries Wyman, then thirty-five years old and the Hersey Professor of Anatomy at Harvard, joined the expedition. Wyman had produced the illustrations for Storer's first edition of the *Report on Fishes* in 1839, and their families were connected through the linked lineages of Boston society, Harvard, and the medical profession—a social world to which Atwood, the poor fisherman's son from Provincetown, had never imagined he would be introduced.[58]

Three years before his voyage to Labrador, Wyman's reputation as a naturalist and anatomist had been burnished publicly by his revelation of a sea serpent fraud. At the Apollo Saloon on Broadway, in New York, Albert Koch, a flamboyant German entrepreneur, assembled fossilized bones from at least five whales to erect a 114-foot-long skeleton of what he called *Hydrarchos sillimani,* literally, "Silliman's master of the seas." The skeleton was supposedly that of a "gigantic fossilized reptile." Koch's name for the beast honored Yale professor Benjamin Silliman, who had followed the esteemed gentlemen of the Linnaean Society decades earlier in recognizing the Gloucester sea serpent. To the disappointment of the great crowds flocking to see the monster, Wyman demonstrated that the vertebrae, which had been cemented together, "not only belonged to more than one individual, but to many ages." He also showed that "the teeth were those of a cetacean, not a reptile." By then Harvard had become the center of natural science in America, with luminaries such as Louis Agassiz and Asa Gray on its faculty. Wyman's report was not the end of sea serpent sightings, but it shifted the natural history establishment away from the Linnaean Society's insistence that its members knew more than fishermen like Captain Rich simply because of their status as gentlemen. Wyman was a gentleman, too. And Storer's expanded second edition, published in 1867 as *A History of the Fishes of Massachusetts,* did not mention the serpent.[59]

Accompanied by the famous Professor Wyman and Dr. Storer's two sons, Captain Atwood sailed for Labrador in July 1849. He later recollected how the voyage easily accommodated both commercial fishing and science. "We started in pursuit of objects of natural history and the manufacture of medicinal cod-liver oil." Atwood made 300 gallons of cod-liver oil, and Horatio R. Storer, just twenty years old that summer, did the fieldwork for a monograph he published two years later on the fishes of Nova Scotia and Labrador. Within a few years Dr. D. Humphreys Storer would honor Atwood as "the best practical ichthyologist in our state."[60]

Eighteen fifty-one was almost a record year for mackerel. Landings were extraordinary, and fishermen had fine paydays. Some mackerel were gill-netted near the shore, in the same fashion that Atwood had netted them as a boy, but the mackerel fishery for the most part relied on jigging. Within the next few years, however, a technological revolution would transform mackerel fishing in Massachusetts and Maine, where virtually all of the American mackerel fleet was based, even as a scientific breakthrough bolstered naturalists' knowledge about mackerel reproduction. In 1853, as armed cutters from British Canada were harassing American fishermen in the Gulf of St. Lawrence, the Massachusetts schooners *Ada, Romp,* and *Vanguard* experimented with purse seining mackerel. Purse seines were a relatively new technology, which in recent years had been used to good effect in the newly expanding menhaden fishery. The purse seine was a long net deployed by two small boats to circle a school of fish. Applicable only to species such as herring, menhaden, and mackerel, which school near the surface, purse seines were about to make Abraham Lurvey's shiny jigs obsolete. They would also multiply the destruction of fish. "The waste during the seining season is enormous," Horatio Storer noted off Labrador during the herring season in 1849, with "many more being taken than can possibly be cured, so that hundreds of barrels are left to rot upon the beach; and . . . for miles around, the water is completely covered by a thick oily scum, arising from the decaying fish."[61]

The second revolution was scientific, and a fisherman spearheaded it. Despite the commercial significance of the mackerel fishery, naturalists understood little about mackerel's spawning. In the spring of 1856 Captain Atwood decided to pursue the subject systematically. By then he was accustomed to the company and the ways of thinking of scientific men, being a regular associate of Storer and Wyman and other members of the Boston Society of Natural History. In 1852 he had been visited by Professor Louis Agassiz. With Augustus A. Gould, Agassiz had recently published the book cementing his fame, *Principles of Zoölogy, Touching the Structure, Development, Distribution, and Natural Arrangement of the Races of Animals.* (It did not include sea serpents.) Impressed by Atwood's contributions to ichthyology, Agassiz traveled to Provincetown to meet the skipper-turned-naturalist. That visit "began an acquaintance that shortly ripened into an intimacy and life-long friendship," noted a contemporary, marked by years of correspondence respecting fishes.[62]

In the spring of 1856 Atwood set drift nets from his new boat, the *Ichthyologist,* taking 2,250 mackerel on May 20 and 3,520 the next night. He determined that their spawn was not yet "free to run," though it looked mature and fully formed. He collected eggs almost daily thereafter, putting them into alcohol, ultimately determining that the fish had finished spawning by June 10, and that June 5 was probably the midpoint of that year's spawning. "Thirty days after I went out into the bay and found any quantity of schools of little mackerel which were, I should think, about two inches long." He collected, preserved, and dated his specimens, then returned twenty-five days later to procure more. As he recounted later with obvious pride, "I called on Professor Agassiz and gave him the specimens. He had that he had never before been able to ascertain these facts so clearly and so well." Atwood persisted with his fieldwork until late October that year, taking tiny mackerel with a fine-mesh net, and recording the growth of what he believed to be that year's class. Appointed by the state that summer as one of three commissioners to study the artificial propagation of fish, he was also elected that year as a member of the Essex Institute of Salem, blurring the boundaries between workingmen and gentlemen in a fashion that would have been difficult to imagine for the members of the Linnaean Society in 1818, when the sea serpent cavorted off Cape Ann.[63]

The five decades before the American Civil War saw both the rise and fall of the jig as the dominant mackerel technology, and the rise and fall of attention to sea serpents by New England naturalists. Belief in the authority of print gave way grudgingly to empiricism, a necessary step in developing systematized scientific observation. Meanwhile creeping concerns about overfishing became palpable, coexisting uneasily alongside the determination to make natural science serve the republic in terms of prestige and profit. No single group monopolized knowledge of natural history, and none determined whether precautionary narratives had merit—such as the Cassandra-like warnings that mackerel would go the way of "penguins," or that seining caused enormous waste, or "that the increasing scarcity of fish of every kind" demanded "Legislative interference." Yet the ability to develop technology to harvest the sea, and to distribute its resources to consumers, far outstripped accumulation of knowledge about sea creatures, including simple baselines regarding commercially valuable species' abundance and distribution.

The Gloucester sea serpent may appear to have played only a bit part in New England's marine environmental history, but something was lost when naturalists and fishermen finally debunked *Scoliophis atlanticus*. For millennia the sea had been imagined as limitless, unfathomable, implacable, and wild. The virtually simultaneous dismissal of the sea serpent, along with invention first of the mackerel jig, and then of the purse seine, tamed and appropriated that limitlessness. One consequence of dismissing the credibility of sea serpents made the ocean more approachable, more objective, more scientific—and supposedly more manageable. During the antebellum decades Americans grew more confident in their ability to rationally comprehend, or even control, the natural world, as revealed by their optimistic attempts to engineer nature. By the late 1850s naturalists and fishermen were increasingly comfortable with the idea that technology would resolve the ocean's mysteries *and* its problems with productivity. But as the midcentury cod fishery soon revealed, such confidence came with costs.

Viking invaders revolutionized Europeans' relationship to the sea by bringing air-dried cod and technologies for catching sea fish. Prior to the Viking invasion in the ninth century, coastal Europeans ate relatively little seafood other than fish such as salmon, sturgeon, and shad— anadromous species that appeared in the rivers each spring. (*Íslendingur*, replica Viking ship; courtesy of the Vikingaheimar Museum, Reykjanes, Iceland.)

Large-scale sea fishing grew as Europe's freshwater fish were overexploited. By the fourteenth and fifteenth centuries, Catholic Europeans were regularly eating cod, plaice, and other sea fish (upper left). Herring appeared so numerous that a bishop claimed: "when they arrive in their shoals an axe . . . thrust firmly into their midst sticks firmly upright" (lower left). Later such superlatives would be used for New World fisheries. Dutch herring vessels (below) could stay at sea for weeks, catching and preserving the fish most commonly eaten in medieval Europe. (Upper and lower left: Olaus Magnus, "Deep-Sea Fishing off Norway" and "Countless Herring," in *Description of the Northern Peoples,* Rome, 1555; reprint London, 1998, quotation on 1061; courtesy of University of New Hampshire Photographic Services. Below: Anonymous, after Jan Porcellis, *Haring Buysen groot omtrent 40 Last 4;* courtesy of Rijksmuseum, Amsterdam.)

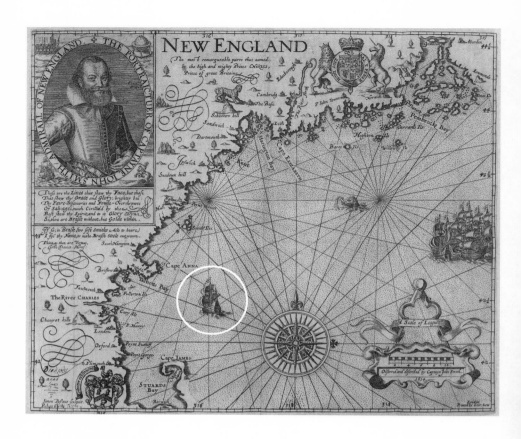

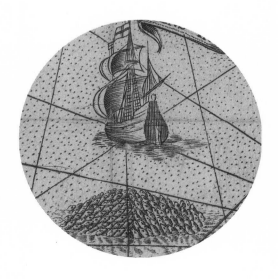

But coastal European ecosystems could not produce enough to satisfy demand. By the early sixteenth century fishermen pushed west across the Atlantic, first to Newfoundland and the Gulf of St. Lawrence, then to New England. Captain John Smith drew this map (top left) in about 1616; a subsequent edition (bottom left) depicted a vast school of fish under the ship—the sort of abundance once seen in European waters. Herman Moll illustrated catching, curing, and drying cod in Newfoundland in 1720 (below). By then that fishery was more than 200 years old, and was removing as much as 150,000 metric tons of cod per year. (Left: John Smith, "Map of New England," 4th state, ca. 1616; and detail from John Smith, "Map of New England," 9th state, ca. 1635; courtesy of the John Carter Brown Library at Brown University. Below: Herman Moll, "A View of a Stage and Also the Manner of Fishing for, Curing, and Drying Cod at New Found Land," 1720; courtesy of the John Carter Brown Library at Brown University.)

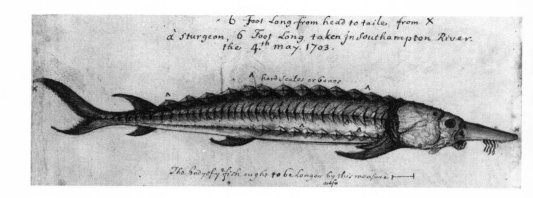

By 1800 harvesting pressure had significantly reshaped the marine ecosystem between Cape Cod and Newfoundland. Some species of coastal whales had been nearly eradicated. Walrus had been exterminated in their southern range and pushed toward the Arctic. It took settlers only two centuries to make sturgeon (top), a large armored fish with few natural enemies, relatively rare in northern New England. Great auks (bottom), the North American "penguin," were well on their way to extinction in 1800. The last one was killed in 1842. (Top: Sturgeon drawn by Jean Barbot, 1703; by permission of National Archives of the United Kingdom, Kew, Surrey, re. ADM 7/830 A&B. Bottom: Aquatint by John James Audubon and Robert Havell, from Audubon's *The Birds of America,* London, 1827–1838, vol. 4, plate 341; courtesy of Errol Fuller.)

Sea serpents had been seen in New England before, but none generated the attention of those reported—and drawn—near Gloucester from 1817 to 1819. Taxonomists classified them as *Scoliophis atlanticus*. The state of fisheries science, fishermen's innovations, and changes in the sea during this era reveal humans' growing confidence in their ability to understand God's marine creation, and their tragic failure to take a precautionary approach in the face of profound uncertainty. (*Monstrous Sea Serpent as Seen at Cape Ann,* ca. 1817; courtesy of MIT Museum.)

Fitz Henry Lane painted Gloucester Harbor in 1848 with the precision of a photograph. The cod and haddock piled on the beach under the cleaning table were 20-to-30-pounders—big fish that could still be caught by day boats near shore. Although the coastal ecosystem had been changed by humans in simple sailing craft and rowboats by 1848, it was still extraordinarily productive. (Fitz Henry Lane, *View of Gloucester Harbor,* 1848; courtesy of Virginia Museum of Fine Arts, Richmond. Adolph D. and Wilkins C. Williams Fund. Photo Katherine Wetzel. © Virginia Museum of Fine Arts.)

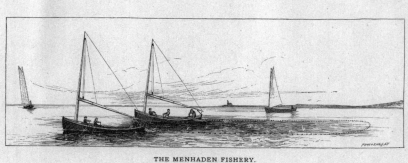

THE MENHADEN FISHERY.

Purse and mate boats encircling a school; carry-away boats in waiting. (Sect. v, vol. i, pp. 334, 368.)

From sketch by Capt. B. F. Conklin

Maine's menhaden wars began around 1850 in the little town of Blue Hill (top). Fishermen in small sailboats and rowboats began to pursue schools of menhaden with handmade nets to render them for oil (bottom). Other fishermen protested vehemently that seining menhaden would destroy the forage base on which cod and mackerel fisheries rested, fisheries that already seemed depleted. (Top: Fitz Henry Lane, *Blue Hill, Maine,* ca. 1853–1857; private collection, Washington, D.C. Bottom: "The Menhaden Fishery: Purse and Mate Boats Encircling a School," engraving from a sketch by Capt. B. F. Conklin, *The Fisheries and Fishery Industries of the United States,* Washington, D.C., 1887, sec. V, plate 101.)

By then the most common fishing boats in northern New England were pinkey schooners, developed during the 1820s. With their "cod's head and mackerel's tail"—meaning that they were full forward and fine aft—they were safe and seaworthy, but unable to sail close to the wind. These simple vessels were the norm during the heyday of mackerel jigging, which included record-setting landings in 1831. (Pinkey schooner *Maine*, courtesy of Penobscot Marine Museum, Searsport, Maine. Boutilier Collection.)

By the time this photo was taken in Maine at the end of the nineteenth century, New World cod had been dried on flakes like these for almost 400 years. Schooners had got bigger and more powerful, but fishing remained resolutely preindustrial. Nevertheless, cod landings from the Gulf of Maine decreased steadily, from about 70,000 metric tons in 1861, to 54,000 in 1880, to

about 20,000 in 1900. The "restoration of our exhausted cod fisheries," championed by the U.S. Fish Commission in 1873, never occurred. (Fish drying at the Cranberry Isles, Maine, ca. 1900, photograph by Fred Morse; courtesy of Marie Locke.)

Spencer F. Baird (top), who directed the U.S.
Fish Commission from its inception in 1871
until his death in 1887, concurred with
Thomas Huxley, Britain's leading fisheries
scientist, that humans could make no impact
on schooling sea fish such as cod, mackerel,
and herring. Baird's assistant, George Brown
Goode (right), who edited the seven-volume
Fisheries & Fishery Industries of the U.S.
during the 1880s, agreed. (Top: Spencer F.
Baird, courtesy of Smithsonian Institution
Archives, image MAH-16607. Right: George
Brown Goode, courtesy of Smithsonian
Institution Archives, image SA-63.)

But most New England fishermen strenuously disagreed. From the 1850s to 1915 they argued that stocks were declining, and that the government should take measures to ensure the availability of fish for the future. (George H. Donnell with a tub of pollock, York, Maine, ca. 1882, photograph by Emma Lewis Coleman; courtesy of Historic New England, Boston.)

By the time Winslow Homer painted this halibut fisherman (top) in 1885, New Englanders were sailing to Greenland and Iceland in search of halibut. Local stocks had already been exhausted. Meanwhile new technologies such as canning (bottom), along with expanding networks of fish dealers and merchants (right), put more pressure on ocean resources. (Top: Winslow Homer, *The Fog Warning*, 1885, oil on canvas, 76.83 × 123.19 cm [30 1/4 × 48 1/2 in.], anonymous gift,

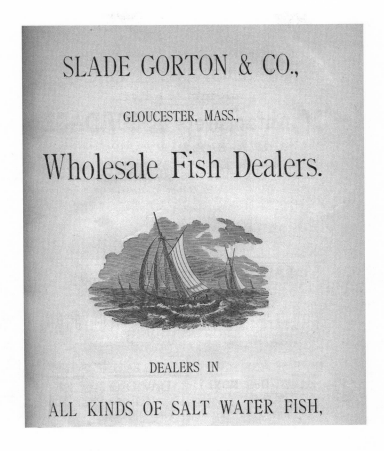

SLADE GORTON & CO.,

GLOUCESTER, MASS.,

Wholesale Fish Dealers.

DEALERS IN

ALL KINDS OF SALT WATER FISH,

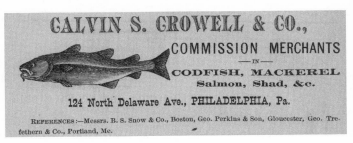

CALVIN S. CROWELL & CO.,

COMMISSION MERCHANTS
— IN —
CODFISH, MACKEREL
Salmon, Shad, &c.

124 North Delaware Ave., PHILADELPHIA, Pa.

REFERENCES:—Messrs. B. S. Snow & Co., Boston, Geo. Perkins & Son, Gloucester, Geo. Trefethern & Co., Portland, Me.

The first federal regulation to conserve sea fish went into effect in 1887. Congress closed the mackerel fishery during the spring spawning season after stocks appeared to collapse in 1886. By then fishermen no longer jigged for mackerel. They sailed powerful schooners to pursue the fish, and used seine boats to encircle the schools (right). Stocks of mackerel, menhaden, lobster, and halibut all crashed during the late nineteenth century. Clam-diggers, photographed rowing peapods and skiffs at Deer Isle, Maine, in the 1890s (above), also saw catastrophic declines in their harvests. (Above: Clam-diggers in peapods and skiffs at Oceanville, Deer Isle, Maine, 1890s; courtesy of Deer Isle–Stonington Historical Society. Right: Mackerel schooner towing seine boats, Gloucester Harbor, Mass., ca. 1890s, photograph by Eric Hudson; courtesy of Maine State Museum, Augusta.)

As landings of cod and other bottom fish declined, schooner fishermen on the western Atlantic banks abandoned handlining from their vessels. During the 1860s they began to set longlines from dories. This practice dramatically increased their number of hooks—and their demand for bait. Meanwhile European fishermen in the North Sea region were already dragging nets along the bottom, first beam trawls from sailboats and then otter trawls from steamers. Fishermen in Nova Scotia and New England feared destructive trawling technology and resisted it. Their initial encounter with a steam trawler took place shortly after the launch, in 1905, of the *Spray*. (Thomas M. Hoyne, *New Ways on Quero Bank*, 1981; courtesy of Doris O. Hoyne and the Peabody Essex Museum, Salem, Mass. Gift of Russell W. Knight, 1982.)

By the turn of the twentieth century, as catches continued to decline, fishermen increasingly adopted technologies that their grandfathers and fathers had resisted as too destructive. Resignation to the new ways replaced concerns about changes in the sea. (Purse seining from a dory, ca. 1890s, photograph by Eric Hudson; courtesy of Maine State Museum, Augusta.)

With the onset of industrialized fishing, the die had been cast. Virtually every previous attempt to conserve fish stocks had failed. In 1911, when only six steam trawlers worked New England's banks, including the three shown above, a Massachusetts congressman introduced a bill to prohibit bottom trawling. Most fishermen and many politicians opposed the new technology. They believed it would destroy fish stocks in America, as it had in Europe. The U.S. Bureau of Fisheries took almost three years to investigate. Its report raised serious questions, but in the intervening years trawling had become more "normal," and opposition to it waned. Seventy-five years later—the blink of an eye in ecological time—the once-storied North Atlantic banks were virtually empty of fish, the result of a 500-year fishing spree. But the warning signals had been there at every step of the way. (Trawlers *Foam, Ripple,* and *Spray,* ca. 1918; courtesy of Naval History and Heritage Command, Washington, D.C.)

Four

MAKING THE CASE FOR CAUTION

> There are doubtless plenty of fish still in the sea, but the
> trouble of capturing them increases daily, and the instru-
> ments of capture have to be yearly augmented, indicating
> but too clearly to all who have studied the subject that we
> are beginning to overfish.
>
> —James G. Bertram, *The Harvest of the Sea:*
> *A Contribution to the Natural and Economic History*
> *of the British Food Fishes* (1865)

Late in 1864, as General William T. Sherman cut a swath of devastation across
Georgia on his notorious march to the sea, Jotham Johnson of Freeport, a village
in the northwest corner of Casco Bay, Maine, lamented devastation in the sea
closer to home. Johnson was frightened. Ruing the day that menhaden oil
factories ("the greates Destruction to the fisheries of any invention Ever got
up") had come to the Maine coast, and complaining that mackerel seiners
would soon "inclose all the shoal ground," he asked the legislature to intervene. "If their is not sumthing don to put a stopt to this Slatter [slaughter], fare
will to the fisheries in Mane."[1]

By the 1850s and 1860s fishermen such as Johnson in New England, Nova
Scotia, and Newfoundland were not using the word "sustainability," but they
were clearly concerned about the future of marine resources. Concerns regarding conservation of sea fish on which coastal communities had long depended
were heard on fishing stages, aboard schooners, and in town meetings. Although

such concerns had been expressed intermittently during the previous thirty years, the intensity of the complaints increased dramatically at midcentury.

Fisheries science, however, barely existed. Fishes' "habits and the laws that govern them are little understood," observed one Massachusetts insider in 1856, "although many facts respecting them have been known for scores of years." So "little progress is being made in observing the natural history of fish," noted James G. Bertram in 1865, "that we cannot expect for some time to know much more than we do at present." No naturalist then knew at what age cod, haddock, or halibut reached sexual maturity, much less whether or not such species wandered randomly—meaning that they might repopulate exhausted fishing grounds—or whether each species consisted of loosely related subraces that spawned only in specific places. Little was known about differences in food fishes' spawning grounds, nursery grounds, and feeding grounds. Systematic landings data, much less landings data with reference to place, simply did not exist in ways accessible to naturalists or politicians. Scientific regulation would be impossible in the absence of such knowledge, yet the 1850s and 1860s were noteworthy not only in New England and Atlantic Canada, but in Great Britain and Norway as well, for fishermen's insistence that governments do *something* to preserve the fish on which their livelihoods depended.[2]

New England and Nova Scotian fishermen making the case for caution at midcentury touched on a number of concerns, including the specter of overfishing, which raised questions about whether humans could affect the sea; human disruption of the marine food web through targeting forage fish such as menhaden; the threats posed by ultraefficient modern gear, including purse seines and longlines; and depletion from the destruction of brood stock. During the early 1850s, even before much technological innovation in the fisheries had occurred, menhaden, mackerel, and cod all seemed diminished or threatened in the eyes of many observers.

In 1852 A. D. Gordon lambasted the shortsightedness of catching spawning mackerel. In a letter to the Nova Scotia Assembly's Committee on Fisheries he argued that "the disturbance, interference and killing the Mackerel when depositing its spawn has contributed to the failure of the fishery, and may eventually destroy it altogether." Gordon wanted the assembly to revive the fishery by prohibiting "spring mackerelling except for home consumption." Cod seemed threatened as well. "There has been great complaint in late years, in the upper part of the Bay of Chaleur, of the falling off in the cod fishery, which is said to be every year decreasing," noted M. H. Perley in his report to the legislature on New Brunswick's fisheries, also in 1852. "At these places there was formerly an abundant supply of fish; but the inhabitants now barely catch enough for their own winter store."[3] In 1856 Joseph Cammett of Barnstable, Massachusetts, confessed culpability in the apparent reduction of Cape Cod fish stocks, even as he insisted that his fellow fishermen must change their ways. On Cape Cod ruthlessly efficient new seines were creating problems. "I have seined for fish outside and inside until I knew by experience that it injured the fishing for everybody. . . . It don't only injure blue fish but has spoilt catching sea bass and scuppaug. They . . . can't come in to our waters till the seining season is over, and then it is too late for them to spawn." For Cammett the lesson was clear: unless seining was stopped, it would "spoil our fishing for us and our children." Other innovative technology seemed just as destructive. In 1859 Nova Scotian fishermen from Digby protested a new "system of fishing called the set-line fishing, or as many term it, trawl fishing." Setlines, also known then as tub-trawls, are referred to now as longlines. Some Nova Scotia and New England fishermen began to emulate the French, and to employ longlines in the cod fishery during the late 1850s, as traditional hand-line catches declined. Yet as the Digby men saw it, long trawl lines bristling with hooks, and set on the bottom, "invariably catch those fish which are most generative or prolific, by means of which the fish are becoming very scarce."[4] Though naysayers scoffed at claims that the ocean was no longer producing, or that puny humans and their puny efforts could affect the eternal sea, a chorus of concern reverberated from Cape Cod, Massachusetts, to Cape Race, Newfoundland, mirrored by similar complaints in northern European fishing communities.

Ecologists now know that the middle of the nineteenth century was exceptionally cold, "the last gasps of the Little Ice Age," as George Rose, a respected fisheries scientist, puts it. As temperatures fell, so did the productivity of cod in the North Atlantic. Western Greenland cod stocks virtually disappeared by 1850, and were largely absent for decades. Newfoundland's inshore cod stocks declined considerably, as is shown by the fact that landings could not keep pace with the growing population of fishermen and increased fishing effort from about 1820 to 1860. Newspapers such as the *Carbonear Sentinel* noted a general collapse in Newfoundland's Conception Bay fisheries during the late 1830s. A decade later the *Weekly Herald* reported that fisheries in Conception Bay, Bonavista Bay, and Trinity Bay, Newfoundland, had failed, too. Seabird distribution reflected the chilling sea and diminished stocks of forage fish in the mid-nineteenth century. Gannet colonies, for instance, abandoned Funk Island, Baccalieu Island, and Cape St. Mary's in Newfoundland for more southerly locations with better forage, returning only as the sea warmed again beginning around 1880. Migratory fish accustomed to warm water, such as mackerel and tuna, also became much less common on the Grand Banks in midcentury. Of course, no one had the ability to make systematic correlations between decadal climate fluctuations and fish abundance in the nineteenth century, though insightful naturalists and fishermen speculated correctly that some migrating species, such as mackerel, timed their arrival in more northerly waters to sea surface temperatures.[5]

Diminished natural productivity in the mid-nineteenth-century boreal North Atlantic marine ecosystem, prompted by falling temperatures, coincided with dramatic fisheries innovations, including purse seines, tub-trawls, pound nets, the targeting of new species, and the capacity to fish more intensively. To some extent declining catches prompted new technologies. As handliners' landings decreased, skippers traded in their handlines for longlines. In other ways the synergy between technological efficiency and climate change was pure coincidence. As temperatures fell in the mid-nineteenth century, mechanization and industrialization took off—for a host of unrelated reasons. Fisheries, like other industries, modernized in the middle of the century, more so in some places than in others, but enough that the effects were widely felt. Fishermen's midcentury case for caution resulted from observations of decreased productivity in the ecosystem coupled with fears that new gear impeded fish reproduction and migration.

Fishermen's complaints regarding depletion during the 1850s, 1860s, and 1870s were different from previous ones in that they were not primarily laments about anadromous fish. Instead, experienced men lined up by the thousands to protest the diminution of menhaden, mackerel, herring, cod, bluefish, tautog, and scup—true sea fish. Some fishermen were increasingly convinced that human activities could affect the migratory patterns of sea fish and their ability to reproduce. "Breaking up the schools" is how they expressed it, articulating their belief that longlines, purse seines, and other gear were affecting fish behavior. Since the Middle Ages everyone associated with fisheries had known that human fishing pressure could reduce stocks of river fish from the sea, such as salmon, shad, and sturgeon. Seventeenth-century New Englanders had worried about depleting gadoids and mackerel, and had imposed rational regulations. But between about 1700 and 1850 few coastal residents had the audacity to imagine that fishermen could leave a perpetual mark on ocean finfish. If so, the future looked bleak. The 1850s and 1860s are the earliest decades (so far, at least) from which records survive that allow calculation of total landings or biomass of any species other than mackerel. Fishermen's laments can be examined in light of measurable indicators of ecosystem productivity. The correlations are striking.

During the years between 1850 and 1880 noticeable changes in the sea and a simultaneous sea change in attitudes about ocean resources defined northern New England's and Nova Scotia's fisheries. Still an age of small sailing vessels and relatively simple equipment—much of it handmade—the era nevertheless saw anything but a continuation of traditional fisheries. The story of fishing in the northwest Atlantic during those decades is one of increasing fishing pressure, valiant attempts at conservation, important regulatory changes, and, ultimately, the creation of new narratives about the ocean. Despite the exuberance of contemporary economic promoters, it is also a story of loss.

PRESERVATION VERSUS THE RIGHT TO FISH

Blue Hill is a quiet hamlet of Federalist houses and tidy capes tucked into the northwest corner of Blue Hill Bay, near Mount Desert Island in Maine. The town has an extraordinarily sheltered harbor for small vessels and an equally extraordinary vista from its namesake hill. Around 1850 Mrs. John Bartlett, an "elderly lady" from Blue Hill, inadvertently began the menhaden wars that would rage up and down the Maine coast for the next forty years. According to Eben B. Phillips, an oil merchant in Boston, Mrs. Bartlett "came into my store with a sample of oil, which she had skimmed from the kettle in boiling menhaden for her hens. She told me the fish were abundant all summer near the shore, and I promised $11 per barrel for all she could produce." Like whale oil, fish oil was a valuable commodity, and it could be produced easily by boiling menhaden. Mrs. Bartlett's husband and son began gillnetting menhaden in earnest, making 13 barrels of oil that summer. Phillips provided bigger nets and large kettles for boiling the fish, and during their second year in the oil business the Bartletts produced 100 barrels. By the standards of Blue Hill Bay, earnings were substantial. Neighbors got involved, and some wondered how much oil was being discarded with the refuse left in the kettles. Experiments in pressing the fish residue paid off, boosting the volume of oil per weight of fish, and Phillips "subsequently fitted out fifty parties on the coast of Maine with presses of the model known as the 'screw and lever press.'" They worked like familiar cider presses. All of this meant that within the space of two or three years, Maine fishermen and seat-of-the-pants entrepreneurs reinvented the lowly menhaden, a familiar summer visitor to their coast.[6]

Menhaden—also known as porgies, mossbunker, and by other names in various shoreside communities—are in the family Clupeidae, close cousins to sea herring, alewives, and shad. They are bony, oily, unpalatable (at least to most people), and, once out of the water, rather smelly. "The mossbunker is an ordinary looking fish," noted Ernest Ingersoll, "and you do not admire it." For centuries New England's fishermen had held them in low repute except for occasional use as bait, a practice that became more common around 1830.[7]

In fact, for most of America's history menhaden had been ignored or considered farmers' fish. In 1792 a prominent Long Island, New York, farmer published an article extolling menhaden fertilizer as the elixir for depleted soils in eastern Long Island and coastal Connecticut. Progressive agriculturalists in New England and the mid-Atlantic states subsequently applied menhaden to their fields for decades. Schools were vast, and their proximity to shore each spring could not have been more convenient. Ripe for taking with beach seines, menhaden came virtually to the dooryards of the farmers who wanted them.[8] From Montauk "acres of them" could sometimes be seen, "purpling the waters of the Atlantic Ocean." Captain Nathanael Smith of Newport, Rhode Island, remembered: "In 1819 I saw a school of menhaden out at sea, when I was going to Portland, that was two miles wide and forty miles long." Crude oil-boiling operations began on the Rhode Island shore in 1811. A handful of experimenters in Rhode Island tried variations on the menhaden oil business during the next few decades until, in 1841, the first factory "built to cook fish by steam in wooden tanks" was built south of Black Point Wharf in Portsmouth, Rhode Island. Reminiscing about those years, famous ichthyologist G. Brown Goode said: "The fish then swarmed the bays and inlets all along the New England coast, and there is good authority for a story that 1,300,000 were once taken with a single haul of a seine in New Haven harbor." That would have been a beach seine, set from rowboats in a bight around the schooling fish, and hauled to shore hand over hand by the men, perhaps assisted by a horse.[9]

Menhaden are filter-feeders. With no teeth or interest in bait-sized morsels of food, menhaden simply will not take a baited hook. They must be caught with nets. Uncaught in the coastal ecosystem, however, menhaden play two special roles. They convert plankton, which they filter from the water column, into the protein and fatty acids on which larger predators rely. Drawn by the lush spring plankton bloom, a filter-feeder's delight, menhaden typically arrived off New England a few weeks earlier than mackerel during the mid-nineteenth century, striking Massachusetts' Vineyard Sound in late April, and reaching Maine by about the first of June. Tuna, bass, whales, and cod followed close behind. "It is not hard to surmise the menhaden's place in nature," wrote naturalist G. Brown Goode in 1880, "swarming our waters in countless myriads, swimming in closely-packed unwieldy masses, helpless as flocks of sheep, close to the surface and at the mercy of any enemy, destitute of means of offense or defense, their mission is unmistakably to be eaten." Menhaden were forage fish par excellence, a crucial link making plankton's primary productivity available to predators higher up the food chain.[10]

Their second special role was not understood until the mid-twentieth century, but, in combination with the first, it has led some to dub them "the most important fish in the sea." Massive schools of filter-feeding menhaden are the coastal ocean's kidneys, filtering out not only plankton, but cellulose and other detritus. They serve the same function in the water column as oysters do on the bottom. Without that cleansing, turbidity in the water blocks sunlight penetration, which hinders the growth of aquatic plants that produce oxygen. Menhaden kept the system in balance.[11]

Hook fishermen in antebellum Maine had no idea about menhaden's contribution to water quality, but they certainly understood pogies' role as first-rate forage. And they were outraged by the new nets and screw presses provided by Phillips, the Boston capitalist, and the novel use of menhaden for oil and industrial applications, rather than for food or bait. Interested parties dug in on both sides, either working to preserve schools of baitfish, which they saw as threatened by this new homespun oil industry, or lobbying hard for the right—and righteousness—of using new technology and creating new markets to bring prosperity to the region.

Opponents of the menhaden oil business initially saw it as a sideshow, but as one that could undermine the lucrative cod and mackerel fisheries on which most midcoast Maine communities relied. In 1852 more than 150 men from Boothbay, one of the two most important fishing towns in the state, petitioned the Maine legislature, lamenting that "taking Menhaden fish (as practiced by many persons) by means of Seines in our Bays, Rivers, and Harbours is very destructive to said fish, and if persisted in will eventually destroy them, or drive them from our coasts, to the detriment of the fishing interests of this State."[12] Fishermen from Surry, a stone's throw across the bay from Blue Hill, asserted in 1853 that seining "tends to break up and destroy" the schools of menhaden. Worse yet, "the practice has utterly broken them up in other places, and if the same result is brought about in this state, it will prove ruinous to the fishing business." Petitioners from Ellsworth argued the same year that seining would "utterly destroy" the menhaden, and that it had already done so "in other places, particularly in Long Island Sound and around Cape Cod." A year later, in 1854, inhabitants of nearby Sedgwick wrote to the legislature that "continuing to catch or take them in such vast quantities as was taken last year . . . will . . . drive them from the Bays and Harbours which they now frequent, much to the disadvantage and detriment of *all* those engaged in the Cod and Mackerel fisheries." The hundreds of fishermen petitioning in this vein during the 1850s believed that menhaden existed to be eaten by more noble fish. As the Surry petitioners put it, "the manufacture of oil" from menhaden was "an unjustifiable waste of the fish." They were convinced that menhaden, as forage, lured cod, mackerel, and other valuable species into coastal waters in the Gulf of Maine. As they saw it, menhaden should be left in the wild to be devoured by predators, or, if caught, used as bait.[13]

Mrs. Bartlett's hungry hens and her home-grown oil business had triggered a tempest. During the early and mid-1850s the menhaden oil business remained a cottage industry, one more way that residents of Hancock and Waldo Counties could make a living from the natural resources around them. Oil boilers set up large kettles outdoors on simply erected brick hearths. Locally cut cordwood fueled the fires. Later simple "try-houses, with two to four kettles each," replaced the outdoor hearths. Processors boiled menhaden for a mere thirty minutes, skimmed the oil, and decanted it into locally coopered barrels, just like the barrels used for mackerel, cod, and grain. No factories rose on the beaches or headlands. No steam machinery broke the early-morning silence. Locally recruited crews sailing diminutive sloops and schooners or handling assorted rowboats caught schooling menhaden near shore with small stationary gillnets and handmade seines. Within a few years of Phillips' involvement, stationary gillnetting gave way to "sweeping," a technique in which several small nets were fastened together and maneuvered near schools by fishermen in boats. The first purse seine in Maine appeared in 1859, when fishermen at Damariscove Island, near Boothbay, bought one for inshore work. But purse seines, which were quite expensive, never became as common in Maine as they were in Rhode Island or Massachusetts or New York. Well into the era of the Civil War, the oil business remained small scale and homegrown.[14]

This new menhaden fishery could not have been more similar to the traditional inshore cod fishery; in fact they mirrored each other in almost every way. In the inshore cod fishery, which had been prosecuted as long as Maine had been settled, small crews of locally based men handlined cod on grounds close to home, gutted and split the fish, and then brought them ashore to air-dry on flakes near the beach, where workers known as shoremen cured the fish, which ultimately were packed in barrels for shipment. In the new menhaden fishery, small crews of locally based men netted menhaden on grounds close to home, then brought them ashore to be boiled on the beach, where boilers skimmed the oil and poured it into barrels for shipment. In every way, the new menhaden fishery could have been—or should have been—understood as a logical extension of traditional patterns of work in a hardscrabble maritime economy. Cash was always welcome in communities such as Blue Hill and Surry and Gouldsboro, whose mixed economies relied to a great extent on barter and self-sufficiency. Why, then, during the mid-1850s, did hundreds of fishermen from more than half-a-dozen communities on the midcoast of Maine raise a ruckus about the impact of the small-scale oil operation that was providing jobs and cash in their communities?

Their impassioned response and the strife it created reflected their deep-seated conviction that catching large volumes of menhaden threatened the cod, haddock, and mackerel fisheries, which were already at a tipping point. Similarly situated fishermen in Nova Scotia and Massachusetts were also afraid that the basis of their age-old livelihood was slipping away. By the early 1850s concerns about the health of cod and mackerel stocks were so pronounced that removal of forage fish (even on a relatively small scale, by neighbors), or continuing capture of spawning fish, threatened to exacerbate the problem. Nothing else explains the fervor of the moment.

Paul Crowell's "Report on the Fisheries" for the Nova Scotia Assembly in 1852 detailed the damage done to the mackerel fishery by catching spawning fish. "As there is no doubt the mackerel are bound to Chaleur Bay for the purpose of spawning," he wrote, "it would lead us to believe that when one fish is taken with the net or seine [in spawning season], thousands are destroyed which would otherwise likely come to maturity. Could the practice of taking fish with their spawn be abolished, it is likely they would be much more abundant."[15] Crowell advocated restrictions on using nets to kill spawning mackerel because he believed mackerel stocks were not infinite, and because he saw the mackerel fishery as crucial to the Nova Scotia economy. Fishermen knew that spawning fish, with something else on their minds, rarely bit at hooks. But nets swept up spawning fish indiscriminately.

A similar debate, prompted by conservationist concerns, occurred in Maine just a few years later. In 1855, as the menhaden wars raged, fishermen from Wells requested the legislature to prohibit seining mackerel within three miles of shore. Shortly thereafter the state enacted a law to prohibit seining mackerel "in any of the bays, inlets, or harbors within the jurisdiction of Maine." It was not quite the protection the men from Wells had sought, because it did not blanket all waters within three miles of the shore, but they considered it a serious step in the right direction. The impetus behind that law was the concern that seiners broke up schools of mackerel, took spawning mackerel before they had reproduced, and were likely to drive mackerel from near-shore grounds into deeper water. Like the battles being waged over menhaden, the restriction on seining mackerel in Maine's bays, inlets, and harbors reflected the commonly held idea that changes in the sea were threatening local livelihoods.[16]

Yet, despite their substantial numbers and the groundswell of public opinion, Maine residents who were worried about the impact of the fledgling oil business on forage fish could not forge a consensus. Hancock County fishermen employed by the menhaden interest claimed in 1854 "that the fears of a dearth of pogies or menhaden . . . are entirely hypothetical." Arguing that the "true question is shall the pogies taken" be used "for bait when they can turn them to a more profitable account in making oil," the pogie fishermen ended with a rhetorical flourish. "We are strongly in favor of free trade in pogies."[17]

Like the Hancock County menhaden fishers, fishermen from Dennis, on Cape Cod, also opposed limits on seining sea fish. Claiming in 1856 that such restrictions "would take away the living of large numbers of the inhabitants of the Cape," they sidestepped arguments that stocks were declining, making a case instead about what "would be best for the good of all" in the short term. Conceding that the legislature might protect "Rivers and Ponds" for "the use of those Towns in which they are located," they lobbied hard that the sea itself should be exempt from legislative interference. In their eyes the coastal ocean remained a great commons available to anyone, using any sort of gear.[18]

Fishermen from Harwich, also on Cape Cod, opposed restrictions on seining for purely economic reasons. Limiting seining would "take away the living from a large number of our honest fishermen," they explained, and force consumers "to pay a much larger price for the fish they consume." Inhabitants of Yarmouth, another town on the Cape, did not deny that fish stocks needed protection, though they discouraged the legislature from limiting seining. "It would be a much better way of protecting the fisheries of the coast of Massachusetts," they wrote, "by paying a bounty of so much per barrel for all the bluefish taken than to stop the seining of them, as it is known by all . . . that they destroy almost all other smaller fish." Defining bluefish as wolves of the sea, and waging war on them, seemed more palatable than "taking from the poor but honest fishermen their means of supporting himself & family."[19] A few years later the *Provincetown Banner,* a Cape Cod newspaper, reported on a petition "now before the Committee on Fisheries, in the House, to abolish the catching of mackerel in seines on our coast," and on the furor it created. "As mackerel can now be caught only in this way," editors noted, conveniently forgetting about decades of successful hookfishing, "and many of our people are interested in the business, it becomes highly important that any such stupid petition should be prostrated at once. . . . One thing is certain, if we do not take mackerel in seines or nets we shall get none at all."[20]

As preservationists lamented depletion of fish stocks, and as advocates of free enterprise insisted that that the sea must remain open to all harvesting, a handful of interested parties struck a middle course. Cod and mackerel fishermen from Duxbury, Kingston, and Plymouth, Massachusetts, who described themselves in 1857 as "almost entirely dependent, of late years, for a supply of bait" from menhaden, were not opposed to seining. They used seines, and wanted to continue using seines. But they were concerned about perpetuating the stock of baitfish on which they relied, and they wanted local control of menhaden resources. In a petition reminiscent of fast-fading norms, more than 140 men from those towns asked the legislature to prevent fishermen from elsewhere from taking menhaden in their harbors. They also protested the pernicious practice of dressing fish right where they were caught, claiming that the discard overboard of menhaden offal had driven away schools of fish. Their desire to exclude outsiders was hardly novel, but during the 1850s it became coupled with concerns about bait and depletion of forage fish. That was new.[21]

Stepping back to gain perspective on the to-and-fro of assertion and counterassertion that defined the fisheries debates during the 1850s, it is obvious that many fishermen perceived deleterious changes in the ecosystem. They seemed to outnumber those who insisted that everything was fine. As demands for conservation reverberated in state and provincial legislatures, opponents rarely countered them by insisting that catches were robust or that stocks were self-perpetuating. Instead, they resorted to arguments that restrictions on fishing would hurt fishermen financially, or raise the price of fish for consumers, or expand the power of the legislature to control the sea itself. Opponents were content with the idea of taking short-term gains, and they deflected— rather than demolishing—arguments that the sea was no longer as productive as it had been.

Against the master narrative of modernization and progress, then, a counternarrative took hold along the coast from Cape Cod to Cape Breton and Cape Race. It spoke of decay and diminution. Based on the firsthand observations of thousands of fishermen, who had made countless fares, it underscored the fear of a future without fish, and an uncertainty of how communities that had relied on the sea would adapt when catches came to naught. Josiah Hardy, a beleaguered fisherman from Cape Cod, told a story in 1856 explaining worrisome changes in the sea that he and his neighbors had witnessed firsthand. It forecast dire consequences should the status quo continue.

"The fisheries in the bays and along the shore which are a great value to the citizens," he began, "have been greatly diminished and are in danger of being wholly destroyed by the practice of setting and using seines between Succanesset Point and Point Gammon. The effect of these seines is to prevent the fish coming into the bays, from which they are driven; and shoals of blue fish, bass, scuppaug, and herring, whose habits bring them annually to seek the bays and inlets along the shore, are turned in their course and forced to pass out into deep water. Every year that the practice of seining has been resorted to, & principally by persons who are not inhabitants, the hook fishing has diminished, and it is the belief of all who are experienced in the habits of the fish that there is no remedy to restore the former abundant good fishing which we and our fathers enjoyed when the hook only was used, but to abolish the use of seines in these waters. Should that be done, abundant fishing by the hook, might be enjoyed by all who would resort to that method of taking fish, whereas the use of Seines gives a present monopoly to the few who can use them, but must result in the destruction of the fishery, and thus deprive them, as well as all the inhabitants of all future benefit or profit to be derived from this source."[22]

The possibility that coastal fisheries would fail catastrophically aroused considerable passion. "There will be enough fishing for all who will use only the hook and line like good fishermen," the selectmen of Mashpee said, "and not murder the fish and drive all off in one season by setting seines, and killing and frightening away every kind of Fish." Taking "fish with the hook," they elaborated, "always leaves enough for seed."[23]

Seed for the future: that was the issue, whether the discussion concerned mackerel, scup, or cod. In the spring of 1861, as longlining gained momentum in the cod fisheries, a Nova Scotian wrote to the provincial legislature's Committee on Fisheries about "the evils of sett line [longline] fishing." The "mother fish," he explained, "during the season of reproduction are very sluggish in their movements, and generally repose on the bottom for some time before and preparatory to depositing their spawn. The baited hooks, therefore, on those sett lines, being barely two feet from them," were "swallowed chiefly by the mother fish, which are generally of the largest size and are thus destroyed in the very act of reproduction. . . . It is virtually killing the goose for the sake of the golden egg." Fishermen had known for centuries that spawning cod rarely took the hook. As tub-trawls came into use, some fishermen believed that "gravid females seize bait lying on the bottom which they will not rise to take when suspended in the water." Fishermen may have seen a higher proportion of spawners landed on longlines. Though not verifiable, that was the implication of men who heard sea stories circulating about diminished hookfishing and new techniques that murdered the fish.[24]

SEA CHANGE ON THE BANKS OF NOVA SCOTIA

What led a generation of fishermen, beginning in the 1850s, to believe that stocks were declining and that new gear was contributing to the problem? One clue appeared on the offshore banks of Nova Scotia's continental shelf, a productive series of grounds frequented by well over 1,000 fishing vessels during the 1850s. By then, those banks had been fished commercially for about three centuries. From east to west they were known as Artimon Bank, Banquereau, Misaine Bank, Canso Bank, Middle Ground, Sable Island Bank, Le Have Bank, Roseway Bank, and Brown's Bank, interspersed with features such as the Le Have Ridges. During the middle of the nineteenth century New Englanders and Nova Scotians fished there, as did the French, at least for a while. Skippers knew the underwater topography intimately, correlating bottom conditions, currents, and depth with the likelihood of finding fish. Given the basic instruments at their disposal, however, and the vagaries of the weather, they sometimes groped to find sweet spots. Larkin West, skipper of the schooner

Torpedo, for instance, noted in his log on August 25, 1852, "this night and morning caught 450 [cod], hove up, tried some time to find rough bottom." A week later he noted that the bottom was "rocky and fish scarce."[25]

Skippers like West had a lot of ground to cover. Banquereau consisted of about 2,800 square miles, measuring approximately 120 miles by 47 miles at its widest point. On the eastern part of the bank lay a shoal called Rocky Bottom, about 110 feet (18 fathoms) deep. The rest of Banquereau was deeper, from 18 to 50 fathoms. Patches of sand and gravel interspersed what was primarily a rocky bottom. A narrow deep channel called "The Gully" separated Banquereau from Western Bank, which was considerably larger, about 156 miles long and 76 miles wide, for a total of 7,000 square miles. Most of that area ranged between 18 and 60 fathoms deep, with a sandy bottom interrupted by patches of gravel and pebbles. Fishermen sounded using leadlines armed with tallow to retrieve bottom samples. In June 1856 the logkeeper on the schooner *Iodine* noted various conditions on Western Bank. On June 9 at latitude 43° 53'N he found "green sandy bottom." Four days later at the same latitude in 35 fathoms he found "moss bottom." Eleven days later, "pumpkiny bottom; here we find plenty of fish." On June 28, anchored in 33 fathoms, still at 43° 53'N, he noted "rough mussel bottom, fish very large." The southern edge of Western Bank was the extremity of the shelf, and depths dropped rapidly there from 80 fathoms to well over 1,000 fathoms. The banks of the Scotian Shelf, with their tricky currents, summer fogs, and frightening shallows near Sable Island, supported extensive stocks of benthic fish, including haddock, cod, cusk, halibut, pollock, and hake. Of course, during the 1850s, when no preservation techniques existed for haddock (a fish that did not salt well, and was the despised "white eye" in fishermen's parlance), when few markets existed for hake or cusk, and when fishermen forfeited their federal bounty if they landed fish other than cod, the profitable target for offshore bankers remained the venerable cod. Fishermen largely ignored other species.[26]

The banks of the Nova Scotian Shelf accounted for just one of six separate geographical locations fished by New Englanders in the mid-nineteenth century. Small boats and some superannuated large ones fished the relatively safe inshore waters of the Gulf of Maine, never straying far from home. A fleet of larger-than-normal vessels from Newburyport and a few other ports pursued a beach-based fishery on the southern coast of Labrador, where they seined small cod during a short summer season. Yet other schooners worked grounds in the Bay of Chaleur and Gulf of St. Lawrence, trips sometimes referred to as "going over the bay." The Georges Bank fishery, which had only begun to be exploited during the nineteenth century by boats from Gloucester and Cape Cod, and the fishery on the Grand Banks of Newfoundland were, like the Scotian Shelf fishery, offshore enterprises. They required well-found boats and resourceful captains. For the most part skippers from specific towns exhibited strong territorial inclinations: the fleet did not distribute itself randomly between home ports and those six fishing destinations. Among the vessels greater than sixty tons hailing from Beverly, a town near Gloucester on the North Shore of Massachusetts, 66 percent fished the Scotian Shelf full-time from 1852 to 1859, and over 90 percent fished there part-time. A treasure trove of cod-fishing logbooks with daily catch data remain from almost all of the Beverly fleet's trips between 1852 and 1859.[27]

This remarkably well-preserved series of 326 logbooks from the Beverly fleet, along with related records, allows reconstruction of the Scotian Shelf fishery during the 1850s, a pivotal decade. On each day of the trips, most of which lasted for about ten weeks, the captain noted the vessel's position and indicated next to each man's initials the number of cod he had landed. Comments about weather, depth, bottom conditions, and the presence or absence of bait species were also common, as were notations of "vessels spoken." That was recognition of the custom by which schooners crossing paths on the banks would hail each other with the name of the vessel and her home port, along with one other prized bit of information—the number of cod caught since leaving home. Sharing information was the norm, whether proudly, apologetically, or matter-of-factly. And in that dangerous occupation, colored by the constant threat of unexpected death, the sentimental values of the larger society dictated a grave commitment to record notice of every passing schooner. Information about 1,313 "vessels spoken" exists in the Beverly logs from 1852 to 1859. The schooners spoken hailed from Portsmouth, Portland, Marblehead, Barnstable, and other New England ports. All these vessels were similar in size, and they all fished with similar gear, meaning that the Beverly fleet was representative of the larger New England fleet working the Scotian Shelf. The thoroughness of this data—day by day, boat by boat, year by year—illuminates the Scotian Shelf fishery in the 1850s with the precision of a satellite camera and continuous-stream data recorder.

The Beverly logs during the 1850s reveal contemporary fishing strategies, declining catch, and technological change. That decade was grim for banks fishermen. Average landings for the Beverly fleet declined from 26,217 fish per schooner per year in 1852 to only 14,414 in 1859—a drop of 55 percent. These salt-bankers from Beverly were full-time fishermen, generally out of sight of land and undistracted by other activities. They were at sea to catch as many fish as possible in as short a time as possible—with the exception of Sundays, maintained as a day of rest. Coming home with half the fish they had expected was discouraging, if not disastrous.[28]

Skippers tried new fishing strategies as catches fell. During the early 1850s the Beverly fleet fished most intensively on Banquereau. Most skippers split their season into two trips, or fares. Schooners departed from home around the end of April, and typically fished the Western Bank for a few weeks before concentrating most of their effort on Banquereau by late May. They fished hard until about the middle of July, landing, gutting, and salting cod until their holds were full; then returned home. Two weeks in port was generally sufficient to unload, clean the vessel, repair, and resupply. By the first or second week of August they were ready to depart again. During the early 1850s Beverly skippers often skipped the Western Bank entirely on their second fare, heading directly to Banquereau instead for another seventy-five-day trip. By late October the fishing was done, and the schooners were home within a few weeks. The best fishing normally occurred in two waves, once from late May to late June, then again from late July to late September. An uncommonly lucky day on Banquereau in 1852 or 1853 might see a schooner landing 1,000 cod or more, though typical daily landings were much less.

At the end of the 1856 season the average Beverly schooner had 7,000 fewer fish than just four years earlier. Captains had begun to adapt to lower catches in 1855 by spending less time on Banquereau and more time on the Western Bank. By the fall of 1857 more of the fleet was on the Western Bank. Moreover, schooners were averaging ten days longer on each fare, increasing their effort and risk. The national financial downturn in 1857 did not lower fish prices. In fact the market remained strong and the price rose twenty-five cents per quintal from the previous year. But most fishermen were catching considerably less than they had the year before, and pocketing less pay. Desperate to make the best of a bad situation, the crew of the *Susan Center* tried tub-trawling, but the skipper's log entries reveal their disappointment. August 25, 1857: "set trawls, found no fish." August 27, 1857: "fished in dories, found fish scarce." September 1, 1857: "Tried on Middle Bank, found no fish."[29]

Confronted by significantly declining catches, fishermen began to augment hand-lining from their schooners with a new method. Deploying handliners in small boats from the schooner allowed a crew to cover an appreciably larger area with their hooks. In time, that practice gave way to tub-trawling from dories. The evolution to fishing a larger area, and then to fishing many more hooks, was a milestone not only technologically but ecologically. It put more pressure on cod stocks. The transition occurred during the 1850s, just as regional cod catches were declining, and as inshore cod fishermen were rattled by what they perceived to be a menacing new menhaden fishery that was undermining the forage base for cod. As hand-lining over the rail of the schooner shifted to tub-trawling from dories, fishermen on specific schooners used various techniques during the same season, and sometimes during the same day. Skilled handliners regarded innovations with skepticism. The new tub-trawls were dangerous and expensive. And they required more bait. Yet no one could deny that seasonal landings were decreasing.[30]

Most cod fishermen in 1850 used gear that would have been familiar to fishermen 300 years before, except that the new clipper and sharpshooter schooners were bigger, faster, and harder to handle. Hand-lining remained the norm. Sailing from ports in New England with barrels of bait, such as salted clams, skippers proceeded east, testing the depths with a lead line until they found the edge of the banks. Sampling for fish as they drifted or sailed over the banks, they anchored when they found abundant cod. Every man, including the skipper, then fished from the deck of the schooner using handlines. Each fisherman tended two to four hooks. Skippers remained in one spot until the fish stopped biting, then hove up the anchor and moved on, following a pattern that had prevailed for centuries.

In the mid-1850s, however, as cod seemed in short supply on Banquereau, a few captains began to send men out to fish in their stern boat while the rest of the crew fished from the schooner. This tactic considerably enlarged the area a vessel could fish while anchored. At first captains sent the stern boat to scout for cod, moving the schooner only if that reconnoitering succeeded. Experimentally minded captains kept track of landings per technique. As fishing from the stern boat caught on, some skippers began carrying several boats, eventually investing in dories, which could be nested on deck and carried to the fishing banks. This shift in technology expanded the region each schooner could fish at a given time, but multiplied threats to the men, who now left the relative security of their schooner to fish from tiny dories. Not long before, such a strategy would have seemed like lunacy. Nevertheless, the age-old practice of handlining from the schooner gave way to hand-lining from dories. In

1853 fewer than 5 percent of the schooners from Beverly cod-fishing seaward of Nova Scotia used dories or small boats. Four years later 35 percent had adopted this innovation.[31]

It is still not clear what caused the catastrophic decline in catches, whether natural fluctuations—possibly caused by lowered sea temperature—or overfishing, or some synergy between them. Fishermen at the time, however, blamed overfishing by French factory ships, each of which set tub-trawls with thousands of hooks. In 1858, as cod landings spiraled downward, and as some New England skippers turned to hand-lining from dories, French trawlers arrived on Banquereau and the Western Bank. Each carried two sizable boats, along with tub-trawls, each of which bristled with nearly 4,000 hooks. The typical New England handliner then fished 14 to 28 hooks at a time. The French ships and brigs, moreover, were huge square-riggers, well financed through generous government subsidies. Compared to little Yankee schooners they seemed ruthless fishing machines. And there were lots of them. On July 8, 1858, the logkeeper of the schooner *Franklin* noted "saw 20 sail of French ships in sight." A few days later the skipper of the Beverly schooner *Lodi* wrote caustically, "fish very scarce today. The French bothers us very much. They run their trawl all around us so they get most of the fish." In September one Beverly skipper "boarded the French ship *Charlotte,* w/160 thousand fish." That discovery was discouraging: the average Beverly schooner landed only 26,000 fish during the best year of that decade.[32]

Overmatched as they were, Beverly skippers hesitated to accept tub-trawling as the answer to their problem. In 1858 fewer than 8 percent of the American schooners were fishing with tub-trawls, although by then almost 42 percent of them had shifted to fishing from small boats. Satisfaction with hand-lining remained the norm, as did its corollary, suspicion of longlining—even though Frenchmen had been fishing tub-trawls since the 1830s at St. Pierre and Michelon, the tiny French islands south of Newfoundland, and a few Yankee skippers had experimented with them off and on for ten years. At Swampscott, Massachusetts, a small town near Beverly from which men fished inshore, old-timers denounced the newfangled tub-trawls. In 1857 and again in 1858 Swampscott fishermen requested the legislature to ban tub-trawls in the inshore waters controlled by the state, because they feared that otherwise "soon haddock would be as scarce as salmon."[33]

Still, New England vessels fishing Banquereau and the Western Bank faced a dire situation by 1859. Landings during the decade had decreased by almost

50 percent. A dramatic shift occurred that year, as many Beverly skippers abandoned the Scotian Shelf altogether, sailing instead to the Grand Banks or the Gulf of St. Lawrence, longer voyages with greater risks. During that dismal season in 1859, the worst in a decade for Beverly schooners fishing the Nova Scotian banks, skippers and owners adopted tub-trawling. That move was revolutionary. No offshore fishermen from Beverly handlined along the rail to the exclusion of other technologies after 1859. All were using dories, and the majority had embraced the French longline technology vilified just a few years before. Yet such measures, once considered extreme, were not a panacea. In 1860, confronted by falling catches, many Beverly vessels withdrew from the fishery altogether.

By 1861, after a decade of shrinking catches on the Nova Scotian banks, much of the New England fleet essentially abandoned those once-favored grounds. This departure was not a result of the Civil War. During the war the Massachusetts cod fleet dropped by only 7 percent. For the most part, fishing vessels persisted in fishing despite the war. New Englanders who continued to fish, however, generally steered for grounds other than Banquereau. As a Nova Scotian put it in 1861, "the effects of this sett line fishing are already being seriously felt. . . . Bank Quereau, one of the best fishing banks to be found, has been completely ruined by sett line fishing." Two decades later, when the United States Commission of Fish and Fisheries produced its magisterial seven-volume *The Fisheries and Fishery Industries of the United States,* the editor remarked that Banquereau was "not much fished at present by Americans." Only a generation previously it had been the favorite fishing ground of Beverly's fleet, and for hundreds of schooners from other New England ports.[34]

It appears that hook-and-line fishing during the age of sail affected cod's distribution and abundance. Specifically, it seems that during the 1850s poor conditions for cod, likely related to seawater temperature, decreased cod stocks. Meanwhile the introduction of tub-trawling, a technique with increased catching power, put more pressure on them. Catches fell catastrophically. With the gear at their disposal, experienced fishermen in the 1860s found the density of cod on Banquereau not worth the trip. More forebodingly, as late as the 1880s New England fishermen still believed that two decades of mild harvesting had not allowed the stock to recover sufficiently to support a robust hook fishery.

Concerns expressed during the 1850s and 1860s in coastal New England and Nova Scotia about the overall state of the fishery undoubtedly originated, in part at least, from the decay of the Scotian Shelf fishery. As W. T. Townsend explained to the Nova Scotia Assembly's Committee on Fisheries in 1862, "Set-line fishing by the French, on the Banks off the coast of Newfoundland, is not only destroying the fishery on these banks, but it is materially affecting the fishery on the coast of Newfoundland—the fish being intercepted in their course toward the shore." This put poor men, who fished close to home from small boats, at a decided disadvantage to those offshore in sturdy ships and schooners. The Newfoundland House of Assembly heard similar testimony that year. Townsend, meanwhile, had been informed that at the Magdalen Islands, in the Gulf of St. Lawrence, setline fishing was "completely destroying the cod-fishery in the neighborhood of those islands, and that the inhabitants had to leave and go elsewhere in search of fish." Townsend's overall findings were clear, at least in his eyes. "Set-line fishing realizes the fatal result of sweeping off all the fish within its reach."[35]

Could humans affect the living ocean? Throughout the seventeenth century, New England magistrates and the most experienced fishermen were quite sure that overfishing was a real possibility, and they took pains to prevent it. During the eighteenth and early nineteenth centuries, however, that conviction had waned, only to reappear at midcentury when landings faltered and technological innovations refashioned the fisheries.

One of the earliest articulations of overfishing occurred in 1850, in a report on cod and ling issued by the Commissioners for the British Fisheries. "By the statements of the fishermen generally, it appears that the boats are almost everywhere obliged to go further from the land than formerly before they find fish; and hence it is assumed either that the fish have changed their runs on account of the fishing that has been carried on, or that the fishing grounds near the shore have been overfished." A few years later, in a paper on the causes of fluctuations in the British herring fishery, John Cleghorn wondered, "May we not have drawn over liberally on our shoals of herring?" He pointed out that herring were then captured with "10,974 boats, [and] 41,045 sailors employing 81,934,330 square yards of netting," and asked: "With such appliances may we not have overfished the sea? That a river or lake may be overfished, or that the whales between the tropics and at the poles may have their numbers so thinned that the fishing would cease to pay, will be readily conceded; but nobody here ever dreams of imputing the failures in the herring fishing to our having overdone it." As he saw it, "the cod and ling fishing in the German Ocean" was already "not worth the prosecuting." As on Banquereau, enough cod had been removed from "the German Ocean," or eastern part of the North

Sea, that with the gear at their disposal fishermen found trips there disappointing. Few English contemporaries shared Cleghorn's pessimistic perspective, and villagers in Wick, where he lived, persecuted him for his ideas. Yet such radically discouraging ideas were then in the air, in some fashion or another, on both sides of the boreal North Atlantic.[36]

By midcentury in New England, Atlantic Canada, Norway, and the United Kingdom, fish merchants and fishermen were feeling the pinch of decreasing catches. In 1856, prompted by evidence of decline, the Massachusetts legislature authorized a commission to investigate the artificial propagation of anadromous fish. In 1859, the first year in which Maine created a fish commission because of concerns regarding depletion (the first state to do so), the Norwegian government asked Axel Boeck to investigate fluctuations in the herring fishery. Two years later a group of Maine legislators had sought appointment of an agent "to report upon the present condition of the sea fisheries on the coast of this state," and in 1864 the Norwegian government hired Georg O. Sars to examine fluctuations in the cod fisheries, an initiative that resulted ultimately in serious fisheries science. Meanwhile, in 1863, in response to the recent rapid expansion of the English beam-trawling fleet (a new technique in which nets were dragged along the bottom by sailing vessels), and to controversies over the impact of beam trawling and the question of whether fisheries were decaying, the British government appointed a royal commission. The commissioners, who included the renowned biologist Thomas Henry Huxley, were charged with examining, "firstly, whether the supply of fish is increasing, stationary, or diminishing; secondly, whether any modes of fishing . . . are wasteful, or otherwise injurious to the supply of fish; and thirdly, whether the said fisheries are injuriously affected by any legislative restrictions." Had the fisheries been in fine shape on both sides of the boreal North Atlantic—had overfishing not been occurring—no incentive would have existed for these costly inquiries.[37]

In the most influential scientific pronouncement regarding North Atlantic fisheries during the middle of the nineteenth century, the British royal commission ran roughshod over hundreds of fishermen who testified that beam trawling caused problems and that fish populations were declining. Controversy had riddled the testimony of experts and fishermen, and the commission had no objective way to measure whether stocks were actually diminishing or whether beam trawling disturbed essential fish habitat. Ultimately they decided that even if beam trawling disturbed the reproduction or maturation of fish, market forces would remedy the problem. Should overfishing occur on any banks, "the trawlers themselves will be the first persons to feel the evil effect of their own acts." The commission forecast that as fish became scarcer and profits diminished, trawling on spent grounds "will cease, and the fish will be left undisturbed until their great powers of multiplication have made good their losses." Stating that "In such circumstances as these, any act of legislative interference is simply a superfluous intervention between man and nature," the commission advised that all British laws regulating or restricting "fishing in the open sea be repealed; and that unrestricted freedom of fishing be permitted hereafter." The case for caution, which had been building on both sides of the Atlantic, took a staggering blow.[38]

John Bertram, a British fisheries expert, openly disagreed with the influential royal commission. "There are doubtless plenty of fish still in the sea," he wrote in 1865, "but the trouble of capturing them increases daily, and the instruments of capture have to be yearly augmented, indicating but too clearly to all who have studied the subject that we are beginning to overfish." With numerous insiders in New England, Atlantic Canada, Norway, and the United Kingdom identifying the possibility of overfishing as a problem by the 1860s, the controversy would not cease. But with the commission's extraordinary report, those who wished to ratchet up fishing pressure seized the opportunity for profit.[39]

BAIT AND OIL

Northern New England fishing communities' demands on their coastal ecosystem changed significantly during the middle third of the nineteenth century. Species previously ignored were targeted, including swordfish, menhaden, lobster, and juvenile herring. As new technologies with more fishing capacity came on line, both the volume and the variety of organisms harvested each season increased. This reduction of biodiversity affected ecosystem functions, including those necessary for human well-being. What seemed obvious at the time, and is now clear in retrospect, is that coastal and continental shelf ecosystems were losing resiliency. Cod's keystone role was already being compromised on some grounds, and economically important fish such as cod, haddock, halibut, menhaden, and swordfish were becoming noticeably less abundant on inshore grounds, reducing coastal ecosystems' "reservoir of biological options."[40]

The immediate problem was bait. Generations of handline fishermen had relied on salted soft-shell clams as the bait of choice when they left for the banks. The typical hand-lining schooner in the banks fisheries circa 1830 to 1850 consumed about fifty barrels of salted clams on each of its three-to-four-month fares, though fishermen happily left the clams in the bait locker if they could obtain fresh capelin or fresh squid, or kill seabirds such as petrels, shearwaters, and puffins. Most of the salted clams originated on the coast of Maine, and Portland became the clearinghouse for bankers seeking salt clam bait. Cape Cod vessels outbound to handline on the banks often carried salted squid in lieu of clams because Cape fishermen found it easier to jig squid or take them in weirs than to dig clams. In any event, cod preferred fresh bait. So did fishermen, when it was available. Nevertheless, in 1840, according to one estimate, American fishermen used approximately 40,000 bushels of salt clams as bait.[41]

Change was in the offing. Halibut fishers began experimenting with longlines during the 1840s. Cod fishers, especially those from Massachusetts, turned to longlines in the late 1850s and 1860s. As they transitioned from tending 4 hooks to 400, or more, the demand for bait skyrocketed. Clams fell out of favor, replaced largely by herring. It took a while to meet longliners' demands. As G. Brown Goode recollected later in the century, during the early days of tub-trawling "the facilities were not so good as at the present time for obtaining and preserving the necessary quantity of bait." The earliest discussions of the bait problem focused on menhaden and clams, two species brought to prominence by the fishing revolution quietly occurring at midcentury. And wrapped up in those discussions were genuine concerns about the preservation of clam flats and menhaden schools in the face of new pressures on the coastal ecosystem.[42]

Towns that had long ignored their clam flats except for subsistence digging turned to them in earnest as the demand for bait rose. In Scarborough, Maine—southwest of Portland—commercial digging to supply bait for banks fishermen began around 1850. "The clam-flats have now become a source of considerable profit to many of the townsmen," noted a resident. "During the winter and spring of the present year [1852] they have procured nearly 2,000 barrels of this bait." Clamming was a winter occupation, and on pleasant winter days, armies of diggers fanned out over the flats.[43]

Deer Isle, Maine, fishermen pointed out in 1852 not only that bait was "indispensible," but that "from the scarcity of clam bait in proportion to the demand—the abovementioned fish [menhaden] have been substituted as bait." Fishermen believed that as gillnetters and seiners in the oil business were reducing menhaden schools, clam diggers were ravaging the flats, heedlessly destroying young clams before they grew to marketable size. Clams were "now growing scarce, in consequence of the supply not being equal to the demand," and so "the fishing interest is likely to suffer," Deer Islanders argued in 1853. Seeking to overturn town-based management of natural resources, and hoping to dig bait clams elsewhere, they requested the legislature to initiate a process whereby state residents could get permits for clam digging anywhere in state waters.[44]

They coupled this expansionary demand, however, with a plea for conservation. They wanted a closed season statewide from "the first day of June until the twentieth day of September." During that period, they explained, "the clams breed, and digging up the flats brings the small ones to the top and exposes them to the heat of the sun, which effectively destroys them." If summer digging continued, they feared, "this kind of bait will be effectually destroyed in a few years." The Deer Islanders' petitions, which did not sway the legislature, articulated their concerns about the future of the fisheries and the depletion of bait species, even as they advocated expansion of clam digging in "places where clams are plenty" because "few are dug." They neatly (or paradoxically) linked their fears that the coastal ecosystem was no longer producing as it had because of human interference, with their desire to ratchet up harvesting pressure.[45]

A different controversy severely divided the town of Harpswell, Maine, in 1857, brought on by the recently heightened value of clams for bait. Families and neighbors split over the question of access to the flats now that banks fishermen from distant ports would purchase limitless barrels of salted clams. One group wanted to "protect the Clams," and they insisted that the current law was "not sufficient to protect our rights to the Clams in our Flats, that they may not be destroyed." As they saw it, customary practices had changed. Noting that "for several years a great demand for Clam bait" had "existed in Massachusetts," and that "the traders will purchase for that market all they can get," the protectionists argued that hundreds of diggers worked "the Flatts against our entreaties & very much against our interests" each spring until the beds "were dug over so often as to entirely destroy them." Supposedly each digger was limited to taking only seven bushels per day, but no mechanism for enforcement existed. The preservationists forecast that "we shall soon be without enough for our own consumption," and enjoined the legislature to forbid outsiders from digging without a permit in Harpswell. Linking the language of local consumption and subsistence with conservation, they fashioned a preservationist discourse in opposition to free-market norms.[46]

But the preservationists could not rally all their townsmen. An opposing group invoked "their antient privileges" and remonstrated "against any additional restrictions on the free fishery for Oysters, Clams, and other shellfish." They pointed out that the privilege of shell-fishing was "invaluable for food and other uses," and noted that it had been the norm "from the early settlement of the country." Suspending attention to depletion of the flats, and to the potentially divisive issue of selling limitless amounts to traders from elsewhere, they sought to maintain the status quo even though the contexts in which shellfish harvesting occurred had changed radically during the past few years.[47]

Mackerel fishing demanded different bait from that used for cod, and clams were less frequently used. Mackerel schooners, with bait mills mounted on their starboard rails, required bait for chumming—what they called "tolling"— and not just any old bait. As a Nova Scotian mackerel jigger explained in 1852, "Your bait must be as salt as possible, well taken care of, and free from rust or bad flavor of any kind—salt herring, menhaden or porgie, No. 1 salt mackerel, or salted clams." Mackerel fishers often seined their own bait underway, or used mackerel too small to fetch a good price; but they also typically departed on each trip with barrels of bait purchased ashore. Mackerel fishers had been the first north of Cape Cod to turn to menhaden as bait, though some worried initially whether menhaden were too bony. But by 1835 or 1840 menhaden were generally preferred as mackerel chum by Massachusetts fishermen, partly on account of their availability, and partly because oily menhaden, ground to a pulp, made a slick on the surface of the water that seemed to attract mackerel. By the early 1840s mackerel jiggers from Boothbay, Portland, and other Maine ports followed suit. This became the first systematic use of the vast schools of menhaden that swarmed into the Gulf of Maine each summer, schools that had been left alone for centuries. As late as 1867, when most of the New England mackerel fleet was still hookfishing, mackerel schooners consumed about 25,000 barrels of menhaden bait annually.[48]

As the Civil War wound down, industrialists erected the first factory for rendering menhaden in Maine in 1864. Capitalized by a Rhode Island fish-oil firm, the factory was built at South Bristol. The buildings, boilers, engine, piping, cooking tanks, hydraulic press, and wharf cost about $12,000, at a time when the average Maine fisherman earned less than $200 annually. The following year a competing company from Rhode Island, already an established center of the fish-oil business, erected a similar factory at Blue Hill, Maine. Rhode Island firms such as Joseph Church and Company were already hammering the summer schools of menhaden near their own coast, and they recognized the potential profit swimming through the Gulf of Maine.[49]

Up and down the Maine coast fishermen cursed the colossus that seemed to be undermining their way of life. This newly invigorated menhaden fishery was not to scale with anything else on the coast. Organizers circulated petitions laying out the threat as they saw it, and hundreds of men such as Sullivan Green, S. S. Lewis, and Henry Eaton queued up to sign. "We the undersigned Citizens of the Several Towns bordering on the Sea Shore," began one, "Respectfully represent that a law is necessary to prevent the destruction . . . of Fish called Pogies or Menhaden." The several petitions then followed a common thread. "People from other *States* come into our waters with *large-seines* and break up the *schools;* preventing our fishermen from taking them in *set-nets;* If this practice . . . is allowed to continue, in five years we shall not have a Pogy (or Menhaden) for Bait." The legislature listened, and in February 1865 passed "An Act to Protect Menhaden or Porgies in the Waters of the Coast of Maine." It prohibited seining menhaden within three miles of the shore in state waters, though it exempted small nets, defining a "seine" as a net more than "one hundred and thirty meshes deep." The law had teeth. Violators convicted of breaking the new law would be fined "not less than four hundred, nor more than one thousand dollars," in addition to forfeiting "all vessels, boats, craft, and apparatus employed in such unlawful fishing." Sensing the mood of the people, the governor signed the legislation into law. It was not a conservation measure pure and simple, because it still allowed coastal residents to net pogies, which could be sold as bait to Massachusetts schooners on their way to the Bay of Chaleur. It prevented out-of-state seiners, however, with more efficient gear, from decimating menhaden stocks.[50]

But out-of-state residents were not the only ones to sense potential in fish oil, and even as the legislature was debating the pros and cons of seining menhaden near shore, instate investors and entrepreneurs (some of whom would join together a few years later as the Association of the Menhaden Oil and Guano Manufacturers of Maine) were combining their capital, and strategizing to vastly increase the production of menhaden oil and fertilizer. Within about a year of the signing of the law to protect menhaden in state waters, local entrepreneurs built eleven oil factories in coastal towns, including Boothbay,

Bremen, Southport, and Bristol. Each cost between $15,000 and $30,000 for buildings and equipment. Resident capitalists who had invested nearly $250,000 were not going to let the previous year's law impede their production of porgie oil and fertilizer, and they mustered sufficient clout to convince the legislature to pass a new act in 1866 "to regulate the taking of menhaden and other fish in the waters of Maine." More open-ended than the precautionary law of the previous year, it redefined a seine as a slightly larger net and reduced the monetary penalty for violations. Most important, it allowed county commissioners to grant permits to seine menhaden. The new law gutted precautionary regulations enforced by the state as a whole, replacing them with "such limitations and restrictions" as the various county commissioners "see fit." Applicants would pay between $10 and $20 for a permit, valid for a year. Prominent well-heeled men simply had to convince county commissioners to grant permits.[51]

Beleaguered small-scale fishermen reacted as they knew how. The day after Christmas in 1866 thirty-one men from Freeport signed a petition praying that the legislature would "Do away" with the menhaden factories. "Sence thease Presses have bin set-up the fishing Business has folen of one third and it is time that we should be awaik in this Business." Forty-nine citizens from Brunswick, led by Thomas Street, asserted that the recent law allowing menhaden to be seined at the whim of county commissioners was "injurious to the people of Maine." The Brunswick petitioners argued that "people who obtained their livelihood from the fisheries" were suffering because coastal waters had "been swept by the seines of the numerous vessels." They predicted that seining menhaden, "if pursued to the extent already practiced, must eventually lead to their extermination," and they hoped that the law giving county commissioners the right to issue seining permits would be repealed. "The interests of the many," they wrote, "demand protection from the monopoly of the few wealthy capitalists, who by this means may appropriate the whole fishing privilege upon the coast." Despite line fishermen's concerns about maintaining a ready supply of bait and forage fish near the shore, legislators refused to act.[52]

But the pressure persisted, and early in 1868 fishermen from Bristol and Bremen, concerned about their livelihood and the prospect that seiners would exterminate pogies, again demanded repeal of the law. By then, however, men from Sedgwick and Southport and other towns working for the oil factories, or supporting the factory owners' right to harvest menhaden, remonstrated against repealing the law. Caught in the crossfire, legislators in 1868 directed their Fisheries Committee "to inquire what legislation is necessary to protect the pogy fishing on the coast of Maine." Their compromise allowed "inhabitants of any town to use seines for porgy fishing within town limits without being subject to a license." In effect the Fisheries Committee told line fishermen to modernize, and to use seines themselves for catching bait. As incentive, men doing so would not need to purchase a license.[53]

Clearly articulated though it was, the precautionary approach to pogies could not prevail in the face of potential profit and extensive capitalization. In 1870 shipwrights launched the first menhaden steamer in the United States. Designed by engineering genius Nathanael Herreshoff, the sixty-five-foot purse seiner, christened *Seven Brothers,* was built for the seven brothers of the Church family, owners of the most prominent fish-oil firm in Rhode Island. *Seven Brothers'* deployment marked the mechanization of the American fishing fleet, though it would be many decades before steam vessels were widely used in fisheries for cod, haddock, mackerel, and other species. They caught on immediately, however, in the menhaden business. As one enthusiast noted, "The advantages of steam are too obvious to need special notice, such as dispatch, economy of time and labor, etc." Larger landings were the natural result. "With the advent of steam vessels, larger factories with more ample equipment became a necessity to handle the larger receipts in shorter time." Line fishermen, who only a few years before had worried about the "extermination" of the menhaden, had more cause for concern. Within just over a decade the largest factory in Maine had gone from being able to handle 500 barrels of fish per day to being able to handle 4,000 barrels. The first steamers to be used in Maine appeared in the summer of 1873. Liberalized state regulations then allowed for much more aggressive seine-fishing than had been the case a few years earlier. By 1877 members of the Association of Menhaden Oil and Guano Manufacturers of Maine had forty-eight steamers in addition to a fleet of thirteen sailing vessels. By then they were employing 727 fishermen on those vessels, and another 300 men at the factories, and their combined operations had been capitalized at over one million dollars.[54]

By the 1870s the menhaden oil and guano interest was publicly promoting the fact that its modern steam-powered purse seiners could catch bait for offshore banks fishermen cheaply and efficiently. Each year the menhaden plants put up a tiny fraction of their catch in barrels and sold it as bait. This practice provided some profit when a glut of fish precluded rendering them into oil and guano before they spoiled. It was also a good public relations ploy, in which managers of oil factories could look out for the interests of neighbors or townsmen in the line fisheries—typically the most vociferous critics of the seiners. Albert Gray & Company of Round Pond; Gallup, Morgan and Company of East Boothbay; and the Pemaquid Oil Works of Bristol all sold hundreds of barrels of pogies annually as bait for mackerel jiggers and cod fishermen. Selling bait to line fishermen, however, barely created a ripple in the ledgers of the oil businessmen. It was really a sideshow.[55]

The million dollars of capital, the 1,000 employees, and the more than one million gallons of menhaden oil produced each year in Maine during the mid-1870s—not to mention the provision of bait to neighbors—did not silence critics' concern that the fish-oil industry would exterminate the menhaden or drive them offshore, to the detriment of other fishing interests. Discussing the plight of Maine's coastal ecosystem in 1873, Spencer F. Baird, the U.S. commissioner of fisheries, referred to "the reduction in cod and other fisheries" and the importance of "the restoration of our exhausted cod fisheries." Baird did not mention menhaden specifically; he skirted that powerful interest. But he listed other forage fish whose abundance he felt would be essential to restoring cod stocks, including alewives, shad, and sea herring. Everyone associated menhaden with that suite of species. The next year E. M. Stilwell and Henry O. Stanley, Maine's fish commissioners, noted that "Our river and harbor fisheries are conducted with too much activity. Other markets opened to us make a demand upon our resources greater than the supply." Like Baird, Stilwell and Stanley did not directly criticize the influential menhaden lobby, but the commissioners' cautionary attitude was unmistakable. And in 1878 the legislature responded to those sorts of concerns with another precautionary law. It prohibited purse seining and drag seining for menhaden, mackerel, and herring in inland waters, defined as "all of the small bays, inlets, harbors, or rivers of this state, where any entrance to the same . . . is not more than one mile in width." Since quite a bit of Maine's many-fingered coast qualified for that exemption, forage fish such as menhaden would remain relatively unmolested in inland waters. Proponents hoped that this move would revive the faltering fisheries. The following year lawmakers revised the law more stringently, prohibiting all seining within one mile of the coast in all state waters.[56]

Fishermen from down-east Maine noted that menhaden had disappeared from Pembroke and Lubec in 1860, and that they had last been seen in Jonesport during the summer of 1873. Fishermen from Nova Scotia and New Brunswick, where menhaden had never been as common, noted their disappearance after 1870. The retreat of the schools southward may have been a function of water temperature, because through the middle of the 1870s robust landings were still reported on the midcoast of Maine, and in central and southern New England. Nevertheless, Maine fishermen's testimony to the U.S. Fish Commission by early 1879 was "almost unanimous" that menhaden "no longer hug the shores, but are found many miles out at sea." W. H. Sargent, for instance, said that "the fish are much less numerous in the creeks, coves, inlets, and rivers," where fishermen of modest means hoped to catch them and the larger food fish that fed on them, though he noted that "outside no decrease is perceptible."[57]

Scientists today know that a coastal fishery's move offshore is often the first indication of stock depletion and overfishing. By the late 1870s, however, despite the fact that menhaden schools were less and less likely to frequent the shores, G. Brown Goode of the U.S. Fish Commission and most of the best fisheries scientists of the era had rallied to the support of industrial menhaden fishing. Dismissing the testimony of fishermen who claimed that the abundance and distribution of menhaden had been affected by the scale of the oil and guano fisheries, Goode insisted: "There is no evidence of a decrease in the abundance of menhaden during a period of fifteen or more years of fisheries conducted on an immense scale. It seems, therefore, that no one can reasonably predict a decrease in the future." Goode had no intention of letting a precautionary approach to forage fish and coastal ecosystem restoration impede the profits of the fish-oil business, an industry demonstrating conclusively the economic importance of the fisheries that he and his colleagues studied, supported by federal funds.[58]

CONCERNS ABOUT INSHORE COD STOCKS

The controversies raging over depletion and preservation of marine resources during the 1850s and 1860s on both sides of the Atlantic reflected genuine concerns about sustainability. However, it is always a challenge for environmental historians, encountering such documentation, to connect historical people's expressions of concern to objective measurements of past ecosystems. The royal commission, for instance, did not have the data to chart quantitative changes in the United Kingdom's coastal fisheries. Sufficiently detailed records were kept about the Gulf of Maine inshore cod fishery during the middle of the nineteenth century, however, that something of the nature of that ecosystem during the 1860s can be reconstructed. The picture that emerges reveals a serious inshore fishery, a robust cod stock supported by considerable populations of forage species, and widespread concern by knowledgeable insiders over recent depletion of the cod on which they depended.

Logbooks generated by inshore Gulf of Maine fishermen from 1852 to 1866 are not as detailed as the ones from the offshore Scotian Shelf fishery, but they still provide the number of fish caught per man per day, sometimes with exact location—and otherwise in places that can be estimated rather accurately. The logs, the fishing agreements (contracts between the vessel's agent and its crew), and the seasonal abstracts (which noted the total days fished and total weight of fish landed) were all official documents, deposited in the customs house at the end of each season so that the vessel could receive its federal bounty. The number of men fishing on each vessel, the vessel's tonnage, its home port, the number of fish landed, and the total weight of the fish landed can all be determined from these documents. Quite remarkably, the data are clean. As with the Scotian Shelf logs and corollary documents, no incentive promoted misrepresentation. There were no taxes to avoid or quotas with which to be concerned. Each man's pay reflected the number of fish he caught, so fishermen made sure their skippers kept an accurate tally. The catch, however, was sold to the merchant by weight, not by number of fish. And the federal bounty payment corresponded to neither the number of fish nor their weight, but to the tonnage of the vessel. The result was a straightforward system of recordkeeping.

Records from the Frenchman's Bay Customs District contain the most complete set of logs and agreements for the Gulf of Maine cod fishery, including a virtually complete run of logs for 1861. That year, 220 vessels from the Frenchman's Bay District, averaging 48.7 tons, landed 3,281,897 cod. This translates to 12,134 metric tons. All of these cod were hooked, mostly on handlines, but some with tub-trawls. And virtually all of them were caught within twenty miles of shore between Penobscot Bay and Grand Manan Island, the area of operations for most of the Frenchman's Bay fleet. Many of the hands in that fleet were schoolboys fishing with neighbors or family members. The trips were short and the vessels small, though these landings—extraordinarily robust by subsequent standards—excluded subsistence fishing from boats smaller than five tons.[59]

The Frenchman's Bay data, along with logbook data from five other customs districts in Maine and Massachusetts, make it possible to estimate fishing effort for the *entire* Gulf of Maine in 1861. No data set or estimate from any other source provides Gulf of Maine cod landings before 1870. Fishing patterns emerged from the logs, as did the geographical distribution of fishing effort. Other federal records provided the tonnage of all the vessels licensed for cod fishing in the gulf, from Cape Cod to the New Brunswick border in the Bay of Fundy. Depending on the conversion factor used to convert cured fish to live fish, *total* cod landings from the Gulf of Maine in 1861 fell between 62,600 and 78,600 metric tons—approximately 70,000 metric tons. Those landings were greater than, but near, Gulf of Maine cod landings reported in 1870, the first year for which published data exist. Thereafter cod landings in the Gulf of Maine continued to shrink.[60]

Cod landings in 1861, combined with observations in the fishermen's logs regarding bait and other species, illuminate the nature of the coastal ecosystem at that time. Essential fish habitat included codfish breeding grounds and nursery grounds. Moreover, robust food supplies were necessary for large stocks of food fish. A healthy benthic community then supported a profusion of crabs, echinoderms (starfish and sea urchins), worms, and shellfish, including the mussels and clams preferred by cod. Large populations of small pelagic fish, such as herring, menhaden, smelt, and capelin, provided forage for multiple stocks of cod, haddock, pollock, and other groundfish, as well as for migrants such as sharks, tuna, and swordfish. Current science suggests that the order Clupidae (including menhaden, alewives, sea herring, and shad) provide the lipids necessary for many demersal (bottom-dwelling) fishes' reproduction. Mollusks and crustaceans, also part of demersal fishes' diet, simply do not contain much fat, including the lipids necessary for procreation.[61] Although anadromous fish stocks, including alewives, shad, and blueback herring, had already been substantially depleted, that gap appears to have been the only significant hole in the food web of the coastal ecosystem. In other words the system, though having experienced significant fishing pressure, was still substantially intact in 1861.

Visual imagery from that prephotography period is rare, but the unparalleled realist paintings of Gloucester native Fitz Henry Lane substantiate inshore waters' productivity at midcentury. Trained as a lithographer, and striving for verisimilitude, Lane became known for exquisitely detailed marine paintings. His *Gloucester Harbor*, painted in 1848, looks toward Ten Pound Island from the beach, revealing a quotidian scene from the day-boat fishery. The ebbing tide has left high and dry a dory and a small Hampton boat, next to which a man is cleaning cod as two other men lug fish up the beach on a handbarrow. The painting is breathtaking in its ability to convey the feel of the midcentury fishery. From the perspective of fisheries science, however, the most stunning aspect is the size of the cod piled at the feet of the man cleaning fish. They

were big, twenty- to thirty-pounders probably, and in 1848 such fish still could
be landed by men rowing out into the harbor. Years later Captain Stephen
J. Martin, who grew up in East Gloucester, corroborated the sort of scene Lane
rendered. "From 1832 to about 1838 Amos Story and Jefferson Rowe would go
out at daylight and be back at 8 A.M. with a dory full of haddock, dress them,
and go out in the afternoon, catch another dory load, and be back at 4 P.M. . . .
In 1851 James Coas and myself loaded a fifteen-foot dory twice in one day
within two miles of the mouth of the harbor." Painters and fishermen alike
testified to harbor fisheries' productivity at midcentury.[62]

Another indication of the overall productivity of the Massachusetts Bay
ecosystem circa 1860 can be found in reports of mass strandings of fish. Goosefish, for instance, weighing from fifteen to seventy pounds, and known for their
capacious mouths and projecting lower jaws, and the spine that dangled above
it, were benthic fish. They spent their lives on the bottom, sluggish except
when darting at prey. According to David Humphreys Storer, "thousands run
ashore at Provincetown every season." Goosefish's life habits could not have
been less like those of the needlefish, a slender surface dweller about eighteen
inches long, and the only one of the billfish family commonly found in the Gulf
of Maine. Yet again, according to Storer, "Large quantities are yearly thrown
upon the shore at Provincetown," while at "some of the other towns upon Cape
Cod it is taken in immense numbers." Such matter-of-fact strandings spoke to
vast populations of fish, indicating in turn that they had plentiful forage and
the habitat essential to sustain large populations.[63]

By any subsequent standards, the coastal ecosystem and the cod fishery were
thriving. But contemporaries did not see it that way. During the 1860s, although
cod were distributed on numerous micro grounds close to shore, and concentrated on larger banks offshore in the gulf, and though the average inshore boat
was landing more than 16,000 fish per season in the Gulf of Maine, fishermen
from New England lobbied hard to reduce overfishing and save their cod. From
the perspective of their generation, the first one from which we have any systematic quantitative data, the fishery was failing. As Spencer Baird put it in 1873,
"Whatever may be the importance of increasing the supply of salmon, it is
trifling compared with the restoration of our exhausted cod fisheries."[64]

Feelings were sufficiently strong that in 1860 both the House and Senate in
Maine passed a conservationist act prohibiting nonresidents from fishing for

any species with seines, drift nets, or tub-trawls within one mile of shore, and on every bank with twelve fathoms or less water at low tide. The act defined a trawl as any line with more than two hooks. It defined a seine as "any net more than two hundred yards in length or more than eight yards in depth," yet would have allowed anyone, resident or not, to take bait for "the ordinary business of codfishing" with a smaller net. Governor Lot Morrill, an attorney and Republican, vetoed it, citing the common right to fish in the open sea and his belief that Maine's legislature did not have the ability "to exclude citizens of other states from this enjoyment of this common right," even though so many constituents were concerned about resource depletion.[65]

By the time news of Banquereau's cod failure became common knowledge, in 1862, Maine legislators proposed prohibiting trawls in state-controlled waters for "taking or destroying any cod, haddock, or other bank fish." Many fishermen were convinced that the new longline gear had the capacity to overfish. But proponents of free enterprise killed the bill in committee. It was remarkably similar in language to a bill introduced in Newfoundland's legislature the same year, which also failed. Both bills reflected the sentiment of Nova Scotia's Committee on the Fisheries, which had come out strongly against tub-trawling the previous year. "The committee feel that this mode of fishing is not only destructive when being carried on along the coast, but is injurious to a much greater degree to the fisheries of the banks lying off the coast of Newfoundland, Labrador, Prince Edward Island, New Brunswick, and this province. It is well known to all persons who are acquainted with the cod fisheries," noted their report, "that if this mode of taking fish is persisted in, that in a few years these banks as fishing grounds will be rendered altogether unproductive."[66]

In 1866 a similar act, "to prevent trawl-fishing [longlining] for the purpose of protecting the cod fishery on our seaboard," died in committee in the Maine legislature.[67] Conceding the failure to restrict tub-trawling in all state waters, two groups of cod fishermen from Frenchman's Bay, led by Robert B. Hamer and J. W. Palmer, resorted to an attempt at local preservation. In 1868 they petitioned the legislature "for an act to prevent trawl fishing in Frenchman's Bay." Their complaint reflected that of fifty-four Nova Scotians from Lower Prospect and France Bay, who just a few years earlier had petitioned their legislature "in consequence of those trawl lines" and their fear that trawls "will eventually destroy our Cod fishery." As evidence of what awaited them, should the legislature not outlaw trawls, they pointed "to the sufferings of our fellow fishermen in Newfoundland owing to the failure of their shore cod fishery." In Massachusetts before 1870 concerned fishermen sent four petitions to the legislature to prevent trawl-line fishing, including the one in 1858 arguing that unless the practice was outlawed, "soon haddock would be as scarce as salmon."[68]

Fishermen using different gear often blamed "the other guy" when things went poorly in a given fishery. To some extent, that age-old pattern character-izes the controversies raging from the 1850s through the 1870s. Hook fishers blamed those with seines. Handliners blamed longliners, with their newfan-gled tub-trawls. Men with mobile gear blamed pound-net and trap fishers, while the pound-net men cried foul when purse seiners swooped in to scoop up schools of fish before they had swum to the pound nets and weirs.[69]

However, complaints about competitors with more efficient gear can only be understood in light of the dramatic depletions evident to many fishermen at midcentury. In 1869 the fish commissioners of the state of Massachusetts raised "the important question on the *possible exhaustion of sea-fisheries*," lambasting the shoddy procedures and assumptions of the British royal commission, which had recently determined that no form of fishing had "been permanently injuri-ous to the supply of fish." The Massachusetts commission pointed out that the royal commission had used no statistics revealing changes in the annual yield of fish from the coasts of the United Kingdom. Moreover, the commission had failed to discriminate between "bottom fishes" (such as flounder), "wandering fishes" (such as herring or mackerel), "white fishes" (such as bass or mullet), and "alien fishes" (such as rays and dogfish), though everyone knew that their habits and susceptibility to different gears varied dramatically. The Massa-chusetts commission argued that "the local and bottom fishes, which are pe-culiar to certain limited areas near the shore, may be greatly reduced or even practically annihilated, in certain places, by improper fishing." They invoked a French study, by Rimbaud, which had established a general principle: if "fishermen have to go further and further, and fish more and more carefully, for their fare, nothing will persuade him (or the fishermen) that fish are as plenty as formerly." In concluding its precautionary approach to the controversial question, the Massachusetts commission noted that "our shore population is beginning to complain of a diminution in many species."[70]

State fish commissioners in Maine did not raise the alarm about the depletion of sea fish until 1872, when Commissioner E. M. Stilwell wrote to Spencer Baird inquiring about "the probable cause of the rapid diminution of the supply of food-fishes on the coast of New England, and especially of Maine." By then Stilwell knew that cod, haddock, pollock, and halibut catches were free-falling. During the five previous years, Maine's fish commissioners had concentrated on anadromous fish. Listing dams, overfishing, and pollution as the three most significant causes of anadromous fish destruction, they lobbied tirelessly for the construction of fishways around dams to allow spawning fish to reach their spawning grounds. Various reports noted the alarming decrease of striped bass, the plight of salmon, and the nearly universal agreement among Kennebec River fishermen "that the time has come for a radical change in some direction or other to save the fisheries from destruction." By 1868 almost all the Kennebec fishermen agreed that shad and alewife stocks had rapidly diminished. And in 1869 commissioners noted "that the smelt-fishery is over-done, and that unless some radical measures are taken, it will soon fall into as great decay as have the salmon and alewife fisheries."[71]

Remedies for this formidable set of problems reflected the precautionary approach prevalent among many concerned citizens in Maine during the 1860s. In 1868 state fish commissioners proposed revising fishery laws to include a number of progressive measures. They would forbid drift nets in any rivers or lakes not only because they "are destructive and wasteful," but because driftnetters—unlike weirs and some seines—could easily elude wardens. The commissioners wished to prohibit weirs from extending below the low-water mark, and thus to reduce their catching power. Their fifth provision, "No weirs or traps to be used in any except tide waters; nor any nets except a dip-net, for five years," was radical, aiming to restore depleted stocks. And they desired closed seasons in which taking salmon, shad, alewives, and smelt would be forbidden. Commissioners Nathan W. Foster and Charles G. Atkins were somber but optimistic. They refused to sugarcoat the problems, but suggested that impassable dams, overfishing, and pollution could be remedied, and that state appropriations were needed. Short-term sacrifices would be necessary, by both taxpayers and fishermen, but "under a wise and liberal policy, there is no reason to doubt that the fisheries of Maine can be restored to something like their former productiveness."[72]

Professor Henry Youle Hind, a Canadian critic, was not so sanguine. A protonationalist who defended the interests of British North American fishermen against American encroachments during the 1870s, Hind had considerably more farsightedness than his contemporaries. He dispassionately explained exactly why coastal New England's fisheries were failing. "In the United States the local control exercised by separate State Governments over the marine and fresh water fisheries within the limits of each State, coupled with powerful lumbering and manufacturing industries, obstructing the free passage of the anadromous fishes to their spawning grounds, has resulted disastrously to the coast and river fisheries, and rendered their restoration not only extremely difficult but tardy, and to a certain extent ineffectual."[73] Although Hind never established himself in contemporaries' eyes as a scientist of the first order, he promoted a sophisticated ecosystem-based approach to fisheries. Inspired in part by an ardent defense of the fishermen of Atlantic Canada, he nevertheless envisioned the fisheries in light of what ecologists today would call the food web.

"The catch of the commercial fishes in the deep sea is dependent upon bait procured in coastal waters," he wrote, "but the spawn and young fry of the bait-fishes are the food of the commercial fishes, and as these diminish, the accessible supply of the commercial fishes diminishes also. . . . Whatever, in a word, affects the abundance of fish life, or of the lower forms, large or small, in coastal waters, affects also in a corresponding ratio the deep sea fishing area lying outside. . . . Hence it is that from whatever point of view we regard the coastal waters, we arrive at the inevitable conclusion that these are at once the source and the mainstay of the deep sea fisheries, both in respect of bait, food, spawning grounds, shelter for young fry, and recuperating nurseries."[74]

In a forecast of what was in fact already occurring, Hind argued that "The movement of certain kinds of fish, especially the cod tribe, farther and farther from the shore, is inevitable, if inshore food supplies are not maintained." N. V. Tibbets, from Brooklin, Maine, had noted precisely that sort of movement in the coastal waters of Eggemoggin Reach between 1855 and 1870. Eggemoggin Reach was an arm of the sea stretching northwest to southeast along the western side of Deer Isle. The town of Sedgwick, whose residents had protested seining menhaden in the strongest terms during the 1850s, lay on the Reach. "Most all farmers, like myself, were fishermen at times, and relied on catching our yearly supply of fish of various kinds, especially codfish and haddock; but these fish have long since deserted Penobscot Bay and Eggemoggin Reach," Tibbets lamented. "We used to row out on the Reach two or three hundred yards from shore, and in a few hours" catch "a few hundred pounds of haddock and some cod."[75]

As weir fisheries proliferated after the Civil War, taking alewives and herring, and as seiners relentlessly pursued schools of menhaden and herring, Hind

reiterated what so many petitioners from the coast of Maine and Massachusetts had told their legislators. Indicting the "indiscriminate and uncontrolled
taking of bait" fish, he predicted that contemporary fishing methods were
going to "rapidly diminish the supply," as a result of which cod and haddock
and other valuable food fish would move farther and farther offshore. Hind
was spot-on, though G. Brown Goode of the U.S. Fish Commission dismissed
him contemptuously.[76]

Fishermen during the Civil War and shortly thereafter had cause for concern.
They were perched on a precipice, and many sensed it. As it turned out, Gulf
of Maine cod landings declined, almost steadily, for the next century. Most
chilling is that from the way contemporary fishermen talked, that decline had
already been under way for years. Estimated Gulf of Maine landings in 1861
were around 70,000 metric tons. Landings in 1870 were about 66,873 metric
tons. By 1902 landings had fallen to 24,579 metric tons. All of these declines
predated dragging. Cod were still hooked, or occasionally taken in gill nets.
By the late 1930s, when steam and diesel draggers accounted for much of the
fish, Gulf of Maine landings totaled less than 10,000 metric tons. And in 2007
commercial landings for the entire Gulf of Maine were a minuscule 3,989 metric
tons, only 6 percent of those in 1861. The "restoration of our exhausted cod
fisheries," which Spencer Baird had declared a priority in 1873, never occurred.
The tipping point had been reached before the Civil War, and inshore fishermen up in arms over the menhaden oil business inspired by Mrs. Bartlett's
hungry hens knew it.[77]

The advent of efficient new gear exacerbated the problem while camouflaging
it. During the late 1850s and 1860s cod fishermen began to set longlines, which
further increased their hook footprint. Some experimented with gill nets around
1880. Gill nets did not rely on bait, and did not attract fish or require them to
act. Fish caught in gill nets had simply blundered into them in the dark. Each
step in this technological parade was marked by vehement protest but eventual complicity—at least from those who remained in the fishery. As each gear
was eclipsed by a more efficient one, fishermen's discussions of diminution and
decrease were silenced by elevated landings (the result of more efficient gear)
and the euphoria always associated with a good fare.

A clipping from the *Gloucester Telegraph* dated March 23, 1870, makes the
point. Illuminating the Portsmouth, New Hampshire, cod fishery, the article
breathlessly explained that ten vessels with forty small boats and 100 men

were then engaged in Portsmouth's fisheries, and that "over a million pounds of codfish have been landed at one wharf in Portsmouth during the past winter." What explained such robust landings? Local men, despite misgivings—their own and their neighbors'—turned to expensive gear, requiring extensive bait, which ratcheted up fishing pressure in ways almost unimaginable twenty years earlier. "In and about the harbor," the reporter explained, "there is now sunk over 63 miles of trawls, on which are hung over 96,000 hooks." Portsmouth harbor is small, just about two miles in length from Whaleback Light, at the harbor entrance, to the navy shipyard and town. The Isles of Shoals, famous as a fine cod fishing ground since the era of Captain John Smith, lay seven miles offshore from the lighthouse. Whether the sixty-three miles of longlines criss-crossed the harbor or reached out to the Shoals and back was immaterial. The forest of baited hooks saturated the grounds in a way impossible for handliners. And while that intensity would have been considered almost criminal not long before, it was now associated with millions of pounds of cod and big paydays.[78]

Farther south, however, at Block Island, off the Rhode Island coast, home to a fleet of small inshore boats, fear of longlining dominated discussions during the late 1870s. "When, a few years since, trawling was begun at Gloucester, Massachusetts, cod were caught in large quantities near the port," fishermen explained, reflecting what had happened at Portsmouth and other places. By "trawling" they meant tub-trawling, or longlining. "Soon the fish could not be caught there, having been either taken or scared into deeper water. The trawlers kept on until now the fish are not caught in quantities, on some of the grounds east of Massachusetts, not except in one hundred and twenty fathoms of water." Overfishing stocks with the new gear did not take long. As failure of the inshore grounds put handliners out of business, the tub-trawlers ranged farther afield. At Coggeshall's Ledge, just twenty miles from Block Island, fishermen previously had taken "four quintals per trip to each man. Since trawlers have been there we cannot catch enough to pay for the trip." It was the same story told about Banquereau fifteen years earlier. As catches declined, handliners despaired. While many worried about ruthless new gear, and some protested it, others decided to experiment or adopt it. Catches rose. They did not rise in direct proportion to the effort expended, but high-line fishermen were not interested in calculating catch per unit of effort. They wanted to catch fish. And if doing so required new gear, they would try it.[79]

Norwegian fishermen had long used gill nets in the coastal cod fishery, and the U.S. Fish Commission—"ever anxious to introduce among the Americans any methods that will result to their advantage"—imported seven deep-sea gill

nets from Norway in 1878. The Fish Commission deployed them in a prelimi-
nary way during the winter of 1878–79, but rough water tore them up among
the rocks, and big fish ripped holes in the nets. Landings were sufficiently
good, however, that Fish Commission employees believed the trial would be
successful if they bought or built nets of heavier twine. Commercial fishermen,
for the most part resistant to change and risk-averse, did not accept the commission's invitation. None invested in gill nets in 1878. A few years later, however, when Captain Joseph Collins, of the Fish Commission, returned from the
Berlin International Fishery Exhibition, he brought home a more nuanced
understanding of how to fish with gill nets. In 1880 the skipper of the schooner
Northern Eagle, of Gloucester, confronted with the high price of bait, decided
to put what would have been a season's expenditure for bait into gill nets.
Experiments that first season were sufficiently rewarding that he purchased
larger and stronger nets, and within a few years was fishing eight dories, each
with a single man and three nets. Each net was fifty fathoms (300 feet) long
and three fathoms deep. Suspended from a headrope buoyed by blown-glass
floats, the nets were small enough that a single man could underrun them in a
dory every morning, picking fish as he went. According to one observer, gillnetters were soon taking catches "three times as large as that of the trawlers
[longliners] fishing on the same ground."[80]

As Spencer F. Baird explained in his annual report, "At first the nets met
with the same opposition from the trawlers that trawls had from the hand-line
fishermen, when they were introduced, some thirty years ago. Although at first
inclined to inveigh against 'building a fence' to prevent the fish from reaching
the trawls, &c., the fishermen soon began to realize its advantages." The American Net and Twine Company of Boston, which already manufactured nets for
herring, mackerel, shad, smelt, and other fish, willingly turned to manufacturing gill nets for cod. But gill-netting cod was slow to take off.[81]

A near total failure of the bait supply in the winter of 1882–83 threatened to
prostrate the cod fishery off Massachusetts and New Hampshire, providing
the opportunity sought by the U.S. Fish Commission to promote gill-netting.
Rather than abandon the shore cod fishery in the absence of bait, fishermen
turned to gill nets in 1882 and immediately landed large catches. A headline
from a Cape Ann newspaper in December 1882 trumpeted: "Good Results of
Net Cod-Fishing." One boat, it explained, "with two men, took 5,000 pounds
of large codfish in seven nets . . . sharing $40 each." Another crew of five men
"shared $320 apiece, clear of all expenses, by the last of December," equivalent
to more than a year's pay for six weeks of work. By December 1882 there were

twenty vessels from Gloucester alone, with 124 men, in the gill-net cod fishery. Captain Stephen J. Martin of the U.S. Fish Commission reported that 2 million pounds of cod were landed in late November and December 1882—a six-week period—in Swampscott, Gloucester, Rockport, and Portsmouth. "The fish caught in the nets were of extraordinary size," he elaborated, "averaging more than 20 pounds each, while some individuals weighed as much as 60 or 75 pounds." During twenty days in January and February 1883, "ten sail of small vessels, which had been fishing in Ipswich Bay" landed "230,000 pounds of large codfish"—a remarkable haul. Ipswich Bay was a prime spawning area, and those were gravid females, the sort of fish that never took a hook. Not long ago, in the era of hook fishing, they would have been exempt from capture. But gill nets captured all cod tangled in the mesh, whether they were spawning or not. Ironically, as officials of the Fish Commission saw it, the beleaguered New England cod fishery was coming back to life.[82]

Shortsightedness existed in abundance, as did misplaced confidence. By 1883 Baird believed that "the day is now not far distant" when Fish Commission hatcheries would be "propagating the cod on a very extensive scale, this having been found perfectly practicable." He was already sure that "the school of cod hatched out at Gloucester in 1878-'79" had reproduced, "as young gray cod of two sizes are now taken on the coast. In 1882 they were abundant off Portsmouth, N.H., the fishermen being satisfied that they were the result of the work of the Commission." From what Baird gleaned from local fishermen, he concluded "that not only have these fish been successfully planted, but also that they have changed their habits and are likely to continue to be an inshore summer fish."[83]

Thanks to the Fish Commission, 4 million "sound eggs" were obtained from live cod brought to Fulton Fish Market in New York City, among other places, "hatched out and deposited" back in the sea. Informants as far afield as Mount Desert Island, in Maine, tried to correlate cod caught nearby with fish hatched by the Fish Commission in Gloucester. Brash speculation of this sort was contagious, and it suppressed the chorus of criticism that for the last generation had been making a case for caution. It is likely that the Fish Commission was barely augmenting the coastal cod stock with its propagation program. But commissioners and their employees, buoyed by self-congratulatory sentiment, would not admit that possibility.[84]

Changes in the sea, such as those noticed by N. V. Tibbets and Henry Youle Hind before the introduction of tub-trawling, purse seining, and gillnetting, prompted a new generation of sea stories. Taking root between the 1850s and 1880, those stories questioned the new practice of gill-netting gravid females. For centuries Yankees and their Puritan forebears had depicted the ocean as a testing ground, but a fruitful one, where challenges could be rewarded with ample catches and good fares. The long swell and the short chop of the sea had never been trustworthy: its perils and hardy fishermen's reactions to them ballasted every tale. But prudent men inured to toil and accustomed to driving their vessels and themselves—whether exhausted or lonely or cold—had faith that the sea would provide in its seasons. Haking or clamming in winter; cod-fishing in late winter and spring; lobstering inshore from March to July; making mackerel fares from July to November; and hooking pollock in late autumn for a few weeks: not every fisherman pursued each fishery each season, but everyone knew what to expect from the bountiful sea. So it had always been. By midcentury, however, the yarns that went round on the fishing stages and aboard the schooners during quiet times contained a more ominous element. Words such as "depleted," "diminished," "decreased," and "over-done" were at the heart of these new tales. And within a few years fishermen's change of tone was being reflected by contemporary writers.[85]

A sailor's sailor, Charles Nordhoff had considerable experience before the mast in merchant ships, whaling ships, and mackerel schooners. A widely read journalist as well, who occasionally rented a quiet room on Cape Cod, Nordhoff kept his ear to the ground between voyages. In 1864 he published a story reflecting erosion of the Cape's ancient ways. "The gradual failure of the fish," he wrote, "and the somewhat rapid increase of the population of the Cape, caused a good deal of uneasiness to the people of that thrifty region. . . . Hitherto there had been abundance for all, according to their frugal expectations; but now the prospect grew dark."[86] As Nordhoff saw it, ecological changes brought unwanted cultural changes in their wake, and residents scrambled to sort out the implications.

In 1870 the editors of *Harper's New Monthly Magazine* raised the specter of the "destruction of sea-fisheries," pointing out the diminution of fish in English waters as a result of dragging trawl nets on the bottom, but pointing out that the "same result" was "following, more slowly perhaps, but with equal certainty, on our own coast, especially that of Maine . . . New Brunswick, Nova Scotia, and Grand Menan." Fine-meshed nets and numerous weirs were taking "not only the mature fish, but also the young fry," preventing herring from spawning, and setting in motion a ripple of depletions of "cod, hake, pollock and other fish." A variation on that theme flowed from the pen of a third-rate New England novelist, the Reverend Elijah Kellogg, a prolific writer of books for boys. In *The Fisher Boys of Pleasant Cove,* published in 1874, Kellogg's narrator looked back on technological and social changes in the mackerel fishery, noting an ominous change following the shift away from jigs. "In this manner mackerel were taken for many years; they were abundant, the schools easily raised, and they were ready to take the hook; but so great has been the havoc made among them that they are now less willing to take the hook, are sometimes caught in nets, and the business has become quite precarious."[87]

Diminution of the fish on which coastal New Englanders relied struck Samuel Adams Drake about the same time. His *Nooks and Corners of the New England Coast,* published in 1875, lamented the plight of fishing hamlets such as New Harbor, in Maine's Muscongus Bay. "Here and elsewhere I had listened to the story of the destruction of the menhaden from the fishermen's point of view. They apprehend nothing less than the total disappearance of this fish at no distant day. 'What are we poor fellows going to do when they catch up all the porgees?' asked one." Drake toured the menhaden rendering factory at Pemaquid Point and "was persuaded the fish could not long support the drain upon them." As he put it provocatively, "The question with which the political economist will have to deal is the expected extinction of the menhaden." By the time Drake wrote that ominous line, other storytellers were wondering about the expected extinction of the lobster, the halibut, the eider, the shad, the salmon, and possibly even the mackerel and the cod. Against that narrative of decline, the misplaced confidence of Baird and his Fish Commission scientists seemed a welcome tonic. Their story had a happy ending.[88]

A FISHING REVOLUTION

The fishing revolution that occurred during the middle of the nineteenth century in the Gulf of Maine and on the offshore banks from New England to Atlantic Canada, including the introduction of controversial new gear, had ecological consequences and mediated a generation's understanding of the future of marine resources. The larger process of which it was just one piece has often been referred to as "modernization," a shorthand way of linking mechanization, technological innovation, product development, market expansion, and the cultural acceptance of—and legal justification for—possessive individualism. But the fishery-specific elements have rarely been considered together in light of their influence on coastal marine ecology, much less on attitudes toward conservation in particular places. Overfishing of sea fish came to be recognized as a problem (both an economic and ecological one) simultaneously with modern techniques' increased pressure on marine resources in the middle of the nineteenth century.

This fishing revolution did not depend on mechanization. Sails and oars still predominated. In the western Atlantic no steam-powered draggers were built before 1905, and the only steam-propelled fishing vessels were menhaden seiners, beginning in 1870. A handful of steam-powered mackerel seiners were launched during the 1880s. Largely in the absence of mechanization, however, the fisheries transformed themselves in ten ways. Those transformations had enormous economic and ecological consequences, which continue to resonate in our own day.

One. Previously underutilized species were targeted intensively as part of nineteenth-century fisheries modernization, including halibut, lobster, menhaden, swordfish, and juvenile herring, rebranded as "sardines." Harvesters put pressure on organisms ranging from herbivorous filter-feeders, such as menhaden, to apex predators such as swordfish, and on both vertebrates and invertebrates. As with every new fishery, fishermen skimmed the cream first, affecting both the distribution and abundance of the targeted organisms, whether lobsters, swordfish, or halibut.

Two. Net fisheries expanded dramatically, with the result that the overall volume of fish withdrawn from the ecosystem increased. Massachusetts' first commercial net shop opened in 1842. Before that all nets were made on an ad hoc basis. The innovation in 1842 intensified netmaking, but those shop-made nets were still constructed by hand. In 1865 the first machine-made nets became available, bolstering the size and catching power of various seines. During the 1850s and 1860s purse-seine technology took off, allowing the construction of nets that could encircle an entire school of pelagic fish. Pound nets, and weirs constructed with netting, also boosted catching power. This new generation of net fisheries thrilled some fishermen and scared others. Maine's Fish Commissioners E. M. Stilwell and Henry O. Stanley complained in 1874 that "new devices and improvements in floating pound nets, and other ingenious methods of capture, endanger our resources of breeding stock."[89]

Three. The hook fishery multiplied itself by several orders of magnitude, as hand-lining with a few hooks per man—the standard gadoid gear since the

Middle Ages—gave way to long-lining (also called tub-trawling, set-lining, and bultow fishing), in which each fisherman deployed hundreds of hooks attached to a long groundline. Tub-trawls could be fished at greater depths than were practical for handliners, opening up new grounds. As fisheries historian Wayne O'Leary explains, "The first primitive Maine trawlers to fish the Gulf of St. Lawrence for cod around 1860 recorded catches that were double or triple those of contemporary hand-liners on the same grounds." Those larger catches, of course, were landed only because the tub-trawlers expended disproportionately greater effort.[90]

Four. Bait fisheries grew exponentially in response to the multiplication of hooks, each of which required salted clams or chunks of menhaden, mackerel, or herring. The proliferation of lobstering called for more bait, too. By 1880 "the total amount of flounders, sculpins, and herring used for bait on the Maine coast" lobster fishery "far exceeded 30,000 barrels." Entrepreneurs responded to this buyer's market for bait by building weirs and pound nets for inshore schooling fish, which rapidly reduced their populations, and by exhausting once-productive clam flats.[91]

Five. New gear with more fishing power, such as tub-trawls, purse seines, and pound nets, increased the volume of fish unintentionally killed and discarded, waste that is now known as by-catch. From some fishermen's perspectives, the incidental mortality of juveniles of marketable species was akin to "killing the goose that laid the golden eggs." By-catch reduced prey and affected biodiversity by killing sharks and other long-lived species with low reproductive rates. It also raised moral questions about wasting resources. Traditional hook fisheries for cod and mackerel had generated considerably less by-catch.

Six. New means of marketing and product development delivered more fish to more consumers, putting greater pressure on resources. New England vessels first began to carry ice to sea in 1845, and fresh iced fish was soon being distributed via an ever-expanding network of railroads. Thus species that did not preserve well with salt, such as haddock and flounder, could be caught and delivered to consumers at a distance. For centuries those fish had been ignored, except for modest landings that could be sold fresh in fishing ports. Specialized fish commission merchant firms, such as John Boynton's Son in New York City, and A. W. Rowe and Brother in Philadelphia, smoothed the interface between the New England fleet and seafood consumers in major American cities. In the fifteen years before the American Civil War tinned seafood, iced seafood, and seafood distributed by railroad became the norm for many consumers, some of whom began to taste varieties of fish previously unknown to them.

Seven. Considerable capital was invested in fisheries, notably in sleek mackerel schooners, in menhaden rendering plants, in menhaden steamers, in canneries, in elaborate purse seines, and in the cod fleet. This phenomenon changed the makeup of those interested in the fisheries. Vertical integration increasingly characterized commercial fishing operations in Rhode Island and Massachusetts, though less so in Maine, Nova Scotia, and Newfoundland. Even so, as the United States lurched toward the Gilded Age, policymakers could not help but be awed (or influenced) by the capital invested in American fisheries.

Eight. Vessel design changed radically with the construction of sharpshooter and clipper schooners during the 1850s and 1860s. The new craft were larger and faster. They were also more weatherly, meaning they could sail closer to the wind. Less safe than the pinkeys that preceded them, they nevertheless could carry more men and gear to deliver more catching power to the fishing grounds.[92]

Nine. The seventy-three-year-old federal subsidization of the cod fishery, known as the cod bounty, ended in 1866, forcing fishermen to squeeze more profit from the ecosystem to prevent financial losses. Well-capitalized fishing firms, including many in Gloucester, did not oppose repeal of the bounty because they did not want to be constrained by its rules, notably the regulation requiring a vessel to fish only for cod for 120 days per year to be eligible. But for many inshore Gulf of Maine fishermen from small villages such as Surry or Gouldsboro, loss of bounty money meant economic hardship. They had to fish harder to stay afloat. Repeal of the bounty promoted consolidation, and worked against independent fishermen.[93]

Ten. Government involvement in New England's fisheries changed significantly. Town-based strategies for resource management, a holdover from the colonial period, were increasingly replaced by state regulation, which was being influenced by input from a new generation of "scientific men." Government-sponsored fisheries science burgeoned during the 1870s and 1880s, with emphasis on basic ichthyological research, fish hatching, and artificial propagation. If nature couldn't make enough fish, government labs would fill the void. The problem was that while hatcheries worked well enough on trout streams, their output was a drop in the bucket in the boisterous North Atlantic. Many coastal fishermen would have preferred to see federal money spent on the old cod bounty.

By 1870 the image of the colonial-era cod fishery, pursued with handlines from shallops or small schooners, seemed as quaint as the idea of gentlemen wearing wigs and hose. By then transformations in the industry were affecting the marine environment and inspiring a controversial series of discussions about the future of fisheries. The case for caution, articulated by experienced men worried that "haddock would soon be scarce as salmon," or that "exterminating" menhaden would lead to "the material injury of the codfishing interests in this State," confronted the exuberance and optimism promoted by new technologies and marketing possibilities.

Fisheries science, still in its infancy, swelled with misplaced confidence. With the exception of some researchers from France—whose Old World coastal ecosystems were considerably more shopworn than New England's—very few men of science stood squarely behind a precautionary approach to fisheries in the middle of the nineteenth century. Spencer F. Baird and G. Brown Goode, among others, were certain that questions regarding the life history of fish would soon be answered, and that rational science would solve the problems of the fisheries. "The fact that particular portions of our sea-coast are frequented by the herring during their spawning-season, while others, apparently equally eligible, remain unvisited by them, induced me to undertake a careful investigation of ocean temperatures," Baird wrote in 1873. However, neither Baird nor Goode nor any of their colleagues was able to learn enough about ocean temperatures, or any other aspects of physical or biological oceanography, to manage ocean fisheries and compensate for the overfishing already occurring, overfishing that they denied. Their fanciful belief that artificial propagation of cod could counteract its massive historical depletion rested on wish-fulfillment, not on facts, though the stories they told reassured listeners that fisheries had a future.[94]

By the middle of the nineteenth century environmental concerns of many kinds were prompting embryonic conservation initiatives by scientists and naturalists worldwide. New England states, followed by others, established fish and game commissions to steward disappearing resources. Vermont-born George Perkins Marsh, who spent considerable time in the Mediterranean, published his influential *Man and Nature* in 1864, arguing that human-induced deforestation and the erosion it caused led to desertification, and that this phenomenon was going to worsen. Meanwhile there was a growing realization by European scientists and surgeons that imperial development on tropical islands had come at heavy ecological cost to fragile island ecosystems. Such observations brought an increasing awareness of how vulnerable certain environments were to human activities.[95]

As naturalists grappled with the ecological impact of economic development on nature's bounty, and recognized slowly, case by case, that the Earth's resources were not limitless, they tended to maintain an exception for the vast and unknowable sea. It was primarily fishermen, hand-hardened and relatively unlettered, who argued that the watery world they knew firsthand was changing, and not for the better. Ironically, though, while they wanted fish for the future, they also wanted to keep fishing. Their well-articulated statements regarding depletion, diminution, and degradation fell on deaf ears, often even their fellow fisherman's, as efficient new fishing technologies and dreams of artificial propagation overwhelmed both their sea sense and their common sense.

Five

WAVES IN A TROUBLED SEA

Destruction will take care of itself. Preservation requires
action and purposeful vigilance.

— *Report of the Commissioner of Fisheries and Game of the
State of Maine for the Years 1891–92* (1892)

For Maine's Commissioner of Sea and Shore Fisheries, B. W. Counce, the
world seemed upside down in 1888. It wasn't just that "the present catch" of
mackerel was "the smallest known for fifty years" or that "many vessels" would
suffer "great loss" or that, as usual, "the cause of this falling off no one seems
to know." The situation had deteriorated beyond that. "To supply the demand,"
he lamented, "many mackerel have been shipped to the States from England,
a thing never known before."[1] As every schoolboy of Counce's generation
knew, the coastal dreamscape from Labrador to Cape Cod had lured fish-
starved Europeans across the western ocean more than three centuries earlier.
The western Atlantic's resource base leveraged individuals and nations to
wealth and greatness. What would it say about the American republic—its spirit
of enterprise, its genius for self-government, and its future—if citizens from
Boothbay and Gloucester were forced to turn to Europe for fish?

Two years earlier, in fact, during another poor year for mackerel, American
fish merchants had imported Irish mackerel, and by 1888, according to the
New York Times, "the principal supply of mackerel for this market has come
from Ireland." Wholesale and commission dealers in fish, such as D. Haley &
Co., No. 6 Fulton Market, New York, were not going to let local shortages

disrupt sales of one of their best-selling products. Mackerel, with its naturally oily flesh, was then America's favorite fish, savored both at upscale restaurants such as Delmonico's and on the kitchen tables of the working class.[2]

By the time Counce lamented the importation of mackerel from Europe, a stunning series of population crashes among commercially important marine species had got the attention of maritime communities in New England and Nova Scotia. No such shortages had ever occurred before. Lobster, menhaden, mackerel, and halibut: like dominoes they tumbled one after the other between 1879 and 1897. Three of the crashes occurred in the decade following 1879. Fishermen and dealers who had depended on those species faced longer trips, empty nets, poor paydays, even bankruptcy. This was a peculiarly nineteenth-century story: except for mackerel, none of those species had been targeted in any systematic way by commercial fishermen before 1800. Redefined as desirable by an expanding economy, lobster, menhaden, and halibut were hit hard by relentless fisheries that pushed stocks toward depletion or commercial extinction. These waves in a troubled sea caused economic hardship, ecological havoc, and the most spirited debates yet about the desirability of taking steps to perpetuate marine resources.

They also marked a milestone in Atlantic history. In the larger Atlantic world, integrated through the movement of commodities, capital, and labor, preserved fish had been shipped only one way: west to east.[3] Until the late 1880s the relatively impoverished marine ecosystems of the Old World and the large human populations concentrated there meant that Old World consumers routinely ate New World fish, but that people in the Western Hemisphere rarely imported fish from Europe. The mackerel failure off the Atlantic coast of the United States and Canada in 1886 not only led to imports of mackerel from England and Ireland, but inspired Cape Cod fishermen to sail to South Africa to seine mackerel. Meanwhile discouraged skippers and crews of Gloucester halibut schooners were sailing to Iceland, the westernmost outpost of Europe, to make their fares. As consumer demand for seafood ratcheted up, and as harvesting and transporting technologies became more efficient, New World consumers began to eat from Old World ecosystems. By 1890 the boreal North Atlantic, east and west, had been integrated by depletion, transportation efficiencies, and market demand. For fisheries and for marine ecosystems, this marked the turning point from the early-modern period to the modern one. Once again, marine ecology was shaping the course of history, creating a new Atlantic world.

Hook fishermen, weir fishermen, men of science, fish commissioners, and well-heeled capitalists all jockeyed for advantage as rancorous Gilded Age conversations unfolded about the future of fishing. Many small-scale fishermen sought to protect the resources, or at least to have it both ways, wanting fish for the future even as they insisted on fishing—often with increasingly efficient gear. The scientific community, for the most part, sided with industrialists and commercial interests, claiming that perceived depletions were simply natural fluctuations, and that nothing humans did could affect oceanic fish stocks, though some scientists' faith faltered as crash followed crash. To some extent, both sides acknowledged the nature of marine systems as variable and complex, as riddled with inherent uncertainties. One set of spokespersons insisted on fishing ever more aggressively and relentlessly despite those uncertainties, while another group—never claiming the mantle of conservation for conservation's sake—argued that the only sensible approach, given the uncertainties, was to throttle back fishing pressure.

The ongoing depletion of the coastal ocean from the end of the Civil War to about 1890 illuminates not only late-nineteenth-century history from the perspective of the living ocean, but the elusive struggle of scientists to understand that ocean in absolute terms even as its structure and function were changing. Ironically, the most outspoken advocates of restrictions were fishermen themselves. And for the first time, they got the attention of the U.S. government. The first federal fishing regulations, adopted in 1887—after menhaden, mackerel, and halibut stocks had crashed—were designed to perpetuate mackerel in a living sea no longer imagined as immortal.

HERE TODAY, GONE TOMORROW

During the late nineteenth and early twentieth centuries, no place in the Union was more closely associated with wringing a living from the sea than Maine's rockbound coast. The high-water mark of Maine's commercial fisheries occurred during 1845–1865, when at least one-third of the American cod and mackerel fleet (and sometimes as much as 46 percent of that fleet) was registered in Maine. By 1870 Maine's share of the fleet had fallen to only 25 percent; by 1900, to a mere 15 percent. Several factors contributed to this decline. Even before the Civil War, as cod fishermen turned to tub-trawls, and mackerel fishers to purse seines, the expense of a season's fishing gear had risen dramatically. By 1870 the typical fishing firm from Massachusetts was worth $18,000, that from Maine only $4,000. The amount of capital required to remain competitive tended to squeeze out small-scale fishermen, especially those from little outports and villages. So the industry consolidated in major ports such as Boston, Gloucester, and Portland. Meanwhile the repeal of the federal cod bounty in 1866 drove fishermen of limited means out of business. Without the bounty, many handliners from down-east Maine could not afford to fish, though larger tub-trawling schooners from Gloucester or elsewhere could land enough cod to make it profitable.[4]

"I have been in the fish business more or less all my life," explained one disenchanted Mainer to an interviewer from the state's Bureau of Industrial and Labor Statistics in 1887. "Fish are growing scarcer every year. Can remember when I could go out in a boat and get all the fish I wanted with hand line; now have to go five to ten miles from home, and fish with trawls having 500 to 1,500 hooks, in order to get any fish at all. The result is it costs about as much for gear as the fish are worth, for very often the hooks get caught and you lose half your trawl." His doleful story of changes in the sea during his own lifetime explained what had happened: fewer fish, more expensive gear, and destructive overfishing had undermined the business. As he lamented, "I have made on a good average fishing year $200 for the last three of four years. I find it hard to meet my bills."[5]

Before the Civil War, the bulk of Maine's fleet pursued cod and mackerel. After the war, cod fishing and mackereling were supplanted by menhaden seining and oil rendering, lobster fishing, sardine canning, and clam digging. As late as 1880, more than 11,000 people still worked in the fishing industry statewide, producing products valued at more than $3,500,000. But Maine's sea fisheries, which for decades had been rather decentralized, generating a competency for numerous small-scale producers, were becoming centralized, funneling more profits into fewer hands. The concentration began with the shift to tub-trawls, to purse seines, and especially to menhaden rendering. Postwar fisheries, increasingly capital-intensive, relied on ever more expensive gear with greater catching power.[6]

Maine fishermen lagged behind those from states to the west when adopting new (and more expensive) technologies. Purse seines, an entirely novel form of net, linked the destinies of mackerel and menhaden around 1850 on the coasts of Rhode Island and New York. Maine's fishermen were slower to adopt them, because of the cost. Purse seines consisted of a curtain of mesh that could be maneuvered to corral an entire school of midwater fish. Stretched out in a pasture, a purse seine in the late 1850s would have been a rectangular net, perhaps 600 or 800 feet long by 75 or 100 feet deep. When deployed at sea, blown-glass floats attached to the headrope provided buoyancy, while weights on the footrope made the net hang vertically in the water. The footrope also had large iron rings attached to it at intervals, through which a stout line was passed. Upon spotting a school of menhaden or mackerel the fishermen would sail as close as practicable without scaring the fish, and then deploy the seine boat carrying the net, along with another small boat, typically a dory. The dorymen grabbed one end of the net. The seine boat encircled the school, returning to the dory so that both ends of the net could be fastened together. "Pursing the seine," or tightly cinching the bottom so the fish could not escape, involved sliding a heavy weight down the line that passed through the rings at the foot of the net. As the rings bunched together, the bottom of the net closed, trapping the fish. A lot could go wrong. Fish could spook. Sharks or porpoises chasing menhaden could tear up a net. Setting a purse seine in shallow water or having it drift into shallows could lead to costly repairs. But, though complicated and expensive, purse seines caught fish—lots of fish.

By the time purse seines were first deployed in Long Island Sound and off the coast of Rhode Island during the 1850s, about the same time Mr. and Mrs. John Bartlett began their primitive menhaden processing in Blue Hill Bay, a half-century of farmers' fishing in Long Island Sound and elsewhere had thinned out menhaden schools, or at least pushed those oily little fertilizer-fish farther off the beach, farther from an increasingly oil-thirsty, industrializing society. Purse seines made it possible to capture the fish far from shore. Overnight, farmers' fish became industrialists' fish. Industrialists rendered menhaden into oil, then dried the scrap to be ground and sold as fertilizer. Menhaden oil dressed leather. It replaced linseed oil in paint. It lubricated the hemp from which rope was manufactured. It contributed to the oil soap used to cleanse wool. It lit lamps, in coal mines and elsewhere. Americans dominated the global whale fisheries throughout the nineteenth century, and whale oil had long served many of those purposes. As whale stocks crashed and whaling faltered, oil from tiny menhaden replaced that from whales. Following the Civil War the bony, oily menhaden, a fish largely ignored for centuries, vaulted into prominence, becoming the third most valuable fish landed in the United States, after cod and mackerel.[7]

The first factory for processing fish oil and fertilizer from menhaden opened in Greenport, New York, on the eastern end of Long Island in 1850. Two or three years later William D. Hall of Wallingford, Connecticut, patented the process of extracting oil from menhaden with steam. In 1857 Spencer Baird noted that "Quite recently several establishments have been erected on Long Island for the manufacture of oil from the mossbunker." During the Civil War, six state-of-the-art factories in Peconic Bay, New York, consumed about two million fish per week, in season. Purse seiners working from small sailboats could catch as many as 150,000 fish per day per boat, selling them to the factories for one dollar per 1,000, a rate of return that "makes a paying business of it," as one journalist noted. Porgy mania gripped communities in Connecticut, New York, Rhode Island, Massachusetts, and Maine. As an enthusiast from Greenport, New York, put it in 1862, "we are a stirring people . . . and if there is anything on land or sea which can be turned into money we are the ones to find it."[8]

But as the Civil War wound down, residents from at least nineteen coastal towns in Massachusetts debated the merits of seining menhaden. The arguments were remarkably similar to those that had divided communities on the midcoast of Maine during the early 1850s, though now the stakes were higher because opponents knew they were confronting an industrial fishery, not a home-grown oil-rendering business. Half of those taking sides opposed seining, and forecast the destruction of the traditional fisheries on which they depended. The other half looked optimistically to the future and to profits from an underutilized resource. In 1865 crusaders traveled from town to town along coastal Massachusetts rallying support. Approximately 1,820 men signed petitions to repeal the state law that prohibited purse seining menhaden, arguing that millions of dollars were unavailable to Massachusetts residents because of the laws. As the petitioners saw it, no "public or private interests are to be injured should this fishery be opened to our citizens." They insisted that purse seines "could not injuriously affect the hookfishery," and that there was an "inexhaustible supply of these fish upon our coasts every season." Removing restrictions would add "largely to the material wealth of the state."[9]

At least 1,886 men saw the issue differently, and argued that repeal of Massachusetts' statutes prohibiting menhaden seining would lead directly to "diminution and destruction of the fish"—not just menhaden, but *all* fish and all fisheries. Menhaden seining not only destroyed forage fish, but inadvertently caught (and wasted) more valuable fish that should have been eaten. Those arguments would characterize much of the menhaden debate for the next thirty-five years.[10]

By 1874, investors had capitalized the American menhaden industry with $2,500,000 paying for, among other things, sixty-four factories and twenty-five steamers. These steamers, the first mechanized vessels in any American fishery, could "surround a school of menhaden in almost any weather," as one opponent noted, "and with a hoisting apparatus operated by steam can empty one of the seines after it has been pursed." From the limited data available it is clear that by 1875 or 1876 the center of the American fish-oil business had shifted from Rhode Island and New York to Maine. Of course cash-strapped fishermen unable to pay for expensive purse seines were not in the vanguard of this movement. Capital-intensive and vertically integrated fisheries were now a fact of life on the Maine coast. In 1876 factories in Maine processed 709,000 barrels of menhaden, while factories in the rest of the nation processed only 826,885 barrels. At 200 pounds of fish to the barrel, that translated to total American menhaden landings of about 307,177,000 pounds, with landings in Maine of 141,800,000 pounds.[11]

Maine's processors capitalized on a fact of nature. Annual cycles of scarcity and abundance meant that most creatures were at their prime in late summer. The Gulf of Maine marked the northern limit of menhaden's range, and by the time they arrived there, about June 1, shortly after the summer plankton bloom, they had been feeding all the way up the coast. "Pogies generally get good and fat about the 1st of July," testified a fisherman, and "keep increasing until August." Moreover, menhaden stratified themselves by size and age, with larger, older fish ranging farther north. Menhaden caught in the Gulf of Maine were thus fatter than those taken anywhere else, much oilier in fact than menhaden taken off mid-Atlantic shores. The Association of Menhaden Oil and Guano Manufacturers of Maine proudly pointed out that in 1876 Maine factories processed 46 percent of the menhaden in the United States, but produced 71 percent of the oil. In the American fish-oil business, identical outlays for equipment and labor generated greater returns in Maine than elsewhere.[12]

Critics protested the slaughter. A journalist touring a Maine menhaden factory during the mid-1870s became convinced that "the fish could not long support the drain upon them." He sympathized with locals, who felt that a resource rightfully theirs was being monopolized by outsiders of a different class. "Although the oil factories purchase the catch that is brought in, the owners are considered intruders. . . . As men of capital, possessed of all needful appliances for their business, they are really independent of the resident population." E. M. Stilwell and Henry O. Stanley, Maine's fish commissioners, agreed. Referring to the 1878 season, they noted that "Fleets of steamers have swept our coasts, bays, harbors, and rivers . . . harrying [and] straining . . . our waters with nets." Stilwell and Stanley believed porgies were needed for bait in the cod and mackerel fisheries, and they supported small-scale enterprises in the face of the menhaden trust. "Money is power; capital needs no more legislative protection," they thundered. "Let us sustain our porgie law, and if possible strengthen it."[13]

Luther Maddocks, a Boothbay fisherman, capitalist, and insider in Maine's menhaden association, pooh-poohed their concerns. "The Menhaden is prolific to a marvel, even among fish," he enthused, and "there would seem to be scarcely any possibility of drawing too heavily upon the stock." By 1877 the Menhaden Association in Maine employed more than 1,000 men (300 at the factories, and the rest fishing), thirteen sailing vessels, and forty-eight steamers. The total capital invested exceeded $1,000,000, an increase of more than $100,000 from the previous year. The average fisherman in Maine then earned about $240 per year, and lived on a shoestring.[14]

Disaster struck in 1879. The most accomplished fishermen could not find menhaden in the Gulf of Maine. The fish simply did not appear north of Cape Cod, though previously they had appeared every year. "The oldest people . . . in the business say they never knew pogies to fail coming on this coast as long as they could remember," said a fisherman named F. F. Johnson, from Deer Isle. Before 1879, that was. Menhaden landings in Maine plummeted from more than a million pounds one year to just 20,000 pounds the next. Factories sat idle, and 1,000 men had no earnings. A fisherman from Portland named Charles Dyer had a pretty clear idea what had happened. "I think I know as much about" pogy-fishing, he testified, "as most anybody that was reared on the shore. . . . There were any quantity of pogies until these steamers commenced operations. . . . Before the steamers we had sailing vessels that seined and carried to these factories, and they destroyed a great many fish, but they did not seem to have the effect that the steam did. . . . A dozen steamers would come into our bay here and there would be thousands of pogies here, and in twenty-four hours you could not see one flip; they would clean them right out." Dyer ended his tale by pointing out that "A great many men in this State get their living fishing in open boats, and they depend on pogies for their bait . . . and when you take the pogies away from them, you take away their bread and butter."[15]

Nature buffers itself with redundancies: the absence of menhaden in the Gulf of Maine for the next six years was compensated to some extent for menhaden-eating species by the presence of herring, sand lance, and other forage fish, though capelin, an occasional visitor to the gulf, made no appearance in that period. Nevertheless, it is likely that the dearth of menhaden meant that fewer transient tuna, swordfish, sharks, and whales summered in the gulf, and that gadoids such as cod, haddock, and pollock—which typically relied on menhaden—were less well fed and possibly less likely to reproduce in abundance. The omega-three fatty acids found so dramatically in menhaden and other clupeids (members of the herring family) are necessary for gadoid reproduction. Of course from the perspective of the gulf's entire ecosystem over the *longue durée* those six years were barely a blip. From the perspective of maritime communities, such as Boothbay and South Bristol, which had come to rely on menhaden landings, those six menhaden-free years were a catastrophe. As one resident of Swans Island, Maine, remembered, "Many of our townsmen lost heavily by this failure, as many had invested nearly all their property in the fishing gear and property that was left useless on their hands . . . others never recovered from these losses." Human reliance on the system was no longer in sync with the system's inherent fluctuations. Human pressure seems to have exacerbated a natural downturn, creating an economic disaster.[16]

Menhaden's disappearance from the Gulf of Maine in 1879 almost certainly resulted from the intersection of the human extractive economy and natural fluctuations in the coastal ecosystem. The gulf had long been a coupled human and natural system, though human legacies were not always evident, in part because of the time lags between cause and effect. While nineteenth-century men of science believed humans were external to the system, commercial fishing by the 1870s was making a mark. In fact menhaden landings in 1878 were greater than those in most years during the next six decades, although catching technology continued to be refined, with bigger ships, stronger nets, and ultimately spotter aircraft as the years passed. In other words, by 1878, right before menhaden disappeared from the Gulf of Maine, fishermen were taking as many out of the system as was humanly possible. And the system was not immune.[17]

Self-appointed stewards of the little fish struck hard and fast, introducing a bill in Congress in 1879 to prohibit menhaden seines with mesh of less than five inches. Conventional mesh was then 2½ inches, and the menhaden trust—which believed such a law would put them out of business—dispatched Daniel T. Church to Washington, where he lobbied to kill the bill. Church owned part of one of the largest menhaden firms in Rhode Island. An outspoken and self-confident man, he was known for strong opinions about the living ocean: "I do not believe it is possible for man to make a perceptible decrease in sea fish." Church insisted it would be "foolish to limit free fishing." Congress had never restricted the fisheries, leaving such regulation to the states, and this bill introduced a number of thorny issues regarding state sovereignty, interstate trade, and the constitutionality of federal fisheries regulations. The legislation died without much fuss.[18]

However, the perception by most fishermen that steam-powered seiners "broke up" the schools; the realization that catching spawners destroyed the foundation of the industry; the jolting reality that menhaden served as crucial forage in the wild for more noble (and tasty) food fish; and the proposition—contentious though it remained—that human fishing *could* destroy sea fish all combined into a cataclysm in 1882. Senator William J. Sewall from New Jersey introduced a bill to restrict menhaden seining along the entire East Coast. He believed seiners were catching valuable food fish, as well as destroying the forage on which commercial fishing and recreational angling relied. "The evil is a crying one," he thundered, "and must be suppressed." The proposed bill would prohibit taking menhaden within two miles of the Atlantic coast or in any arm of the sea not within the jurisdiction of a state.[19]

As congressional hearings proceeded in 1882, journalists squared off. On September 7 one argued that "wherever the catches of menhaden have been the greatest the decrease in striped bass and bluefish has been the most marked." On September 24 another wrote that from "the immense power of destruction these vessels possess, few of the shoals of fish escape." Biologists now know that menhaden "inhabit pelagic, euryhaline waters of estuaries and bays, as well as polyhaline coastal waters on the inner continental shelf," meaning they tolerate a wide variety of salinities. Fisheries scientists have also learned that even when offshore, menhaden "are seldom far from land." As a *New York Times* journalist saw it in 1882, "a hundred steamers, with an average speed of eight knots an hour, following the mossbunkers day and night," would make "an absolute cordon of vessels." "Think what a very poor chance the fish would have to escape the net." But another writer saw the situation very differently. He felt that "facts" were "very much wanted"; that "the truth is we know next to nothing of these subjects"; and that—while menhaden landings were admittedly down—"whether by overfishing the menhaden men have killed their own goose which laid the golden eggs is not, however, clearly proved." That writer had more tolerance for risk than the other journalists, and a tendency to dismiss worries about the unknown as trivial. Such an attitude encouraged fishermen to press on, regardless of possible consequences.[20]

Yet by the 1870s once-prolific hauls from beach seines in Long Island Sound were a thing of the past. Porgies had been farmers' fish, but they no longer conveniently swam in vast schools to the farmers' dooryards, in Long Island Sound or anywhere else. S. L. Boardman of Maine noted that "Parties engaged in taking menhaden now go off ten or twenty miles from shore, whereas they formerly fished near the coast." A few years later another expert stated that "Constant fishing on the northern coast has driven the fish out to sea." Remembering fishing off Long Island, New York, Lorenzo Dow Moger explained in 1882 that "we used to have fish pretty close to the shore." But currently, as he fished Virginian waters, the menhaden were "in the middle of the bay or out of the bay." Captain C. S. Morrison agreed: "I have not fished very near it [shore] for two or three years; there have not been many fish inshore." This was something about which virtually everyone agreed. The age-old behavior of menhaden to swarm near the shore had been altered in just a few decades of intensive fishing.[21]

Scientists today agree that the systematic movement offshore of any fish stocks formerly abundant inshore indicates overfishing and population depletion. Although fish stocks fluctuate naturally in terms of both abundance and distribution, those dynamics can be affected by human pressures. During the 1870s menhaden's consistent movement offshore along the coast of Virginia, in Long Island Sound, and in the Gulf of Maine was not simply a function of biological variability, but the result of relentless day-and-night pursuit by a flotilla of vessels equipped with gigantic purse seines, a form of pressure that had never before existed.[22]

As discussions about the nature of the ecosystem and the state of American fishing heated up, interest groups wrangled for position. A witness from Boston testified in 1882 that a closed season "would materially affect the quality" of both menhaden *and* mackerel, in a positive way. "When the fish first come on here in the spring for spawning they are in very poor condition; they are thin and almost tasteless." Moreover, he continued, taking fish "at that early season . . . destroy[s] a great number of the spawn which they contain." Were fishing prohibited until "after the spawning time is over, of course year by year the quantity of fish in the waters must increase, and very rapidly." As he saw it, those fish were "very much more valuable taken at a later season," and delay-ing harvest would be "more profitable for the fishermen." A closed season during spawning time would create a win-win situation.[23]

The food-fish interest, represented by dealers and commission merchants, wanted to ensure a steady supply of cod, haddock, bluefish, striped bass, mackerel, and the like. New York dealers did not want to impose limitations on harvesting mackerel, especially early spring mackerel, even if they were thin and relatively tasteless; but steps for preservation of menhaden stocks seemed necessary. Samuel B. Miller, a fish dealer from Coney Island, testified "that it is injurious to the food fish to catch them [menhaden] the way they catch them now. We all know that fish follow the bait. If there is no bait on our coast, you will find but very little fish there." Other dealers concurred. "In my opinion," said Eugene G. Blackford of the Fulton Fish Market in 1882, "the great amount of fishing that is carried on for menhaden all along the coast breaks up the schools of fish which are followed by the striped bass and bluefish. . . . That quantity [of bass and bluefish] has been steadily diminishing year by year, and this year the scarcity is more marked than ever before." He recom-mended to the U.S. Senate that Congress impose a closed season "extending from the 1st of April to the 1st day of July" to "cover the spawning season of the menhaden."[24]

By every measure of efficiency, menhaden landings in 1881 were disastrous compared to those of 1874. During that seven-year interval the number of fish caught by Americans in the industry fell slightly, from about 493 million to 454 million, and the amount of oil rendered fell far more, from over 3 million to only 1.2 million gallons. The latter was an ecosystem indicator. It meant the fish had not found sufficient forage to fatten well as the season advanced. The extraordinary drop in efficiency, however, could be measured as well by the larger number of men employed (5,211 in 1881 compared with 2,438 in 1874), the larger number of steamers required (seventy-three versus twenty-five), and the larger amount of capital invested ($4.75 million versus $2.5 million)—all to catch fewer fish and produce much less oil. By every measure, catch per unit effort had fallen sharply.[25]

The well-capitalized and well-connected United States Menhaden Oil and Guano Association fought tooth and nail against limitations on menhaden fishing. Its secretary, Louis C. D'Homergue, ridiculed as "absurd" the "charges made that we catch up large quantities of food or game fish in our nets with menhaden." He referred to Spencer F. Baird's and George Brown Goode's assertions that capturing menhaden for oil and fertilizer would not damage other fisheries, and wondered, rhetorically, "what are the allegations set up against the largest fishing interest of the country, involving about four millions of dollars, mostly owned in New York State, employing over 90 steamers, 250 sailing vessels, and some 5,000 men?" Baird and Goode were the most respected fisheries scientists in America at the time, and leaning on their expertise could not but help bolster D'Homergue's position.[26]

Colonel Marshall McDonald, who sided with the industrialists, represented in person the U.S. Commission of Fish and Fisheries at the hearings. McDonald, a former Confederate officer and professor at the Virginia Military Institute, had been appointed to the state fish commission in Virginia in 1875; from there he went to the U.S. Fish Commission. Admitting that most fishermen would favor a national law for a closed season on mackerel and menhaden prior to June 20 to allow spawning, he nevertheless argued from his position as a scientific man that "legislation should be directed not so much to prohibition of fishing during the spawning season, about which we are not yet fully certain, but rather as to such general regulations as will contribute to maintain production." In other words, he wanted to fish harder and increase landings until scientists definitively demonstrated that a closed season during spawning time would be advantageous.[27]

It had taken only thirty years for what would become the classic manifestations of overfishing to occur in the New England menhaden industry. Within the experience of sea fishermen, the time frame had never been so compressed. Unfortunately the sequence would become typical for overfished species. The resource, long ignored, was redefined with commercial potential. That happened for menhaden around 1850, when farmers' fish became industrialists' fish. Robust fishing pressure quickly followed, putting strain on the resource. In the menhaden fishery that pressure came with purse seines, steamers, and rendering plants hungry to process every possible fish. It was America's first industrial fishery. As the menhaden fishery's productivity declined, with more effort required to land fewer fish, critics advocated reducing fishing pressure. Meanwhile oil and guano interests insisted that nothing untoward was happening; after all, the ocean produced fish in "natural" ways largely unknowable to humans, and in ways—they believed—that should be beyond the compass of law. As productivity continued to decline, effort increased more than commensurately. The trend became evident in the menhaden fishery during the late 1870s, when output flattened despite considerable increase in effort. Collapse in the Gulf of Maine came in 1879. Diminished likelihood of profit subsequently reduced effort enough for the resource to rebound at least partially, before fishing pressure resumed to shrink it once again. Here was a new template for the relationship between harvesters and living resources in the coastal ocean.

Following hearings in 1884, the U.S. Senate Committee on Fisheries recommended closing the spring menhaden season and legislating larger mesh. "While the industry is an important one and should not be capriciously or needlessly obstructed," the senators wrote, "it is at the same time evident to your committee that in so far as it has a tendency to lessen the supply of food-fish a reasonable regulation to avoid that result is demanded by the highest considerations of public policy."[28]

They had connected the dots. But the firestorm sputtered out as the menhaden trust flexed its muscle. Congress did not follow the recommendations of its Fisheries Committee. Unregulated purse seining of mackerel and menhaden continued, despite the protests of fishermen and fish dealers, and the insistence of respected ichthyologists, such as Seth Green, the superintendent of New York's Fish Commission, that protracted fishing could destroy sea fish. Though no one yet knew, the menhaden crisis that had spread from the Gulf of Maine to Capitol Hill during the early 1880s was setting the stage for a larger drama, the mackerel failure of 1886.

CLOSE TIME FOR MACKEREL?

Common wisdom during the nineteenth century was that mackerel's abundance "varied greatly from year to year." Sometimes, as one expert put it, "their numbers have been so few that grave apprehensions have been felt lest they should soon depart altogether." By contrast cod seemed phlegmatic, and cod fishing relatively dependable. Bumper years in the mackerel fleet could be followed by lean ones, making planning difficult for both business interests and individual fishermen. "The highest stock I ever made in the Gulf of St. Lawrence mackereling was $7000.00," testified Captain Peter Sinclair, who had fished for decades. That was 1859. "My poorest year I stocked $150, gone six weeks. This was in 1860." Boats that shifted to mackerel from the more predictable cod fishery sometimes could not even pay for their season's outfit. As the century progressed, arguments raged about whether fluctuations in mackerel and menhaden landings could be attributed to fishing pressure or to "natural causes, such as temperature, currents, the presence or absence of food, and the like, over which man has little or no control," as fisheries biologist R. E. Earll put it in 1887. No one considered the synergistic impact of human pressure and natural downturns, much less the notion that ecology, economic production, and law were inextricably intertwined. Fluctuations in the coastal marine ecosystem did not sit well with a laissez-faire economic system that assumed ever-expanding productivity, and a supposedly stable nature.[29]

The mackerel fleet's catching power expanded dramatically during the fifteen years after the Civil War, putting more pressure on stocks. Progressive mackerel fishers adopted purse seines during the 1850s, and seining began to account for a larger percentage of the annual catch. As late as the 1870s a handful of holdouts—especially from poorer communities in Maine—stuck with the less expensive jigs. For the most part, however, purse seines had become almost universal by then, and net-builders had improved them significantly. During the 1860s engineers had developed the first knitting machines for nets. No longer would they be assembled by hand, mesh by mesh. By the mid-1870s the largest seines were 1,350 feet long and 150 feet deep, enormous compared with those of 1850. Glass floats on the headropes had largely been replaced by corks— hundreds of them, and some quite large. Rings for the cinching line on the footrope had been replaced on the most sophisticated nets with galvanized blocks (pulleys), through which ropes ran with less friction. The bunt of the net, which took most of the strain, was knitted from the stoutest twine, while the wings and sides were lighter to save weight. Innovators secured numerous patents for improved gear during the 1870s and 1880s. Fishing reflected New Englanders' mechanical genius and can-do spirit as much as any other industry. Seine boats grew larger to accommodate the ever-growing seines. In 1857 all seine boats in New England had been twenty-eight feet long, modeled on whaleboats. By 1872 the standard was thirty feet; by 1873 boat shops had lengthened them to thirty-one feet. By 1877 new seine boats were generally thirty-four feet, though a few thirty-eight-footers had been built. Until 1872 all were lap-strake, or clinker-built, their external planks overlapping like the clapboards on a house; after that, most were carvel-built, with the planks meeting flush at the seams so that the smooth sides were less likely to catch the nets. Between the nets it shot and the boats used to deploy them, a modern purse-seining mackerel schooner in the late 1870s was an entirely different sort of fish-killer from the jiggers common in 1850.[30]

During the 1850s, when the fleet first shifted to seining, each schooner towed one seine boat. By 1880 most of the larger mackerel schooners carried

two seines and two seine boats. That year the American mackerel fleet numbered 468 vessels. "The mackerel schooners," wrote Goode and Collins, "as a
rule, spread more sail, in comparison with their size, than any vessels in the
world, except, perhaps, the extreme type of schooner-rigged yacht." They
"should be seen beating into the harbor with a spanking breeze," noted another
aficionado. "Their long sharp graceful hulls, taut jaunty spars, flat trim sails,
and lively manoeuvering would suggest an ocean regatta of clever yachts." Naval
architects such as Edward Burgess and Joseph Collins vied to innovate, and
by the 1880s American mackerel schooners were the strongest, fastest, and most
close-winded fishing boats in the world.[31]

Innovation did not stop with nets and vessels. Ironically, one bane of fishermen was an abundance of riches: sometimes they seined so many mackerel
they could not dress them fast enough to prevent their dying in the seine or,
worse yet, being ravaged by sharks. Voracious predators could rip an expensive seine to pieces, scattering or killing the fish trapped right alongside the
schooner, as bleary-eyed fishermen worked to clean and salt the catch. The
patented "spiller pocket," designed by H. E. Willard of Portland in 1878, and
refined by Captain George Merchant Jr. of Gloucester in 1880, solved the problem. Spillers were large net bags, thirty-six feet by thirty feet by fifteen feet,
made of exceptionally stout twine, and attached to the side of the schooner by
wooden poles or outriggers. A spiller pocket could hold 200 barrels of live
mackerel. Seiners with a big haul would funnel the live fish into the spiller and
then haul the seine back aboard to keep it safe from sharks. Dogfish, large
sharks, and porpoises found it much tougher to tear the extra-stout twine of
the spiller. Spillers allowed a seined school of mackerel to be kept alive and safe
from sharks for hours while the crew systematically processed the fish.[32]

Night seining began in the 1870s. Mackerel were notorious as capricious,
fickle fish; often they thwarted fishermen by not showing themselves on the
surface for days. Mackerel came to the surface routinely in the dark, however,
following the diurnal migration of plankton and squid on which they fed. On
dark nights bioluminescent organisms betrayed the presence of the fish by firing
the water with brilliant phosphorescent displays. Keen-eyed fishermen with
considerable experience could read the trace and discern, even in the dark, if
the disturbance indicated menhaden, mackerel, or herring. By the mid-1870s a
number of ambitious skippers had commenced night seining, and by 1881 it
was the general custom. Night fishing was difficult and dangerous. Seine boats
and dories carried oil lanterns, but the slap of a wave could extinguish lights
in an instant, making it difficult for the skeleton crew left aboard the schooner

to retrieve seine boat and seine. Skippers took the gamble: increased catches offset risks. In the fall of 1881 the *Cape Ann Advertiser* noted, "It would not greatly surprise us if the mackerel fleet next year were supplied with powerful calcium lights, to be carried at the masthead, and that the fishery will be extensively prosecuted in the night-time."[33]

Fishing pressure also increased during the 1870s by extending the season at its beginning, with early spring trips. During the 1879–80 season at least 64 schooners from Maine and Massachusetts sailed south in early or mid-March to intercept mackerel schools returning to the continental shelf after wintering in deep water. By 1885 the *spring* mackerel fishery fleet had ballooned to 184 schooners. Before the 1870s there had been occasional spring trips, but no concentrated or systematic effort to fish mackerel off Cape Hatteras, or the Virginia coast, or in the New York Bight. Before the Civil War, New York City had been supplied with fresh mackerel primarily by Connecticut-based smacks, whose crews jigged summer fish and carried them to New York markets. By 1880, however, the New England fleet of modern, well-equipped purse seiners had the ability to fish early in the year, to fish in the dark, and to handle and process very large catches. Entirely sail-powered, it was a juggernaut of efficiency.[34]

Mackerel landings in 1881 were enormous, larger than in any previous year except 1831. Fishermen attributed the high catches and mind-boggling payoffs to the modernization of the fishery. "Never within the previous history of the fishing business of New England," explained two insiders, had so much money been "made by a single vessel in the mackerel season." The schooner *Alice* of Swans Island, Maine, took 4,900 barrels and earned $28,000. The *Edward E. Webster* of Gloucester caught 4,500 barrels and earned more than $26,000. Others did less well, but very well indeed.[35]

Purse seines were not universally welcomed. In 1878 a group of fishermen from Portland and Gloucester lobbied Congress in person, but unsuccessfully, for prohibition of purse seines in the mackerel fishery. Critical of seines' wanton slaughter of juveniles and their propensity to take fish before or during spawning, opponents predicted that "without immediate and radical change" the fishery "must soon come to ruin." According to one experienced seiner, during the 1876 season "there were more thrown out of the seines than were saved." Market gluts, and bad weather, which prevented schooners from landing catches fresh, contributed to staggering discards.[36]

Innovation continued to boost fishing pressure, however, and in the summer of 1882 the first steamer in pursuit of mackerel departed Tiverton, Rhode Island. The vessel provided a twofold innovation: not only was this the first instance of a steamer's being engaged in any fishery besides menhaden, but the mackerel caught were to "be manufactured into oil and guano and diverted from their use as food." The steamer was a menhaden boat, repurposed for mackerel. With menhaden catches plummeting, its owners risked innovation. But their assets and connections were all in the guano and oil business. Rather than gearing up to pickle mackerel for human consumption, they opted simply to render them at oil and guano plants in lieu of menhaden. Critics immediately protested that purse-seining steamers had already "driven off the menhaden," and that "the same effect will be produced on the mackerel." According to the *New York Times,* there was a "general feeling that stringent laws should be at once enacted for the protection of the mackerel fishery, which gives employment to thousands and is an important food industry."[37]

Within several months a small fleet of menhaden steamers, from three to five vessels, according to different reports, was seining mackerel from Cape Cod to the Bay of Fundy. As a newspaperman put it, "since the menhaden has grown scarce there will be every inducement for more of the menhaden steamers to enter into mackerel catching." Most of the menhaden boats seining mackerel that fall landed their fish in Portland. Fish of good quality were sold fresh; others went to canneries. Critics worried, however, that steamers would be tempted to make huge hauls, knowing that any fish unsuitable for human consumption, fresh or canned, could be discharged at the rendering plants. The tactic would prevent waste, long a concern in the mackerel industry. But using such a fine fish for anything other than food struck many people as immoral, "a wicked waste of good material."[38]

Value judgments aside, if mackerel could be taken more cheaply by steam than by sail, fishermen would use steam. The first steamer fitted out expressly for mackereling slid down the ways at Kennebunk, Maine, in the summer of 1885, and was towed to Portland for outfitting with engines. The *Novelty,* as she was called, measured 275 tons when mackerel schooners averaged about 80 tons. She was too far ahead of the curve: even a skilled skipper such as Hanson P. Joyce could not make a profit with her, and the vessel was "sold to the Haytians for a war cruiser."[39] But although sail would remain the norm for decades, gigantism and mechanization had insinuated themselves into the mackerel fleet.

Mackerel landings in 1884 set a record; it would be eighty-four years before landings from the western Atlantic would match it. But although landings in 1884 were close to those of 1831, exact catch per unit effort cannot be compared, because the technologies employed varied considerably. In 1831 all mackerel were individually hooked by men jigging aboard small schooners. A catch of 1,000 fish per man per day was considered very good. During that jigging era, however, when vessels were smaller, the overall fleet was more numerous. In 1831 the mackerel fleet had at least 600 vessels. By 1851, when it was still jigging, the American mackerel fleet consisted of 940 vessels, employing 9,998 men. By 1880 individual schooners were larger and faster, though considerably more expensive and less numerous. The American mackerel fleet consisted of only 460 vessels that year. Virtually all fished with purse seines, which could land 100,000 fish in a good set, and virtually all were equipped with spiller pockets. All had the benefit of accumulated scientific knowledge of mackerel's movements. Most fished at night, and about half the fleet sailed south early in the season, which had not been the case in the jigging era. To compare the effort expended by the hand-jigging fleet and the purse-seining fleet would be to compare "apples and oranges": precise standardization is impossible. Nevertheless, it appears that the huge catch of 1884, only a bit larger than that of 1831, was obtained with bigger schooners, more-efficient gear, a longer season, and night fishing. Effort appears to have increased.[40]

After the record year, catches crashed. In 1886 landings were lower than at any time in the previous forty-five years. Moreover, mackerel landings did not rebound for decades. As had been the case with Gulf of Maine menhaden a few years earlier, intensive fishing pressure in 1881 and 1884, coupled with a natural downturn in productivity or some sort of regime shift, appears to have slashed the stock dramatically.

Fearing the worst, mackerel men lobbied Congress to close the spring mackerel fishery. J. H. Freeman, general manager of the Boston Fruit Company, wrote in 1886: "After a lifetime spent in the fishing business, and for fifteen years as acting agent of one of the largest mackerel firms in Massachusetts, I feel a deep interest in any movement to save or promote the business." O. B. Whitten, a veteran fisherman and fish dealer from Portland, agreed: "We believe the taking of fish during the spawning season will finally prove disastrous to the species." Moreover, "It is the men who are engaged in catching mackerel who ask for this close time. In the state of Maine I can get 99 out of every 100 fishermen to sign a petition for close time." Abner Rich, a fish dealer from Provincetown, concurred. "Everyone taken in this condition full of spawn is wholesale slaughter to the supply."[41]

Immature mackerel were routinely destroyed by seines and traps before they were large enough to be sold or to reproduce. Waste also resulted from vast spring catches that could not be processed or brought to market sufficiently fast to prevent spoiling. W. A. Wilcox, manager of the American Fish Bureau in Gloucester, testified in 1886 that during the previous spring "the aggregate amount thrown away from all vessels" had been "from 70,000 to 100,000 barrels," about 20 million pounds.[42] Asked how fishermen regarded the bill in favor of a closure during spawning season, he came right to the point. "The bill is a step in the right direction, and ought to become a law unless we wish to kill and drive the mackerel from our shores entirely. It is regarded with favor by all engaged in mackerel fishing." A fishing agent from Wellfleet, Massachusetts, concurred. "We have thirty five sail of mackerel fishermen from this port and they *all* both *fishermen* and *owners* are desirous for this bill to pass."[43]

The strongest opposition came from fishmongers and wholesale dealers at New York City's Fulton Fish Market. Fresh-fish dealer Eugene G. Blackford argued that the bill "came into existence through the salt fish dealers, as I understand it, on the coast of Maine." Everyone in the business knew that early spring mackerel salted poorly, being so deficient in fat, and that they would never "rate as a No. 1." So salt-fish dealers could afford a spring closure. But early spring mackerel could be consumed fresh, and Blackford insisted that "we ought to allow the people to have the mackerel because they are cheap, they are wholesome, and they are desirable food." He felt that closing the spring fishery would "take 1000 barrels a day of fresh mackerel out of the supply"—equivalent to 100 tons— and would drive up the price of other fish. Denying sales was not in the interests of commission merchants such as Blackford, who earned 12.5 percent.[44]

During the hearings scientific men from the U.S. Fish Commission defended two decades of scientific inquiry, its expense, and its conclusions. The official line, as promulgated by Professor Thomas Huxley in his investigations of European herring, was that human activities could not affect sea fish. Congressman Hewitt, who opposed the bill, quoted Huxley's views on herring, and argued that "the habits of herring and mackerel are almost identical." Initially Baird, head of the U.S. Fish Commission, situated himself squarely with Huxley. In written testimony he said, "I have never been convinced that the abundance of mackerel has been in any way affected through the agency of man." Confessing, however, that "Naturalists are obliged to admit their ignorance in regard to many portions of the life-history of the mackerel," he hedged, and said that he was unsure whether the bill "would have a beneficial effect." George Brown Goode, Baird's assistant, did not hedge a bit. He was sure that fishing had not affected mackerel or that "spring mackerel fishing will lead to its own destruction." Part of the scientists' opposition to restrictions on the fishery was face-saving: they did not want to be "laughed at by the men of science in England, Scotland, and France," as one said, should they capitulate to the clamor of fishermen.[45]

Congressman Thomas B. Reed of Maine, who had introduced the legislation for a closed season, and who within a few years would become the famously influential Speaker of the House of Representatives, was having none of it. "While Professor Goode says he does not know whether such a measure is necessary . . . or not," Reed told other members of Congress on May 21, 1886, "I am bound to say to you that every fisherman engaged in the business does know, and all of them are here before you with hardly a dissenting voice urging upon the ground of their personal experience that it will be the destruction of the fisheries not to have a close time."[46]

Reed knew his history, and he pitted it openly against the best science of the day. "In the face of scientific authorities I will not undertake to say we can prove that the destructive agency of man will extirpate the whole mackerel tribe from the face of the earth," lectured Reed, "but I will say this, every man on the New England coast knows that the lobster has almost disappeared. You can now only catch lobsters about 10 or 12 inches long, and I can remember when the ordinary size of the lobsters was pretty nearly twice that size. . . . We know that the supply of halibut is thinned out, and that the case is the same in regard to a great many other kinds of fish. I am aware that Professor Huxley says there is no proof that the herring has been diminished by the hand of man. But while I cannot absolutely prove the necessity, I say all these considerations put together render it exceedingly desirable that this experiment should be tried."[47]

As evidence poured in for and against closing the spring mackerel season, congressmen and senators became increasingly sympathetic to protecting the fish. Senator Palmer, chair of the Senate Committee on Fisheries, reminded his colleagues of seiners' ruthless efficiency—"as high as 1500 barrels had been taken on a single haul. One would imagine that they could empty the ocean in the course of time at that rate." Senator Eugene Hale drew analogies from the menhaden question, recently argued in the Senate. "Have not the menhaden, which used to be in countless millions on the New England coast, by this steam fishery purse net and all that, been practically driven away, whether annihilated or not?"[48]

Congressman Seth L. Milliken of Maine represented constituents vociferously in favor of the bill. He saw the issue plainly. "It seems to me to be a question whether we will legislate to save the source of supply of a valuable article of food, the source of a great industry, or allow people for immediate gain to kill the goose that lays the golden egg."[49]

As Reed had done, he treated his colleagues in the House to a history lesson, and to a story about protecting lobsters, something the state legislature had done through a closed season and a minimum-size law. "But this law, while it has arrested the destruction, and I hope may prevent the extermination of the lobster, came too late to save it from being so seriously diminished, both in numbers and size, that this fish, once so plentiful and cheap, is now comparatively rare and dear, and will average less than one half its size of twenty years ago. Still, we had the same experience obtaining legislation to preserve the lobster that we had in trying to save the menhaden, the same we have here today in our efforts to prevent the extermination of the mackerel. Our opponents quoted from scientific gentlemen, produced the testimony of theoretical experts, and talked of the enormous number of eggs which the fish deposited, but what the practical fishermen said proved to be correct."[50]

Efforts at the state level to restrict fishing reflected ongoing discussions in Washington. During the summer of 1886 petitioners in Massachusetts alerted their legislature to the "danger of the exhaustion of the food-fishes formerly so abundant" and argued it was "due partly to overfishing." The genie was out of the bottle. For the first time in New England's centuries-long discussion of fisheries, the term "overfishing" played a part. Petitioners insisted that catching fish had "been monopolized by a few, to the injury of the rights which belong to all, and to the probable exhaustion of the fisheries themselves." They sought a trial closure. They wanted the legislature to approve an experiment outlawing "use of traps and all nets" during certain seasons, to determine "whether the fisheries may not be wholly or partially and gradually restored."[51]

As discussions raged, the mackerel fishery continued to collapse. Towns such as Swans Island and Pulpit Harbor, both in Maine, never recovered from the one-two punch of the menhaden collapse in 1879 and the mackerel collapse in 1886. Maine's Bureau of Industrial and Labor Statistics published a report in 1887 on the condition of Maine's fisheries and fishermen. "The effect of large seining operations on the mackerel fishery is apparent everywhere. The business is virtually ruined and will have to be abandoned if the existing conditions continue." Referring to the mackerel fleet of North Haven, consisting of sixteen vessels, carrying "on an average, fifteen men each," the reporter noted that most had been fishing for eight months "and had not even wet their seines. . . . I have talked with owners, captains, and with men who have been in the business and studied it all their lives, and they all agree on this point, that the seining has ruined the business, and until it is stopped and the old method of catching on the hook adopted there can be nothing better expected." In larger ports bankruptcies and consolidations were the order of the day.[52]

After months of testimony Spencer F. Baird and his usually loyal lieutenant, George Brown Goode, split on the mackerel bill. While Goode toed the official scientific line that humans could do nothing to affect fish in the open sea, Baird wrestled with testimony to the contrary by fishermen, who had considerable traditional ecological knowledge. Ultimately Baird changed his tune. Noting that he "did not feel clear" about the legislation, he nevertheless "thought it was wise to pass this bill, because it might have a favorable effect upon the mackerel" in the future, and that "he was in favor of trying the experiment." The scientific community had never ceded so much to fishermen.[53]

Confronted by the catastrophic mackerel failure, and remembering its unwillingness to intervene on behalf of menhaden, Congress responded with the United States' first federal fishery law. As of March 1, 1887, landing or importing mackerel caught between March 1 and June 1 (understood, by some, as the spawning season) was prohibited for five years, except for those mackerel caught by hook and line or those taken in open rowboats whose keels were less than twenty feet long. In other words, exceptions were allowed for small-scale subsistence fishing during the spawning months. Powerful schooners with modern purse seines, however, would remain secure at the wharves unless they fished close inshore. The new federal law had no influence over waters within three miles of the coast, which remained under states' control. But given mackerel's whereabouts between March 1 and June 1, when they were never close to shore, the new federal law would, in effect, shut down spring fishing. Preservationists had won a major round.[54]

REVERSING THE TRAJECTORY OF HISTORY

The combination of closing the spring mackerel fishery in 1887, following poor landings in 1885 and disastrous landings in 1886, created a seller's market the likes of which had never been seen. Prices skyrocketed. A barrel of fish that had sold in New York City for six dollars several years earlier rose to twenty dollars, and occasionally to fifty. New Yorkers were not concerned with the ocean's vagaries. Their demand for food remained insatiable, however, and they could not abide inconvenience. If local supplies failed, commission merchants could remedy the situation with the steamship or the railroad. In 1886 fish dealers at Fulton Market began to import Irish mackerel in considerable quantities for the first time.[55]

Fishermen from elsewhere in the Old World had been targeting Irish mackerel for centuries. Early in the seventeenth century Spanish license-holders, Dutch license-holders, and Swedish fishermen (who avoided paying for licenses) deployed substantial fleets with liberty to fish Irish waters. In 1671 Robert Southwell of Kinsale, a small port in County Cork, at the southwest corner of Ireland, complained that before French mackerel fishermen had begun working local waters, it had been "usual for the hookers and fishermen of Kinsale, with about three men and a boy in each boat, to take 3000 or 4000 mackerel a day." French competition reduced local landings. Complaints about the French resurfaced in 1739. Local fishermen testified that "French fishing boats quite ruin their business; the nets of each boat, reaching near a league in length, break the shoals and drive the fish from the coast, so that this, which was a flourishing fishing, is destroyed and the fishermen reduced to beggary." In 1770 more than 300 French vessels pursued mackerel off County Cork with great success. Surviving evidence suggests that for well over a century small-scale Irish fishing operations were overwhelmed by foreign distant-water fleets, which timed their arrival each spring to match that of the fish.[56]

The great famine of 1846–1847 further prostrated the Irish fishery. Ironically, rather than turning to the sea for food as crops failed ashore, Irish cottagers sold their boats and tackle. Desperation for money for food overwhelmed all else. Irish fisheries took decades to recover. Meanwhile drift netters from Scotland, the Isle of Man, Cornwall, and France pursued mackerel in Irish waters each year from March to June. While Galway Bay fishermen netted herring, few Irish fishermen pursued mackerel until the 1870s, despite robust shoals on the Galway and Mayo coasts, primarily because Irish boats and gear remained at subsistence level. But change was in the wind. According to the Irish *Annual Report of the Fishery Inspectors for 1870,* almost 100,000 boxes of mackerel were sold at Kinsale that year. Catches dipped during the next few years, but in 1873 120,000 boxes (equivalent to 12,000 tons of mackerel) were sold, the aggregate landings of Irish and foreign vessels. In 1879, reflecting rapid growth in the Irish mackerel fishery, 218 Irish vessels joined 308 vessels from the United Kingdom (England, the Isle of Man, and Scotland) in the spring fishery. Most fish taken were packed in ice, then transported by steamship to urban English markets. Until 1880 Kinsale remained the center of the Irish mackerel fishery, and by the late-1880s, as American mackerel fisheries were collapsing, government inspectors reported total Irish mackerel landings of 20,000 tons. In 1887 Boston fishmongers learned from telegraphic dispatches that Irish mackerel were selling in London and Liverpool for two pence a pound. Merchants hankering for mackerel, such as D. F. DeButts, a wholesale fish dealer in Boston, knew where to turn.[57]

During the early 1880s natural factors and human decisions changed the center of gravity of the Irish mackerel fishery. To the surprise of fishermen, who still wished to imagine nature as predictable, migrating mackerel shifted their customary route closer to Baltimore, in County Cork. In response, part of the mackerel fleet, both foreign and Irish, moved westward from Kinsale, and that port lost its monopoly of the Irish mackerel fishery. By 1881 four other Irish ports besides Kinsale and Baltimore were reporting mackerel landings, and as the decade unfolded twelve other towns in Cork and Kerry staked out a piece of the mackerel fishery. Demand for spring mackerel remained high in England. By the time the American mackerel fleet took its staggering body blow in 1886, British and Irish fishing companies had spent the previous decade developing infrastructure for catching, processing, and shipping Irish mackerel throughout the British Isles.[58]

The failure of the American fishery created demand for prime Irish mackerel caught in the fall. As in the western Atlantic, the first schools of mackerel to close with the coast each spring were scrawny and underfed. Sufficiently suitable for sale as fresh fish, especially to undiscriminating buyers, they simply did not stand up well to preservation. After foraging all spring and summer, however, Irish mackerel, like those in the Gulf of Maine, were fat and perfect for salting. But Irish packers were accustomed to icing the fish and sending them straightaway to England. Few Irish packers knew how to clean and salt mackerel to preserve it long-term. Some coastal communities, such as Cape Clear, cured mackerel for their own consumption and for local sale, but quality control was poor and unscientific at best. The first Irish mackerel to arrive in America met a decidedly mixed reception. New Yorkers desperate for their favorite fish could not help but note with dismay that "the Hibernians did not know how to cut the fish for the American market, and the earlier cargoes did not arrive in satisfactory condition."[59]

Confronted by disastrous landings at home, American fish merchants traveled to County Cork in 1887 to cultivate Irish mackerel suppliers. Offering competitive prices, they shared insiders' information on packing fall mackerel, and worked with Irish and British firms to arrange shipping to Boston, New York, and Philadelphia. Fall mackerel caught near County Cork was cleaned and salted locally, packed in barrels, shipped to Liverpool by steamer, and then transshipped to American destinations. Within a few months American incentives contributed to the opening of the Baltimore Fishery School in August 1887. School trustees financed a purpose-built curing facility and trained boys for jobs in the fish industry. Private firms such as the Baltimore and Skibbereen Fishing Company turned to mackerel curing as well, though as late as 1890, when thousands of barrels were being exported to America, quality control remained problematic. As in the western Atlantic, ecological fluctuations prevented accurate predictions about supply. In August 1891 an American agent who had been purchasing mackerel in western Ireland for three years reported the catch as less than half that of the previous year. Quoted prices were high. The peak of Irish mackerel exports to American markets came in the mid-1890s. "The waters of the west coast of Cork are at present almost alive with fish," noted the *New York Times* in the fall of 1894. "The glut is so great that for want of hands to cure them for the United States, thousands of [mackerel] were thrown back again from off the piers into the sea."[60]

As American fish merchants hungry for mackerel set up shop in County Cork during the late 1880s, an entirely novel transatlantic venture in the mackerel business took shape on Cape Cod. Old fishermen there hoped it would "revolutionize that business." Captain J. A. Chase spent September 1889 outfitting the eighty-five-ton schooner *Alice,* a staunch Bath-built mackerel vessel, for a trip to South Africa. For many years old Provincetown sailors had reported that vast schools of mackerel "struck on" at the Cape of Good Hope about December 1 each year. Like mackerel arriving off New England in June, they were thin and ravenous, but they fattened fast as the season advanced. According to a reporter, "They have been seen in such immense schools that a vessel might be filled from them in three days." Cape Codders regarded South Africa's virtually unexploited mackerel stocks in 1889 as eagerly as English and French mariners had regarded unexploited fish stocks off Cape Cod three centuries earlier. As supplies of mackerel in home waters dwindled, then disappeared, men from Cape Cod became willing to cross the North Atlantic *and* South Atlantic to fish the productive upwelling off South Africa. Captain Chase equipped the *Alice* with two fine linen seines. He lashed his seine boats upside down on deck for the Atlantic crossing, and hoped optimistically to return in six months with a profitable load of No. 1 and No. 2 mackerel. As it was, he sold seven-eighths of his first season's catch elsewhere, but consigned one-eighth (99 barrels) to buyers in Provincetown.[61]

This was not the first time New England skippers had tried fishing the eastern Atlantic. Mackerel had been scarce in New England in 1839, and the following year Captain Nathaniel Atwood, from Provincetown, felt discouraged about his prospects in the Gulf of Maine and Gulf of St. Lawrence. He had heard stories about mackerel schooling in the Azores, and he ventured a trip. But Atwood came up empty-handed and did not repeat the attempt. A generation later, in the spring of 1878, Captain Knud Markurson cleared from Gloucester in the schooner *Notice,* bound on an experimental fishing trip off the coast of Norway. Markurson had fished Norwegian waters before. He hoped to create a winning combination by pairing his knowledge of the Norwegian Sea with a modern American purse-seining schooner. Nothing came of it.[62]

With the exception of specialty items such as French sardines, shipments of fish westward across the Atlantic were almost unheard of until the 1880s, as were flighty attempts by Yankee skippers to fish the eastern Atlantic. American merchants imported fish, but the vast majority of those fish originated in Canadian waters, which, ecologically speaking, were part of the same large marine ecosystem as the waters of northern New England. Between 1821 and 1853, 94 percent of the total value of fishery products imported to the United States came from the British North American Provinces that would later become Canada—all part of the large marine ecosystem stretching from Cape Cod to Newfoundland, whose abundance of boreal fish had dazzled European mariners three centuries earlier.[63]

Congress changed the tariff laws in 1854, and for the next twelve years fishery products from the British North American Provinces were allowed into the United States duty-free. During the first few years of the Civil War, 80 percent of the foreign fish imported into the United States originated in those British North American Provinces. Eighteen sixty-six saw a major increase in imported fish products, partly from a substantial importation of French sardines and foreign whale oil. From then until the 1880s brine-salted fish (such as herring and mackerel) remained the most important class of fish products imported to the United States, but even in years such as 1878 to 1881, when merchants imported considerable mackerel, most originated in Canada. Nothing yet had prompted coastal Yankees to consider reversing the course of history and turning to Europe for fish.[64]

Circumstances changed for good during the late 1880s with the simultaneous failure of several New England fisheries. When Maine's commissioner of fisheries, B. W. Counce, lamented imports of English mackerel in 1888, he foresaw an alarming trend. During the years from 1890 to 1894 the increase in value of imported fish to the United States was 176 percent greater than in the years 1869 to 1873. Moreover, by 1894 only 42 percent of fishery products imported had origins in the Western Hemisphere. (If imports of miscellaneous items such as ambergris, shells, coral, and sponges are subtracted, a more accurate figure is 52 percent.) By 1894 Americans regularly were eating from European marine ecosystems. In that year Americans consumed substantial imports of French sardines, Scandinavian mackerel and herring, Dutch herring, and English and Irish mackerel. As an economist from the U.S. Fish Commission explained, "Prior to 1888 almost the entire supply of brine-soaked mackerel imported into the United States was received from Nova Scotia, but the recent decrease of this fish on the American coasts has resulted in large importations from Norway, England, Ireland, and, to a less extent, other European countries."[65]

Most commentators saluted the ingenious reach of international commerce, the alacrity with which American merchants had been able to establish footholds in Ireland, and the indefatigable work of the U.S. Fish Commission promoting linkages between American fish merchants and counterparts abroad. A perceptive minority, including Counce, worried about the implications of Americans' eating from distant marine ecosystems, and what that meant for coastal states such as Maine and Massachusetts, where tens of thousands of citizens worked in the fisheries.

In 1890 the "long-talked-about consignment of African mackerel arrived" at Provincetown. The ninety-nine barrels seined by the *Alice's* crew were inspected at the Union Fish Company's packing sheds. Experts testified they were "sweet and in first-class order," dismissing naysayers who had not imagined it possible to pack mackerel in South Africa and have it arrive satisfactorily in Cape Cod. Later, naturalists at the U.S. Fish Commission determined that the fish were *Scomber colias,* commonly called the bull's-eye, chub, or thimble-eye mackerel, a species distinct from *Scomber scrombrus,* the common mackerel of the western Atlantic, but good eating nonetheless. Despite the quality, however, Cape Cod skippers did not repeat the experiment of sailing to South Africa for mackerel. Even in an era of fisheries collapse, there were economic limits to what a schooner could do.[66]

During the 1880s, as menhaden and mackerel fisheries crashed in New England and Atlantic Canada, halibut crashed, too, and it became worthwhile to pursue them in Old World waters. In 1866 the first New England halibut skipper willing to risk a long voyage sailed to Greenland—2,000 miles away, halfway to Europe. In 1884 and 1885 a small fleet of Gloucester halibut schooners began fishing off Iceland, even farther to the east. Tucked at 64° North, between Norway's Svalbard archipelago and the east coast of Greenland, Iceland was Europe's westernmost outpost, a rugged island populated by descendents of Viking settlers who had arrived to stay in the ninth century. In the saga of North Atlantic fisheries, medieval Iceland had been known for its stockfish. Iceland had come to prominence in about 1407, when English cod fishermen, discouraged by poor fares in the North Sea, began to sail there each February or March for spring cod. From Iceland, Renaissance fishermen had pushed west to Greenland, Newfoundland, and New England, searching for more lucrative grounds. By 1884, North Atlantic fisheries had come full circle. With home grounds virtually picked clean of halibut, but with fishmongers clamoring for more, New England skippers reversed the trajectory of history and sailed to Europe in search of the giant flounder.

THE FLASH-IN-THE-PAN ATLANTIC HALIBUT FISHERY

Among North Atlantic fishes only bluefin tuna, swordfish, and some of the larger sharks were larger than Atlantic halibut, the largest member of the flounder family. Halibut was not a fish with which to trifle. But because it was large and slow to mature, and because—unlike tuna or swords—it congregated in vast, densely packed schools, sometimes "four tier deep" as nineteenth-century fishermen said, Atlantic halibut, like American bison, could be easily exterminated. The flash-in-the-pan halibut fishery, which proceeded from localized depletion to serial depletion to near-extinction in about one human lifetime, revealed how technologically sophisticated, scientifically based, and utterly relentless American fisheries had become by midcentury.

A cold-water fish, though not an Arctic species, halibut normally lived in latitudes above 40° North, frequenting fishing banks but also being found at great depths seaward of the shallows. Like all flatfish it had both eyes on one side; like some, it had sharp curved teeth and a relatively large mouth. Halibut were brown, "chocolate to olive or slaty brown on the eyed (upper) side," and whitish, ranging from pure white to mottled gray, on their lower sides. Record-breaking halibut occasionally exceeded 700 pounds. Three-hundred-pounders, which fishermen claimed were average in virgin stocks, were seven to eight feet long. As local stocks were fished down, typically full-grown females came to average about 100 to 150 pounds, with males a bit smaller. A typical large fish might weigh about 200 pounds.

Halibut were voracious predators. On the basis of stomach content analysis, Bigelow and Schroeder explained that they routinely eat "cod, cusk, haddock, rosefish, sculpins, grenadiers, silver hake, herring, launce on which they often gorge in northern seas, capelin, flounders of various sorts (these seem to be their main dependence), skates, wolfish and mackerel. Halibut are also known to eat crabs, lobsters, clams, and mussels; even sea birds have been found in them." Preferring sand, gravel, or clay bottoms, halibut—uncharacteristically for flatfish—were known by fishermen to come to the surface on occasion. Captain Marr testified that in the early days of the Georges Bank halibut fishery he had seen a "solid school of them as thick as a school of porpoises" feeding on sand lance. Another time, he recollected, "the whole surface of the water as far as you could see was alive with halibut."[67]

Like Captain Marr, whose recollections dated to the 1840s, the first generation of Europeans had found the western Atlantic thronged with halibut. "There is a large sized fish called a Hallibut, or Turbut," Captain John Smith wrote in 1624, "so bigg that two men have much a doe to hall them into the boate; but there is such plenty [of better fish], that the fisher men only eate the heads & fines, and throw away the bodies." During the 1630s William Wood noted that "halibut is not so much unlike a plaice or turbot, some being two yards long, and one wide, and a foot thick. The plenty of better fish makes these of little esteem, except the head and fins which stewed or baked is very good." Diners then enjoyed glutinous foods. One expert points out that halibut fins "were a gloopy delicacy. The halibut's lateral fins have dozens of spines. At the fin's base, in between each spine, are two muscles—one on top, one on the bottom. The flesh where fin connects to body has a higher fat content than the rest of the flesh. Additionally, between each individual muscle is a layer of fat. When cut off laterally, the cross-section is honeycombed between flesh and fat layers." Fatty and succulent, fried halibut fins were seventeenth-century delicacies. Halibut heads' gelatinous flesh was likewise tempting. Seventeenth-century fishermen did not target the giant flounders, but if they hooked one by chance, they sometimes finned it, or headed and finned it, before discarding the rest.[68]

From the time Renaissance seafarers first arrived in the western Atlantic until the 1830s virtually everyone disdained halibut, occasional delicacies notwithstanding. Cod fishermen considered them a decided nuisance: muscular halibut took valuable bait and fought like fury. Halibut's only saving grace was that it did not mix promiscuously with cod or haddock. Fishermen learned that the appearance of a school would drive away the cod. Skippers knew to shift their berth rather than struggle with the giant pests.

Captain Epes Merchant recollected that before 1830 halibut were an "annoyance." Cod fishers in Massachusetts Bay or on Middle Bank (now known as Stellwagen Bank) "would often string up on a rope, at the stern, all the halibut caught" and keep them there until ready to sail for home "to prevent them from annoying the fishermen again." Samuel G. Wonson remembered that before 1830 a few halibut "were taken to Charlestown, Mass., and traded off to the farmers for produce." Around 1835 John F. Wonson set out to bring live halibut to the Boston market from Georges Bank. Vessels from New London, Connecticut, occasionally fished the Nantucket shoals for halibut at about the same time; by 1840 a handful of New London skippers regularly fished halibut on Georges Bank. Halibut's transition from worthless by-catch to valuable commodity began in the late 1830s, after cod fishermen had brought home sufficient halibut for experimentally minded merchants to process and sell.[69]

Relying on an unpublished memoir by a Newburyport fish dealer named John G. Plummer, historian Glenn Grasso effectively reconstructed halibut's refashioning during the 1830s. Beverly schooners sailing to the Grand Banks for codfish, according to Plummer, "used to Bring Home Some Halibut Salted in With the Codfish." "The First Fresh Halibut that Was Ever Cut and Smoked in this Country, Was Cut & Cured by Harry Merchant and Moses Lufkin & Smoked in Lufkins Dog House in Lufkins yard at Gloucester. They had Hard Work to Sell it at any Price." Plummer recollected that a fish merchant named David Crowell also bought halibut in the 1830s for two dollars a quintal, dried it on his flakes, and shipped it west for sale. Whether smoking or drying the halibut, those pioneers were trying to market a fish long overlooked. In 1839 one observer noted that "Before the construction of the Providence and Stonington Railroad the whole number of halibut caught and brought into Cape Ann did not exceed 2,500." Halibut were not "in demand when cured in any manner," he continued; "in fact, so worthless were they considered as salted fish that the owners of vessels . . . generally instructed the crews to cut" them adrift.[70]

Early halibut entrepreneurs discovered that the thick flesh of halibut did not salt well. Alfred Beckett, a fisherman aboard the schooner *Mirror,* kept track of the fish he landed between April 10 and May 11, 1840. His tally comprised eighty-two cod, twenty-three haddock, and fourteen halibut. Beckett also noted that he was "drying halibut to smoke," a clear sign of its increasing commercialization. Gone were the days when every hooked halibut would be discarded or finned. Some New London and Gloucester vessels sailed directly to New York with halibut during the early 1840s, helping to create a market. By then halibut had become targeted, along with pollock, hake, and haddock. None yet had cod's panache, but all fetched a price, although pollock, hake, haddock, and halibut did not salt as well as cod.[71]

Increased consumer demand for seafood and several other developments during the 1840s redefined halibut as a valuable commodity. Fishermen's initial use of ice to preserve catches fresh occurred during that decade, as did railroad connections linking New England seaports with the American hinterland. Sawn blocks of ice harvested from New England ponds increasingly were packed into the holds of outbound schooners. Fish no longer had to be salted or delivered to port within twenty-four hours; they could be iced. It took several years for fishermen to get the hang of icing. The concept of refrigeration did not come naturally. But suddenly edible fish such as halibut, which salted poorly, and which had never been part of the dried fish economy, earned a second look. Halibut's dense flesh actually stood up better to icing than that of cod, haddock, pollock, or cusk.

Veteran fishermen from Connecticut to Maine turned to halibut, saving fish that would have been discarded on cod trips only a few years before, and increasingly fitting out vessels specifically for halibut trips. That meant rebuilding holds to include icehouses, and purchasing trawls. Halibut fishermen handlined for a few years, but they shifted to trawls (longlines) before anyone else. Hand-lining those giant fish was simply too difficult. It is fair to say that halibut remained by-catch through most of the handline era. The first trawling for halibut occurred in 1843; by the late 1840s halibut fishers were routinely setting trawls. The longline revolution, which in the cod fishery did not occur until the late 1850s and early 1860s, took off first in the early days of halibut fishing. Halibut schooners typically carried six dories, each of which set one to four tubs of trawl. A tub, or half-barrel, conveniently held a groundline with 150 hooks, one every fifteen or twenty feet.[72]

The Gloucester halibut fleet switched to ice in 1845. No "halibut fleet" had existed a decade previously. But "fresh fish" increasingly meant either locally caught species or halibut, which could be transported great distances on ice. The icing revolution transformed the market for fish. Salted fish had been a staple of western civilization for almost 1,000 years. During the middle of the nineteenth century fresh fish gained market share, especially among middle-class consumers, while "salted fish began to be associated with immigrants, the urban working classes, and the southern black population." As more prosperous white Americans cultivated their taste for fresh fish, relatively unexploited stocks of halibut were ripe for plucking.[73]

Gloucester entrepreneurs' attempt to dislodge Boston's fish merchants from preeminence in the new halibut business triggered a financial and ecological catastrophe. Gloucester got a railroad connection in 1847, and the Gloucester Fishing Company tried to force retailers to travel to Gloucester by train for halibut. But Boston was the established market, and luring buyers to Gloucester proved difficult. In 1848 the company took a huge gamble and agreed to purchase the fleet's entire yearly catch. The northwest Atlantic ecosystem and human endeavor were about to collide. To the chagrin of company officials, Georges Bank yielded as it never had before in 1848. The fledgling company remained contractually obligated to purchase what was then a huge volume of fish. Desperate to avoid financial ruin, the Gloucester Fishing Company created a system of high-grading to undermine its contracts with fishermen.[74]

Company executives invented three grades of halibut: "white," "gray," and "sour." Mature fish with a completely white underside got the highest grade. Fish whose lower side was mottled or drab got the middle grade. Sour fish, so-called, were those "slightly tainted in the vicinity of the abdominal cavity." Buyers agreed that some justification existed for the third ranking: fish that had not been iced well deservedly brought a lower price. The distinctions between "white" and "gray," however, were entirely fanciful. Mature halibut in nature have varied coloration. Color differential has no relationship to the firmness or flavor of the flesh. Beginning in 1848, however, when "sour" halibut sold on the wharf for 1.5 cents per pound, "gray" sold for 3 cents and "white" for 5. Fishermen suddenly had incentive to discard "gray" halibut, leaving space in their ice rooms for "white" only. The system was doubly bankrupt. Not only did it promote massive discards, but retailers charged consumers exactly the same for "gray" or "white," though fishermen had been paid only half as much for the supposedly lower grade.[75]

The Gloucester halibut fleet had ballooned from twenty-nine vessels in 1846 to sixty-five in 1848, the year the Gloucester Fishing Company promised to buy all halibut landed. The glut overwhelmed it. "Sometimes," Goode noted, "there would be twenty vessels, each with 30,000 or 60,000 pounds of halibut in its hold lying at the halibut company's wharf, waiting to unload, while there was no possible sale for any." The company suspended operations in April. But the high-grading system persisted for years, to the detriment of fishermen and fish. Apparently abundant, and caught in enormous quantities, the supposedly lower grades were discarded routinely, sometimes right in Gloucester harbor. Mismanagement followed mislabeling.[76]

The immense halibut harvest on Georges Bank in 1848 marked a sober turning point. Stocks decreased rapidly, and after about 1850 the Georges Bank fishery ceased to be profitable. Captain Marr believed that the halibut had "shifted off" into deep water. He could not comprehend that they had been largely eradicated. It took only fifteen years for a small fleet of small schooners (averaging sixty-two tons), nearly to wipe out most of the halibut stock on a bank approximately equal in area to the combined size of Massachusetts, Rhode Island, and Connecticut. Following that localized depletion fishermen moved east, but not very far east. From then "to 1861," Goode noted, halibut "fisheries were prosecuted chiefly on the shallow parts of Seal Island Ground, Brown's Bank, and Western Bank." Ironically, by the time Lorenzo Sabine's 1853 *Report on the Principal Fisheries of the American Seas* referred to New England's halibut business as "a new enterprise," the Georges Bank halibut stock was already gone, as was that of Massachusetts Bay.[77]

Captain Knud M. Markuson later told a tale of halibut exploitation characteristic of that flash-in-the-pan fishery. In 1868 he discovered a new halibut ground called the Southern Shoal Water on the southeast end of St. Peter's Bank. "For four years I . . . made three trips to the Shoal Water each season. . . . We averaged about 30,000 pounds of halibut to each trip." Then the fleet followed him, and after one season's fishing the ground became unprofitable. The serial depletion proceeded from Massachusetts Bay to Georges Bank, then to Le Have and Western Bank, then to the Eastern Shoal Water of the Grand Banks and the grounds around the Magdalen Islands. Fishermen hit the shallows first, and then the deeps. It did not take long.[78]

Provincetown whalers told fishermen hungry for halibut that Greenland's waters teemed with the big fish, and in 1866 the American halibut schooner *John Atwood* chanced a fare. Her pioneering skipper returned from the west coast of Greenland in October with $5,500 worth of halibut, a modest success. Several other Gloucester vessels made trips to Greenland in subsequent years, but the first bonanza fare came in 1870, when Captain John McQuinn returned with halibut worth $19,000. During the next several years five or six Gloucester schooners sailed to Greenland each summer. By 1884 most of the halibut schooners from Gloucester, the port dominating that fishery, worked in

Greenland. The obstacles were formidable. Not only was the 2,000-mile trip daunting, but no reliable charts existed of Davis' Strait and the Greenland coast.[79]

Overfishing caused the Gloucester-based halibut fleet to shrink considerably from its early glory days. By 1880 it consisted of twenty-three vessels, down from forty-eight the previous year, and down from sixty-five—its high point—in 1848. Grounds off New England, Nova Scotia, Newfoundland, and in the Gulf of St. Lawrence had been fished out, and skippers had to either sail farther from home for halibut or go back to fishing cod or haddock.[80]

The great circle route to Europe proceeds stepping-stone fashion from Newfoundland to Greenland to Iceland, and with the dearth of halibut nearby it seemed inevitable that some skipper would sail farther east. As early as 1873 the first American schooner to look for halibut in the western fjords off Iceland made a trip there; over the next decade a few others fished Icelandic waters now and again. By then Massachusetts fish merchants were experimenting with a halibut cure that involved initial salting and subsequent smoking. The fresh halibut fishery in the northwest Atlantic had lasted only a few decades. Once halibut had been fished out close to home, schooners had to range as far afield as Greenland or Iceland, and doing so involved returning to salting the catch, a cure that had gone out of fashion. Consumers, however, would take halibut steaks salted if that was the only way to get them. During the summer of 1884, when most of the American halibut fleet was fishing in Greenland, three enterprising skippers sailed to Iceland determined to make a killing, and two of them hired experienced Icelandic fishermen in Reykjavik. The schooner *Concord* fished the western fjords that summer, on white sand and clay bottoms, in about sixty fathoms. Her crew set tub-trawls from dories, wetting their hooks for about six hours, and generally catching 300 fish per day, often 400 or 500, and occasionally 800. The halibut averaged 300 pounds each. Once again Gloucester crews had found a virgin halibut ground.[81]

Predictably, the next summer (1885) twice as many schooners sailed to Iceland for halibut, including the *Concord*. The U.S. Fish Commission noted proudly the "establishment of the Iceland halibut fishery as a profitable undertaking for American fishermen." The commissioner thought this "all the more gratifying, too, in view of the marked depletion of the halibut on the old grounds and the practical failure of the supply."[82]

Statistics on total American halibut landings from the North Atlantic were not kept before 1875, but thereafter they told a tale of woe. Between 1875 and 1880 annual landings ranged between 9 million and 16 million pounds, with

1879 the high point; thereafter landings fell. The halibut fleet that year was only 74 percent of its size in 1848, and it is quite likely that halibut landings in 1848 exceeded those of 1879. In any event, by 1887 and 1888 landings were down to approximately 11 million pounds—a decrease of 31 percent from the high point in 1879. Moreover, landings of salted (as opposed to fresh) halibut more than doubled between 1887 and 1888. Schooners had to range farther afield to find halibut, so ice would not suffice; fishermen had to salt their catches to preserve them. By 1901 New England's diminished halibut landings were just over 5 million pounds, and continuing to decline.[83]

One apologist for the fishery in 1885 maintained a sense of optimism in the face of facts. Newton P. Scudder, librarian of the Smithsonian's National Museum, admitted the harmful "effect produced by the fishing of one year upon the abundance of the fish in the same place in succeeding years." He conceded that "fishermen complain that the halibut . . . must be sought in deeper water year after year," but it perplexed him. "If we consider the halibut as of a roving disposition, why should they shun their former haunts because they have been fished on," he mused; "or if, on the other hand, they are not rovers, how can they, considering their great fecundity, be so easily exterminated?" Scudder himself had calculated that the ovary of a six-foot halibut contained 2,782,425 eggs. That precision, and his certainty of its implications, flew in the face of everyone's observations regarding the halibut's demise. As one of the foremost American scientific librarians of his age, Scudder had internalized the buoyant assumptions of the U.S. Fish Commission, then administering what was probably the largest scientific research and publishing program in the United States.[84]

From the lowliest of field assistants to Baird himself, at its pinnacle, employees and supporters of the Fish Commission knew that they were at the forefront of natural science and simultaneously providing a crucial social service—building the fishing industry along modern scientific lines to provide cheap wholesome food for the masses, even as they grew its revenues and expanded its employment base. The sea would have to cooperate to fulfill their vision, but they were confident that it would, even in the face of nagging observations that might suggest otherwise. Scudder was sure that banks "where the halibut are more abundant" would be discovered. He insisted that "These banks must be more numerous than is at present realized, for the halibut is a wide-spread species, and may be circumpolar in distribution." He could not believe that fishermen could eradicate halibut with a hook-and-line fishery, though much of the damage had already been done.[85]

Greenland and Iceland were not the only distant sources of halibut. As early as 1880 "a few carloads" of Pacific halibut were introduced to eastern markets by rail. The halibut fishery on the Pacific coast began in earnest in 1888, when the two Massachusetts schooners *Oscar and Hattie* and *Mollie Adams* rounded Cape Horn, bound for Puget Sound. They landed over half a million pounds in their first season, and the enterprise took off. In 1890 about 740,000 pounds of halibut were landed in Puget Sound; by 1892 the amount had doubled; by 1895 it had almost doubled again, to 2.5 million pounds. A few experimental steam-powered dory-trawlers sailed from Vancouver, British Columbia, pursuing halibut during the mid-1890s. Encouraged by the prospect of profits, a Boston firm outfitted a steamer for catching halibut with tub-trawls set from dories in the North Pacific in 1898; encouraged by the success of the enterprise, they fitted out another in 1902. By then the total catch of halibut by Massachusetts vessels was 12,155,934 pounds. Only a little more than 7 million pounds came from the Atlantic; the other 5 million originated in the Pacific.[86]

A dirge for halibut echoed throughout the U.S. Fish Commission's magisterial seven-volume set, *The Fisheries and Fishery Industries of the United States,* published during the 1880s. Its extensive essay "The Halibut Fisheries" was at once heroic and wistful, an account of men in a fishery the likes of which would not be seen again, an account of bumper catches, vast stocks, pioneering skippers, enterprising merchants, and the best vessels in the world. "The fishermen employed upon the halibut schooners are chosen men," noted the authors, at the outset of a string of superlatives. "It is not a rare occurrence to find among the crew of a halibut schooner several men who have been masters of vessels." The schooners themselves numbered "among the staunchest and swiftest in the Gloucester fleet." Each one, able "to anchor in great depths of water and ride out furious gales . . . is provided with a cable of great size and strength. This cable is of manila, 8½ to 9 inches in circumference, and from 375 to 425 fathoms in length." No other commercial fishing vessels carried an anchor cable like that, almost half a mile long, because no other fishery in the world existed in which fish were sought at such great depths.[87]

The triumphant tone could not hide the tragedy. In the same essay Captain Joseph W. Collins lamented that "halibut are being reduced in numbers very fast, and if the present style of fishing is pursued will in a few years become extremely scarce, if not almost extinct." Collins worried about the loss of a valuable branch of the fishery. Yet fatalism prevailed. Fishermen, he noted, "feel obliged to catch as many fish as possible when they go after them, and whatever the result may be on the abundance of halibut in future years, the present time must be improved to the best advantage." Fifteen years earlier, in 1870, Captain Nathaniel Atwood had testified to the Massachusetts state senate that halibut "have greatly diminished." Ticking off the banks on which they were targeted—"George's Bank, and also on Brown's Bank, the western coast of Nova Scotia . . . the banks of Newfoundland, and . . . the western coast of Greenland"—he generalized from the evidence. "They seem to be decreasing on all the fishing grounds."[88]

THE MOST VALUABLE CRUSTACEAN

Like halibut, lobster had largely been ignored as a commercially valuable species until the nineteenth century. Like halibut, lobster was redefined as marketable and targeted intensively beginning around 1830. And like halibut stocks, lobster stocks crashed in the late nineteenth century, despite fractious debates in northern New England and Atlantic Canada on the need for lobster preservation. Removal of vast numbers of lobsters and halibut, as well as of most animals of certain age-classes within those species, refashioned benthic communities on the banks of New England and Atlantic Canada. Ecologically, the repercussions were lasting. Sociologically, the process revealed an ambiguous world in which experts and interested parties recognized openly the demise of lobster resources on which they depended, even as their political systems failed to respond in credible ways for the long term. Ultimately markets masked the ecological damage, compensating for that political failure. Pierside prices for lobster rose as catches plummeted, so that lobstermen could still earn a living.

Coastal Europeans from Norway to the Mediterranean were familiar with the European lobster, classified by Carl Linnaeus in 1758 as *Cancer gammarus,* and later reclassified as *Homarus gammarus.* Linnaeus initially lumped lobsters together with crabs; thus the genus *Cancer.* Few fishermen or coastal dwellers cared much about those taxonomic niceties. Lobster was good eating, and people near the shore, especially in Norway and the British Isles, had easy access. Evidence from the seventeenth century indicates that Norwegians took lobsters with six-foot tongs and with gaffs in shallow water. Lobsters could be taken so easily that concerns about their vulnerability to overfishing existed early. The kingdom of Sweden imposed the first regulations in Europe to conserve lobsters in 1686.

Like many crustaceans, lobsters spoil quickly after death; to be moved any distance they have to be kept alive. That biological distinction and logistical difficulty kept lobsters from becoming an important article of commerce. Nevertheless, when Europeans arrived in North America they found a lobster that appeared to be identical with the well-known European one, except—as with many American marine creatures—it grew considerably larger. *Homarus americanus,* the American lobster, is in fact a distinct species from its European cousin, but striking similarities make them virtually indistinguishable. Anthony Parkhurst claimed from Newfoundland in 1578, "I may take up in lesse than halfe a day Lobsters sufficient to find three hundred men for a days meate." In Penobscot Bay in 1609 Robert Juet and his men "found a shoald with many lobsters on it, and caught one and thirtie." Every early raconteur had similar reports. Lobsters were astonishingly numerous among the northwest Atlantic's littoral fauna.[89]

Seventeenth-century settlers and fishermen fed lobsters to hogs and servants, pitch-forked them into fields as fertilizer, and used lobster flesh as bait to catch the more desirable striped bass, or to bait eelpots. No one imagined a commercial fishery. Problems preserving and shipping lobster meat seemed insurmountable, though live lobsters wrapped in wet seaweed occasionally made it to markets in seaports such as Newport, Portsmouth, and Boston. Lobsters were cheap, and coastal residents of all classes ate them. By the end of the eighteenth century in Boston and New York, where pollution and overfishing had already made lobsters something of a novelty, demand grew. A market was being born.[90]

Traps were not required for the commercial lobster fishery to expand in coastal ecosystems near Boston and New York. Lobsters were still sufficiently plentiful around the turn of the nineteenth century that a man could lash a scrap of net to a barrel hoop, add a stone sinker and a bit of bait, and by lowering it briefly to the bottom haul in lobster after lobster. Boys still gaffed them in the shallows. Captured lobsters could be held for weeks in floating crates. But transportation to markets remained the chief challenge in an age during which the only good lobster was a live lobster. Well smacks solved the problem. Shipwrights built watertight bulkheads in the cargo holds of small vessels, then drilled holes through the bottom planks, allowing oxygenated water to circulate freely between the surrounding sea and the built-in tank. Live lobsters could be transported for days or even weeks. Long Island Sound smackmen freighted lobsters to New York City during the early nineteenth century, as smackmen from Cape Cod served the Boston market. Smacks were rigged as sloops and schooners. The first sign of decline came in 1812, when voters in Provincetown, Massachusetts, alarmed by the depletion of local stocks,

convinced the state legislature to limit lobstering in those waters to Massachusetts residents.

By 1820 smackmen with an eye on urban markets were frequenting harbors
in western Maine, prompting an outcry by aggrieved locals, whose petition
reminded legislators "that the lobsters on our coast & shores invite the cod &
other fish thereto, and afford to our fishermen bait." Maine's legislature passed
a law forbidding nonresidents from catching lobsters anywhere in state waters
without a permit from town selectmen. A rush for permits followed, and the
new business took off. As it evolved, part-time or superannuated fishermen
caught lobsters and stockpiled them at prearranged pickup points for smackmen. In 1841 Captain Elisha Oakes of Vinalhaven made ten trips between Harpswell, Maine, and Boston, carrying a total of 35,000 lobsters. By 1855 the trade
had spread down-east to the New Brunswick border. As fishing pressure increased, half-round lobster traps built of lath, with net headers, replaced
the primitive hoop-net pots and gaffing techniques. Local control remained
the norm, and as the fishery expanded, attracting able-bodied full-time fishermen by the 1860s, territorial claims determined who had the right to fish in
certain waters.[91]

Soldered, cylindrical, metal canisters, soon known as "tin cans," changed
the nature of the lobster business dramatically during the 1840s. Lobster canneries lasted in Maine for less than half a century; the last one closed in 1895.
Their impact on the coastal ecosystem, however, was immediate and lasting.
William Underwood had experimented with hermetically sealed glass jars as a
means to market a variety of foodstuffs, including lobster, during the 1820s and
1830s. Obstacles abounded. The process took decades to refine, and inspired
competitors, but by 1844 Underwood had a profitable lobster cannery in Harpswell, Maine. The next year competitors opened a cannery in New Brunswick,
and the following year one in Nova Scotia. Canneries proliferated rapidly in
Maine, eventually packing corn, lobster, poultry, soup, mackerel, clams, and
succotash. By 1880 twenty-three factories were canning food in Maine. Tinned
lobster in cases obliterated the impediment to shipping lobster meat that had
existed since the Middle Ages. Canned lobster revolutionized the market.

No time series of lobster landings exists prior to 1879, but "scuttlebutt in
the eighties had it that the industry's peak had come and gone about 1870, and
both the number and profitability of Maine's canneries was declining." In 1880,
the first year reliable figures were compiled, about 2 million pounds of lobster
meat were packed in Maine, which would have required about 9.5 million

pounds of live lobster. That same year, only 4.7 million pounds were sold as live lobsters to restaurants, boardinghouses, and summer people. In other words, total landings were just over 14 million pounds.[92]

What was required to catch 14 million pounds of lobster in Maine in 1880? Close attention to the boats and gear reveals quite a bit about the coastal ecosystem's productivity, even after it had staggered under an onslaught of lobster fishing during the previous forty years. Unlike late-nineteenth-century menhaden, mackerel, and halibut fisheries, prosecuted with the most advanced fishing schooners and gear in the world, Maine's lobster fishers in 1880 relied entirely on rowboats, small sailboats, and simple hand-fashioned equipment. A prolific ecosystem more than compensated for primitive gear.

The largest boats typically employed were the Muscongus Bay boats, centerboarders with lines otherwise similar to what would later be called Friendship sloops. In 1880 those boats ranged from sixteen to twenty-six feet in length; they all measured well under 5 tons. With small cuddy cabins and floored-over ballast, and with large cockpits and built-in benches, square-sterned Muscongus Bay sloops could be easily handled by one man tending lobster traps. Sometimes two men worked together. An eighteen-foot boat of that design then cost $80; a twenty-five-footer, $200. The average boat in the Maine lobster fleet set 58 traps in 1880, though the number used by each fisherman or each boat ranged from 10 to 125. As the biggest boats in the fleet, Muscongus Bay boats probably set more traps than did men lobstering from peapods or dories. Some traps were set singly, and others connected in strings, which the fishermen called "trawls." All hauling was hand-over-hand, and men knew that hauling at low tide and slack water was considerably easier than at high tide or with the current running hard. Ominously enough, Fish Commission naturalist Richard Rathbun noted as early as 1880 that "The fishermen claim that they are obliged to set a greater number now than formerly in order to obtain the same catch."[93]

In addition to the Muscongus Bay boats, some simpler "two-sail lobster boats," fourteen to twenty feet in length, were favored by lobstermen in Maine during the 1870s and 1880s. They were rigged with a boomed mainsail and a lug foresail, but they had no bowsprit or jib. These boats were decked forward and aft, and wide washboards ran along the sides, leaving an oval-shaped cockpit in the center for the men and the lobsters. Such boats could be rowed or sailed; but all stayed close to home. Single-handed lobstermen often removed the mainmast and mainsail, carrying only the lug foresail. When reverting to ground-fishing later in the season they rerigged the mainmast. Another craft extensively used by lobstermen in that era was the "Maine Reach boat." About fourteen feet long, these were entirely open, and could be rowed or sailed. Around 1870 the double-enders that became known as "peapods" were introduced, and quickly became a favorite of inshore lobstermen, especially in lower Penobscot Bay. Generally arranged only for rowing, peapods were about 15½ feet long, with a 4½-foot beam. The rocker in their keels made them very maneuverable under oars, and with a lineage descended from double-ended Viking ships, they were wholesome in nasty conditions. Peapods could accommodate one or two men, plus traps. Lobstermen in the northern reaches of Penobscot Bay, however, favored the Cape Roseway wherry, a lapstrake boat with a sharp bow, round bilge, narrow flat bottom, and narrow heart-shaped stern. A sleek variant of the dory, these boats were twelve to eighteen feet long, but insufficiently forgiving to be sailed safely. However, they were easily driven under oars. The simplest boats from which Mainers lobstered commercially were common dories, sturdy fourteen- to eighteen-foot rowboats that could be bought for as little as ten dollars. Finally, Maine's lobster fleet in 1880 included eight well smacks, sloops or schooners between five and twenty tons that supplied the canneries and market centers by freighting lobsters.

Simple traps complemented the simple boats. The earliest were hoop-net pots, essentially a simple ring (often a hogshead hoop from 2½ to 3 feet in diameter) to which a shallow net bag was attached. "Two wooden half hoops were bent above it, crossing at right angles in the center about 12 or 15 inches above the plane of the hoop," explained one of the agents of the U.S. Fish Commission in Maine. "Sometimes these half hoops were replaced by short cords. The bait was suspended from the point of crossing of the two wooden hoops and the line for raising and lowering the pot was attached at the same place." Fishermen added a few rocks for ballast. They simply lowered the baited hoop net over the side, waited a while, and hauled it back—often with a lobster or two. Of course lobsters came and went at will, and the men were limited to tending only a few pots at a time. Moreover, the system seemed to work best at night. All these inconveniences led to the development of the lath trap, an apparatus that fishermen believed would hold lobsters after they entered it, and would thus require only occasional visits for tending. Built of the common rough-sawn laths used in plaster walls, lath traps were typically 4 feet long, 2 feet wide, 1½ feet high, and semicylindrical in shape. Funnel-shaped openings at each end of the trap, knitted of coarse twine, tapered to an iron ring or wooden hoop. Lobsters crawled up the tapering net funnel, through the ring, and into the trap to eat the bait. Fishermen thought it was difficult for trapped lobsters to escape. Recently that assumption has been disproved; lobsters seem to come and go as they wish. Nevertheless, the ecosystem was sufficiently productive in the late nineteenth century that crude lath traps, weighted with rocks, retained enough lobsters to make the arrangement work.[94]

The composition of the fleet and the equipment used reveal just how much of an inshore fishery this was. Even with a strong back and a fair current, a man cannot get very far in a heavy wooden rowboat laden with traps. Fishing primarily in the summer, and setting traps in water sufficiently shallow to haul them by hand, lobstermen in Maine and Atlantic Canada (where similar gear prevailed) found enough lobsters to supply canneries and dealers with millions of pounds a year for several decades. But they were skimming the cream, and each year that skimming became more difficult. Boats got bigger, traps more numerous, and depths fished greater as the lobster population shrank.

By the 1870s laments about the future of lobsters had become commonplace. In 1872 W. L. Faxon wrote to Massachusetts' fish commissioners that "this valuable crustacean has been pretty closely fished in Massachusetts waters for the last ten years, and the value of the catch is decreasing yearly and rapidly." Faxon regretted that the state had no laws whatsoever for the protection of lobsters, and that large numbers were sold "of less than one pound each, and also many spawn lobsters." In 1873 Spencer F. Baird wrote from Washington to Maine's fish commissioners advocating a closed season on lobster, and arguing that "unless something be done to regulate this branch of industry, it will before long become practically worthless." Baird noted the rapid expansion of the fishery for canning and admitted that the decline of lobster stocks had "come at an earlier period than was anticipated." The ecosystem simply did not have the reserve buoyancy to withstand fishermen's incessant demands. That same year a principal in the firm of Johnson and Young in Boston lamented the "falling off in catch, and decrease in size" of lobsters taken in Massachusetts, and pointed accusingly at the canneries, "which use everything, without regard to size or condition, leaving nothing to grow or reproduce."[95]

Canners' interests diverged sharply from those of fresh-lobster dealers, and the early skirmishes over lobster conservation in northern New England pitted proponents of one against the other. Cannery operators were content with a closed season between August 1 and October 15, when canneries concentrated on the summer vegetable harvest and avoided lobsters (some of which were shedding, and were disdainfully referred to as "soft shells"). Those months were vital, however, for the summer resort live lobster trade. That business favored the plate-sized ten-and-a-half inch animals, while the canners preferred to pay less per pound for "snappers," the shrimpy-sized immatures. Maine's legislators responded to the growing crisis in the lobster fishery in 1872, with a prohibition on keeping, buying, or selling "berried" females. (After mating female lobsters extrude fertilized eggs, carrying them externally on their abdomens, where the eggs look like berries.) That law could easily be evaded; an enterprising fisherman just had to scrape off the eggs. In 1874 Maine's legislature deferred to the canners and imposed a closed season for lobsters between August 1 and October 15. That same year, however, the Massachusetts legislature, influenced more strongly by the live-lobster dealers, imposed a minimum size of ten-and-a-half inches. Maine experimented with a similar law in 1879, and passed a ten-and-a-half-inch law in 1883.[96]

Those laws spelled the beginning of the end for lobster canneries in Maine, the only New England state where they had existed. Between 1889 and 1892 the number of lobster canneries decreased from twenty to eleven. In 1895 lobster canning ceased altogether in Maine, though by then much of the canneries' expertise and capital had relocated to the Maritime Provinces of eastern Canada. By 1885 employees in nearly 400 canneries were busily at work in Prince Edward Island, New Brunswick, Nova Scotia, and Quebec, many underwritten by Americans. By 1892 more than 600 factories were canning lobster in those provinces, served by lobstermen fishing more than 750,000 traps.[97]

Canneries had been a big part of the problem, with their willingness to devour immatures. Nevertheless, conservation laws of every stripe were routinely ignored by Canadian and New England fishermen during the 1870s and 1880s, as lobster stocks continued to shrink. Fishermen protested that it was "difficult" to measure lobsters as they were taken from the traps; moreover, that unscrupulous fishermen would keep the shorts and scrape eggs from the spawners, so why should anyone comply with the law? A Boston police chief noted in 1884 that the lobster law was a joke: "It is alleged by many honest dealers, that large numbers of short lobsters are taken in every catch." Rarely were they thrown back. For a while New York had no size limit, and smackmen from the Empire State could buy short lobsters with impunity in Massachusetts or Maine. Some fishermen snapped the tails off shorts and boiled them right on their boats, selling the meat to tourists and summer boarders. Most did not regard themselves as beyond the pale for such behavior, so commonly was the law flouted. By 1887 W. H. Proctor, one of Massachusetts' deputy fish commissioners, admitted that the law restricting size simply was not working to protect lobsters. Arrests and convictions occurred, but in light of the extent of the coast, and the numbers of men involved, arrests were minimal. Wardens felt that the only effective regulation would be a closed season, when all catching or selling of lobsters would be illegal.[98]

Eastern Canada's lobster industry lagged behind that of the United States during the 1840s and 1850s. As late as 1869 it was worth only $15,275—a fraction of the New England harvest. Dr. Lavoie, a Canadian fisheries officer, noted ominously in 1876: "The ruin of the lobster fishery on the shores of the United States ought to warn and at the same time teach us a lesson which we should take advantage of; that is, to regulate, with as little delay as possible, the mode of carrying on this fishery." By then lobstering in New Brunswick, Nova Scotia, and Prince Edward Island was taking off. The value of the business skyrocketed from just over $15,000 in 1869 to $2,250,000 in 1891. As proceeds went up, lobster stocks and the size of individual animals went down. Ex-Inspector J. H. Duvar, from Prince Edward Island, tabulated returns showing that it took three and a half lobsters to fill a can in 1874, five in 1884, and six or seven in 1892.[99]

Mutually reinforcing indications demonstrated lobsters' plight. Everyone knew that the average size of lobsters landed was free-falling. "When lobster canning was first started at Eastport," Rathbun noted, "the lobsters were said to have ranged in weight from about 3 to 10 pounds; after 3 or 4 years time however, the average weight was reduced to about 2 pounds, and for a considerable period no lobsters weighing less than 2 pounds were considered fit for canning." By the mid-1880s, when he was gathering that information, most lobsters going into cans weighed only one pound each, far from sexual maturity. Experts likewise agreed that the effort expended to catch lobsters had risen dramatically. In 1864 lobsters were so abundant at Mussel Ridge, the southwestern extremity of Penobscot Bay, "that three men tending from 40 to 50 traps would catch all the lobsters which one smack was able to carry to market" each week. Those men fished from rowboats. By 1879 "the same smack had to buy the catch of 15 men in order to obtain full fares." Meanwhile lobstermen were fishing deeper and deeper waters. "On the coast of Maine, the evidences of decrease are very strong," explained the fish commissioner, "but the rapid extension of the grounds into comparatively deep water has made the actual decrease less apparent."[100]

It was the same story, in the same decade, told of menhaden and halibut. As demand escalated, fishermen put more pressure on stocks, and they quickly found themselves fishing in much deeper water than anyone had imagined possible just a decade earlier. Commercially valuable species' depletion from the shallows was palpable, immediate, and profound.

The state of Maine began to compile consistent landings data for lobster in 1880. In 1886 23 million pounds were landed; in 1888, 21.7 million pounds. Peak landings occurred in 1889, with 24.4 million pounds. Of course, everyone at the time remembered that the real boom had been back during the early 1870s, long before records were kept. In any event, lobster landings in Maine spiraled downward after 1889. By 1899 landings were only half as large as a decade previously. More ominously, the number of traps set had nearly tripled. Maine's lobster landings rose briefly at the turn of the century, then fell to a new low of 11.1 million pounds in 1905. Modest recovery occurred in the next decade, but by 1919 landings were down to 5.7 million pounds—one-fifth of those of 1889. Maine's lobster landings would not reach the 1889 level again until 1957. By then effort expended had risen astronomically. Fishermen had larger motorized boats with mechanical haulers, and they set 565,000 traps to catch the same weight of lobsters landed from just 121,000 traps in the age of sail and oar, when traps were hauled by hand in shallow water.

A generation of reckless harvesting during the middle of the nineteenth century had driven to its knees one of Maine's most valuable fisheries, although the ecological damage was masked by market forces. While Maine's lobster landings had fallen by 50 percent from 1889 to 1898, lobstering remained the most profitable fishery in the state in 1898, with total proceeds of $937,239. Thus, as supplies fell, the price received by fishermen rose. Their bottom line was not in as tough shape as the benthic community, though by 1898 the average Maine lobster trap caught only 78 pounds of lobster, compared to 136 pounds only twelve years before. In that coupled human-and-natural system, what mattered most to humans was the price-point. By 1900 there was "much satisfaction expressed among fishermen as to the present condition of the lobster fishery." Yields from their traps had improved from the previous year, though they were still far from those of 1886. More importantly, the total return to Maine's fishermen had risen by $66,059, an increase of almost

7 percent. Complacency with the system as it was overshadowed memories of how much more productive it had been just fifteen years earlier.[101]

Eastern Canada's lobster saga closely followed that of Maine. An initial high point in lobster landings from New Brunswick, Nova Scotia, and Prince Edward Island (but not including Newfoundland, which was not yet part of the Dominion of Canada) came in 1886, with 15,286 metric tons—equivalent to 33.7 million pounds, approximately one-and-a-half times the landings in Maine that year. Everyone knew the fishery could not sustain that sort of pressure. Nova Scotia's inspector of fisheries, W. H. Rogers, noted in 1883 "that the natural source of supply is being overtaxed." The following year Inspector Duvar, from Prince Edward Island, wrote: "The lobster fishery has taken another year's step toward its early extinction." In 1886 Cape Breton's fisheries officer, A. C. Bertram, stated that the lobster fishery had attained its "limit of expansion." Canada's maximum lobster landings came in 1898. Then stocks crashed, and landings fell almost steadily for twenty years, bottoming out in 1918, and remaining low until the 1950s. Total lobster landings reported in eastern Canada did not reach their 1898 level until 1987—a slump of almost ninety years. By then, of course, the effort expended to land those lobsters had increased exponentially, and the nature of the coastal ecosystem had changed dramatically.[102]

Removing organisms from a system changes ecosystem structure and function, and ultimately influences that system's ability to provide goods and services. Every fisherman noted how the geographic range and distribution of many valuable organisms had changed; notably, that such organisms had "retreated" to deeper water, or given up frequenting coasts and bays where they always had been found. The makeup of marine communities thus changed dramatically within a very compressed time frame, both in narrowly circumscribed places such as Eggemoggin Reach or the Mussel Ridge Channel, and on vast underwater plateaus such as Georges Bank. Removing most of the halibut and lobsters, for instance—including virtually all of those species' large individuals—affected the nature of predator-prey relations in the benthic marine ecosystem. Adult lobsters preyed upon crabs, mollusks, worms, amphipods, urchins, algae, and some fish. In turn, lobsters were eaten by rays, crabs, sharks, and numerous fish, including cod, goosefish, wolfish, tautog, and sea bass. Removing lobsters from much of the system distorted the food web.

Halibut ultimately were nearly exterminated. Their ecological niche was later filled by other species, and halibut never regained their foothold in the benthic ecosystem in which they had been apex predators for millennia. Other fluctuations induced or accelerated by human activity are more difficult to establish. Turbidity, for instance, may have increased in sections of the Gulf of Maine as a result of absence of menhaden for years; menhaden normally filtered the water column. Yet menhaden's sudden and inexplicable return to coastal Maine in 1890 suggests, at least, that even as mackerel and lobster stocks continued to decline, some dimensions of the system could be self-healing. Certainly the natural biological diversity, age distribution, and geographic distribution of organisms in shallow water throughout the Gulf of Maine and eastern Canada had been significantly affected by human activity by 1900.[103]

Commercial fishing pressure in the late nineteenth century removed considerable biomass from the northwest Atlantic ecosystem, and the implications are still not fully understood. Not only did the cod fishery continue to remove hundreds of thousands of metric tons each year, but newly invigorated fisheries targeting menhaden, mackerel, halibut, haddock, and lobster withdrew biomass from the system. How such removals affect nutrient cycling and primary productivity, much less productivity of the more complex organisms desired by people, is not yet precisely measurable, though it is difficult to imagine that such removals are meaningless in terms of long-range resiliency and ecosystem productivity. During the late nineteenth century those observers who did not assume that the natural system was inscrutable or eternal, nevertheless imagined it in fairly mechanistic or linear terms. Professor Francis H. Herrick, then the most prominent lobster biologist in the United States, noted in 1897 that "The [lobster] fishery is declining, and this decline is due to the persistence with which it has been conducted during the last twenty-five years." He argued that killing fewer lobsters would allow more to reproduce, giving fishermen a larger stock from which to draw.[104]

Marine ecosystems function in terms of multiple timescales, simultaneously tidal, seasonal, life-span (which can range from days to decades, depending upon the organism), and in light of multidecadal fluctuations, such as the North Atlantic Oscillation. There is no "normal." Confronted by the serial collapse of menhaden, mackerel, halibut, and lobster stocks during the 1870s, 1880s, and 1890s, none of the best and brightest minds from within fishing communities or fish commissions imagined the possibility that the legacy of human actions in one decade on one part of the ecosystem might not be felt until decades later, and possibly in another part of the ecosystem. Constrained by the tools at their disposal and the assumptions of their age, which included new-found faith in objective scientific investigation, they could not imaginatively stay ahead of changes occurring in the sea around them.

Rathbun's tortured composure, as he sought to present his findings on the "relative abundance of lobsters" in 1885 "without prejudice or undue comment," reflects how rapidly such depletions had overwhelmed scientific, regulatory, and fishing communities. He did not allow himself to sound an unseemly alarm. "The only satisfactory way of determining the question," he observed coolly, after reiterating chapter and verse on the decline of lobster stocks, "would be to institute a thorough and careful investigation of the entire lobster region under the authority of the National Government or of the several States."[105] As mackerel, lobster, and halibut landings continued to free-fall during the early 1890s, the federal act prohibiting mackerel-fishing during the spring was due to expire on June 1, 1892. Would the fishery be opened again without restriction, and what would influence the debate?

Despite the mackerel preservation law, landings of America's favorite food fish continued to fall. From 1884 to 1888 the annual catch of mackerel by American and Canadian fishermen had fallen from 478,000 barrels to 48,000—a decline of 90 percent. The catch in 1890 was lower than that of any year since the War of 1812, when the commercial mackerel fishery with hand jigs had been in its infancy, and when British fleets blockading the coast had bottled up fishermen in port. Critics of the closed season noted that since the imposition of the law in 1887 until 1890, catches had steadily worsened. Although they crept up incrementally in 1891 and 1892, catches at the end of the experimental five-year closed season were still lower than any since 1817—a catastrophe for what had been America's most lucrative fishery.

Skeptics insisted that the five-year reduction in effort had made no impact whatsoever on replenishing mackerel stocks. "To justify such repressive laws," argued J. M. K. Southwick, one of Rhode Island's fish commissioners, "it should be made to appear that continued free fishing was working an injury to somebody or something, or destructive to the fish." As far as Southwick was concerned, fishermen could no more exterminate sea fish than annoyed humans could eradicate mosquitoes. "The number of fish in the sea is as far beyond our estimation as the insects and can be no more influenced by legislative acts." He believed all impediments to fishing simply denied hard-working Americans profits to which they were entitled. Many in Congress agreed, and the federal prohibition on spring mackerel fishing was not renewed. Meanwhile, fishermen ignored other restrictions, such as Maine's ban on night fishing in state waters. Fishermen desperate for a fare sought mackerel wherever they could find them.[106]

In 1892 capitalists from the oil and guano industry not only helped derail interest in renewing the closed season on mackerel, but determined to stack the deck in their favor. The Lapham Bill, as it became known (for Rhode Island's two-term, undistinguished Democratic congressman Oscar Lapham, who introduced it on behalf of menhaden oil and guano interests), sought to transfer control of coastal fishing from state to federal authority. The oil and guano interests assumed, rightly, that it would be infinitely easier to influence Congress to throw open coastal waters to industrial fishing than to lobby state legislatures one by one. Claiming superior knowledge, and insisting that science and progress were on their side, advocates of the Lapham Bill marshaled an imposing array of witnesses to testify in Washington, including principals from the U.S. Fish Commission, editors of prominent newspapers, representatives from the wholesale fish associations of Boston, Philadelphia, and New York, spokesmen from the boards of trade of Gloucester and other cities, and delegations from the oil business, the fertilizer interests, the shoe and cotton trades, and the net and twine associations. Arrayed against them and their abundant financial resources were a few congressmen from Maine and Massachusetts, an attorney retained by Maine's Commission of Sea and Shore Fisheries, and Maine's fish commissioner, acting on behalf of boat and weir fishermen with limited means. It appeared to be a classic David-and-Goliath struggle.[107]

The Lapham Bill would revolutionize control of state fisheries and, as critics pointed out, "throw them all open to indiscriminate slaughter." It was an open secret that the Lapham Bill had been proposed and supported by the Church brothers, from Tiverton, Rhode Island, convicted lawbreakers as some saw it, because their menhaden steamers had been caught illegally seining porgies in waters controlled by Massachusetts in 1889. Convicted in lower court, the Churches appealed to the Massachusetts Supreme Judicial Court, and ultimately to the U.S. Supreme Court. After losing every step of the way they determined to rewrite the rules of the game and to bypass the onerous state prohibitions that had troubled their skipper. The Churches and others in the menhaden guano and oil business assumed that uncaught fish were wasted; they assumed as well that fish in the coastal ecosystem rightly belonged to those who got them first, without restraint of a meddling government. Opponents feared that the Lapham Bill, if passed, would not only nullify state laws regulating schooling fish such as menhaden and mackerel, but might well be applied to oysters, alewives, salmon, shad, and all other fish.

Marshall McDonald, who had replaced Spencer F. Baird as head of the U.S. Fish Commission, backed the bill not only in the interest of streamlining regulation and enhancing the influence of the Fish Commission, but because he fervently believed in deregulation and in expanding American commercial fisheries. One critic lamented the "radical change in the policy of the commission" following Baird's death, noting that in its early days the Fish Commission had been directed to "preservation of the natural bounties" and "the interest of the consumer." In comparison, the commission's most recent report "reserves its highest encomium for the greatest number of fish killed. . . . All increase in the destructive power of the apparatus used is warmly welcomed. . . . No eventual scarcity; no incidental injury to worthy shore fishermen, trouble such bright tabulators." The U.S. Fish Commission had been founded in 1871 because of fears that valuable fish were diminishing. Commissioner McDonald's determination to back the Lapham Bill revealed him as less a trustee for threatened resources than an advocate for industrial expansion.[108]

Conservationists believed state control of coastal waters would be better for preservation of marine resources. Arguing that states had always been vigilant in protecting the resources on which citizens depended, Charles F. Chamberlayne, an attorney who opposed the bill, claimed that from the states' perspectives "the end was always the same—preservation; the dangers to be guarded against were always the same—extermination by indiscriminate and excessive fishing." His interpretation did not conform exactly to the facts, but he and his allies feared worse to come. Invoking the right of states to manage their own resources without federal meddling, Chamberlayne painted a grim picture of what would happen should the bill pass. "Congress can open Chesapeake Bay to all comers; can ruin every herring fishery in New England; can sweep all spawn-bearing food fish into the guano crusher."[109]

Opponents claimed rightly that "organized capital, to the amount of millions of dollars," was arrayed "against unorganized and poor fishermen along our coast." The "Menhaden Trust"—opponents' derisive term for the fish-oil and guano industry, and its lobbyists—was imposing. Organized at the national level and in some states, it would become more influential in a few years with incorporation of the American Fisheries Company in New Jersey. Capitalized with $10 million in 1898, that company bought the menhaden fleets and factories on eastern Long Island. Among its major stockholders was John E. Searles, of the so-called "Sugar Trust." The Standard Oil Company owned a considerable piece as well, having devised a method to mix petroleum refuse and menhaden oil to produce illuminating oil. The menhaden oil and guano interest was wealthy, organized, politically sophisticated, and accustomed to prevailing. It also operated the sole industrial fishery in the United States, as menhaden were the only fish routinely pursued with steam vessels, and one of the few processed in factories. (Other than oil and guano rendering plants, lobster and sardine canneries were the only factories processing seafood.) The Lapham Bill would open the door to industrial fishing.[110]

Confronted by the implications, Edwin W. Gould, Maine's fisheries commissioner, made a poignant case for caution. Gould attacked what he considered to be an unholy alliance of the Menhaden Trust and the U.S. Fish Commission. The menhaden interest opposed all regulations, and worried that restrictions on mackerel fishing would lead to restrictions on menhaden fishing. "Their points are always few and simple," Gould wrote. "To them fish are of limitless fecundity, and no efforts of man can have any appreciable effect upon the result." Gould articulated simple principles that he believed should guide fisheries policy. "The fecundity of fish is not a defense against man's rapacity." Then, "Fish obey laws such as to render protection essential." Furthermore, "Menhaden fisheries can and do diminish the supply." Increased effort and decreasing catches made the case. "In 1881," he pointed out, "it took three times as many men and three times as many steamers as in 1874 to get less fish and one-third the oil."[111]

Accusing the U.S. Fish Commission and the menhaden trust of being blind to "eventual scarcity," Gould invoked the lessons of history. "Probably the persons who made our buffalo a reminiscence thought that with the enormous herds on our prairies no hunting for skins could materially affect the supply. The men who practically exterminated the whale fishery may have felt that, in the power of the whale's escape into inaccessible depths, a refuge was provided which set a limit to the effects of their own energy. The Canadian seal fishers off the Aleutian Islands may feel a serene confidence that they are operating upon an unlimited field. It is the same old story. The buffalo is gone; the whale is disappearing; the seal fishery is threatened with destruction." For Gould the situation was clear: "Fish need protection."[112]

Gould and his allies won the battle but lost the war. Congress chose not to surrender state control to federal authority, but the telling arguments were more about states' rights than fisheries conservation. Meanwhile mackerel catches remained poor, and critics continued to protest. "Nature sends them to us," noted a science writer concerned with the mackerel supply in 1893, "and we should profit by their approach; but we must not use unnatural methods or times to reap the harvest." A critic in 1901 accused the "Greed of the Fish Trust" of "Destroying the Mackerel Industry." As he saw it, "the decline of the mackerel industry is primarily due to the method of catching the fish, and really due to insufficient legislation and laxly enforced laws."[113]

By then the U.S. Fish Commission had existed for thirty years and could point to a prodigious output of publications, reports, and bulletins—studies of both natural science and "economic ichthyology," or the social science of fisheries. Considerably more was known about fish and fisheries than had been the case thirty years earlier, but despite indefatigable work by the federal fish commission and various state fish commissions, many fish stocks had continued to decline. While some individual fisheries, such as the mackerel industry, faced catastrophic losses, most fisheries, such as those for lobster and menhaden, found compensation for ecological depletion through rising prices. The market masked the mess.

One lesson from the virtually simultaneous crashes of menhaden, mackerel, halibut, and lobster eluded commentators at the time. Those four fisheries represented an extraordinary spectrum of gear, a range of appliances and boats so vast that it barely seemed worth discussing in the same breath. Lobstermen fished from dories, peapods, and tiny sailboats, hauling homemade traps by hand in shallow water. Halibut and mackerel crews manned what were then the finest sail-powered fishing vessels in the world, schooners that could navigate horrific conditions and fish at great depths. Menhaden fishers were pioneering the industrial fisheries of the future. With their steamers, their mighty purse seines, their steam-powered hoisting apparatus, and the rendering plants to which they delivered fish, menhaden fishers represented an industrial colossus about as far removed as possible from a lone lobsterman rowing his peapod against the tide. Of course, it was not the gear that determined whether a species such as lobster or halibut would be pushed to the brink, but the animating spirit behind it, the sense that nature existed separately from humans, that ecological depletion would naturally accompany economic expansion, and that the immortal sea would buffer itself somehow from human-induced catastrophe. By the turn of the century American and Canadian fishermen, representing their societies' values and dreams and ambitions, were depleting coastal resources from both peapods and steamers, looking to short-term profit and capital accumulation at the level of village, company, and trust, and delaying their day of reckoning despite jeremiads by Edwin Gould and like-minded conservationists who foresaw the implications.

Six

AN AVALANCHE OF CHEAP FISH

———

Trade in fish is in its infancy.
—*Fishing Gazette,* March 7, 1914

Hₒw could Marshall McDonald, the U.S. fish commissioner in 1895, not feel appreciated? Imitation is the sincerest form of flattery, and distinguished Europeans then sought to emulate the successes of American scientists. "Knowing the good results which have been obtained in your country with the artificial propagation of cod," wrote Msr. Principe DiGangi from Palermo, "I beg that you will give me a detailed description of the methods and apparatus employed, as it is desired to try the experiment in the Mediterranean with the tunny and other marine fishes, which have for some years been very rare . . . America may well be the teacher of Sicily."[1]

As DiGangi sensed, American experts at the turn of the century seemed determined to augment the once-fabled productivity of the sea, and capable of doing it to boot. Exuding the confidence of men with a robust research program of national importance, and a budget to match, they pushed "economic ichthyology" to its limits. Congress appropriated $589,480 in 1901. By 1914 the commission's annual budget exceeded one million dollars. One-third went to propagating food fishes. Each year commission employees cultivated juvenile cod, lobster, flounder, and other valuable species at hatcheries, and experimented with seeding clam beds, raising oysters, and transplanting marine species to potentially promising habitats. A report in 1901 proudly explained that "Up to and including the season of 1896–97, the number of cod fry liberated by the Commission on the east coast was 449,764,000. . . . The unmistakable economic results which have attended these efforts warrant all the time and money devoted to them." In 1907, as part of a transplantation initiative, 1,011 mature lobsters (many bearing eggs) were shipped by rail from the Atlantic coast to Seattle and released around the San Juan Islands. A milestone in scientists' relentless efforts to bolster the nation's supply of seafood, it was "the largest plant of adult lobsters ever attempted."[2]

That national strategy of assisting an enfeebled nature seemed logical to Massachusetts officials in 1905. "The true solution lies not in limiting the demand through prohibition of . . . nets, traps, beam and otter trawls," they argued, "but rather in developing methods likely to secure an increased supply of fish, such as artificial propagation." So brood cod were retained in pools at Woods Hole for spawning. Simultaneously spawn-takers working at collection stations in Kittery Point, Maine, and Plymouth, Massachusetts, obtained eggs from ripe fish caught commercially, eggs that otherwise would have been destroyed as the fish were gutted. Dressed to resist the March cold that swept across unprotected decks of fishing smacks, spawn-takers massaged the soft white abdomens of gravid cod, squirting their roe into wooden buckets of seawater, before handing the doomed fish to the gutters who butchered them. Floating in buckets, the orphaned eggs looked like clusters of clear, round, glass beads, each about as big as the head of a large pin. Salvaged eggs were transferred by the millions to hatcheries at Gloucester and Woods Hole, along with containers of creamy white milt squeezed from the males. After fertilization, in which a little milt went a long way, and hatching under the watchful eye of technicians, the government-assisted cod fry were liberated along New England's coast.[3]

Participants considered this process more sensible than farming; after reintroduction to the sea, juvenile fish required no further care, shelter, or food from their handlers. Ichthyologists convinced themselves that enough would mature and be caught by fishermen to justify the effort. Meanwhile they studied what they could. Mother fish in U.S. Fish Commission pools, for instance, fared better than breeders caught commercially. After spawning they were numbered, tagged, and recorded before being returned to the ocean. Naturalists hoped that data from tagged fish would help them understand cod's migration and growth rate.[4]

Scientists and bureaucrats at the U.S. Fish Commission believed they were doing everything humanly possible to preserve commercially valuable fish from extermination and—by simultaneously keeping detailed statistics of landings and effort—to assess the changing nature of wild fish stocks. Problems persisted, however, and they were hard to ignore, despite the folk wisdom of rustic fishermen, such as the old-timer "of wide experience" who, when asked why catches were down, opined, "Fish have fins and tails with which they can come and go as they please, and that is all I know about it." More-systematic thinkers attributed the paucity of fish to other causes. In 1900 a biologist's requiem on the British fisheries appeared in the *Fishing Gazette,* the trade paper of the American industry. "Now every nook and corner of the sea, every bank and pit round the British Isles, is known and fished over, again and again. Nature cannot produce fishes fast enough to balance the quantity man removes," Walter Garstang explained. As he saw it, "New grounds cannot be found out forever, and steamboats are being built so fast nowadays that in a few more years fish will be so scarce on the new grounds as they now are on the old." A Bostonian put it more succinctly: "Man has not yet ceased to regard the ocean as an inexhaustible mine."[5]

An intermittent drumbeat of concern reverberated against turn-of-the-century Americans' optimistic faith in science, success, and the blessings of modern improvements, at least where fisheries were concerned. In 1906 the federal fish commissioner insisted that states with migratory anadromous fishes should "promptly enact the legislation necessary to insure that a certain proportion of each season's run shall be permitted to reach the spawning grounds." He knew that insufficient fish were being allowed to breed. That same year Massachusetts' commissioners of fisheries and game insisted that the nation needed to confront "the degree and kind of protection which must be extended to the marine food fishes, *e.g.* the mackerel, menhaden, herring, alewife, striped bass, bluefish, and other important species, which are not, like the shad, known with certainty to be rapidly approaching commercial extinction, but which nevertheless appear to be in danger on account of the tremendous inroads made by man." By then everyone knew that Atlantic salmon, sturgeon, and shad populations were free-falling. It looked as though other species would follow. A former game warden from Maryland published an extremely critical essay in 1908 lamenting the lack of fisheries protection nationwide, and highlighting the incongruity of spending hundreds of thousands of dollars on fish propagation while persistently neglecting protection. Only protection, he insisted, could save "from extermination one of the greatest natural food products of the world." Even trade publications such as the *Fishing Gazette* occasionally toned down their untrammeled promotion of the industry to raise a cautionary flag. An issue from 1911 had a feature story whose headline and subheaders said it all:

NOW IS THE TIME TO CONSERVE OUR ALASKA FISHERIES.
Capt. H. B. Joyce Sounds Note of Warning in Behalf of
Pacific Ocean Halibut and Salmon.
*Do Not Repeat, He Urges, on the West Coast, the Experience of
Our Fishermen along the Atlantic Shore.*

Wherever one turned, the need for conservation of fisheries resources seemed extraordinarily pressing, despite the aggressive federal program of artificial propagation.[6]

By 1911 the U.S. Fish Commission had existed for forty years and had spent millions of dollars on research, propagation, and protection of fish. Several of the New England states' fish commissions were even older, and though state budgets were less expansive, those agencies had been working to perpetuate sea fish for half a century. That said, all their pronouncements remained Janus-faced at best, alternating between the light of hope and the shadow of despair. A great deal of uncertainty attended artificial propagation. Optimistic fisheries professionals tried to put a positive spin on their accomplishments, but everyone knew that stocks appeared to be decreasing in spite of the efforts. Observers could not help but believe that "the despoliation of this great national resource will continue to its ultimate destruction," as one *New York Times* reporter wrote, unless radical steps were implemented. The state of the living ocean had never seemed so precarious.[7]

In July 1914, shortly after the assassination of Austria-Hungary's Archduke Franz Ferdinand, that same *New York Times* reporter forecast an inexorable march to disaster: "Extermination Threatens American Sea Fishes—Cost to Consumer Has Risen between 10 and 600 Per Cent Because of Decrease in Supply." By then the U.S. Fish Commission (subsequently the Bureau of Fisheries) had been compiling data for decades to chart the condition of the nation's fish supply. The bureau's own statistics provided a series of dots that were easy to connect, dots that told a decidedly somber story to the investigative reporter and those willing to listen.[8]

From 1880 to 1908 the number of American fishermen had increased by 50 percent, the capital invested had increased by 80 percent (not including shore properties), and the value of boats and gear had increased by 65 percent—

during which time there had been a *decrease* of 10 percent in the total quantity of fish landed annually. The actual story was more complicated than such a summary suggests. The tonnage of the fleet registered for the cod and mackerel fishery had declined during those years (in part because the shortage of mackerel led fishermen to withdraw from mackereling), but the number of weirs, pound nets, and fish traps along shore had exploded during the same period. The human population had grown. Catching power had expanded. During those years—the high point of artificial propagation of fish—the *catch* of cod had fallen by 8 percent; clams, 10 percent; mackerel, 25 percent; menhaden, 30 percent; New England lobsters, 50 percent; bluefish, 56 percent; Atlantic halibut, 65 percent; shad 80 percent; Atlantic sturgeon and New England salmon, even more. Despite largely increased effort, and sophisticated technology to catch and propagate fish, landings were down. Fishermen traveled farther, fished deeper, and brought home less. The only logical conclusion was not that the fish had swum away, but that fewer fish were to be found.[9]

Bright spots, indicated by increased landings of certain species, were all too easily explained. The flounder catch, for example, rose 360 percent from 1880 to 1908. Flounder had rarely been targeted by hook fishermen. Flounders' mouth tissue was insubstantial and their mouths small. Hook fisheries weren't particularly successful. But with the beam trawls introduced at Cape Cod just before the turn of the century, towed by sailing smacks, flounders could be captured en masse. Flounders were taken in weirs, too. Increased landings resulted from more efficient technology, not from flounders' generative abilities. Similarly, pollock landings had risen a whopping 380 percent, because pollock (previously fished with hooks) were now taken in purse seines.[10]

The increase in Pacific halibut catches, up 230 percent, told a different story. After overfishing Atlantic halibut the industry shifted its base from Gloucester to Puget Sound, in the state of Washington. Let loose on virgin Pacific stocks, fishermen increased their catches. No matter where one looked, whether at benthic fish, pelagic fish, or shellfish, few commercially fished stocks seemed able to keep up with the demands placed on them in the early twentieth century. The real compensation for decreased catches came in prices. Though landings were down, market value of the annual catch increased 54 percent between 1880 and 1908. With consumers paying more, fishermen could still make a living. And, clearly, there were still fish in the sea. But given the U.S. Fish Commission's carefully gathered statistics, and its tale of woe despite the aggressive research and propagation program, what did the future hold?[11]

Human pressure on ecosystem goods and services always reflects human population size, available technology, custom (including culture and law), desire, and the degree to which people are willing to acknowledge the consequences of their actions. Capitalism does not encourage harvesters to respect the limits of renewable resources, though the same can be said for many other forms of political economy. In the historically specific situation of coastal New England and Atlantic Canada at the turn of the century, the human population of seafood consumers and the catching power of fishing technology were growing willy-nilly, ratcheting up pressure on resources. Profits were substantial. Offsetting that trend was nearly a century of knowledge accrued by harvesters showing that fish stocks were not limitless, and that human pressure (even from small societies with marginally efficient technologies) could affect the long-term health of ecosystems on which people relied. Admittedly, most fisheries scientists persisted in shortsighted convictions despite considerable evidence to the contrary: human technologies could not genuinely affect sea fish; fish stocks might become locally depleted, but nature would replenish them when harvesters moved elsewhere; and artificial propagation in the lab could more than compensate for shortages in nature.

Meanwhile the industry continued to consolidate and become more vertically integrated. In 1906 the Gorton-Pew Fisheries Company incorporated in Gloucester through a merger of the former firms of John Pew & Son, Slade Gorton & Company, Reed & Gamage, and David B. Smith & Company. Owning fifty-five vessels, fifteen wharves, and thirty-five buildings in Gloucester and six other plants in Boston, Maine, Cape Breton, and Newfoundland, and employing 2,000 workers at sea and ashore, Gorton-Pew Fisheries Company had considerable clout. The W. J. Knox Net and Twine Company boasted in 1907 of the efficiencies of vertical integration. Full-page advertisements touted their "cotton twine plant at Mountain Island, North Carolina, and the Flax Thread Mills of W. J. Knox, Ltd. at Kilbirnie, Scotland," which provided fibers and twine for their Baltimore factory, "90,000 square feet of Floor Space, New, built for netting purposes only." Between net and twine companies, wholesale dealers in fish, menhaden oil operations, and other substantial fishing corporations from Baltimore to Nova Scotia, the fish business—as a related set of industries—was thriving.[12]

This was the environment in which decisions would need to be made about appropriate technologies. On the one hand lay citizens' desire for security, short-term profit, and capital accumulation, not to mention the prevailing belief that people had a legitimate (perhaps God-given) right to fish: on the other, two concerns shared by many coastal residents: the long-term viability of the marine ecosystem, and that system's ability to produce food and jobs in the future.

THE END OF THE AGE OF SAIL

"The history of the Gloucester fishery has been written in tears," observed an anonymous reporter in 1876. Fishing made coal mining look safe. No other occupation in America came close to the deep-sea fisheries for workplace mortality. It was as if fishing ports' populations were constantly at war at sea, with news of casualties trickling in year-round. In 1850 four Gloucester vessels were lost, with 39 men, including the schooner *William Wallace,* which disappeared with all eight hands. The infamous "Yankee Gale" of 1851 broke scores of hearts in New England, noted a veteran skipper, after "the northern shores of Prince Edward Island were strewn with broken wrecks and drowned or maimed fishermen." In the twenty-four years between 1866 and 1890 more than 380 schooners and 2,450 men from Gloucester were lost at sea—a chilling average of more than 100 fatalities per year from that single occupation in a town of between 15,000 and 16,000 residents. As Captain Joseph Collins asked in the *Cape Ann Weekly Advertiser* in 1882, "When will the slaughter cease?" The year 1892 was unusual in that no Gloucester vessel was lost with all hands: only 46 fishermen on Gloucester vessels died. Two years later was more typical: Thirty vessels and 135 men went missing from Gloucester. Every fishing town in New England and Atlantic Canada knew the sea as a cruel mistress, and every inhabitant felt personally Sir Walter Scott's words: "It's no fish ye are buying; it's men's lives." Anything to lessen the toll would be welcome.[13]

Improvements in fishing schooner design during the 1880s made schooners stiffer and safer. Still, sailing vessels knocked down by squalls could fill and sink. Monstrous seas on the banks could overwhelm a schooner, causing it to founder. Collisions at night or in the fog inadvertently turned fishermen into their brothers' killers. Among all calamities, the most catastrophic involved sudden gales that caught the fleet exposed on a long lee shore with no harbors of refuge, "when," as a hardened skipper remembered, "the rush of the storm-demon intensifies the blackness, filling the air with mist and driving sea-spume; when death stares each fisher in the face, and nothing can be done except to courageously meet the conditions and make a desperate attempt to work to windward, away from the dangerous breakers and foaming reefs that stretch along the lee beam for miles and miles—a nearly hopeless task, as too often has been proved." By the late nineteenth century, although New England fishing schooners designed by naval architects such as George McClain and Thomas F. McManus were as close-winded and seaworthy as any commercial sailing vessels the world had ever seen, they still confronted the limitations of every sail-driven ship. A schooner could not make headway through many points of the compass in the direction from which the wind blew, at least not in close quarters or gale conditions. But fishermen routinely took risks, pursuing their quarry into places that could become death traps if the wind changed suddenly and violently. Clawing off lee shores, the men knew they were doomed if a crucial bolt broke or a spar carried away. So it had always been.[14]

Reliable steam propulsion radically improved the chances of threatened mariners. A well-found steamer could make headway to windward, sometimes right into the eye of a gale. But while during the late nineteenth century steamboats regularly plied western rivers, and steamships regularly crossed the Atlantic, the expense of a steam engine and the space consumed by engine, coal, and smokestack simply did not make steam propulsion possible in American fishing boats. For fishermen, the bottom line could not accommodate steam, no matter its life-preserving properties. While a few skippers experimented with steam in the 1880s and 1890s, the newspapers of the day insisted that steamers would not replace sail in the fishing fleet because they were too expensive to run. So untimely deaths persisted. As late as the mid-1890s only a handful of American fishing vessels (in a fleet of about 65,000 tons) had auxiliary power.

Gasoline engines revolutionized the fisheries. They offered security, efficiency, and ease from the backbreaking labor of rowing or handling sail. And like the answer to a prayer, they provided headway in frustrating calms and frightening gales. In 1897 Gardner D. Hiscox extolled the future of "Explosive Motors," arguing that "seekers for small power will find in the explosive motor the economical prime-mover so much desired." He called it right. The first two-cycle marine engine built on the east coast of the United States is thought to have been built by Frank and Ray Palmer, in Cos Cob, Connecticut, in 1894. The Palmer brothers built their first production model the next year, a 1½-horsepower engine initially mounted with a propeller in a fifteen-foot Whitehall, a fine-lined rowing boat. She made headway around the harbor without an oar in sight. The Palmer brothers began turning out three or four engines a week in a small factory at Mianus, Connecticut. Among their first satisfied buyers were Long Island Sound oystermen, who found that motorized boats could pull oyster dredges far more efficiently than sailboats. What soon would be known as "internal combustion engines" seemed readily adaptable for marine propulsion. Hiscox referred to at least eight manufacturers producing marine engines in the United States by 1897, including Sintz, Daimler, Wolverine, L. J. Wing & Company, and the Palmer brothers. Every little fishing port soon had a story about its first engine. On Nantucket, Charlie Sayle remembered that the first engine arrived on island in 1902 or 1903 and was installed in one of the catboats used there for scalloping. Sayle soon installed a 1½-horsepower one-lunger in his own dory even as other fishermen converted their vessels. Forman Hawboldt demonstrated the first marine engine in Nova Scotia when he motored around Chester Harbor in 1902. Lunenburg Foundry was soon producing gasoline engines for fishermen.[15]

An article in 1906, "Motorboating at Portland," spotlighted the phenomenon in Maine's largest port. "This city is motorboat mad. New boats appear so rapidly that it is impossible to keep track of them all," enthused the reporter. "About the only craft here that are not fitted with motors are the big coastwise coal-carrying schooners and a few canoes." He exaggerated a mite, but the overall trend was unmistakable. A representative advertisement that year in *The Motorboat* (a new magazine) said "To Owners of Fishing and Working Boats: Models A and D, Two-cycle Lozier Motors from 3 to 15 H.P. are unexcelled for use in Fishing and Working Boats. Heavy and strongly built. Give rated horsepower at low speeds. . . . Make and break, or jump-start ignition." Acadia Two Cycle Engines had an early brochure whose cover illustration featured lobstermen with traps in an open boat propelled by a gas engine, and the slogan "Always Dependable." The message was clear. Here was a revolutionary new means of doing business that no fisherman could afford to be without.[16]

Captain Solomon Jacobs, Gloucester's high-line mackerel fisherman, was first to install a gasoline engine in a substantial schooner. In 1900 the sails of the *Helen Miller Gould* were supplemented by a 35-horsepower engine, replaced shortly thereafter with a 150-horsepower engine, which drove the 149-ton *Gould* at ten knots. As the *Cape Ann Advertiser* proudly explained, "The catch of fish on the American coast is more and more being marketed fresh, and it is to meet these changing conditions that auxiliary power has been installed, that the vessel may make port without being subjected to the calms." Moreover, "by the use of gasoline in a compact space, a smokestack, coal bunkers, and the usual accompaniments of power propulsion are avoided." She was a splendid success—briefly. The *Gould's* early catches broke records, but at the end of October in 1901 she burned to the waterline in Sydney, Nova Scotia, a casualty of an improperly installed fuel system. Knowing that her tanks held 2,000 gallons of gasoline, the crew prudently abandoned ship rather than staying to fight the fire. But the main engine was not Sol Jacobs' only innovation. He also installed a 5-horsepower gas engine with a power takeoff in the seine boat. His crew no longer had to purse the seine or pump the boat by hand; they were convinced of the benefits. Despite the uncertainties of working with gasoline, with the possibility that misfires, backfires, and fuel leaks could create explosions or fires, fishermen raced to adopt internal combustion engines. They also began to reassess the prospects and economies of using steam. Shortly after the *Gould* burned, Captain Jacobs— "the king of the mackerel killers"—ordered a new purpose-built mackerel steamer. The Story shipyard in Essex launched her in March 1902.[17]

By 1902 Massachusetts' mackerel fleet of 108 vessels included 5 steamers and 9 schooners with auxiliary gasoline engines, as well as 94 sailing-only schooners. At Provincetown the 226 boats in the shore fisheries included 11 with steam or gasoline. At Gloucester 15 gasoline-powered boats used chiefly in the lobster, mackerel, and herring fisheries were among the fleet of 148 boats in the shore fisheries. The *Quartette* of Lynn, a fifteen-ton herring boat with a naphtha engine, also featured an electric light for attracting herring at night, reputedly "very satisfactory, more so than the old method of 'torching' the fish with a fire at the bow." Fishermen coined a new term: "power dories." By 1905 14 percent of the inshore fishing boats registered in Maine, and 20 percent of those in Massachusetts, had gasoline engines. Catches rose immediately. "Such boats can make immensely larger catches than the old-fashioned oar-propelled craft," noted one observer. "Owing largely to the greater efficiency of the lobster equipment by the introduction of motor boats, there has been an increase in the quantity of lobsters," noted another.[18]

Massachusetts' fish commissioners waxed romantic about the changing nature of the fisheries in 1905. "The up-to-date Captains Courageous," they noted, "no longer brave the storm in sail-driven boats, but escape the peril by the aid of power-driven craft. Not alone is human life safer (if proper precaution is observed concerning fire), but more regular connection can be made with daily express trains and steamers, by which the day's catch can be in the Boston or New York market in the morning following the catching. The longer time upon the fishing grounds means more fish. The better condition of the fish means higher prices. Less labor at the oars is necessary in case of unfavorable winds. And finally, the year's total profit, barring accident, is certain to be a handsome excess over that of the sailing craft under identical conditions. Instances are not uncommon on our coast where a boat, when equipped with suitable 'auxiliary' engine and screw, has yielded an increased profit of $5,000 or over."[19]

Fishermen's safety, security, and bottom line all demanded that sail give way to internal combustion or steam engines. By 1917, 55 percent of the fleet in Gloucester, 59 percent in Boston, and 80 percent in Provincetown had engines. Motors allowed men to fish longer, harder, and deeper. But if motorized vessels would be the way of the future, the gear that fishermen deployed from them, and the way those lifesaving engines were used, were yet to be determined. Ecologically speaking it was not just the means of propulsion that mattered but the manner in which fish were caught.[20]

OTTER TRAWLS AND THE FUTURE OF THE SEA

As the yield of western Atlantic ecosystems declined around the turn of the century, it became almost inevitable that Americans would turn for advice to Europeans, who had confronted depleted fishing grounds for some time. The ironies were profound. Four hundred years earlier a report on John Cabot's pioneering voyage to Newfoundland had extolled American ecosystems' productivity by arguing that "they could bring so many fish that this kingdom would have no further need of Iceland" or its stockfish. A century later Captain John Smith had marveled about New England's coastal ocean, comparing it to Old England's, whose fisheries' "treasures" had been "wasted" and "abused." For Smith, New England's pristine ocean awaited men on the make. By the time another century had passed, profits from fishing, and the economic linkages associated with it, were propelling the New England colonies to prosperity and paving the way for what would become the Industrial Revolution.[21]

But a 400-year fishing spree, in the context of fluctuating cold and warm periods, had changed the equation. The northwest Atlantic, still productive, was far from the marine dreamscape it had been, even though warming temperatures by 1900 were increasing fish stocks compared to those fifty or sixty years earlier. This was especially true in Newfoundland and Labrador. There, at the northern edge of the western Atlantic boreal marine ecosystem, the combination of improved climate conditions and simple fisheries technology meant that the ecosystem was rebounding, or at least holding its own. In New England and Atlantic Canada, however, given the price structure for seafood and the depletion of inshore grounds, turn-of-the-century fishermen needed to fish harder or find stocks that had not yet been exploited with the gear at their disposal. That necessity put them on the cusp of the trawling revolution.[22]

"Trawl" is one of those confounding nautical terms seemingly coined by sailors to disorient landsmen. During the 1850s and 1860s, the first revolution in American bottom-fishing gear saw handlines superseded by longlines called "trawls." That innovation prompted fears of overfishing, and acrimonious verbal attacks on French factory ships (and then on progressive Americans) who fished with those "tub-trawls." At midcentury every state and provincial assembly with oversight of a commercial sea fishery received petitions to out-law "trawling" (longlining). Shore fishermen from Swampscott, Massachusetts, remember, had argued during the 1850s that "trawling" (longlining) would make haddock scarce as salmon. Later in the century lobster fishers who attached multiple traps to one groundline referred to the device as a "trawl." But "trawl" had always meant something else, too; a net towed across the bottom by a vessel above.

Commercial fishermen historically had waited for fish to come to them. Fish bit a baited hook, explored a cunning trap, or swam into a drift net or weir. Fishermen knew that hooks of a certain size, baited in a certain way and set at a certain depth, were likely to attract a certain kind of fish. Traps, such as lobster pots or eel traps, targeted specific organisms. So did drift nets and gill nets. Constructed with a set mesh size, and deployed in the water column at a certain depth, drift nets and gill nets generally caught the types of fish that fishermen sought, such as herring, mackerel, menhaden, or pilchards. By-catch, the unintentional destruction of nontargeted creatures, was always a consequence of fishing, but it remained minimal in most of those traditional, passive fisheries. Weirs were an exception. They captured everything. But weirs were still passive: the fish had to come to them. Purse seines, coming into vogue in the middle of the nineteenth century, worked differently. Seiners aggressively encircled schools they had spotted, corralling them in a curtain of mesh. Of course purse seining required seeing the fish ahead of time, identifying them, and keeping that targeted school in sight as the seine boat and dory worked to encircle it. For the most part, fishermen using all the techniques prevalent in the western Atlantic before 1895 had a good idea of what they were catching.

A vessel towing a net along the bottom radically redefined the relationship between fisher and fish. Such nets scooped up everything in their path. Young fish and old fish, spawning and spent fish, precious and worthless fish—all were taken, along with weed, coral, rocks, anemones, sea stars, crabs, and anything else in the way. Nets dragged in this fashion had weighted footropes to keep them on the seafloor and gaping mouths with a pronounced overbite. Beam trawls, the first type of this gear, and then otter trawls, a refinement that allowed much larger nets to be fished, did not wait for the fish to come to them. That they were towed through the water marked them as novel; their indiscriminate catching and collateral damage to benthic habitats marked them as radical.

Beam trawls had medieval origins, but they were not deployed on a large scale until the nineteenth century, in part because they caused so much controversy, and in part because they harvested huge volumes of fish that could not be marketed or preserved in that prerefrigeration era. Beam trawls first appear in the historical record in 1376, when Edward III of England heard from aggrieved subjects seeking a ban on a wondrously destructive new form of fishing gear:

> The commons petition the King, complaining that where in creeks and havens of the sea there used to be plenteous fishing, to the profit of the Kingdom, certain fishermen for several years past have subtily contrived an instrument called "wondyrechaun" made in the manner of an oyster dredge, but which is considerably longer, upon which instrument is attached a net so close meshed that no fish be it ever so small which enters therein can escape, but must stay and be taken. And that the great and long iron of the wondyrechaun runs so heavily and hardly over the ground when fishing that it destroys the flowers of the land below water there, and also the spat of oysters, mussels, and other fish upon which the great fish are accustomed to be fed and nourished. By which instrument in many places, the fishermen take such quantity of small fish that they do not know what to do with them; and that they feed and fat their pigs with them, to the great damage of the commons of the realm and the destruction of the fisheries, and they pray for a remedy.

That medieval net was eighteen feet long and ten feet wide, spread open by a ten-foot wooden beam attached to an iron frame at each end. The two frames ran along the bottom like the runners of a sled. Fishermen nailed the top of the net to the beam and weighted the footrope so it dragged on the seafloor. As the frame and the footrope startled the fish, they were scooped into the open maw of the net. A royal commission investigating the complaint decided that the "wondyrechaun" should be restricted to deep waters, and not used near shore or in estuaries. Apparently all parties were satisfied. At least no law or official ruling followed the inquiry. As ecologist Callum Roberts has pointed out, "What is striking about the commoners' petition is that, even at the very beginning, the trawl was perceived as a destructive and wasteful fishing method. Also remarkable is the evident understanding of the biology of the animals people fished and of how these animals relied on biologically rich habitats for survival."[23]

Occasional references to bottom trawls during the late medieval and early modern periods reveal their sporadic use in England, Flanders, and the Netherlands, where they created anger and resentment. For the most part, more traditional hook-fishery methods sufficed. Nevertheless, by 1785 seventy-six sailing trawlers were working out of Brixham, sending fish to London, Bristol, Bath, and Exeter. Brixham supported England's only substantial fleet of beam trawlers at that time. During the early nineteenth century Brixham men fanned out with their trawlers to Channel ports such as Hastings, Ramsgate, and Dover, near which they found large stocks of turbot, brill, and sole, readily taken in trawls. The 1820s were boom times. Each sailing smack could land 1,000 to 2,000 turbot per trip—unimaginably large hauls. Trawlers plucked the low-hanging fruit quickly. By 1840 experienced men claimed that it was very difficult to find a sole or turbot on those grounds. But beam trawling grew in popularity. By the 1870s between 1,600 and 1,700 sailing trawlers fished from Britain. They squabbled with fishermen using longlines, traps, and nets, whose gear the trawlers often destroyed. During the 1870s the set-gear men and the trawler-men learned to work around each other. Trawlers worked the sandy flats, set-gear men the rougher ground that could damage the large, expensive nets. But the ultraefficient trawls, towed for the most part by gaff-rigged yawls, were making a mark. Fisheries scientist G. L. Alward later assessed annual catches of plaice and haddock by four Grimsby smacks. Charting their landings against their effort revealed a dramatic decline in stock density of those two species between 1867 and 1880.[24]

The protoindustrialization of British fishing began during the late 1860s, when paddle-wheel tugs idled during a downturn in shipping were rigged with beam trawls to fish inshore between Sunderland and North Shields. Hauls (and profits) were substantial. By 1878 about fifty paddle-wheel steam tugs were fishing, despite the fact that they were insufficiently seaworthy to go very far offshore. The first British purpose-built steam trawlers, *Zodiac* and *Aires,* were launched in 1881. Designed to go to sea, to fish aggressively with beam trawls, and to retrieve those trawls with steam winches rather than with brute strength, they were revolutionary. Observers noted that they caught four times as much per day as sailing smacks. *Zodiac* and *Aries* had traditional wooden hulls, but soon steam-powered trawlers were built of iron, and then steel.[25]

Trawling unfolded differently in America. In the western Atlantic, scientists surpassed commercial fishermen in promoting the new technology. Spencer F. Baird referred to the beam trawl in 1877 as "a favorite piece of apparatus with the U.S. Fish Commission for capturing specimens," and forecast "that at no distant day" American fisheries might be "prosecuted to a very considerable degree by its aid, although hardly to such an extent as it is employed around Great Britain and off the coasts of France, Holland, and Belgium." Baird noted that on the coasts of Great Britain most of the turbot and sole reaching the market was taken by beam trawls, and he wrote that "it is not too much to say that without its use it would be impossible to furnish the English markets with fish." He did not pause to consider why. Older methods no longer returned sufficient catches because of diminished stocks. But Baird shared Thomas Huxley's assessment of beam trawls, believing they did no damage because it was impossible (as those scientists saw it) for human contrivances to affect the limitless sea.[26]

Captain Alfred Bradford of the schooner *Mary F. Chisholm* pioneered beam trawling in New England. A transplanted Englishman with trawling experience in the old country, he had also longlined from Gloucester and Boston. In 1891 Bradford experimented with a beam trawl aboard the *Chisholm.* Sufficiently satisfied with the results, he persuaded investors from the firm of Benj. Lowe & Son to construct a ninety-five-ton sailing beam trawler, a near replica of the best English models, plumb-stemmed and yawl-rigged. *Resolute* made four trips to Middle Bank, Ipswich Bay, Georges Bank, and the Great South Channel during the fall of 1891. The learning curve was steep. Torn nets and lost fish were the norm, though she landed 28,000 pounds of twenty different species on one trip, including haddock, plaice, witch soles, lemon soles, turbot, butterfish, cod, hake, and sturgeon. The problem was that the fish "were of terrible quality . . . mangled and crushed, and not only scaled, but skinned," as one wag put it. The nets were insufficiently rugged, and when they came up full the men dispiritedly watched them burst. One tow during the final trip filled the trawl so full it stopped the vessel's headway, and then, as the breeze died, Captain Bradford and his men sat becalmed for forty-eight hours with their fish aging under their noses, unable to proceed to market. Bradford's investors had had enough; they forced him to abandon the experiment. After *Resolute* turned to longlining halibut, no large vessels used beam trawls in New England for the next fifteen years.[27]

Instead, commercial beam trawling in American waters began as part of the expansion of the flounder fishery during the 1890s on Cape Cod. In 1897 twenty-seven sailing beam trawlers, all small craft, landed just over 750,000 million pounds of flounder. By 1904, when Cape Cod's Barnstable County was still the only place in the United States where commercial fishermen used beam trawls, there were sixty-five of them, and the trawlers' annual flounder catch had risen to 1.4 million pounds. With the average fish weighing a pound, that meant 1.4 million fish. In 1908 the catch rose to an astonishing 7 million pounds, most of which was winter flounder. Beam trawls got results. The wooden beams spreading the nets were about 25 feet long, the nets 75 feet long, and the mesh 3½ inches. Crews heaved in the towing warps by hand, along with the nets full of fish. Good results always entailed backbreaking work.[28]

Flounder are peculiar-looking fish that swim on one side, and have both eyes on their upper side. Their mouths appear to open sideways. Fourteen different species were then found in the Gulf of Maine, including the giant Atlantic halibut. Some species, such as summer flounder, are "left-eyed." Most are "right-eyed." The flounders targeted by the new beam-trawl fishery included winter flounder, summer flounder (also known as fluke), yellowtail flounder, witch flounder, and American plaice. Fishmongers regarded winter flounder as the "thickest and meatiest," except for the halibut, of course. Windowpane and other varieties, such as four-spot flounder, were caught and marketed less commonly. Flounder are generally white on their blind side, with variations of brown, gray, blue, green, and black hues on their upper side. Some are spotted. They prefer sandy bottoms or mud, where they feed (depending on the species) on chaetognaths, squids, small mollusks, polychaetes, amphipods, salps, silversides, mummichogs, and sand lance. Winter flounders, for instance, consume soft-bodied invertebrates, while summer flounder and windowpane eat larger and higher-order organisms, such as small fish. Flounders, in turn, provide important prey for sharks, skates, cod, hake, goosefish, and spiny dogfish. Like herring and mackerel, flounder reside in the middle of the food chain, transferring energy from herbivores and small predators to larger carnivores. Unlike herring and mackerel, flounder had rarely been fished commercially before.[29]

Flounder don't salt or smoke well. They need to be iced or sold fresh. For centuries only limited local markets had existed for them. It took the combination of railroads, iced delivery, and commission houses in inland cities specializing in fresh fish to develop voluminous markets for flounder. And it took weirs' and beam trawls' catching capacity to meet that demand. One of the U.S. Fish Commission's proudest discoveries, generated through exploratory research with beam trawls, revealed vast populations of various flatfish in the sandy habitats around Cape Cod and in the New York Bight. For a government agency determined to bring cheap, wholesome seafood to the masses and to promote industrial fishing, revelation of this unfished mother lode went a long way to justify its existence. Gasoline engines appear to have been paired with beam trawls on the Cape for the first time about 1903 or 1904, giving the boats greater range and allowing them to work in various conditions. During the next decade a significant number of small sailboats in the inshore fisheries were retrofitted with gas engines to drag beam trawls, especially in the winter flounder fishery. Fishermen called them draggers, and began to use the terms "dragger" and "trawler" somewhat interchangeably, though conventionally smaller inshore boats were "draggers," while larger offshore vessels were "trawlers." Catches rose dramatically. Barnstable County men, remember, took 1.4 million pounds of flounder in 1904, but 7 million pounds in 1908. Engines made the difference.[30]

Meanwhile editors of state fish commission reports and fishing trade magazines promoted English-style trawling and steam power, arguing that commercial fishing's success depended on satisfied consumers and expanded market share. Fresh fish was all the rage; old-fashioned salted products had become déclassé. And sailboats limited by the vagaries of the breeze could not be relied upon to land first-rate fish. As promoters saw it, delivering the freshest fish in tip-top condition would create a market for more. Immigrants, many of whom were fish eaters, as well as other Americans, could be encouraged to eat more seafood. Industry insiders were sure of it. But developing the industry would require modernization, following the British example.

In 1903 the *Fishing Gazette* printed a report written by the American consul in Hull, one of England's great fishing centers, about the revolution in British fisheries. Twenty years earlier, it explained, "there sailed from the ports of Hull and Grimsby less than 20 steam fishing vessels and about 1,000 sailing trawlers, smacks, yawls, and luggers." But by the time he wrote, only four sailing vessels still fished commercially from those ports because "the catching power of a modern steam trawler" was "estimated by practical men as equal to that of at least eight or ten of the old sailing trawlers."[31]

Hull and Grimsby were somewhat atypical, but the trend in British fisheries was unmistakable. Statistics compiled by the British Board of Agriculture and Fisheries reveal that 1899 was the last year in which more sailing trawlers were registered in the United Kingdom than steam trawlers. Sail then accounted for 53 percent of the fleet of "first class trawlers." In 1900 more steamers were registered than sailing trawlers. By 1905 trawlers powered by sail accounted for only 44 percent of the fleet. By 1906 nations abutting the North Sea had 1,618 steam trawlers. Several hundred hailed from Belgium, Germany, and the Netherlands, but 84 percent were British.[32]

Steam propulsion alone did not explain all the efficiencies. British fishermen also had begun to replace beam trawls with otter trawls. Rather than employing a long beam of elm or other hardwood to spread the mouth of the net, otter trawls used two "doors" towed through the water column and fastened to the net by a bridle. Brackets for attaching the towing warps to the doors were offset so that as the vessel made headway, the doors veered out on either side in its wake, spreading the net. Ultimately much larger nets could be flown with otter gear than with beam trawls. Otter trawls were easier to manage, too. Although the doors were heavy, and dangerous when swinging wildly above the deck in a confused sea, fishermen no longer had to deal with a cumbersome beam, thirty or forty-five feet long, or longer. Otter trawling was the way of the future.

Steam-powered otter trawlers made their New England debut in 1905, when John R. Neal commissioned construction of the *Spray* in Quincy, Massachusetts. His firm, John R. Neal and Company, of Boston, was one of the largest dealers in fresh and frozen fish in the United States, famed for their award-winning brand of finnan haddies (smoked haddock). As one admirer observed,

"Their connections extend throughout this country from the Pacific to the Atlantic coast, Gulf Coast states, and Canada. Their plant is a model one, with every facility for handling stock in unlimited quantities." Traveling occasionally for business in England, Neal witnessed firsthand the reinvention of British fisheries, and the avalanche of fish landed by modern trawlers. An astute businessman, he saw that trawlers produced lots of product. Neal claimed, as well, that trawling was the only "humane" method of deep-sea fishing. If fishermen stayed aboard their trawler to work, rather than departing in dories to hookfish, he argued, the death toll would fall. Neal also hoped to do well by doing good. Always fiscally prudent, he separated his visionary otter-trawling scheme from the established John R. Neal and Company. He found partners and investors among Boston's first families. They incorporated the Bay State Fishing Company and used their capital to construct a new trawler. *Spray* was steel, 283 tons, and 126 feet long—a giant fishing boat by American standards, though she simply imitated the best British designs of the day. She cost about twice as much to build and equip as a first-class fishing schooner, but her investors believed she would pay by landing huge fares of fish. Steam-propelled and outfitted with steam winches, *Spray* introduced otter trawling to the offshore banks of the western Atlantic.[33]

The first steam trawler in Atlantic Canada appeared shortly thereafter, in 1907, at Halifax. *Wren* was a British vessel, brought to Nova Scotia by an enterprising firm. Canadian fishermen protested so vehemently, however, that an order in council in 1908 prohibited steam trawling in Canadian waters. One legislator said, "I am convinced from what I have read on the subject that steam trawling is a serious menace and danger to our fisheries on the Atlantic coast, and I presume on the Pacific coast as well, and if persisted in must lead to the destruction of the fisheries." But the law was not stringently enforced, and for the next few years *Wren* and several other trawlers worked surreptitiously off the coast of Nova Scotia.[34]

Whether steam trawling would pay in North American waters remained an unsettled question. The *Spray* disappointed her investors at first. Her fares were small, and the fish landed poor in quality. For the first year and a half, under several skippers, she simply ran up bills for her owners. Yankee crews had not yet got the hang of trawling. But Neal and his partners were not the only ones interested in trawling the western Atlantic. "The dried fish merchants of northern France believe that steam trawling will yet save the decaying industry at St. Pierre, Miquelon," noted the *Fishing Gazette* late in 1906.

"They are going to send over forty steam trawlers this next year to engage in the bank fishing." The French fleet arrived during the winter of 1908, arousing considerable ire. "The young cod destroyed by them and thrown back into the sea," wrote a reporter from the *Gloucester Daily Times,* "would amount to thousands upon thousands." One skipper asked: "How long will such a slaughter last?" He answered his own question: "Not long, as in a few years there will not be much left to slaughter." An editorial in *The Standard,* a newspaper from Harbor Grace, Newfoundland, said pointedly, "As for Newfoundland, the people of this country are as one in opposition to the employment of such steamers in our fisheries, inshore or in deep water." The editor wondered why the governments of Canada, Britain, the United States, and France could not "do something in the way of regulation or restriction so as to protect our bank fisheries from being depleted."[35]

Congressman Augustus P. Gardner of Massachusetts agreed. "The time to stop this thing is while it is in its beginning," he argued, introducing a bill into the U.S. Congress in 1911 "prohibiting the importing and landing of fish caught by beam trawlers." (Fish caught by otter trawlers, too, or by any other method involving dragging a net along the bottom, would be prohibited.) By then Neal's Bay State Fishing Company was thriving. Its skippers had learned to handle the new gear, and it had six steam trawlers operating out of Boston, all similar to the flagship, *Spray.* For Congressman Gardner, the crucial question was "whether this method of fishing destroys the species." He admitted openly that it was more economical, at least for those who could afford the substantial capital investment, but he pushed the issue to its logical end point. "Assuming that you can fish a little cheaper by this method," he said, "if it destroyed your supply you are going to be a great deal worse off in the long run."[36]

Fishermen and politicians convinced of the destructiveness of the new otter-trawling technology demanded to be heard. J. Manuel Marshall, representing the Gloucester Board of Trade, spoke forcefully to the congressional committee at a hearing in May 1912. By then seven steam otter trawlers were based in Massachusetts. "This style of fishing will tend to deplete the fisheries off our coast," Marshall said. "Our fishermen apprehend that what has happened on the other side of the Atlantic, particularly in the North Sea, will happen here if something is not done at this time to prevent beam trawling or otter trawling. In the North Sea," he pointed out, "it is agreed by responsible authorities that there has been a great depletion in the fisheries, particularly in the size of large fish." Marshall also grasped the workings of the political economy. "If this goes on as has been going on in the North Sea, in continental Europe, and the British Islands, these beam trawlers will multiply and grow." Then "the question of vested interests will arise, and then it will be almost impossible to stop it. . . . What has happened in the North Sea will happen here."[37]

Marshall understood basic ecology and catch per unit effort, as well as political economy. He knew how to generalize from evidence and interpret data, and he understood that the avalanche of cheap fish landed by trawlers was anything but inexhaustible. "When the otter trawl came into existence the steamers increased in size and numbers, and they fished the North Sea with such intensity that they have grabbed up practically all of the large ones. . . . So that now they are obliged, in order to get sufficient fish . . . to go to Iceland, to the Bay of Biscay, and in fact away down to the coast of Morocco. . . . If you will look at the statistics of the fishing ports of England and of Scotland, you will find, I think, that if the supply of fish has doubled, over half of those fish are caught outside of the North Sea, and that less than half caught in the North Sea are caught with four times the catching power that they used previous to the adoption of this otter trawl." Marshall hammered the point home. Otter trawls overfished. Otter trawls depleted species. The problem with otter trawls simply was "catching too many; by catching the small fish, the immature fish, the undersized fish; by catching them all—the large fish, the mother fish, the father fish, and the children," they assured the destruction of stocks.[38]

John F. Fitzgerald, the mayor of Boston, introduced himself at the hearing by saying, "I represent the biggest fish port of the western world." Fitzgerald explained that the Chamber of Commerce and the City of Boston had not yet taken an official stance on the pending bill to prohibit trawling, but they were "very anxious" that the right thing be done, and concerned "about the imminent danger of wiping out the fish industry in our city." Fitzgerald personally favored the prohibition of trawling, and requested that if it was not stopped, "a complete investigation of the whole business be made." Fitzgerald had firsthand experience with fishermen and fish on the wharves of Boston, and he got the committee's attention by comparing them to European ones. "I was across the water last year and was astonished at every place I went to see the character of the fish," he began. "I did not see any fish that compared with our fish. I visited a great many fish markets in London and Liverpool, Paris, and Cork, in Ireland, and other different places . . . and . . . was surprised to see the conditions as they were. The fish were small and I can bear out the testimony that has already been given and can state that the fish across the water are getting smaller every year."[39]

Henry D. Malone also had experience on both sides of the Atlantic. Unlike Fitzgerald he was not a politician, but a professional fisherman, with thirty-two years of experience hand-lining, tub-trawling from dories, and otter trawling. He had been the first skipper on the Bay State Fishing Company's *Spray*. At Neal's request, Malone had gone to England in 1905 and made three trips on a state-of-the-art North Sea trawler to learn from his British counterparts. The experience was eye-opening. "They dragged the net night and day," he said wistfully. "They would save down to a haddock 7 or 8 inches long," he remembered; "what we would call scrub." When he talked with British trawlermen, he recounted, "They said fish were getting scarcer. When we first started in with steam trawlers, the otter trawlers, they got in any quantity of fish above the old trawler, where they formerly used the beam trawl and depended altogether on sail. The reason they attribute for that was because the steamer was going all the time, and with the sailing vessel, and the big long beam, the wind, of course, didn't always give them the power to drag over the bottom." When asked by a congressman, "Did you find a single man over there who thought there were more fish in the North Sea than there used to be?" Malone replied, "No, I did not." And when asked whether North Sea fish were "larger or smaller," Malone replied, as had Mayor Fitzgerald, that they were "very much smaller."[40]

A Scot named William Main testified that he had fished for twenty-eight years in the North Sea, mostly for haddock and whiting, and some cod. It was the same story: the fish now were "a good deal smaller" than when he had first gone in the boats. Main vilified steam trawling. He had made just one trip on an otter trawler, and when asked to recount what the trawlers did with cod and haddock less than eight inches long, he was visibly shaken. "I may say with shame I never did it before, but I was the man that put them overboard." The memory of shoveling those juveniles into a watery grave still rattled him. Trawling was capital-intensive, and the combination of capital against hard-working individuals also stuck in his craw. "The fishermen along the east coast of Scotland as a rule were their own masters," he said, "and since this trawling came in force and steam fishing came in they have been compelled to leave their own homes and seek a livelihood elsewhere."[41]

Captain William G. Thompson of Boston, who had spent most of his thirty-year career line fishing, but who had recently made five trips on an American otter trawler, was convinced of the destructiveness of the new technology. "In my experience I would say that about one third of the fish hauled from the bottom are unmarketable. They are too small, and some of them are shellfish. I have seen lots of them thrown back into the sea." He compared the practice to hook-and-line fishing, where "we do not catch nearly as many small fish, because their mouths are small and they do not bite to that size of a hook." But that was not the worst of it. "If you drag with a heavy piece of wire, and if every piece of vegetation on the bottom is brought up to the surface of the water, it must destroy the bottom."[42]

Representing the 14th Massachusetts district, which included Cape Cod, Congressman Robert O. Harris polled his constituents regarding the proposed ban on trawling. Line fishermen from the Cape were adamant. They opposed otter trawling, fearing "the passing of the deep sea fishing into the control of two or three corporations, and . . . the speedy exhaustion of the fishing grounds." That said, Cape Cod men wanted an exception made for the winter flounder fishery, conducted by small, gasoline-powered draggers. Their flounder fishery was relatively new, quite prosperous, and possible only because of beam and otter trawls. They could not imagine giving it up, much as they wanted to perpetuate the old ways in cod and haddock fisheries on the banks.[43]

In addition to fishermen and politicians, other experts responded to questions by the House committee, including journalists with experience covering the fisheries. James B. Connolly of Gloucester, who had made quite a name for himself as a writer of nautical fiction, claimed to have known New England fishermen firsthand for decades. Connolly based his fictional sea stories on hard-won experience and investigative journalism. In 1902 *Scribner's Magazine* had sent him to the North Sea to look into otter trawling. The following year *Harper's* had sent him back to Europe for another fishing story. During those two trips Connolly had spent months with European fishermen—with Germans flatfishing in the Baltic Sea, with Norwegians fishing cod and haddock north of the Arctic Circle, and with Englishmen aboard state-of-the-art North Sea trawlers.

"The thing that struck me most forcibly in the North Sea," he began, "was the wastefulness of the methods. . . . Those little fish that they throw away, if allowed to remain and get their full growth, would reach several times the bulk . . . [of] the fish that are saved." "I talked with fully a dozen captains," he continued. One of them said "that they tore the bottom off—that they 'raised the devil with the bottom'—and the other thing was they told me they can fish in almost any kind of grounds." By carrying two trawl nets, Connolly explained, British skippers would not need to interrupt fishing if one came up damaged. They fished day and night, nonstop, hauling back every three hours, and if one net went out of commission they used the other while repairing the torn one. That redundancy gave skippers confidence to fish rougher ground than otherwise would have been possible.[44]

In the Baltic, Connolly could not believe what small flounders fishermen kept. "I had never before in my life seen a flounder" as small as they were landing. "Six inches," he said; "years ago that was the ordinary size, but not there now. That was the result of this dragging, because nothing escaped." British fishermen in the North Sea "told me since the steam trawler has operated the fish have decreased noticeably in size."[45]

Proponents of the new method, however, could be found in New England, none more vocal than William F. Garcelon, who represented the Bay State Fishing Company. Garcelon disputed all the testimony presented in opposition to trawling as "statements of fishermen whose experience and knowledge of this method of fishing was limited to a very short period, and a few unsubstantiated statements as to the effect of such fishing during the last 40 years on the fisheries of the North Sea." He insisted, "The sea is not depleted." He also cast aspersions on the motivation of those who would prohibit trawling, insisting that the bill had been introduced "primarily in the interest of the New England fishermen who operate sailing vessels and employ means other than trawling as methods of catching deep-sea fish." As he saw it, "the complaint is based upon the individual interests of a particular class . . . rather than upon a disinterested regard for the welfare of the people as a whole."[46]

For the most part, however, opponents of the proposed prohibition on trawling brilliantly refrained from going toe to toe with their adversaries. Garcelon did not want to sully himself by getting down into the mud with mere fishermen. Rather, he and his supporters would offer objective evidence, including "the statements of the greatest scientists of the world and of other investigators who have made a special study of marine life and its productivity." Moreover—and this was their ace in the hole—they would not presuppose that they, themselves, or anyone else, knew all the answers yet. Rather, the question, "a very large one," as another proponent of trawling explained to the congressional committee, should be submitted "to the United States Bureau of Fisheries for careful investigation and report." Something so large, so complex, and so important deserved more than a hurried congressional hearing.[47]

Such a strategy was welcomed by many congressmen, for whom it would provide cover. They could delay, and then defer to the learned opinion of fisheries scientists. Of course, Garcelon and other trawling supporters had read the statement to the committee by Dr. Hugh M. Smith, the U.S. deputy commissioner of fisheries, in which he said, "I do not see that the condition of trawling in the North Sea or elsewhere has strict or definite bearing on the American question." They had heard him testify, more neutrally, that his agency did "not feel in a position to express any opinion upon the subject now. Steam-trawling in America is new, and there has been no evidence presented to the committee or accumulated by the Bureau of Fisheries . . . regarding the effects and conditions of this trawl fishery." Yet they knew full well that the bureau's official position for decades had been that puny humans could not affect the limitless productivity of the sea, and that bureau scientists had never seen a contraption for taking fish that they did not like.[48]

More than two and a half years would elapse between the initial hearing on Congressman Gardner's proposal to prohibit trawled fish from being landed or sold in the United States, and presentation of the Bureau of Fisheries' *Report on the Otter-Trawl Fishery*. Meanwhile an expanding fleet of steam trawlers continued to fish from American ports. The Bay State Fishing Company had built a fleet of near sister-ships to *Spray—Foam, Ripple, Crest, Surf,* and *Swell*—at a cost of $50,000 each. Equipped with a 450-horsepower triple-expansion steam engine, outfitted with electric lights supplied from a dynamo in the engine room—so they could fish night and day—and towing a net 100 feet wide, each of those trawlers swept approximately 73 acres of seafloor on every tow. (They typically towed for one and a half hours at four miles per hour, thus covering a strip six miles long and 100 feet wide, equivalent to 72.7 acres.) They might make as many as ten tows per day, scraping 730 acres of benthic terrain. The Heroine Company of New York City was operating a steam trawler, *Heroine,* converted from a 160-foot steam brig yacht. Other firms saw looming profits from a fresh-fish business in its infancy. The Trident Fisheries Company of Portland, Maine, refitted a menhaden steamer for otter trawling and put her to work in 1914. Modernization seemed to demand otter trawling, and trawling's momentum was building. Opponents of the ban on trawling had checked their adversaries with an astute political maneuver; they were about to check-mate them.[49]

MANAGED FISHERIES?

Meanwhile, environmental consciousness was maturing in the United States. "It has become a matter of common knowledge," noted Massachusetts officials in 1905, "that the activities of civilized man have in many cases seriously disturbed the biological equilibrium. For example, by killing the hawks and owls, we have permitted the undue increase of the English sparrow. . . . In a similar way we appear to have disturbed the equilibrium of marine fishes." Concerns about songbirds, game birds, sport fish, food fish, whales, seals, and American bison, among others, were common at the turn of the century, and Progressive reformers were trying to engineer a new approach to resource use based both on science and on the fear that business as usual was not sustainable.[50] Ironically, the lack of resilience in coastal ecosystems was becoming more apparent at exactly the same time that beam trawls, gasoline engines, and steam-powered otter trawlers were multiplying human impacts on the ocean. During the first decade of the twentieth century, the living ocean in New England and Atlantic Canada appeared squarely in a crosshair defined by declining yield and increasing effort, at least to astute observers.

At that point, the total catch of marine food fish in the Canadian Maritime Provinces and New England states was valued at more than $20 million. Given the importance of the fisheries, and the productivity of the ecosystem on which they rested, turn-of-the-century legislators and regulators experimented with management. Rejuvenating an incapacitated nature by propagating fish, farming clams, and destroying pests remained politically more palatable than forcing fishermen to reduce catches, even though fishermen themselves often were the most vocal proponents of saving the sea. Take, for instance, the case of clams.

A century before, barrels of salted clams had provided the primary bait aboard New England schooners in the salt-cod fishery. But the era of clam bait had largely passed. By 1901 consumers longed for clam chowder, steamed clams, fried clams, and minced clams. In Maine that year the volume of clams sold in the shell was twenty-five times greater than the volume sold for bait. And people's appetite showed no sign of abating. "The drain on our clam supply is very large and the demand for the Maine clam still increasing," wrote Maine's commissioner of sea and shore fisheries in 1902. "To conserve and increase the yield is the all important question."[51]

By 1902 Maine had a closed season from June 1 to September 15, in which the shipment of clams out of state was forbidden. Harvest was still allowed for in-state canneries and restaurants, although some wardens believed the closed season had "helped to replete our clam flats." Others thought the closed season should be extended to six months. Warden J. F. Goldthwaite of Biddeford, Maine, had an alternative solution. "I have looked this matter up very carefully and I have come to this conclusion, that about the only way to keep up the supply is to seed the flats—that is, to take very small clams that grow near the marshes and that never grow large there, and put them in low flats, and in a year they will be large clams." Like artificial propagation of fish, clam farming was meant to reinvigorate down-at-the-heels natural output.[52]

In his report covering 1903 and 1904, Maine's commissioner noted with alarm that the clam and scallop industry had "already got to the danger point." He was appalled that in the previous two years Maine's clam and scallop production had decreased by 2.3 million pounds. Worse yet, "if our production for the present year *was doubled* the market demand would not be supplied." He wanted the state to put resources behind clam farming and to close "a certain portion of the clam flats" absolutely for at least two years to allow stocks to rebound.[53]

The situation in Massachusetts mirrored that of Maine. In 1901 several bills were introduced in the legislature authorizing clam cultivation with legal protections. The state's fish commissioners wanted the right to cultivate soft-shell and long-neck clams. Such a program would require towns to cede management of clam flats, or at least part of them, to the state. The commissioners hoped to set aside areas, never more than one-third of any town's clam beds, for farming protected clams. They envisioned transplanting young or undersized clams to the reserves, and then policing those reserves to prevent unauthorized digging until the clams matured. Ultimately rejuvenated beds would be opened for public harvesting. Those bills failed. Legislators feared they would lead to privatization of clam flats. For the most part, residents of the commonwealth still adhered to the rights of the commons, believing "that all citizens have constitutional rights, so far as clam digging is concerned, that should not be legislated away for the benefit of any private person or corporation."[54]

By 1905 the shellfish crisis in Maine and Massachusetts had reached the tipping point. Legislatures in both states acted. An act in Maine directed the commissioner to spend up to $1,000 in each of the next two years to "conserve, extend, encourage, develop, improve, and increase the shellfish industry," and also granted him the authority to take control of parcels of "shore rights, flats, and waters" not exceeding two acres in any single location on which to conduct experiments in raising clams. Three clam reservations were immediately established, one each in Knox County, Hancock County, and Sagadahoc County. The commissioner optimistically predicted that with these grounds under state supervision, "production may certainly be increased ten-fold . . . within a few years." The two-pronged strategy consisted of transplanting juveniles to formerly productive flats, and closing certain flats to diggers. Milton Spinney, who oversaw the operation in Sagadahoc County, recognized the necessity of giving the clams a chance.[55]

"If a part of the flats of the state could be set off for a term of years until they had a chance to propagate as they did formerly, then open them up to the diggers and close the other flats that had been left open until they, too, had repopulated," and then open the flats to harvesting "under suitable state laws," Mainers could solve their clam problem. A top-down solution that might have worked—if nature cooperated—Spinney's solution would have required towns to surrender their control to the state, required the state to hire clam farmers and clam wardens, and required citizens to set aside what many considered to be a constitutional or God-given right to harvest the commons. Those challenges were insurmountable. The problem was not biological, but political. As Spinney noted, "The clams will propagate if given a chance."[56]

A Massachusetts official recognized clamming's political quagmire in the commonwealth. "By the system of town control," he argued, "we have escaped neither the dangers of monopoly nor of continued depletion of the supply." Meanwhile, as he saw it, the public misunderstood their "ownership of the shellfisheries." And soon there would not be any shellfish about which to quibble. The state's biologist, D. L. Belding, put the blame squarely on people's demand for more than the system could produce. "There can be no doubt but that wasteful exploiting by man has been the chief cause of the destruction of our clam flats." The combination of overharvesting and reckless destruction of juveniles had depleted the state's beds. Yet Belding was optimistic that man could remedy what man had ruined. "Large portions of these, once bearing immense numbers of clams, now lie unproductive," he wrote, "and yet the conditions appear just as favorable for the growth of clams as in former days." As a scientist Belding wanted to ascertain the actual yield per acre of various clam flats in the state, and to determine clams' rate of growth to marketable size. As a public servant he wanted his work to demonstrate conclusively "that methods of successful clam culture are easier than oyster culture, and that by assisting nature the yield of clam flats can be greatly increased and that profitable clam farming can be conducted."[57]

The Commonwealth of Massachusetts established the Powder Hole Reservation at Monomoy Point on Cape Cod in 1905. The place seemed well suited "for the study of the natural history of the lobster, clam, quahaug, scallop, oyster and winkle." The immediate goal was to "devise a commercially practicable method of rearing lobsters to a marketable size," in part through "controlling the ravages" of predators on the young lobsters. Raising shellfish so that spent areas "can again be made to produce the normal yield" ranked second in importance, though promoters explained that "opportunities for development are alluring." Commissioners began experiments "to determine the most practical methods of increasing the yield of shellfish under different conditions of tides, soils, etc." Given the plight of the shellfish industry, their optimism seemed unfounded. But they believed that reengineering the beds to speed up natural processes would pay off. "The conditions parallel those of agriculture," the commissioners argued buoyantly, "except that in case of marine farming the crops are more certain, *i.e.* are not subject to so many fatalities." Other lessons could have been drawn from several centuries of fishing history in the commonwealth, but the seduction of statistics, measurable outcomes, and progressive management blinkered the promoters of shellfish farming. They felt they could restore the equilibrium that man had compromised, and assist a crippled nature. In addition to the Powder Hole Reservation, artificial clam beds were established in 1905 at Slocum's River in Dartmouth, at Wheeler's Point on the Annisquam River, at Onset, Monument Beach, Woods Hole, Harwichport, Nantucket, Chatham, Provincetown, Gloucester, and Essex. Unfortunately, shellfish reservations did not produce tenfold gains.[58]

State efforts in Maine and Massachusetts to promote shellfish farming complemented the relentless federal effort to propagate fish at dozens of hatcheries and subhatcheries nationwide. Pike, perch, whitefish, black bass, and catfish were being raised in inland states; humpback and blueback salmon in Alaska; chinook, silver, and dog salmon in the state of Washington; and many other fish, including rainbow trout and steelhead trout, in other states. Federal hatcheries raised cod, haddock, flounder, mackerel, pollock, and lobster at Boothbay Harbor and Portland, Maine; and at Gloucester, Plymouth, and Woods Hole, Massachusetts. Candid ichthyologists sensed that releasing trout fingerlings into a stream was more likely to result in measurable success than releasing cod fry into the mighty North Atlantic. Nevertheless, lab-based production, not protection of wild stocks, remained the chief strategy of both federal and state governments when it came to fish.

If most species of sea fish seemed depleted around the turn of the century, despite the best intentions of fish commissioners, one appeared excessively abundant. *Squalus acanthius,* the spiny dogfish, which fishermen contemptuously called "dogs," had always been a nuisance. Seasonal visitors to the Gulf of Maine, dogfish arrived in the spring and then disappeared in the fall to winter offshore. They had no friends. Far and away the most common shark in the western North Atlantic, spiny dogfish outnumbered other sharks—perhaps by a thousand to one. They were the only shark to rival in numbers well-known food fishes such as cod and haddock. Dogfish were small: adult males ranged from 2 to 3 feet long; adult females were a little larger, from about 2½ to 3½ feet, but the average mature female was only seven to ten pounds. Nevertheless, spiny dogfish had a well-earned reputation as voracious. They schooled in huge packs, stole bait, destroyed fish on the hook or mackerel in the seine, and drove desirable species of bottom fish from the grounds. Fishermen had complained about them since the era of Captain John Smith, before permanent European settlement in New England. But around the turn of the twentieth century the dogfish population seemed to be exploding.

Given the nature of their reproduction, that explosion struck some observers as remarkable. Unlike most other fish, spiny dogfish bear live young. Females carry their young for eighteen to twenty-two months, typically bearing them on the offshore winter grounds. Their reproductive cycle meant that adult females caught along the coast of New England in late summer contained early embryos (less than an inch long) or much larger pups (seven to eleven inches long), nearly ready for birth. Fishermen amused themselves by slashing the bellies of females and watching the pups swim away. Litters averaged six to eight but could range from one to fifteen. Like many sharks, spiny dogfish are slow-growing and long-lived. Females do not reach sexual maturity until they are about twelve years old. By the turn of the century, when fisheries experts knew that a gravid cod or halibut contained millions of eggs, but that dogfish bore very limited numbers of live young, the proliferation of the dogfish population seemed perplexing. Of course, once born, dogfish pups were sufficiently large to fend quite nicely for themselves, unlike embryonic fish.[59]

Every fisherman easily recognized dogs by their distinctive large sharp spine alongside the forward edge of each dorsal fin. These slender little sharks with flattened heads and snouts tapering to a blunt tip could arch their backs around like a bow, inflicting a painful puncture with their rear spine. So hook fishers tried to release caught dogs as quickly as possible, avoiding spines and aggravation.

Dogfish usually were slate colored on top, sometimes tinged with brown, shading to white or gray underneath. A row of small white spots adorned each side and were especially noticeable on younger specimens. Their small sharp teeth, like serrated blades along each jaw, led fishermen to think of them as slashers. "Long and lean, they have all the lines of aristocratic racers," gushed a reporter from the *New York Sun* in 1905. Fishermen shared none of that admiration. Most would have willingly exterminated every dog in the sea.[60]

Dogfish are extremely efficient predators, feeding on virtually all species of fish smaller than themselves. They eat squid, crabs, worms, and shrimp. Mollusks form a significant part of their food. In other words, they essentially compete for the same species as cod, haddock, and halibut. But it was their impact on fish desired by humans for which they were notorious. Fishermen told stories of packs of dogfish creating havoc among other schooling fish, for instance by surrounding a school of mackerel on all sides and underneath before devouring or maiming the entire school. They told stories of dogs ravaging every food fish on trawl lines. They told stories of dogs chasing valuable fish off the grounds. Large cod, hake, and goosefish occasionally preyed on dogfish, but dogs' primary natural predators were larger species of sharks, which were relatively limited in numbers. As far as fishermen were concerned, not enough predators existed to keep the dogfish population in check.

Although dogfish were routinely landed and sold in northwestern Europe, no market for their meat existed in the United States or Canada. Dogfish livers could be rendered for oil; dried dogfish skin provided serviceable sandpaper; tanned dogfish skin could be used "for the grips of fine swords and dirks" or as a "covering for handbags, valises, and small trunks"; and dogfish bodies could be converted in factories into fertilizer or protein supplement for poultry feed. None of those uses, however, provided sufficient incentive for a targeted dogfish fishery in the western Atlantic. So as cod, haddock, and halibut were hit increasingly hard, dogs were largely left alone.[61]

Fishermen at the turn of the century were convinced that populations of the obnoxious dogfish had grown dramatically. Barton Evermann, of the U.S. Fish Commission, wrote: "Dogfish appeared on the coast in and near Penobscot Bay in unwonted numbers in 1902." John N. Harriman, who fished regularly in lower Penobscot Bay, near Matinicus and Isle au Haut, stated "that he never knew dogfish so plentiful. They came into the bay early, about June 1, and remained until late in the season." During the summer of 1904, according to the Massachusetts commissioners on fisheries and game, "the dogfish became unusually and remarkably troublesome to the fishermen of Cape Cod. Capt. Benjamin R. Kelley, of Provincetown, a fisherman of great experience, found them far more plentiful in that vicinity than ever before." And fishermen knew that Massachusetts was not suffering the plague of dogfish alone. Newfoundland, the Canadian Maritime Provinces, Great Britain, Ireland, and the European countries facing the North Sea—in every locale, boreal North Atlantic fishermen confronted spiny dogfish cutting into their bottom line. The situation deteriorated to such an extent that in 1904 the Massachusetts legislature passed a resolution calling upon the U.S. Congress—as if Congress had the answers—"to protect the food fish of our coast from these sharks or dogfish." The request was as unprecedented as it was unrealistic. But it had not sprung from thin air.[62]

Fisheries officials in Massachusetts at the time attributed the problem to human behavior, to the serious "mistake of killing many other species of fish and permitting the dogfish to escape." Everyone knew that fishermen tried to get rid of the worthless dogs as quickly as possible. Relatively few were killed. Meanwhile "the tendency is to diminish the other species of fish by relentless killing of old and young, and to make no efforts to diminish the numbers of dogfish; consequently the number of dogfish in proportion to the number of marketable fish is constantly increasing." The solution as the officials saw it was to find effective ways "to kill every dogfish which is hooked or netted"; otherwise "the evil is bound to increase." In their "Report upon the Damage Done by Dogfish to the Fisheries of Massachusetts," state fish commissioners proposed that the government pay fishermen for landing dogfish. The dogs would be rendered into oil and fertilizer. Profits would offset the payments, though the commissioners candidly argued that a "bounty, or other governmental assistance" would be money well spent. Following an inundation of petitions to Congress in 1906 a bill was introduced providing for a bounty of two cents on every dogfish killed between Cape Hatteras, North Carolina, and Eastport, Maine. It died in committee. As late as 1916, however, the U.S. Senate Fisheries Committee was debating the dogfish problem, and contemplating whether it would be appropriate for the federal government to support dogfish extirpation or to encourage dogfish consumption among Americans.[63]

At this distance it is impossible to know whether dogfish stocks in fact exploded at the turn of the century and, if so, whether human activity had anything to do with the dramatic increase. Natural conditions throughout the boreal North Atlantic, including warming waters as a result of climate change, may have conspired to boost dogfish populations. However, given the dramatic increase in harvesting pressure during the final third of the nineteenth century on coastal oceans as far apart as the North Sea and the Gulf of Maine, it is clear that human disturbance had shifted species composition within heavily fished areas. Removing species of high commercial value (such as cod and halibut) from the trophic level shared by spiny dogfish may have allowed the dogfish to increase. That is certainly how fisheries experts at the time imagined the situation. Nearly a century later, when Georges Bank had been fished much more intensively, fisheries scientists made precisely that claim. Following the decline of groundfish populations to historically low levels, "a subsequent increase in the abundance of species of low commercial value was documented, with an apparent replacement of gadid and flounder species by small elasmobranchs (including dogfish sharks and skates). Examination of feeding guild structure suggests that this switch in species dominance may have been linked." Turn-of-the-century fishermen may well have contributed to the problem that plagued them.[64]

Marauding dogfish were not the industry's only problem. Lobster landings in 1913 were down 60 percent from those of 1889. Meanwhile fishermen were lobstering harder. "In all the States more pots are set now than in the earlier years," a federal commissioner wrote in 1915, "and the average yield per pot is much less."[65] The state of Maine passed a law in 1915 requiring every lobster fisherman, as well as dealers and transporters of lobsters, to be licensed. That was an unprecedented step. Lawmakers hoped that licensing would improve data collection, rational management, and enforcement. Licensing lobstermen, giving wardens enforcement power equal to that of sheriffs (including allowing them to act without warrants), and streamlining procedures to measure legal lobsters were all part of management efforts in the face of slumping catches.[66]

By 1915 fisheries management at the state and federal levels included massive propagation of sea fish and lobsters, clam transplantation and cultivation, oyster-bed seeding, occasional closed seasons on the harvest or transport of shellfish, some licensing of lobster fishers and dealers, and attempts to eradicate spiny dogfish—everything *except* reducing fishing pressure. Yet statistics compiled by the Bureau of Fisheries made plain the continuing depletion of sea fish and edible mollusks, despite elaborate schemes to replenish the eviscerated coastal ecosystem. That was the situation when the U.S. Congress asked experts at the Bureau of Fisheries to referee the contentious dispute regarding the introduction of beam trawls and otter trawls to the western Atlantic. Given the declining productivity and increasing effort that characterized American fisheries during the first decade of the twentieth century, all other fisheries-related management decisions would pale in significance.

THE VERDICT

In the summer of 1912, concerned by testimony about the destructiveness of bottom trawling, Congress appropriated funds for the Bureau of Fisheries to investigate "whether or not this method of fishing is destructive to the fish species or is otherwise harmful." Two and a half years later the bureau presented its report, with recommendations. Measured and fair, the report nevertheless was rife with internal contradictions. It contained substantial evidence of overfishing—especially among English and Scottish fisheries in the North Sea, where beam trawling and otter trawling had been the norm for forty years. And it conceded that the situation in the western Atlantic was potentially dicey. "While the facts before us show no proof or presumption of any depletion of the fisheries on the banks frequented by American otter trawlers," the scientists wrote, "it is possible that the seeds of damage already have been sown and that their fruits may appear in the future."[67]

Given the bureau's historical enthusiasm for larger catches and more efficient equipment, its lukewarm response to otter trawling was nothing short of remarkable. Extensive research had revealed extensive problems, and bureau investigators had become undeniably leery. Proponents of trawling, including the Bay State Fishing Company and its allies, had expected a more robust defense. Nevertheless, as careful and restrained men of science—who also understood that considerable capital investment and future profit by American citizens hinged on their decision—the Bureau of Fisheries scientists simply could not recommend, with a clear conscience, absolute prohibition of trawling, predicated on what they knew. Nor would they endorse restricting entry to the otter-trawl fishery by regulating the number of vessels or nets. Doing so would promote monopoly, which seemed un-American. So they recommended restriction of trawling "to certain definite banks and grounds." That concession opened the door to large-scale otter trawling; more specifically, it closed the door on Congressman Gardner's proposal to "stop this thing . . . while it is in its beginning."[68]

Careful examination of the *Report on the Otter Trawl Fishery*, prepared by scientists in 1915, reveals a host of concerns that would not emerge again in a significant way until the end of the twentieth century, when the fisheries were reeling, even though the Bureau of Fisheries investigators in 1915 implored policymakers to keep close tabs on future developments. Their report stated candidly that "excessive use of the otter trawl" already had "caused injury to the North Sea," and they imagined such damage as possible in the western Atlantic. But it had not yet happened. Monitoring the situation would be crucial, however; it was the only responsible way to proceed, now that the trawling genie was out of the bottle. Had the scientists who prepared the report (and who chose objectivity over advocacy, despite their gut feeling about trawling's long-term impact) been responsible for the next steps, they would have monitored constantly, though they feared—quite presciently—that "economic" considerations would "make rectification difficult or impossible" at a later date.[69]

But bureau scientists were not responsible. Congress was. And the people's representatives did not take time to read every page of the report, much less to read between its lines and identify its authors' qualms. Moreover, trawling had expanded considerably in the two and a half years that had intervened between the initial hearing, which raised so many concerns, and finalization of the bureau's report. It had become more normative, and more profitable, just like the ongoing importation of mackerel from Norway and Ireland, and of herring and anchovies from Holland. During the 1880s, importation of European fish had raised eyebrows and caused alarm. By the turn of the century importers in Philadelphia, New York, and elsewhere routinely distributed fish harvested from boreal European ecosystems.[70]

So, despite serious reservations by fishermen and politicians about otter trawling's impact on fisheries of the future, trawling insinuated itself into the fleet. It became part of the working waterfront. The Bay State Fishing Company, for example, had six trawlers in 1911, nine in 1913, and twelve by 1915. Competitors outfitted otter trawlers as well, beginning in 1912. In 1913 the nine Bay State Fishing Company trawlers landed 16 percent of Boston's fish. They made 326 trips that year, generally fishing the South Channel and Georges Bank. Each trawler averaged thirty-six trips per year, a turnaround time of ten days—a rate virtually impossible for a schooner under sail. In 1914 the fleet landed 18 percent of Boston's fish. By then steam-powered otter trawlers accounted for 18 percent of the net tonnage of Boston's fishing fleet. They were no longer an anomaly. The baseline for what was "normal" in the fleet had shifted. In June 1915 the otter trawler *Long Island* landed 280,000 pounds of fish in Portland, Maine, on one trip; the following month the same vessel brought in a fare of 300,000 pounds. Those were the largest hauls ever made by an American otter trawler, and they turned heads. As trawling became commonplace, and exciting, the keen edge of opposition was blunted.[71]

Politicians rarely come down on the side of farsighted actions when measurable outcomes are decades in the offing. Had the eighty-four-page report produced by the bureau categorically denounced otter trawling's destructiveness, prohibition still would have been difficult. The English were trawling. So were other Europeans, including the French, who were trawling the western Atlantic, as well as the North Sea and Bay of Biscay. A handful of Canadians had started. Fishing was big business, nowhere more so than in Boston, where the fish dealers on T Wharf were more likely to be major corporations than mom-and-pop operations—notwithstanding the quaint ring of the term "fish dealer." Elsewhere, American net and twine companies, fish wholesalers, big packing firms, engine manufacturers, and other corporations with investment in commercial fishing—some of which were extraordinarily well capitalized and influential—had no desire to impede the progress in modernizing American fisheries. They could easily paint opponents of steam-powered otter trawling as relics from a bygone era.[72]

In retrospect, what stood between the marine ecosystem of the western Atlantic and the destructive new trawling gear in 1915 were three scientists with qualms, and a group of beleaguered hook-fishers increasingly out of step with current developments—hardly enough to stop industrial fishing. Nevertheless, the bureau scientists' findings about boreal North Atlantic fisheries at the end of the age of sail warrant attention. Had the investigators been trained historians they might have generalized more thoroughly from their data, for some of the patterns they revealed concerning changes in the sea had very deep roots.

A. B. Alexander, H. F. Moore, and W. C. Kendall, who oversaw the investigation and wrote the report, recognized that they stood at a crossroads. "The introduction of a new class of vessels, having greater speed and superior sea-going qualities than were possessed by the old type, has made it possible to prosecute the fisheries on a larger scale at all seasons, especially during the winter months," they noted. "In consequence of the increased size of the modern type of vessels, much more fishing gear is now operated per vessel than was customary 30 or 40 years ago." Such progress brought problems in its wake. "On Grand Bank, Western Bank, Quereau Bank, and other grounds where halibut were at one time very plentiful, there has, in recent years, been a decided falling off in the catch," they continued. "This condition is thought to have been brought about by overfishing." That bleak term, coined in Great Britain during the 1850s but rarely used on American shores until the 1880s, had become part of the everyday vocabulary associated with fishing.[73]

Developments in the North Sea ecosystem alarmed the investigators. As recently as 1903, 79.4 percent of demersal fish landed by English and Welsh vessels had been caught in the North Sea, relatively near ports such as North Shields, Yarmouth, Lowestoft, Grimsby, and Hull, where the fleets were based. In 1906 North Sea landings fell to 54.7 percent of the total. Skippers were ranging farther afield. In 1912 North Sea landings had fallen to only 43.2 percent. By then, much of the United Kingdom's fleet of steam otter trawlers traveled regularly to Iceland, the White Sea, the Faroes, the Bay of Biscay, and waters off Portugal and Morocco. Most English skippers no longer found it profitable to fish the North Sea, preferring instead to steam for days, or even a week, before shooting their nets. The North Sea—birthplace of trawling in the age of sail, and the nursery where steam trawlers cut their teeth—simply was not begetting many fish any more, as testimony to Congress in 1912 had made abundantly clear.[74]

After reviewing official English reports, the Bureau of Fisheries investigators found that "since 1891 there has been a material decrease in the quantities of fishes caught." They also noted that otter trawling had become the predominant form of fishing in England by 1898. "Exact data respecting the activities and catch of this fleet, which are available since 1902 only, show that the average catch of demersal fishes, per voyage and per day's absence from port, has materially decreased between 1903 and 1912, and this decrease has occurred in both round fishes and flat fishes." The apparent pattern was clear. "We believe, therefore, that there is overfishing in respect to both haddock and plaice, and that in consideration of its overwhelming predominance the otter trawl is responsible. The cod," they thought, "being a rapacious, more nomadic fish, and less distinctly a bottom dweller, is not affected."[75]

Besides pursuing paper trails through British records, the American scientists dispatched assistants to make observations on Boston-based steam trawlers. Owners of the Bay State Fishing Company, which brashly felt it had everything to gain through investigation of otter trawling, willingly put its vessels at the disposal of Bureau of Fisheries investigators. Each observer carried "printed forms on which to record full data respecting the date, location, duration, and length of each haul; the numbers and sizes of each species of commercial fish taken; and the numbers and sizes of edible fish of species never, or not usually, placed on the markets." They also were meant to note whether discarded fish were living or dead, whether the trawlers were damaging line fishermen's gear, and "the amount and character of the bottom material brought up in the trawls." Meanwhile some men in the employ of the bureau made trips on sailing line trawlers to observe their practices and the character of their catch.[76]

Comparing otter trawl with hook-and-line fisheries revealed distinctive disparities. Otter trawlers took "a much larger proportion of commercial fishes too small to market." Moreover, "practically all of the immature fishes of marketable species are dead when thrown over from the steamers," the report stated, calling it "an absolute waste. The young fishes taken on the lines have a much better chance to live, as they have not been subjected to the pressure to which the netted fish are exposed, and are immediately returned to the water, although some of them are killed or injured by being 'slatted' against the sides of the dories." The investigators' data sheets allowed them to compile tables comparing "total waste, all species." Otter trawlers surveyed averaged 55 percent waste; line trawlers, just 36 percent—a substantial difference.[77]

Still, as the investigators saw it, otter trawlers did not cause all the problems that critics attributed to them. For instance, the investigators believed that "otter trawls do not seriously disturb the bottom over which they are fished nor materially denude it of the organisms which directly and indirectly serve as food for commercial fishes." Most researchers today would disagree. While some substrates, such as broad sandy plains, lend themselves to otter trawling with minimum disruption, most bottom habitats are seriously altered by repeated trawling.[78]

One wrinkle ultimately would undermine most of the report's careful research. "We have been unable to discover from an examination of official records, extending from 1891 to 1914," the scientists wrote, "any evidence whatever that the banks frequented by the American otter trawlers are being depleted of their fishes." They immediately qualified that finding by noting that those "conclusions" were "necessarily inconclusive for the reason that the otter-trawl fishery in American waters is too recently established and relatively too small to have had a very material effect on the fish supply." The situation struck them as problematic, clearly in need of ongoing assessment. Nevertheless, how could a government agency in a democratic, capitalist society of educated people tell its citizens that they could not, or should not, use a type of gear to make a living from the sea, if no evidence existed that the gear in question had ever caused problems in American waters? The best the worried authors could do was to establish a case by analogy. "Considering the English and Scotch fisheries in the North Sea together, there is a strong presumption of overfishing in the case of the plaice [a flatfish, and] considerable evidence of the same thing in respect to the haddock. . . . As the steam trawler is overwhelmingly predominant, it must be held responsible."[79]

The investigators were quite confident that bank fisheries in the western Atlantic faced "little danger" of "depletion by line fishing as at present conducted"—which, today, would be considered a controversial finding in its own right—but reiterated that "there is no such accumulation of data respecting the recently introduced otter trawl." For an indication of what the future might hold, however, "we must have recourse to the history of the fishery in other places. Otter trawling has been practiced longest and has attained its greatest development in the North Sea where there appears to be ample evidence that it is being carried on to excess and that the fisheries for certain fishes have suffered in consequence." The challenge for Americans, then, was to prevent "the development of similar conditions in the American fisheries."[80]

That was a political, not a scientific test. As the investigating scientists saw the situation, "it is not fishing with the otter trawl but overfishing which is to be guarded against. The fact that it is undoubtedly more destructive than line fishing is not sufficient for its condemnation." Hindsight suggests otherwise. Had the three authors known that neither the Bureau of Fisheries nor Congress would return to the question of otter trawling's destructiveness for decades, they might have sounded more of an alarm. But as scientists in an advisory capacity, they did not make policy; they made suggestions. And once the secretary of commerce forwarded their report to Congress on January 22, 1915, the issue was out of their hands. Soon thereafter the Government Printing Office published the report, including its recommendation that otter trawling be restricted "to the regions to which it" had so far "been confined," namely "Georges Bank, South Channel, and part of Nantucket Shoals"—a tiny slice of the western Atlantic's fishing grounds.[81]

No legislation was introduced to that effect. All of Mayor John F. Fitzgerald's concerns disappeared in an avalanche of cheap fish. Outrage remained, but became more muted as time passed, and as otter trawlers became an accepted feature of picturesque fishing wharves. In 1926 an editor of the *Atlantic Fisherman* sympathized with hook-fishers and schooner owners affected by the expansion of trawling, but observed that "somehow we cannot but feel that our good friends, in protesting against the trawler, are bucking the inevitable."[82]

Copious photographs from around 1920 reveal a moment in time in which an eclectic fleet of schooners and smacks, most of them aging, but some newly built, shared the banks with a growing armada of motorized wooden draggers and steel steam trawlers. Fished commercially by then for 400 years, the venerable grounds from Cape Cod to Newfoundland, and the fishing ports from which men departed, still presented as charming a scene as any talented watercolorist could desire. Stunningly beautiful gaff-rigged schooners (some with auxiliary power), whose hard-bitten crews fished from little dories, plied the banks along with Portuguese square riggers, also dory-fishing. Lofty mackerel schooners, increasingly outfitted with gasoline or steam auxiliary engines, and all towing graceful seine boats, cruised the grounds with keen-eyed men at the masthead and seines at the ready. Crisscrossing the banks, with stacks belching smoke, otter trawlers flying American, Canadian, British, and French flags made systematic tows every few hours where schooners fishing adrift had once reigned supreme. The proximity of staunch schooners (whose designers and builders were still making refinements) and modern trawlers (which fished with clockwork precision) signaled that the age of sail was not yet finished, though it was passing rapidly.

Closer to shore, squat little menhaden steamers with plumb stems, pole masts, and jaunty pilothouses chased shrinking schools of pogies, while transom-sterned draggers—increasingly designed and built without any sails—dragged for flounder, fluke, haddock, and cod on the near-shore grounds. Closest to the beach, where eddies swirled, and the suck of the tide surged around rocks fringed with bladder wrack, enterprising lobstermen worked from open gasoline-powered launches. Young boys, old men, and ne'er-do-wells still hunkered over the oars and hauled their traps from wooden dories or peapods.

As had been the case for centuries, individuals from the maritime communities of New England and Atlantic Canada were hard at work upon the unforgiving sea. But craft and gear that would have been considered immoral not long before were increasingly common. The fisheries were modernizing, like virtually every other aspect of contemporary life at the outset of the Roaring Twenties, and the meaning of "normal" was changing—although painters and photographers still found the fleet romantic, heroic, and wistfully traditional. Of course, the vessels differed dramatically from those of 1820, and even more dramatically from those of 1720 or 1620.

Had equipment yet existed for underwater photography, images from beneath the surface would have revealed other historically specific scenes—the nature of the communities of marine species on which the prosperity of fisheries and maritime communities rested. Much had changed in 400 years. In fact it is arguable that changes in the sea below the surface were as compelling, as pervasive, and as transformative as those above the surface, although many contemporaries liked to imagine that they were at work upon the same immortal sea known to John Cabot and Jacques Cartier. Fishermen's baselines had shifted, but even the best-informed did not realize how much. As men baited hooks with herring, pitch-forked flounder and bluefish from weirs, or dumped haddock, skates, and redfish from draggers' nets, it was still easy to imagine that the sea would always produce in its seasons. It was harder to imagine that the abundance and distribution of valuable marine species, and the relative composition of the ecological community, had changed, sometimes drastically; or that the bottom terrain was being altered more radically every day. The sea was not immortal, it was not as "equally wild" as it had been in antiquity, despite Henry David Thoreau's musings decades before on Cape Cod's desolate beaches. The living sea was inextricably entwined with the decisions and fate of the people who dared to do business in its great waters.

Epilogue

Changes in the Sea

———

Even in the vast and mysterious reaches of the sea we are
brought back to the fundamental truth that nothing lives
to itself.

—Rachel Carson, unpublished notebooks

In its immensity and fragility the sea has never been equaled. Well before
industrialized and mechanized fisheries took their toll, harvesters working
from simple wooden boats affected the mighty North Atlantic, leaving biological marine communities and the human maritime communities that depended
upon them in deep disarray. The contemporary plight of the world's living
ocean is comprehensible only in light of that long history. Nothing conveys the
sea's vulnerability as effectively as the realization that men first vexed it using
gear that in hindsight looks extraordinarily primitive. Put another way, future
technological marvels will strip all defenses from creatures of the deep. Restoration of our exhausted seas, to the extent that is possible through management,
will require extraordinary vision, commitment, and action. Generations of
nineteenth-century Newfoundlanders, who lived at the sufferance of the sea,
and who understood its secrets like few others, had a common proverb: "We
must live in hopes, supposing we die in despair." Now *we* must live in hopes—
that the living sea's resilience and potential for recovery are equal to its immensity and fragility. The future of the Earth hangs in the balance.

Testifying before Congress in 1912 concerning the introduction of otter trawling in American waters, Boston's Mayor John F. Fitzgerald, who favored banning the controversial new technology, referred to the plight of generations unborn. "If we are going to permit a situation which is going to harm the fish supply of the country," Fitzgerald said, "I think we are committing a grave injury to the people of the future." Among those affected were his descendants, including his namesake grandson, John Fitzgerald Kennedy.[1]

Just a few years after Fitzgerald testified, Captain Sylvanus Smith of Gloucester echoed the mayor's sensibilities. Smith was eighty-six years old in 1915, a veteran mackerel-killer and high-liner with more than half a century of fishing under his belt, but the old man was concerned about the impact of beam trawls and purse seines, about "man's devastating and destructive methods." Contemplating what he called "the decline of the fisheries," he reminded people that "As a people, a country, we owe something to future generations, to those millions of people who shall come after us." As Smith saw it, the ocean of the future would be "an important factor in the world's food supply." He asked plaintively, "Shall we continue to do our best to destroy this heritage?"[2]

The mayor of what was then the largest fishing port in the Western Hemisphere and the grizzled old skipper understood that policy decisions about commercial fishing were always financial—about jobs and profits—but that such decisions had ethical implications. No one could label the mayor or the skipper an opponent of business. Each had been successful; each was closely connected to the world of capitalists and corporations. Nor could anyone accuse either man of being overly sentimental. But as the otter-trawl revolution loomed on the horizon, Fitzgerald and Smith sensed that they were at a critical turning point. As fisheries insiders, they refused to stick their heads in the sand, deny obvious problems, and pretend that everything would work out. Searching, instead, for a strategy that would ensure a vibrant fishery in the future, they pitched appeals for reform in light of the immorality of destroying the rightful inheritance of generations unborn.

A contemporary of theirs, Captain William G. Thompson, saw the future in more dire terms. A resident of Boston, Thompson had fished for thirty years, line fishing and, more recently, otter trawling. He feared the onslaught of newfangled steam otter trawlers, with their voracious nets. Asked by congressional investigators in 1912 what effect he thought trawling would have upon the supply of fish, he cut right to the chase. "I think in seven or eight years we would have no fish; they would all be destroyed."[3]

Thompson was wrong, but not by much. It took seventy or eighty years, not seven or eight, for his prediction to come true. From the perspective of ecosystems through time, seventy or eighty years is effectively the same as seven or eight years. Yet that was the gap, just eighty years, between Captain Thompson's alarming testimony opposing the legalization of otter trawling and the closure of the Grand Banks cod fishery off Newfoundland. Canadian Minister of Fisheries and Oceans, John Crosbie, pulled the plug in 1992. Shortly thereafter American officials closed extensive areas of Georges Bank and the Gulf of Maine to bottom fishing. The impossible had occurred. People had killed most of the fish in the ocean. It turned out to be a lot easier than killing all the biting insects on land.

What changed during those years from 1912 to 1992 was simply the scale of humans' impact on the living ocean, in both time and space. The prevailing pattern had been established long before, as had criticism of the fisheries' self-destructiveness, often by fishermen whose intuition told them that what they were doing was wrong. During the 1850s and 1860s fishermen in New England and Nova Scotia feared the newly identified specter of overfishing, and worried openly about it among themselves and to their elected officials. Fishermen wondered whether human actions could affect the sea, specifically whether overfishing of forage fish could disrupt the marine food web and whether the destruction of brood stock would lead to depletions in the future. From then until about 1915 many fisheries insiders feared the consequences of increasingly rapacious gear. If stocks were already declining, what would be the impact of gear that fished deeper, faster, and more vigorously? Would there be fish for the future?

As early as 1914, when the jury was still out on otter trawling, the efficiencies of the new method seemed obvious, despite reservations about its destructiveness. Boston-based otter trawlers were landing an average of 43,000 pounds of groundfish per trip, compared with tub-trawlers' 27,000 pounds. As fishing communities grudgingly accepted the once-controversial trawlers, industry turned to them with alacrity. By 1925 more than 100 otter trawlers were fishing from New England ports. One casualty of the avalanche of cheap fish accompanying the shift to otter trawling was the sea story that had resonated in fishing towns in New England and Nova Scotia for three-quarters of a century, the story predicated around troubling terms such as depletion, diminution, and overfishing. As the age of sail faded, so did many of those concerns.[4]

Consolidation became the norm as the fishing industry evolved, as did the capital-intensive investments required for modern trawlers and state-of-the-art processing facilities. In 1910 the Commonwealth of Massachusetts entered into an agreement with the Boston Fish Market Corporation, a newly formed company of fish dealers looking to relocate from their antiquated base on T Wharf. Under the agreement the state constructed a new fish pier, at a cost of more than one million dollars, and leased it to the new corporation. The lease stipulated the agreement would last for at least fifteen years, with the possibility of subsequent fifteen-year extensions to 1973. Upon opening in 1914 the Boston Fish Pier was the largest and most modern fish distribution facility in the world. The Bay State Fishing Company (builder and operator of the largest otter trawlers) and the Boston Fish Pier Company (dealers arrayed together against Bay State's strength) made vast profits until 1918. The federal government and the Commonwealth of Massachusetts then prosecuted the duopoly. High-profile fish dealers were indicted for monopoly and restraint of trade, and seventeen were fined or imprisoned. Federal prosecutors, relying upon the Sherman and Clayton Anti-Trust Acts, overhauled the industry, imposing size limits on fish companies and other regulations. The potential for profits nevertheless remained substantial.[5]

Fishermen responded to industrial consolidation with strategies of their own. In 1915 William H. Brown organized the Fishermen's Union of the Atlantic, affiliated with the American Federation of Labor's International Seamen's Union. By 1920 nearly all fishermen working on larger boats from Boston and Gloucester were members, and the union had prevailed in arbitration with the large trawling companies to raise wages substantially. An ill-conceived strike in 1921 and relentless opposition to the union by management gutted the union, and by the early 1930s it had collapsed, only to be reinvented in 1937 as the Atlantic Fishermen's Union, an arm of the Congress of Industrial Organization's National Maritime Union. The union boasted 4,000 members by 1947.[6]

Meanwhile, the introduction of filleting by processors, in 1921, gave a huge boost to modern, mass-marketing of whitefish, such as cod, haddock, and pollock. Until then filleting had been done by hand at retail outlets—meaning the corner fish market, whether in Boston or St. Louis. Head, tail, and bones, for which most consumers had little use, accounted for a substantial share of the total weight of a fish even after it had been gutted. Yet fresh fish had always been delivered to retailers with head, tail, and bones, a package deal rooted in ancient practices. Filleting obviated freight charges for the waste and gave rise to packaging fish that could be frozen for distribution and branded with eye-catching labels. The innovation prompted chain stores and supermarkets to stock more fish. It also allowed processors to sell fish waste for animal feed or fertilizer. The combination of otter trawling, filleting, and quick-freezing—developed by Clarence Birdseye in Gloucester during the 1920s—rapidly ratcheted up pressure on bottom fish.[7]

Haddock stocks crashed in 1930. The catch per day on Boston trawlers dropped nearly 50 percent from the previous year. Federal fisheries biologists explained that haddock spawning had been poor from 1925 to 1928, as a result of natural phenomena over which people had no control. Meanwhile fishing pressure, which industrialists and politicians could influence, increased dramatically, more than tripling from 1925 to 1935. Otter trawling led the way. In 1935 otter trawlers landed more fish than the combined landings from all other methods used by the New England fleet. Only twenty-five years before, the destructive technique had been vilified by virtually all fisheries insiders in New England and Atlantic Canada. But by the 1930s, although some hook-fishing schooners still plied the banks, otter trawling had become the norm. As the norm, it was no longer protested by the fishing community, but protected.[8]

Investigations during the 1930s revealed that millions of pounds of baby haddock were being caught by otter trawlers and thrown back dead into the sea, too small to market. Alarmed by the implications, American biologists recommended in 1936 that the industry adopt a larger mesh size to allow juvenile haddock to escape. Bureau of Fisheries scientists' experiments with commercial otter-trawling gear indicated that the mesh then prevalent caught about five times as many juvenile haddock as the larger, recommended size. Calls for conservation went unheeded. While many fisheries scientists remained convinced that their mission was to promote commercial fisheries, the 1930s saw the beginning of a split between biologists, who counseled caution, and the industry, which seemed hell-bent on expansion regardless of the long-term consequences. In 1938 a social scientist's study of contemporary fisheries noted alarmingly that New England fishermen were "fishing out haddock, flounder, and redfish more intensively than [they] ever fished lobster, salmon, and shad. We think back with contempt for depletions which earlier generations brought on, yet we go on quite blind to the effects of our present activity."[9]

The industry rebuffed scientists' suggestion to fish with larger mesh. Vessel owners feared that competitors would use smaller mesh clandestinely, and that regulation and enforcement would be difficult. American fishing interests insisted that a requirement to adopt larger mesh would provide advantages to unregulated foreign fishermen, notably Canadians, who not only produced fish more cheaply, but flooded the American market with it duty-free. By the late 1930s, despite Bureau of Fisheries arguments that larger mesh size would perpetuate haddock stocks, American fishing interests scoffed at the idea of conserving fish for foreign competitors. The industry fished harder than ever, increasing total landings at Boston from just under 100 million pounds in 1914 to nearly 340 million pounds in 1936.[10]

"Scrod" had not even been part of fishermen's vocabulary until otter trawls began to slaughter juvenile haddock, but by the 1930s scrod became the target of choice. They fitted nicely on a dinner plate. This creatively named new seafood consisted of baby haddock (or occasionally cod) weighing between $1\frac{1}{2}$ and $2\frac{1}{2}$ pounds. These were tiny creatures with tiny mouths, ones that rarely had taken a hook during the heyday of line fishing because hooks were sized for much bigger fish. Otter trawlers scooped up large and small fish indiscriminately. As the daily catch of large haddock remained relatively low, between 1931 and 1941, the daily catch of scrod increased sixfold.

Stocks rebounded to some extent during World War II. Governments requisitioned trawlers on both sides of the Atlantic for the war effort. Trawlers were just the right size to serve as minesweepers. Meanwhile the menace of German submarines kept part of the American and Canadian fleet in port. The reduction in fishing effort allowed depleted fish populations to rebuild. But the development of new technologies during the war, including radar, sonar, and polyester fibers (adaptable for nets), meant the respite would be short-lived.

Fisheries scientists at Woods Hole assessing the "Current Haddock Situation" in 1948 argued that destruction of juvenile haddock through targeted scrod fishing had reduced the haddock stock on Georges Bank to one-third of its previous size. Those scientists estimated that between March and October 1947 approximately 15 million baby haddock (averaging less than one pound each) were discarded dead on Georges Bank by American otter trawlers. A Boston economist calculated that "If these fish had not been caught until the next spring, they would have increased the catch by at least 20 million pounds. Assuming 1947 prices, this would have brought an additional $1.5 million to the industry's fishermen and vessel owners." But the industry had cast caution to the wind.[11]

During the 1930s and 1940s advertisements, feature articles, and photographs in trade publications such as *Atlantic Fisherman* emphasized fishermen's heritage, invoking sleek schooners, dorymen, and the romance of sail. But as the unprecedented consolidation and unionization proceeded, "fishing" came to mean something very different from what it had conveyed just forty years before. Despite New Englanders' association with fishing as the longest-running commercial enterprise in the New World, and despite publicists' attempts to promote its romantic heritage, the business arrangements, labor arrangements, regulatory structure, and relationship of the industry to the resource base on which it relied all had been transformed. The future looked bleak. Fish dealers, vessel owners, and fishermen remained at one another's throats. Charges and countercharges of cheating and corruption echoed in the auction halls in Boston and other ports. Meanwhile stocks of commercially valuable species continued to decline. As one economist explained in 1954, "The operation of market forces has led New England interests to exploit recklessly the limited self-renewing stocks of these species on New England banks and to join with foreign fishermen in 'mining' relentlessly the banks in northwest Atlantic international waters." Reasonable catches were now "obtained only by fishing more intensively in New England waters or by making much longer trips to more distant banks." That necessity raised the cost per pound of fish landed. It also signaled clearly (as it had during the mackerel, menhaden, halibut, and lobster crises of the late nineteenth century) that overfishing had become the norm.[12]

No one noted the most telling internal change in the fishery. During the late nineteenth century *fishermen* in New England and Atlantic Canada had insisted that overfishing was occurring. Industry insiders then demanded that governments protect fish stocks for the future with reasonable regulations. By the middle of the twentieth century the industry routinely treated with contempt government biologists' recommendations to promote conservation of the resources on which they relied.

This was the situation in 1954, when the world's first factory-equipped freezer stern-trawler arrived on the Grand Banks from England. "They're fishing out there with ocean liners!" is the way astonished Canadian and American fishermen described the moment. *Fairtry,* the ironically named first of those ships, measured 280 feet long and 2,800 tons. "The floating Ritz, we called her," one of the original crew members recollected. She had showers, modern toilet rooms, and a cinema, amenities to which fishermen had never been exposed. A factory ship such as *Fairtry* could land as much fish in one lucky hour as a seventeenth-century vessel could have landed in a season.[13]

Fairtry's success soon inspired construction of two sister-ships, *Fairtry II* and *Fairtry III*. Meanwhile, in a dramatic instance of industrial espionage, Soviet fisheries managers acquired the plans, and the Soviet Union and other Eastern Bloc nations began to build factory-equipped freezer stern-trawlers. These vessels shared four features that rendered them distinctive from all previous fishing boats. Each had a sloping stern ramp so that nets would no longer be hauled over the side, as they always had been, but from astern. Each had a factory below decks, equipped with an assembly line of machines to gut, clean, and fillet fish; no longer would the crew labor to clean fish by hand on the exposed weather deck of a North Atlantic fishing boat. Each had an ammonia or freon freezer system to quick-freeze fish and store them indefinitely. Freezer equipment replaced the chopped ice most fishermen still used in the 1950s, a cumbersome system requiring considerable space and limiting the length of a trip to the period in which the ice remained intact. Finally, each of these ships was outfitted with machinery to process fishmeal from the factory residue and nonmarketable fish. Fishmeal, for fertilizer and animal feed, added profit. Captain Harald Salvesen, the architect of this revolutionary fishing behemoth, borrowed its essential elements from the whaling ships run by Christian Salvesen Limited of Scotland. Those ships could stay at sea for months, and hoist entire whales aboard for processing. The only problem was that by 1950 whale populations were in free-fall as a result of rapacious overharvesting. Salvesen accurately saw little future in whaling profits, but as a man ahead of his time, he envisioned adapting lessons from international whaling for a brave new frontier in the fisheries.[14]

From 1875 to 1955 cod landings off the east coast of Newfoundland had ranged between 160,000 and 300,000 metric tons per year. Some years saw catches of less than 200,000 tons. While most years' landings were larger, fishermen attained the 300,000-metric-ton mark only twice during that eighty-year period. Freezer-equipped factory trawlers changed the equation. In 1960 cod landings off eastern Newfoundland expanded to 500,000 metric tons; in 1968, to 800,000. By then factory trawlers from Japan, Spain, the United Kingdom, Russia, Poland, East Germany, and other nations were jockeying for position on the Grand Banks. Americans and Canadians, in contrast, appeared to be fishing in mom-and-pop operations, from antiquated side-trawlers and small wooden draggers. The vessels built by the Bay State Fishing Company fifty years before had long since passed their prime. Many Newfoundlanders still fished from open skiffs and dories, tending cod traps close to the shore.

The huge catches in 1968 were an ominous milestone. Stocks crashed, and during the next nine years cod landings fell steadily to a low point of about 150,000 metric tons—about the same amount landed in that area during the 1860s by hook fishermen in schooners—even though a huge fleet of freezer-equipped factory trawlers still crisscrossed the banks each year. By the 1970s and 1980s precious few cod were finding their way past the gauntlet of factory trawlers to Newfoundlanders' cod traps. Landings rebounded slightly during the 1980s, but then crashed to virtually nothing in 1992, prompting the Canadian government to close the fishery.[15]

During the early 1970s the Boston-based fleet faced hard times. Its boats were old. So were the men who manned them. Youngsters resisted recruitment. Only about seventy-five men continued to work the offshore boats from Boston in 1972, though twenty-five years earlier the New England union had had 4,000 members. Those aging fishermen landed a mere 27 million pounds of fish that year, whereas in 1935 the Boston-based fleet had landed 305 million pounds. Stocks of once-profitable groundfish had been devastated. Conditions on Georges Bank, fished regularly by foreign factory ships, were somewhat akin to those on the Grand Banks of Newfoundland. Cod landings fell steadily from 1968 to 1978. Haddock landings dropped even more dramatically. The Gulf of Maine provided the only bright spot for New England's fleet. The gulf, tiny by comparison with the Grand Banks, avoided the worst inroads of foreign factory ships. Most of the boats fishing there were relatively small, home-ported in Maine, Massachusetts, and Nova Scotia. In 1976 those boats landed just over 12,000 metric tons of cod from the gulf. Less than one-fifth of what hook fishermen had taken in 1861, it seemed pretty good by mid-twentieth-century draggermen's standards. The fishery was free-falling. By the mid-1970s about 93 percent of the groundfish eaten in the United States was imported. An industry and a way of life once central to New England had been driven to its knees.[16]

Change was in the wind. In 1976 the Fishery Conservation and Management Act revolutionized management of American fisheries. Known as the Magnuson Act, after Senator Warren Magnuson, of Washington, the federal legislation established eight regional councils to manage fishing, including the New England Regional Council. Its goals included "Americanization"—the promotion of the U.S. fishing industry. It also required that all commercially fished stocks be regulated to provide "optimum yield," a close cousin to "maximum sustainable yield," the primary management concept during the middle of the twentieth century. The law defined "optimum yield" very broadly, however, as the amount of fish that would "provide the greatest overall benefit to the Nation." In effect, the Magnuson Act gave regional councils tremendous latitude to set catch levels. The councils, consisting of political appointees, essentially were accountable only to the U.S. secretary of commerce, whose position, of course, existed to promote business. The fishing industry lobbied effectively so that most appointees to the councils came from within its ranks. No henhouse had ever been guarded by a more willing fox.[17]

Among its accomplishments, the Magnuson Act asserted a 200-mile Exclusive Economic Zone (EEZ) seaward from the shore of the United States, to be controlled by the federal government. (The major exception was that each state would continue to regulate all fishing in waters under state jurisdiction, which in most cases meant 3 miles from the coast.) Nations around the world were insisting on their right to control the sea—and its resources—within 200 miles of their shores. In the United States, the Magnuson Act stipulated "full domestic utilization," translated as exclusion of foreigners from American waters. Newly energized American managers sought to boost the American fishery. As late as 1977, foreign vessels still caught 71 percent of the fish landed within the United States' new EEZ. From then on, however, in both Canada and the United States, governments worked to expel foreigners from the 200-mile zone. Fishing interests in both nations were jubilant, feeling that they were finally going to have access to fish that they regarded as rightfully theirs, fish that had been scooped up by foreigners for decades.

In that flurry of Americanization, the number of boats fishing from New England rose dramatically, from 825 in 1977 to 1,423 in 1983. No need for more fishing capacity existed. Stocks had already been drastically overfished. Yet under federal tax rules, a new fishing boat could be amortized within five years. In effect, many of those boats were paid for by the federal government. In theory, fish resources were a public asset, owned by all citizens. In practice, fish resources were owned by no one until they had been caught, meaning that the industry not only regulated the fishery through its presence on regional councils, but derived nearly all the benefits from it. Meanwhile taxpayers got no benefits from nationally managed fish resources, but paid to accelerate overfishing. By 1992 foreign ships were not taking any fish from within the United States' EEZ, but by then there were few fish to take.[18]

With foreign fleets effectively gone, both Canada and the United States could have recreated a sustainable cod fishery beginning in 1977. Neither did. The bold outlines of the stories are similar. The details vary. Canadian fisheries biologists from the Department of Fisheries and Oceans made unrealistically optimistic assumptions about cod recruitment, influencing the government to increase the cod quota. During the 1980s department managers hoped to reach a harvest of 350,000 metric tons of cod in Atlantic Canada, but after decades of foreign factory trawlers vacuuming up fish, cod were few and far between. Canadian biologists and managers acted recklessly, mirroring the behavior of nineteenth-century fisheries "experts," who had always been in industry's vest pocket. A different story unfolded in New England, where open hostilities between fishery scientists and fishermen dominated the waterfront during the late 1970s and 1980s. As stocks declined and fish mortality rose, New England's fisheries biologists implored the New England Regional Council to reduce fishing. In 1989 National Marine Fisheries scientists predicted the "collapse" of cod, haddock, and yellowtail flounder. The council dithered. Meanwhile a fishing supply company in Portsmouth, New Hampshire, produced bumperstickers that frustrated fishermen stuck on their trucks: "National Marine Fisheries Service: Destroying Fishermen and Their Communities since 1976." Nothing encapsulated better how far the aims of government fisheries scientists and New England fishermen had diverged.[19]

Trying to seize the initiative in 1989, the National Marine Fisheries Service asserted its right, under the federal Fisheries Conservation and Management Act, to impose guidelines for preparation of regional fishery management plans. The service published what came to be called its "602 Guidelines," because in that year's Code of Federal Regulations, it was Part 602. The 602 Guidelines finally provided a formal definition of overfishing, and required that all regional councils' management plans be amended to include quantifiable definitions of overfishing for each stock managed. The guidelines also directed regional councils to create plans for rebuilding devastated fish stocks. This step provided the leverage that activists needed. In 1991 the Conservation Law Foundation sued the U.S. Department of Commerce, claiming that the New England Fishery Management Council was not obeying the federal mandate regarding overfishing. The conservationists won their case. Under court order, the New England council drafted regulations forcing fishermen to reduce their number of days at sea by 10 percent, a small step toward reducing fishing mortality. Discussions were acrimonious. But by 1995, when a further amendment to the New England Groundfish Management Plan was being discussed, the mood had become somber. By then even industry insiders admitted that the fishery was in ruin. In the interim Canada had closed the Grand Banks to cod fishing, and the U.S. government had closed more than 5,000 square nautical miles of prime fishing grounds in the Gulf of Maine and on Georges Bank. Regulators and fishermen put on game faces, but the situation had never looked so grim.[20]

Congress passed the Sustainable Fisheries Act in 1996, calling for fish populations to be "rebuilt," even as congressional representatives from the New England delegation pressured the National Marine Fisheries Service to ease constraints on the fleet. In 1999 a report by the Multispecies Monitoring Committee insisted that previous cuts had been insufficient to meet congressionally mandated goals, and called for further reductions in groundfish harvests. Headlines from the *Boston Globe* in 2003 captured the glum assessment of both industry and fisheries biologists: "The New England Fishing Crisis: For all sides, goal is preservation. Inevitable steps may put way of life in the balance."[21]

Arguments about the accuracy of stock assessment and management techniques raged on.[22] In 2010 the New England Fishery Management Council abandoned regulating fishermen by limiting the number of allowable days at sea, exchanging that strategy for a new sector-based management plan. A "sector" would consist of a group of fishermen with multispecies permits who would be allowed to fish until their sector reached a "total allowable catch." Red tape, monitoring practices, and ill will were in abundance. Fish were not, at least according to most fisheries biologists and managers, even though in the official parlance of the National Marine Fisheries Service, several stocks had been "fully rebuilt," a notion that derived more from limited management targets than from ecological or historical understanding. As sector-based management became law, New England fishermen insisted that many stocks were in good shape, and certainly capable of being fished harder than current limits allowed.[23]

The question is one of scale. Most fishermen and scientists agree that 1992 was probably the low point (so far) for New England fisheries. Men who have fished for the last twenty years say that circumstances are better now, citing recent harvests of haddock to make their case. Their hard-earned experience is not to be denied; the uptick they note is genuine. Their observations, however, when set against the histories of the fishery and of the coastal marine ecosystem recounted in this book, appear "N.T.S."—not to scale. If marine ecology and fisheries management are to contribute substantially to rebuilt ecosystems and fisheries, they will need to incorporate historical perspectives. Nothing else conveys the magnitude of what has been lost and what might be restored. Without the crucial context provided by historical frames of reference fisheries management will remain captive to the two-year or four-year political cycle, a scale irrelevant to ecological time.

Industrialized fishing merely accelerated a process of overexploitation already set in motion by centuries of policy decisions, market transactions, and human desires. Clearly, many different societies and types of societies share responsibility. Medieval pagans (such as the Vikings), medieval Christians (such as the County of Zeeland in the Holy Roman Empire, now part of the Netherlands), capitalistic democratic republics (such as the United States), and parliamentary democracies (such as the United Kingdom) have all been guilty of overharvesting the sea. During the twentieth century, communist states (such as the Soviet Union), fascist states (such as Franco's Spain), and social democracies (such as Denmark) also played their parts. American-style industrial capitalism does not get a pass, but it has been far from the sole offender.

Seeking explanations, some concerned individuals have imagined that powerful people always were on the dark side of this story; that while courageous activists in various generations spoke "truth to power," power always prevailed. It's not that simple. During the seventeenth century, as colonists were struggling to establish a foothold along the Atlantic edge of the American continent, the most outspoken preservationists were the magistrates, men such as Governor William Bradford of Plymouth Colony and the elders on the General Court of the Massachusetts Bay Colony. They sought to conserve cod, haddock, mackerel, striped bass, and other valuable fish in the sea of plenty lapping at their feet.

During the eighteenth century, provincial legislative bodies, followed by revolutionary legislative bodies, debated the righteousness of perpetuating river fish swimming upstream from the sea to spawn, and passed statute after statute to do just that. Prominent local citizens of the early republic, such as Judge Benjamin Chadbourne of South Berwick, Maine, and Reverend Jeremy Belknap, an Enlightenment intellectual and author of a famous multivolume history of New Hampshire, spoke candidly about the ongoing depletion of coastal ecosystems and the implications for their contemporaries and their contemporaries' children. During the early and mid-nineteenth century, provincial legislatures in Nova Scotia and Newfoundland and state assemblies in Maine and Massachusetts strove to protect sea fish. Subsequently governments in Norway, England, New England, and Atlantic Canada paid for inquiries into the depletion of the sea, by then both an ecological and an economic problem. By the late nineteenth century prominent statesmen, including Thomas B. Reed—soon to be one of the most powerful Speakers of the House of Representatives ever to hold that office—spoke forcefully about the need to preserve sea fisheries. Congressman Augustus P. Gardner introduced legislation to outlaw otter trawling, and Mayor John F. Fitzgerald, a prominent Boston politician, supported prohibition of industrialized otter trawling. At every step of the way, well-heeled and influential men tried to redirect the defining relationship between living people and the living ocean, to stop the myopic slaughter that led each year to emptier nets and emptier oceans.

Naturalists, scientists, journalists, commercial fishermen, fish wholesalers, and other insiders—with varying degrees of articulateness and influence—also lent their voices to the struggle to conserve marine resources, especially after 1850. Evidence, both obscure and obvious, shows that citizens from various walks of life, many with vested interests in the fisheries, recognized what was happening and tried at different times to stem the tide. Their efforts failed. The situation continued to worsen. Insiders understood as early as 1850 that the coastal ecosystem was not yielding the abundance it once had. By 1890 a barrage of evidence, some of it quite sophisticated and statistically grounded, demonstrated that human fishing effort had increased, while natural productivity had decreased. Congressional hearings on otter trawling in 1912 and the Bureau of Fisheries report on otter trawling in 1915 did not pull many punches. Crystal-clear data, at once historical, anecdotal, traditional, and statistical, made the case that otter trawling lent itself to excesses, and that overfishing had occurred even before steam or gasoline engines powered the fleets.

It is not as if one constituency—whether fishermen, or scientists, or politicians—ever spoke with consistency on the issue. They did not. There is plenty of blame to go around; and some accolades, too. At certain times well-informed, moral, or farsighted individuals, including fishermen, scientists, and politicians, spoke openly about how their friends and neighbors (along with others, sometimes not so friendly or neighborly) were destroying the resource base on which a great business rested, not to mention food and jobs for the future. If there is any lesson in this saga, it is not that the fishermen were (or are) to blame, or that the scientists were (or are) to blame, or that the politicians were (or are) to blame. The interlocked system was (and is) to blame. That system, with its checks and balances, its desire for prosperity and security, its willingness to honor a multiplicity of voices, its changing sense of "normal," and its shifting ecological baselines, was (and is) insufficiently nimble to stop the desecration of commonly held resources on which the long-term good of everyone depended (and depends).

Of course, no one is to blame if everyone is to blame. That attribution of responsibility, or lack of attribution, does not provide a solution. The epic story of boreal North Atlantic fisheries does, however; it provides a compass heading into the murk of the future. In a nutshell, that cardinal heading is the precautionary approach to resource management. When presented with a choice regarding the ecosystem of our blue Earth, even when not all of the relevant evidence has yet been assembled, pick the least destructive option.

At every step of the way recounted here, from the arrival in Iceland about 874 A.D. of Viking settlers, who confronted vast herds of walrus, to the American controversy over otter trawling from about 1912 to 1915, the precautionary approach could have made a difference. Modest short-term sacrifice of profit and prosperity would have perpetuated renewable resources for the future. "Sacrifice" is actually too strong a term; and its emphasis is all wrong. "Stewardship" is more appropriate. Modest stewardship would have perpetuated renewable resources for the future. Resources such as fish, marine mammals, and seabirds, harvested sustainably, can return a dividend almost perpetually—within the natural fluctuations, of course, that characterize ecosystems through time. Stewardship pays dividends.

The precautionary approach is especially germane when evaluating new technologies. In this realm, lessons from the past are quite appropriate for the future. The labor-saving and lifesaving properties of some technologies (the substitution of netfishing for hookfishing from dories, for instance; or the installation of engines in fishing boats) could be seen as the answers to generations of prayers. Once developed, engines were bound to go fishing; they saved lives. The largely unspoken corollary, however, shadowed by enthusiasm for engines' and nets' reduction of risk and labor, is that each new generation of more efficient technology, when applied to harvesting resources, masks ongoing depletion. One theme that runs the course of this history, like the lay-line in a length of rope, is that more efficient harvesting technology, while not a problem itself, is a shortsighted and poor substitute for resource management. It is possible to have *both* innovative technologies *and* responsible resource management if citizens and leaders recognize two simple rules that emerge from 1,000 years of fishing history. Those rules are very straightforward. Humans have limited ability to control nature; they cannot engineer exactly the outcomes they desire. And humans have an established record of fouling up nature, of compromising the natural resources and services they need. Our challenge is to pilot ourselves within those rules. The precautionary approach provides the course.

"Sustainability" has become all the rage in the last decade or so, at least in certain quarters. For some, it is a term charged with nobility. But it is not exactly new. For centuries, many fisheries insiders promoted sustainability. Anything else, they knew, was madness. That attitude changed during the first two-thirds of the twentieth century. As the story of boreal North Atlantic fisheries shows all too painfully, the Earth's resources—even its apparently most abundant ones, such as North Atlantic cod—are not limitless. Sustainability, like so many other things, rests on a shifting baseline. Each generation must assess its needs and resources; each responsible generation will do so in light of conscious under-standing of those resources' changes through time. Historical perspectives are essential.

Now, fifty years after publication of Rachel Carson's game-changing *Silent Spring*, human beings face a daunting list of challenges as they continue to exploit the ecological system on which they rely. Climate change, and the extent to which it is human-induced through emission of fossil-fuel exhaust, typi-cally leads the list, although the scarcity of potable water in many parts of the world (including both developed and underdeveloped nations) may soon vie for top billing. Habitat destruction and reckless waste disposal by garbage-generating societies clamor for attention. For example, dense concentrations of tiny plastic fragments now exist in several convergence zones in the North Atlantic and North Pacific, a phenomenon only several decades old, and whose implications have yet to be determined. Some recent plankton tows in the Sargasso Sea have revealed as much weight in plastics as in biomass.[24] In addition to such new problems, old problems remain. The ongoing destruc-tion of sea fish, notably big, long-lived, and slow-to-reproduce fish, such as bluefin tuna and sharks, remains sobering. In light of the "pressures on their populations"—a euphemism for killing them early and killing them often— those big fish cannot beget sufficient offspring to survive.

While concern for the interrelated web of life that underpins human existence has grown in many quarters since publication of *Silent Spring,* naysayers remain vocally opposed to a precautionary approach. Most ideologies invoked by opponents of stewardship make no sense in light of a historically based assessment of the situation; the notion, for instance, that the Earth will heal itself no matter what is done to it, or that future generations will sort out the problems, or that short-term profits are justified despite long-term ecological costs. Contemporary fishermen's laments testify poignantly to the limitations of natural resources. Today's fishermen are descendants of the oldest continually operated business enterprise in the New World, one predicated on renewable resources, and one with a centuries-old history of conversations about conservation. Yet today both fishermen and fish are in crisis. Dean Travis Clark, editor of *Sport Fishing* and *Marlin* magazines, summed it up with a headline in 1998: "So Long, Oceans. Thanks for All the Fish."[25]

Yet the issues faced today by policymakers, fishermen, and ecologists are hardly new. Conceptually, the terms of the debate are quite similar to those of many nineteenth-century controversies, and some seventeenth-century ones, although the stakes are higher now because the plight of the ocean has worsened exponentially. It has been too easy to forget that the director of the U.S. Fish Commission made "restoration of our exhausted cod fisheries" a priority in 1873, and too easy to assume that rapacious trawlers with sophisticated electronics emptied our oceans only recently. But the warning signals have been there at every step of the way. Ultimately the scale of this story, spanning centuries and stretching across the North Atlantic, reveals, as few other tales can, the tragic consequences of decisionmakers' unwillingness to steer a precautionary course in the face of environmental uncertainties.

A remarkable cast of characters strides through this history of the sea: Jacques Cartier, Samuel de Champlain, James Rosier, William Wood, George Cartwright, Abraham Lurvey, Captain Rich, John James Audubon, Captain Nathaniel Atwood, Dr. David Humphreys Storer, Jotham Johnson, Spencer Baird, George Brown Goode, Captain Solomon Jacobs, and A. B. Alexander, to name just a few. Each felt deeply that people were meant to fish, even that they had to fish; each took seriously the challenge of navigating the relationship between human harvesters and the living ocean. Each knew the sea, used the sea, and changed the sea. By no means, however, did all of them agree with one another; by no means could all of them be described as conservationists. Still, it is likely we can agree on at least one thing concerning them all: were they to return now to the fishing ports and banks where they spent their days, they would be devastated by the catastrophic changes in the sea they knew. Had their generations steered a precautionary course, circumstances would be better. Now it's up to us.

APPENDIX

NOTES

GLOSSARY

ACKNOWLEDGMENTS

INDEX

APPENDIX

Figures

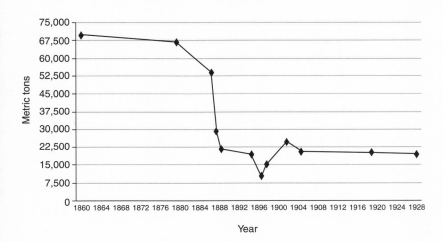

Note: All Massachusetts reported catches after 1879–1880 are reduced by 60 percent to account for percentage caught beyond Gulf of Maine, because *Census of the Commonwealth of Massachusetts: 1885* (p. 1439) indicated 39.5 percent of Massachusetts catch was taken in American waters.

Sources: Courtesy, University of New Hampshire Gulf of Maine Cod Project. Karen E. Alexander et al., "Gulf of Maine Cod in 1861: Historical Analysis of Fishery Logbooks, with Ecosystem Implications," *Fish and Fisheries* 10 (2009), 428–449; Francis A. Walker, Superintendent of the Census, *Ninth Census—Volume III. The Statistics of the Wealth and Industry of the United States, Embracing the Tables of Wealth, Taxation, and Public Indebtedness; of Agriculture; Manufactures; Mining; and the Fisheries* (Washington, D.C., 1872); *FFIUS*, sec. 2:11, 106, 120; USCFF, *Part XVI: Report of the Commissioner for 1888* (Washington, D.C., 1892), 291–296; *Bulletin of the U.S. Fish Commission, Vol. X, for 1890* (Washington, D.C., 1892), 94–119; Horace G. Wadlin, Chief of the Bureau of Statistics of Labor, *Census of the Commonwealth of Massachusetts: 1895* (Boston, 1896); USCFF, *Part XXVI: Report of the Commissioner for the Year Ending June 30, 1898* (Washington, D.C., 1899), CLXV–CLXVIII; USCFF, *Part XXVI: Report of the Commissioner for the Year Ending June 30, 1900* (Washington, D.C., 1901), 167–177; U.S. Department of Labor and Commerce, *Report of the Bureau of Fisheries 1904* (Washington, D.C., 1905), 247–305; *U.S. Bureau of Fisheries Document 620* (Washington, D.C., 1907), 14–68; *U.S. Bureau of Fisheries Document 908* (Washington, D.C., 1921), 132–145; U.S. Bureau of Fisheries, *Report of the United States Commissioner for Fisheries for 1929* (Washington, D.C., 1931), 789–790.

FIGURE 2. *Mackerel landings, United States, 1804–1916*

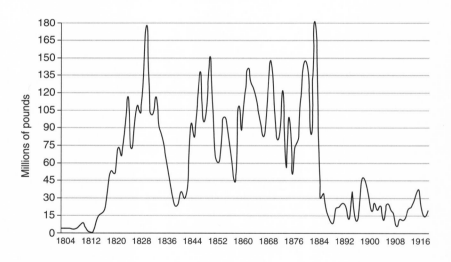

Source: Oscar E. Sette and A. W. H. Needler, *Statistics of the Mackerel Fishery off the East Coast of North America, 1804 to 1930,* U.S. Department of Commerce, Bureau of Fisheries, Investigational Report No. 19 (Washington, D.C., 1934), 24–25.

FIGURE 3. *Comparison of mackerel landings and registered tonnage of the American mackerel fleet, 1830–1860. (Estimated landings indicated as thousands of pounds of fresh, round mackerel. Tonnage expressed as total registered tonnage.)*

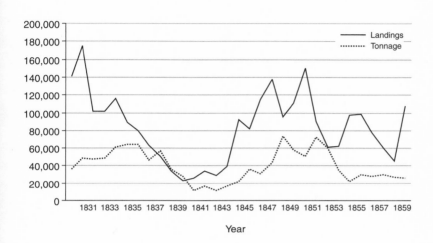

Note: Statutes at the time did not recognize any fisheries other than cod, mackerel, and whale fisheries for purposes of documenting tonnage. Vessels engaged in catching other fish were aggregated with the mackerel fleet. Thus the actual mackerel fleet tonnage was somewhat less than indicated.

Sources: Oscar E. Sette and A. W. H. Needler, *Statistics of the Mackerel Fishery off the East Coast of North America, 1804 to 1930*, U.S. Department of Commerce, Bureau of Fisheries, Investigational Report No. 19 (Washington, D.C., 1934); *Report of the Secretary of the Treasury, Transmitting a Report from the Register of the Treasury of the Commerce and Navigation of the United States for the Year Ending June 30, 1860* (Washington, D.C., 1860), 670–671; U.S. Bureau of the Census, *Historical Statistics of the United States, Colonial Times to 1970*, 2 vols. (Washington, D.C., 1975), 2:745.

FIGURE 4. *Menhaden landings, Maine, 1873–1920*

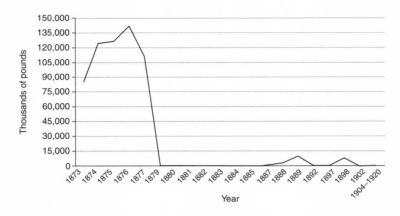

Sources: The Menhaden Fishery of Maine, with Statistical and Historical Details, Its Relations to Agriculture, and as a Direct Source of Human Food (Portland, 1878), 22–26; Douglas S. Vaughan and Joseph W. Smith, "Reconstructing Historical Commercial Landings of Atlantic Menhaden," SEDAR (Southeast Data Assessment and Review) 20-DWO2 (North Charleston, S.C., June 2009), South Atlantic Fishery Management Council, NOAA, 8.

FIGURE 5. *Menhaden landings, New England, 1880–1920*

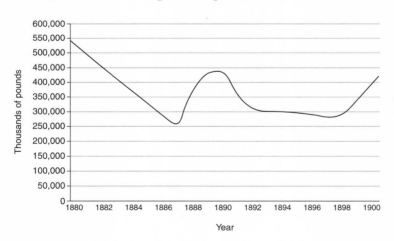

Source: Douglas S. Vaughan and Joseph W. Smith, "Reconstructing Historical Commercial Landings of Atlantic Menhaden," SEDAR (Southeast Data Assessment and Review) 20-DWO2 (North Charleston, S.C., June 2009), South Atlantic Fishery Management Council, NOAA, 16.

FIGURE 6. *Halibut landings, United States Atlantic Coast, 1848–1915*

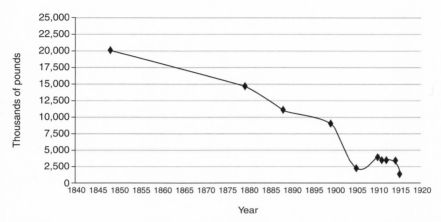

Note: Halibut landings in 1848 are estimated, while those from subsequent years are taken from published federal and state reports. The estimate was created by juxtaposing two discrete observations. In 1905 Massachusetts' Commissioners on Fisheries and Game noted that annual catches of halibut had been "upwards of 20,000,000 pounds" for some years, though by 1905 they had "dwindled" considerably. Fisheries insiders had always remembered 1848 for its immense halibut landings, but no systematic statistics were compiled that early. It is likely that in the early years of the targeted halibut fishery, circa 1848, landings in New England were at least 20,000,000 pounds per year.

Sources: Estimate, *MFCR* (Boston, 1906), 28; USCFF, *Part XVI: Report of the Commissioner for 1888* (Washington, D.C., 1892), 289–325; *FFIUS,* sec. V, 1:3; A. B. Alexander, H. F. Moore, and W. C. Kendall, "Report on the Otter-Trawl Fishery," Appendix VI in Bureau of Fisheries, *Report of the U.S. Commissioner of Fisheries for the Fiscal Year 1914* (Washington, D.C., 1915); Bureau of Fisheries, *Report of the U.S. Commissioner of Fisheries for the Fiscal Year 1915* (Washington, D.C., 1917), 44; Bureau of Fisheries, *Report of the Commissioner of Fisheries for the Fiscal Year 1912 and Special Papers* (Washington, D.C., 1914), 37.

FIGURE 7. *Lobster landings and effort, Maine, 1880–1919*

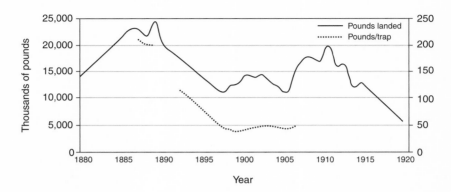

Source: Maine Department of Marine Resources, http://www.maine.gov/dmr/rm/lobster
/lobdata_files/sheet001.htm (accessed August 26, 2011).

NOTES

ABBREVIATIONS

FFIUS U.S. Commission of Fish and Fisheries, *The Fisheries and Fishery Industries of the United States,* ed. George Brown Goode, 5 secs. in 7 vols. (Washington, D.C., 1884–1887)

MeFCR *Report of the Commissioner of Fisheries* (Augusta, 1867–1879); *Report of the Commissioner of Fisheries and Game* (Augusta, 1880–1894); *Report of the Commissioners of Inland Fisheries and Game* (Augusta, 1895–1924)

MeSA Maine State Archives, Augusta

MeSSF *Report of the Commissioner of Sea and Shore Fisheries of the State of Maine* (Augusta, 1898–1924)

MFCR *Annual Report of the Commissioners on Inland Fisheries* (Boston, 1867–1885); *Annual Report of the Fish and Game Commissioners* (Boston, 1886); *Annual Report of the Commissioners of Inland Fish and Game* (Boston, 1887–1901); *Annual Report of the Commissioners of Fish and Game* (1902–1919)

MHMF G. Brown Goode, Joseph Collins, R. E. Earll, and A. Howard Clark, "Materials for a History of the Mackerel Fishery," Appendix B in USCFF, *Part IX: Report of the Commissioner for 1881* (Washington, D.C., 1884)

MSA Massachusetts State Archives, Boston

NARA National Archives and Records Administration, College Park, Md. and Waltham, Mass.

NOAA National Oceanographic and Atmospheric Administration

NSARM Nova Scotia Archives and Records Management, Halifax

NYT *New York Times*

RG Record Group

USCFF U.S. Commission of Fish and Fisheries

PROLOGUE

1. Tony J. Pitcher, "Back-to-the-Future: A Fresh Policy Initiative for Fisheries and a Restoration Ecology for Ocean Ecosystems," *Philosophical Transactions of the Royal Society B* 360 (2005), 107–121.

2. Richard W. Unger, *The Ship in the Medieval Economy, 600–1600* (Montreal, 1980); E. M. Carrus Wilson, "The Iceland Trade," in *Studies in English Trade in the Fifteenth Century*, ed. Eileen Power and M. M. Postan (New York, 1933), 155–183; Kenneth R. Andrews, *Trade, Plunder and Settlement: Maritime Enterprise and the Genesis of the British Empire, 1480–1630* (Cambridge, 1984); Brian Fagan, *The Little Ice Age: How Climate Made History, 1300–1850* (New York, 2000); Fagan, *Fish on Friday: Feasting, Fasting, and the Discovery of the New World* (New York, 2006).

3. Michael S. Reidy, *Tides of History: Ocean Science and Her Majesty's Navy* (Chicago, 2008); Alain Corbin, *The Lure of the Sea: The Discovery of the Seaside in the Western World, 1750–1840*, trans. Jocelyn Phelps (Berkeley, 1994).

4. Margaret Deacon, *Scientists and the Sea, 1650–1900: A Study of Marine Science* (London, 1971); J. A. van Houte, *An Economic History of the Low Countries, 800–1800* (New York, 1977); Jan de Vries and Ad van der Woude, *The First Modern Economy: Success, Failure, and Perseverance of the Dutch Economy, 1500–1815* (Cambridge, 1997); J. Sherman Bleakney, *Sods, Soil, and Spades: The Acadians at Grand Pré and Their Dykeland Legacy* (Montreal, 2004); Mart A. Stewart, *"What Nature Suffers to Groe": Life, Labor, and Landscape on the Georgia Coast, 1680–1920* (Athens, Ga., 1996).

5. Kenneth Sherman and Barry D. Gold, "Large Marine Ecosystems," in *Large Marine Ecosystems: Patterns, Processes, and Yields*, ed. Kenneth Sherman, Lewis M. Alexander, and Barry D. Gold (Washington, D.C., 1990), vii–xi; Lewis M. Alexander, "Geographic Perspectives in the Management of Large Marine Ecosystems," ibid., 220–223. Although the area that had been known as the northeast continental shelf LME was reclassified into three smaller LMEs in 2002, with one in American territorial waters and two in Canadian waters, the region's history and ecology suggest that envisioning it as one unit still makes considerable sense. See www.lme.noaa.gov.

6. Callum Roberts, *The Unnatural History of the Sea* (Washington, D.C., 2007).

7. For a useful chronology of the decline of shore whaling, constructed from eighteenth-century documents, see John Braginton-Smith and Duncan Oliver, *Cape Cod Shore Whaling: America's First Whalemen* (Yarmouth Port, Mass., 2004), quotations 143–146; William Douglass, *A Summary, Historical and Political, of the First Planting, Progressive Improvements, and Present State of the British Settlements in North America* 2 vols. (Boston, 1755), 1:58–61, 1:294–304, 2:212.

8. H. W. Small, *A History of Swans Island, Maine* (Ellsworth, Maine, 1898), 194; Philip W. Conkling, *Islands in Time: A Natural and Cultural History of the Islands in the Gulf of Maine* (Rockland, Maine, 1999), 26–28; B. W. Counce, "Report of the Com-

missioner of Sea and Shore Fisheries," in *MeFCR for 1888* (Augusta, 1888), 37; Counce, "Report of the Commissioner of Sea and Shore Fisheries," in *MeFCR for 1889–1890* (Augusta, 1890), 28.

9. Robert S. Steneck and James T. Carlton, "Human Alterations of Marine Communities: Students Beware!" in *Marine Community Ecology* ed. Mark D. Bertness, Steven D. Gaines, Mark E. Hay (Sunderland, Mass., 2001), 445–468.

10. Henry D. Thoreau, *Cape Cod* (1865), ed. Joseph Moldenhauer (Princeton, 1988), 148; Heike Lotze et al., "Depletion, Degradation, and Recovery Potential of Estuaries and Coastal Seas," *Science* 312 (June 23, 2006), 1806–09; Lotze, "Rise and Fall of Fishing and Marine Resource Use in the Wadden Sea, Southern North Sea," *Fisheries Research* 87 (November 2007), 208–218; J. B. C. Jackson et al., "Historical Overfishing and the Recent Collapse of Coastal Ecosystems," *Science* 293 (July 27, 2001), 629–638.

11. Bruce Robertson, "Perils of the Sea," in *Picturing Old New England: Image and Memory,* ed. William H. Truettner and Roger B. Stein (Washington, D.C., 1999), 143–169; Franklin Kelly, "Deflection of Narrative—Works of American Painter Winslow Homer," *Magazine Antiques,* November 1995; Paul Raymond Provost, "Winslow Homer's *The Fog Warning:* The Fisherman as Heroic Character," *American Art Journal* 22 (Spring 1990), 20–27; Glenn M. Grasso, "What Seemed like Limitless Plenty: The Rise and Fall of the Nineteenth-Century Atlantic Halibut Fishery," *Environmental History* 13 (January 2008), 66–91.

12. Joseph Dow, *History of the Town of Hampton, New Hampshire, from Its Settlement in 1638 to the Autumn of 1892* (Salem, Mass., 1893). Author's interview with Robert Nudd, Hampton, N.H., October 24, 2007.

13. Author's interview with Robert Nudd.

14. Sarah Orne Jewett, *The Country of the Pointed Firs* (1896; reprint, Boston, 1991).

15. Daniel Pauly, "Anecdotes and the Shifting Baseline Syndrome of Fisheries," *Trends in Ecology and Evolution* 10 (October 1995), 430.

16. Andrew A. Rosenberg, W. Jeffrey Bolster, Karen E. Alexander, William B. Leavenworth, Andrew B. Cooper, and Matthew G. McKenzie, "The History of Ocean Resources: Modeling Cod Biomass Using Historical Records," *Frontiers in Ecology and the Environment* 3 (March 2005), 84–90. For the Swampscott petitioners, see *FFIUS*, sec. V, 1:159; G. Brown Goode Collection, series 3, Collected Material on Fish and Fisheries, box 14, folder "Misc Notes, Mss, Lists, Statistics," RU 7050, Smithsonian Institution, Washington, D.C.

17. Ove Hoegh-Guldberg and John F. Bruno, "The Impact of Climate Change on the World's Marine Ecosystem," *Science* 328 (June 18, 2010), 1523–28. In a media interview after this article was published, the lead author referred to the ocean as the Earth's "heart and lungs." Gerald Sider, *Culture and Class in Anthropology and History: A Newfoundland Illustration* (Cambridge, 1986), 158.

1. Depleted European Seas and the Discovery of America

1. Antonio Pigafetta, *The First Voyage around the World 1519–1522: An Account of Magellan's Expedition,* ed. Theodore J. Cachey Jr. (Toronto, 2007), 3, 7, 76.

2. Ibid. 48; Christopher Columbus, *The Log of Christopher Columbus,* trans. Robert H. Fuson (Camden, Maine, 1987), 84; Gonzalo Fernandez de Oviedo y Valdes, *The Natural History of the West Indies* (1526), in *The Fish and Fisheries of Colonial North America: A Documentary History of Fishing Resources of the United States and Canada,* ed. John C. Pearson, *Part 6: The Gulf States and West Indies,* NOAA Report No. 72040301 (Rockville, Md., 1972), 1103; Anthony Parkhurst, "A letter written to M. Richard Hakluyt of the middle Temple, conteining a report of the true state and commodities of Newfoundland, by M. Anthonie Parkhurst Gentleman, 1578," in Richard Hakluyt, *The Principal Navigations, Voyages, Traffiques & Discoveries of the English Nation,* 8 vols., ed. Ernest Rhys (London, 1907), 5:345.

3. David B. Quinn, "Sir Humphrey Gilbert and Newfoundland," in Quinn, *Explorers and Colonies, America, 1500–1625* (London, 1990), 207–223; Samuel Eliot Morison, *The European Discovery of America: The Northern Voyages, A.D. 500–1600* (New York, 1971), 555–582.

4. Robert Hitchcock, *A Pollitique Platt for the honour of the Prince* (London, 1580), n.p.; D. J. B. Trim, "Hitchcock, Robert (*fl.* 1573–1591)," in *Oxford Dictionary of National Biography* (Oxford, 2004), http://www.oxforddnb.com/view/article/13370 (accessed November 12, 2007).

5. David B. Quinn, "Newfoundland in the Consciousness of Europe in the Sixteenth and Early Seventeenth Centuries," in Quinn, *Explorers and Colonies,* 301–320; Martin W. Lewis, "Dividing the Ocean Sea," *Geographical Review* 89 (April 1999), 188–214; Joyce Chaplin, "Knowing the Ocean: Benjamin Franklin and the Circulation of Atlantic Knowledge," in *Science and Empire in the Atlantic World,* ed. James Delbourgo and Nicholas Dew (New York, 2008), 73–96. On the multiplicity of names for the Atlantic, see James Atkinson, *Epitome of the Art of Navigation; or a Short and Easy Methodical Way to Become a Compleat Navigator* (1686; reprint, London, 1718), 156.

6. Olaus Magnus, *Description of the Northern Peoples* (Rome 1555), 3 vols., trans. Peter Fisher and Humphrey Higgens, ed. Peter Foote (London, 1998), 3:1081–1156, esp. 1095.

7. Michael Berrill and Deborah Berrill, *A Sierra Club Naturalist's Guide to the North Atlantic Coast, Cape Cod to Newfoundland* (San Francisco, 1981), 6–29; Nicholas J. Bax and Taivo Laevastu, "Biomass Potential of Large Marine Ecosystems: A Systems Approach," in *Large Marine Ecosystems: Patterns, Processes and Yields,* ed. Kenneth Sherman, Lewis M. Alexander, and Barry D. Gold (Washington D.C., 1990), 188–205; Á. Borja and M. Collins, eds., *Oceanography and Marine Environment of the Basque Country* (Amsterdam, 2004), 493–511; Hein Rune Skjoldal, ed., *The Norwegian Sea Ecosystem* (Trondheim, 2004); Daniel Pell, *Pelagos, nec inter vivos, nec inter mortuos, neither*

amongst the living, nor amongst the dead, or, An improvement of the sea (London, 1659), 209; Christopher Levett, "A Voyage into New England, Begun in 1623 and Ended in 1624," in *Collections of the Massachusetts Historical Society*, 3d ser., vol. 8 (Boston, 1843), 161. For shipmasters' preferred routes across the Atlantic see Edward Hayes, "A report of the voyage and successe thereof, attempted in the yeere of our Lord 1583 by sir Humfrey Gilbert," in Hakluyt, *Principal Navigations*, 6:7–11; Ian K. Steele, *The English Atlantic, 1675–1740: An Exploration of Communication and Community* (New York, 1986), 79.

8. Invocations of the sea's timelessness have been a staple in western culture. See T. S. Eliot, "The Dry Salvages," in *Four Quartets* (New York, 1943); Henry D. Thoreau, *Cape Cod* (1865), ed. Joseph J. Moldenhauer (Princeton, 1988), 148; Herman Melville, *Moby-Dick; or, The Whale* (1851; reprint, New York, 1972), 685; Joseph Conrad, *The Nigger of the "Narcissus"* (1897; reprint, New York, 1985), 17, 80, 87, 135, 143; John Peck, *Maritime Fiction: Sailors and the Sea in British and American Novels, 1719–1917* (Houndsmill, U.K., 2001), 80.

9. John H. Steele, "Regime shifts in Fisheries Management," *Fisheries Research* 25 (1996), 19–23; Steele, "Regime Shifts in Marine Ecosystems," *Ecological Applications* 8, no. 1, suppl. (1998), S33–S36; Nancy Knowlton, "Multiple 'Stable' States and the Conservation of Marine Ecosystems," *Progress in Oceanography* 60 (2004), 387–396; A. J. Southward, "The Western English Channel—an Inconstant Ecosystem?" *Nature* 285 (June 5, 1980), 361–366, quotation on 366.

10. Jürgen Alheit and Eberhard Hagen, "Long-Term Climate Forcing of European Herring and Sardine Populations," *Fisheries Oceanography* 6, no. 2 (1997), 130–139. A recent history drastically misinterpreted this phenomenon. See Brian Fagan, *Fish on Friday: Feasting, Fasting, and the Discovery of the New World* (New York, 2006), 125–127. The analogy to "signal" and "noise" is Jeremy B. C. Jackson's. See Jackson, "What Was Natural in the Coastal Oceans?" *Proceedings of the National Academy of Sciences USA* 98, no. 10 (May 8, 2001), 5411–5418.

11. The arrow worms favored by herring are *Sagitta elegans;* those favored by pilchards are *Sagitta setosa*. Arrow worms are in the phylum Chaetognatha. See Southward, "Western English Channel"; Wendy R. Childs and Maryanne Kowaleski, "Fishing and Fisheries in the Middle Ages," in *England's Sea Fisheries: The Commercial Sea Fisheries of England and Wales since 1300,* ed. David J. Starkey, Chris Reid, and Neil Ashcroft (London, 2000), 19–28; Michael Culley, *The Pilchard: Biology and Exploitation* (Oxford, 1971), 37–56.

12. My discussion of marine productivity is based on K. H. Mann, *Ecology of Coastal Waters with Implications for Management* (Oxford, 2000), 3–7; Berrill and Berrill, *North Atlantic Coast, Cape Cod to Newfoundland,* 45–59; Deborah Cramer, *Great Waters: An Atlantic Passage* (New York, 2001), 27–43; Raymond Pierotti, "Interactions between Gulls and Otariid Pinnipeds: Competition, Commensualism, and Cooperation," in *Seabirds & Other Marine Vertebrates: Competition, Predation, and Other Interactions,* ed. Joanna Burger (New York, 1988), 205–231.

13. Hayes, "A report of the voyage and successe thereof," 24.

14. Charles Yentsch, Janet W. Campbell, and Spencer Apollonio, "The Garden in the Sea: Biological Oceanography," in *From Cape Cod to the Bay of Fundy: An Environmental Atlas of the Gulf of Maine,* ed. Philip. W. Conkling (Cambridge, Mass., 1995), 61–76.

15. Magnus, *Description of the Northern Peoples,* 3:1062.

16. Benthic species live on the bottom of the sea. Pelagic species live in the water column or are associated with the open sea, such as pelagic birds. Polychaetes are a class of segmented marine worms, including the sandworms often sold to anglers as bait. On comparative primary productivity in European and American boreal seas, see T. Laevastu, "Natural Bases of Fisheries in the Atlantic Ocean: Their Past and Present Characteristics and Possibilities for Future Expansion," in *Atlantic Ocean Fisheries,* ed. Georg Borgstrom and Arthur J. Heighway (London, 1961), 18–39, esp. 19–20; Heike Lotze et al., "Depletion, Degradation, and Recovery Potential of Estuaries and Coastal Seas," *Science* 312 (June 23, 2006), 1806–1809, table 1; Simon Jennings, Michael J. Kaiser, and John D. Reynolds, *Marine Fisheries Ecology* (Oxford, 2001), 21–38.

17. Geoff Bailey, James Barrett, Oliver Craig, and Nicky Milner, "Historical Ecology of the North Sea Basin: An Archaeological Perspective and Some Problems of Methodology," in *Human Impacts on Ancient Marine Ecosystems: A Global Perspective,* ed. Torben C. Rick and Jon M. Erlandson (Berkeley, 2008), 215–242; Sophia Perdikaris and Thomas H. McGovern, "Codfish and Kings, Seals and Subsistence: Norse Marine Resource Use in the North Atlantic," ibid., 192–199. Analysis of stable carbon and nitrogen isotopes in bones of the deceased can indicate the relative proportion of marine protein and terrestrial protein in a human's diet.

18. Lotze et al., "Depletion, Degradation, and Recovery Potential"; Richard C. Hoffmann, "Economic Development and Aquatic Ecosystems in Medieval Europe," *American Historical Review* 101 (June 1996), 631–669; James H. Barrett, Alison M. Locker, and Callum M. Roberts, "The Origins of Intensive Marine Fishing in Medieval Europe: The English Evidence," *Proceedings of the Royal Society of London B* 271 (2004), 2417–2421; Inge Bødker Enghoff, "Fishing in the Southern North Sea Region from the 1st to the 16th Century A.D.: Evidence from Fish Bones," *Archaeofauna* 9 (2000), 59–132.

19. Anton Ervynck, Wim Van Neer, and Marnix Pieters, "How the North Was Won (and Lost Again): Historical and Archaeological Data on the Exploitation of the North Atlantic by the Flemish Fishery," *Atlantic Connections and Adaptations: Economies, Environments and Subsistence in Lands Bordering the North Atlantic,* ed. Rupert A. Housley and Geraint Coles, Symposia of the Association for Environmental Archaeology no. 21 (Oxford, 2004), 230–239.

20. C. Anne Wilson, *Food & Drink in Britain: From the Stone Age to the 19th Century* (1973; reprint, Chicago, 1991), 18–59; Bailey et al., "Historical Ecology of the North Sea Basin," 215–242, quotation on 231; Perdikaris and McGovern, "Codfish and Kings, Seals and Subsistence," 192–199.

21. Sophia Perdikaris, "From Chiefly Provisioning to Commercial Fishery: Long-Term Economic Change in Arctic Norway," *World Archaeology* 30 (February 1999), 388–402;

Perdikaris and Thomas H. McGovern, "Cod Fish, Walrus, and Chieftains: Economic Intensification in the Norse North Atlantic," in *Seeking a Richer Harvest: The Archaeology of Subsistence Intensification, Innovation, and Change,* ed. Tina L. Thurston and Christopher T. Fisher (New York, 2007), 193–216; Perdikaris and McGovern, "Codfish and Kings, Seals and Subsistence," 187–214.

22. Bailey et al., "Historical Ecology of the North Sea Basin," 215–242; Perdikaris and McGovern, "Codfish and Kings, Seals and Subsistence," 187–214.

23. Perdikaris and McGovern, "Codfish and Kings, Seals and Subsistence," 192–199, quotation on 194.

24. Jeffrey S. Levinton, *Marine Biology: Function, Biodiversity, Ecology* (New York, 2001), 424; K. S. Petersen, K. L. Rasmussen, J. Heinemeier, and N. Rud, "Clams before Columbus?" *Nature* 359 (1992), 679; Alfred W. Crosby Jr., *The Columbian Exchange: Biological and Cultural Consequences of 1492* (Westport, Conn., 1972). The common periwinkle is known by scientists as *Littorina littorea.* Softshell clams are *Mya arenaria;* the common cockle is *Cardium edule.*

25. Fagan, *Fish on Friday,* quotation on xiii; Wilson, *Food and Drink in Britain,* quotation on 38.

26. D. H. Cushing, *The Provident Sea* (Cambridge, 1988), 77–101; Maryanne Kowaleski, "The Commercialization of the Sea Fisheries in Medieval England and Wales," *International Journal of Maritime History* 15 (December 2003), 177–231.

27. Childs and Kowaleski, "Fishing and Fisheries in the Middle Ages," 19; Richard W. Unger, "The Netherlands Herring Fishery in the Late Middle Ages: The False Legend of William Beukels of Biervliet," in Unger, *Ships and Shipping in the North Sea and Atlantic, 1400–1800* (Aldershot, U.K., 1997), 335–356; Hoffmann, "Economic Development and Aquatic Ecosystems," 648. For the intensification of estuarine and coastal fisheries in the west country of England during the late Middle Ages, see Harold Fox, *The Evolution of the Fishing Village: Landscape and Society along the South Devon Coast, 1086–1550* (Oxford, 2001).

28. C. J. Bond, "Monastic Fisheries," in *Medieval Fish, Fisheries, and Fishponds in England,* ed. Michael Aston, 2 parts, BAR British Series 182(i) (n.p., 1988), 1:69–112, quotation on 86–87.

29. This paragraph closely follows Bond, "Monastic Fisheries." See also S. Moorhouse, "Medieval Fishponds: Some Thoughts," in Aston, *Medieval Fish, Fisheries and Fishponds,* 2:479–480. The seminal study of the impact of medieval economic activity on aquatic ecosystems is Hoffmann, "Economic Development and Aquatic Ecosystems."

30. Bond, "Monastic Fisheries," 79; Moorhouse, "Medieval Fishponds," 479–480; Kowaleski, "Commercialization of Sea Fisheries," 190.

31. Kowaleski, "Commercialization of Sea Fisheries," 190; Bond, "Monastic Fisheries," 79; Wilson, *Food and Drink in Britain,* 21; Colin Platt, *Medieval England: A Social History and Archaeology from the Conquest to 1600 A.D.* (London, 1994), 187–188.

32. Heike K. Lotze, "Rise and Fall of Fishing and Marine Resource Use in the Wadden Sea, Southern North Sea," *Fisheries Research* 87 (November 2007), 208–218.

33. Childs and Kowaleski, "Fishing and Fisheries in the Middle Ages," 19; Maryanne Kowaleski, "The Expansion of the South-Western Fisheries in Late Medieval England," *Economic History Review* 53, no. 3 (2000), 429–454; Kowaleski, "Commercialization of Sea Fisheries," 177–231; Unger, "Netherlands Herring Fishery," 335–356.

34. Edward Sharpe, *England's Royall Fishing Revived or A Computation as well of the Charge of a Busse or Herring-Fishing Ship* (London, 1630), p. E 3.

35. Bo Poulsen, *Dutch Herring: An Environmental History, c. 1600–1860* (Amsterdam, 2008), 40–80.

36. A. Rallo and Á. Borja, "Marine Research in the Basque Country: An Historical Perspective," in Borja and Collins, *Oceanography and Marine Environment of the Basque Country,* 3–26, esp. 5; Survey of Fisheries, 1580, reproduced as app. 3.1 in Todd Gray, "Devon's Coastal and Overseas Fisheries and New England Migration, 1597–1642" (Ph.D. diss., University of Exeter, U.K., 1988), 357–358; Alex Aguilar, "A Review of Old Basque Whaling and Its Effect on the Right Whales *(Eubalaena glacialis)* of the North Atlantic," *Reports of the International Whaling Commission (Special Issue)* 10 (1986), 191–199, quotation on 194; Wim J. Wolff, "The South-eastern North Sea: Losses of Vertebrate Fauna during the Past 2000 years," *Biological Conservation* 95 (2000), 209–217; W. M. A. De Smet, "Evidence of Whaling in the North Sea and the English Channel during the Middle Ages," in *Mammals in the Seas,* FAO Fisheries Series no. 5, vol. 3: *General Papers and Large Cetaceans: Selected Papers of the Scientific Consultation on the Conservation and Management of Marine Mammals and Their Environment* (Rome: Food and Agricultural Organization of the United Nations, 1981), 301–309; Richard Mather, *Journal of Richard Mather* (Boston, 1850), quoted in Joe Roman and Stephen R. Palumbi, "Whales before Whaling in the North Atlantic," *Science* 301 (July 25, 2003), 508–510.

37. Wolff, "The South-eastern North Sea: Losses of Vertebrate Fauna," 210–213.

38. Ibid., 211; Cornelis Swennen, "Ecology and Population Dynamics of the Common Eider in the Dutch Wadden Sea" (Ph.D. diss., Rijksuniversiteit, Groningen, 1991); Lotze, "Rise and Fall of Fishing and Marine Resource Use."

39. Hoffmann, "Economic Development and Aquatic Ecosystems," 649–650.

40. Jennings, Kaiser, and Reynolds, *Marine Fisheries Ecology,* 242–243; Tony J. Pitcher, "Fisheries Managed to Rebuild Ecosystems? Reconstructing the Past to Salvage the Future," *Ecological Applications* 11, no. 2 (2001), 601–617; Poulsen, *Dutch Herring,* 40–80.

41. David B. Quinn, ed., *New American World: A Documentary History of North America to 1612,* 5 vols. (New York, 1979), 1:93–98.

42. Ramsay Cook, ed., *The Voyages of Jacques Cartier* (Toronto, 1993), 8, 12, 25; Robert Mandrou, *Introduction to Modern France, 1500–1640: An Essay in Historical Psychology* (London, 1975), 239. For Europeans' attitudes to nature during the Renaissance and

early modern eras see Clarence J. Glacken, *Traces on the Rhodian Shore: Nature and Culture in Western Thought from Ancient Times to the End of the Eighteenth Century* (Berkeley, 1967); Keith Thomas, *Man and the Natural World: Changing Attitudes in England, 1500–1800* (London, 1983).

43. Cook, *Voyages of Jacques Cartier,* 48.

44. Quinn, *New American World,* 4:343–344.

45. Carl N. Shuster Jr., Robert B. Barlow, and H. Jane Brockman, eds., *The American Horseshoe Crab* (Cambridge, Mass., 2003), 5–32, 133–153.

46. Farley Mowat, *Sea of Slaughter* (Boston, 1984), 300–323; Tony J. Pitcher, Johanna J. (Sheila) Heymans, and Marcelo Vasconcellos, "Ecosystem Models of Newfoundland for the Time Periods 1995, 1985, 1900, and 1450," *Fisheries Centre Research Reports* 10, no. 5 (Vancouver, Fisheries Center, University of British Columbia, 2002), 5, 44–45.

47. *The Ice Regime of the Gulf of St. Lawrence,* Enfotec Monograph no. 1 (Ottawa, n.d.), http://www.amac.ca/enfotec1.htm (accessed January 5, 2009).

48. Perdikaris and McGovern, "Codfish and Kings, Seal and Subsistence"; Niels Lund, ed., *Two Voyagers at the Court of King Alfred: The Ventures of OTHERE and WULFSTAN together with the Description of Northern Europe from the OLD ENGLISH OROSIUS,* trans. Christine E. Fell (York, U.K., 1984); Mowat, *Sea of Slaughter,* 300–323.

49. Cook, *Voyages of Jacques Cartier,* 46; Hayes, "A report of the voyage and successe thereof," 32.

50. For walrus in coastal Europe, see Sir Alister Hardy, *The Open Sea: Its Natural History,* Part II: *Fish and Fisheries, with Chapters on Whales, Turtles and Animals of the Sea Floor* (Boston, 1959), 287, 291; Charles Leigh, "The Voyage of M. Charles Leigh, and divers others to Cape Briton and the Isle of Ramea" (1598), in Hakluyt, *Principal Navigations,* 6:101; Thomas James to Lord Burghley (September 14, 1591), in Quinn, *New American World,* 4:59–60; Richard Hakluyt, "A briefe note of the Morsse and the use thereof," in Hakluyt, *Principal Navigations,* 4:60.

51. Leigh, "Voyage of M. Charles Leigh," 101, 107, 113; John Brereton, "A Briefe and True Relation of the Discoverie of the North Part of Virginia" (1602), in *The English New England Voyages, 1602–1608,* ed. David B. Quinn and Alison M. Quinn (London, 1983), 152.

52. For reference to "Bunyanesque" exaggerations see Patricia Cline Cohen, *A Calculating People: The Spread of Numeracy in Early America* (Chicago, 1982), 50. Stephen Greenblatt refers to the authors of the first anecdotes about the New World as "liars." See Greenblatt, *Marvelous Possessions: The Wonder of the New World* (Chicago, 1991), 7.

53. Leigh, "Voyage of M. Charles Leigh," 114.

54. Brereton, "Briefe and True Relation," in Quinn and Quinn, *English New England Voyages,* 171; Gabriel Archer, "The Relation of Captaine Gosnols Voyage to the North Part of Virginia" (1602), ibid., 118.

55. John Smith, *A Description of New England* (1616) in *The Complete Works of Captain John Smith (1580–1621),* 3 vols., ed. Philip L. Barbour (Chapel Hill, 1986), 1:347;

Leigh, "Voyage of M. Charles Leigh," 101, 107, 113; Frederic A. Lucas, "The Bird Rocks of the Gulf of St. Lawrence in 1887," *The Auk: A Quarterly Journal of Ornithology* 5 (April 1888), 129–135.

56. James Rosier, "A True Relation of the Most Prosperous Voyage Made this Present Yeere 1605, by Captain George Waymouth, in the Discovery of the Land of Virginia," in Quinn and Quinn, *English New England Voyages,* 260, 264.

57. Marc Lescarbot, *History of New France,* 3 vols. (1616; reprint, Toronto, 1914), 3:236; Robert Juet, "The Third Voyage of Master Henry Hudson, Written by Robert Juet, of Lime-House," in *Sailors' Narratives of Voyages along the New England Coast, 1524–1624,* ed. George Parker Winship (1905; reprint, New York, 1968), 179–192.

58. For bone analysis of large cod landed in prehistoric eras, see Bruce J. Bourque, *Diversity and Complexity in Prehistoric Maritime Societies: A Gulf of Maine Perspective* (New York, 1996); Catherine C. Carlson, "Maritime Catchment Areas: An Analysis of Prehistoric Fishing Strategies in the Boothbay Region of Maine" (M.S. thesis, University of Maine, Orono, 1986). For seventeenth-century fishmongers' categorization of cod by size, see Cushing, *The Provident Sea,* 60; John Mason, *A Briefe Discourse of the New-found-land, with the situation, temperature, and commodities thereof, inciting our Nation to goe forward in that hopefull plantation begunne* (Edinburgh, 1620), n.p.

59. My discussion of numeracy and estimates is based on Frank J. Swetz, *Capitalism and Arithmetic: The New Math of the 15th Century* (La Salle, Ill., 1987); Alfred W. Crosby, *The Measure of Reality: Quantification and Western Society, 1250–1600* (Cambridge, 1997); David Hackett Fischer, *The Great Wave: Price Revolutions and the Rhythm of History* (Oxford, 1996). While Patricia Cline Cohen's assessment of "the narrow scope of numeracy" among seventeenth-century Englishmen in America is spot-on, her dismissive attitude with regard to the "extravagant claims" in promotional tracts about the coast of North America is not warranted. Cohen, *A Calculating People,* 47–51.

60. Darrett B. Rutman, *Husbandmen of Plymouth: Farms and Villages in the Old Colony, 1620–1692* (Boston, 1967), 19.

61. Richard Hakluyt, "A Briefe Note Concerning the Voyage of M. George Drake," (1593), in Hakluyt, *Principal Navigations,* 6:97; Parkhurst, "A letter written to M. Richard Hakluyt," 5:344; Sylvester Wyet, "The Voyage of the Grace of Bristol" (1594), ibid., 6:98–100; Laurier Turgeon, "Bordeaux and the Newfoundland Trade during the Sixteenth Century," *International Journal of Maritime History* 9, no. 2 (1997), 1–28. See also Selma Huxley Barkham, "The Mentality of the Men behind Sixteenth-Century Spanish Voyages to Terranova," in *Decentring the Renaissance: Canada and Europe in Multidisciplinary Perspective, 1500–1700,* ed. Germaine Warkentin and Carolyn Podruchny (Toronto, 2001), 110–124.

62. These chroniclers include, but are not limited to, Jacques Cartier (1534), Anthony Parkhurst (1578), Gabriel Archer (1602), John Brereton (1602), Martin Pring (1603), Samuel de Champlain (1603), James Rosier (1605), Marc Lescarbot (1612), Captain John Smith (1614), *Mourt's Relation* (1622), Francis Higginson (1630), Thomas Morton (1632), William

Wood (1634), Roger Williams (1643), William Bradford (1620–1650), John Winthrop (1630–1649), John Josselyn (1638–1671), and Samuel Maverick (1660).

63. Gray, "Devon's Coastal and Overseas Fisheries," 27, 357–358.

64. Lotze, "Rise and Fall of Fishing and Marine Resource Use"; Lotze et al., "Depletion, Degradation, and Recovery Potential"; J. B. C. Jackson et al., "Historical Overfishing and the Recent Collapse of Coastal Ecosystems," *Science* 293 (July 27, 2001), 629–638; Barry Cunliffe, *Facing the Ocean: The Atlantic and Its Peoples, 8000 B.C.–A.D. 1500* (Oxford, 2001), 109–158.

65. Pierre Biard, "Relation of New France, of Its Lands, Nature of the Country, and of Its Inhabitants" (1616), in *The Jesuit Relations and Allied Documents: Travels and Explorations of the Jesuit Missionaries in New France, 1610–1791,* ed. Reuben Gold Thwaites, 73 vols. (New York, 1959), 3:20–283, esp. 79–81; Lucien Campeau, "Biard, Pierre," in *Dictionary of Canadian Biography Online,* http://www.biographi.ca (accessed January 14, 2009).

66. "Martin Pring's Voyage to 'North Virginia' in 1603," in Quinn and Quinn, *English New England Voyages,* 212–230, quotation on 226.

67. Nathalie Fiquet, "Brouage in the Time of Champlain: A New Town Open to the World," in *Champlain: The Birth of French America,* ed. Raymonde Litalien and Denis Vaugeois, trans. Käthe Roth (Montreal, 2004), 33–41.

68. Tim D. Smith, *Scaling Fisheries: The Science of Measuring the Effects of Fishing, 1855–1955* (Cambridge, 1994), 8–37, quotation on 8; Gray, "Devon's Coastal and Overseas Fisheries," 107, 126–127; Brian Fagan, *The Little Ice Age: How Climate Made History, 1300–1850* (New York, 2000), 69–78; E. M. Carrus Wilson, "The Iceland Trade," in *Studies in English Trade in the Fifteenth Century,* ed. Eileen Power and M. M. Postan (New York, 1933), 155–183. For the complicated relationship between climate fluctuations and marine ecology, see Jean M. Grove, *The Little Ice Age* (London, 1988), 379–421; Geir Ottersen et al., "The Responses of Fish Populations to Ocean Climate Fluctuations," in *Marine Ecosystems and Climate Variation: The North Atlantic, A Comparative Perspective,* ed. Nils Chr. Stenseth and Geir Ottersen (Oxford, 2004), 73–94; Holger Hovgård and Erik Buch, "Fluctuation in the Cod Biomass of the West Greenland Sea Ecosystem in Relation to Climate," in Sherman, Alexander, and Gold, *Large Marine Ecosystems,* 36–43.

69. John Brewer and Roy Porter, eds., *Consumption and the World of Goods* (London, 1993), ignore the environmental impact of globalization and consumer culture. Peter E. Pope, *Fish into Wine: The Newfoundland Plantation in the Seventeenth Century* (Chapel Hill, 2004), 19–20; Pope, "The Scale of the Early Modern Newfoundland Cod Fishery," in *The North Atlantic Fisheries: Supply, Marketing and Consumption, 1560–1990,* ed. David J. Starkey and James E. Candow (Hull, U.K., 2006), 27–28; George A. Rose, *Cod: The Ecological History of the North Atlantic Fisheries* (St. John's, Newf., 2007), 241, 286.

70. Richard C. Hoffmann, "Frontier Foods for Late Medieval Consumers: Culture, Economy, Ecology," *Environment and History* 7 (May 2001), 131–167, quotation on 133;

Gary Shepherd and James Walton, *Shipping, Maritime Trade, and the Economic Development of Colonial North America* (Cambridge, 1972), 3.

2. PLUCKING THE LOW-HANGING FRUIT

1. William Wood, *New England's Prospect* (1634; reprint, Amherst, Mass., 1977), 107; Bernard Gilbert Hoffman, "The Historical Ethnography of the Micmac of the Sixteenth and Seventeenth Centuries" (Ph.D. diss., University of California, Berkeley, 1955), 151–171, 235; Carolyn Merchant, *Ecological Revolutions: Nature, Gender, and Science in New England* (Chapel Hill, 1989), 44–50; Kathleen J. Bragdon, *Native People of Southern New England, 1500–1650* (Norman, Okla., 1996); Harald E. L. Prins, *The Mi'kmaq: Resistance, Accommodation, and Cultural Survival* (Belmont, Calif., 2002).

2. Christopher Levett, "A Voyage into New England, Begun in 1623 and Ended in 1624," *Collections of the Massachusetts Historical Society,* 3d ser., 8 (Boston, 1843), 184–185; John Smith, *A Description of New England* (1616), in *The Complete Works of Captain John Smith (1580–1631),* 3 vols., ed. Philip L. Barbour (Chapel Hill, 1986), 1:330, 333.

3. Everett Emerson, ed., *Letters from New England: The Massachusetts Bay Colony, 1629–1638* (Amherst, Mass., 1976), 33.

4. Wood, *New England's Prospect,* 62–63.

5. Wood, *New England's Prospect,* 58, 64. On alewives as passenger pigeons of the sea, see William Cronon, *Changes in the Land: Indians, Colonists, and the Ecology of New England* (New York, 1983), 23; Captain Charles Whitborne, in *The True Travels of Captain John Smith,* quoted in Henry B. Bigelow and William C. Schroeder, *Fishes of the Gulf of Maine* (Washington, D.C., 1953), 102; Karin E. Limburg and John R. Waldman, "Dramatic Declines in North Atlantic Diadromous Fishes," *BioScience* 59, no. 11 (December 2009), 955–965.

6. Nathaniel B. Shurtleff, ed., vols. 1–8, and David Pulsifer, ed., vols. 9–12, *Records of the Colony of New Plymouth in New England,* 12 vols. (Boston, 1855–1861), 1:17; Isaack De Rasieres to Samuel Blommaert (ca. 1628), in *Three Visitors to Early Plymouth: Letters about the Pilgrim Settlement in New England during Its First Seven Years by John Pory, Emmanuel Altham, and Isaack De Rasieres,* ed. Sidney V. James (Plymouth, Mass., 1963), 75–76. The "shad" at Plymouth to which De Rasieres referred were probably alewives.

7. Edward Johnson, *Wonder-Working Providence of Sions Saviour in New England (1654) and Good News From New England (1648),* ed. Edward J. Gallagher (Delmar, N.Y., 1974), 173.

8. Genesis 49:25.

9. Kenneth Sherman, Lewis M. Alexander, and Barry D. Gold, eds., *Large Marine Ecosystems: Patterns, Processes, and Yields* (Washington, D.C., 1990), vii; Smith, *Description of New England,* 360. For the global reorganization of Large Marine Ecosystems in 2002 see http://na.nefsc.gov/lmetext/htm.

10. John Noble, ed., vols. 1–2, and John F. Cronin, ed., vol. 3, *Records of the Court of Assistants of the Colony of Massachusetts Bay, 1630–1692,* 3 vols. (Boston, 1901–1904), 2:37; Pulsifer, *Records of New Plymouth,* 11:5, 16; Shurtleff, *Records of New Plymouth,* 1:17.

11. William Bradford, *Of Plimouth Plantation, 1620–1647,* ed. Samuel Eliot Morison (New York, 1953), 122–123, 130–131.

12. Wood, *New England's Prospect,* 55; John Smith, *Advertisements for the Unexperienced Planters of New England, or Anywhere* (1633), in Barbour, *Complete Works of Captain John Smith,* 3:282.

13. Average weight of twentieth-century fish from Bigelow and Schroeder, *Fishes of the Gulf of Maine,* 390. Wood corroborated Smith's observations on bass landings, noting that "sometimes two or three thousand" bass were taken in one set of a net. Wood, *New England's Prospect,* 55. Samuel Eliot Morison, *The Story of the "Old Colony" of New Plymouth, 1620–1692* (New York, 1956), 122.

14. Bradford, *Plimouth Plantation,* 122, n. 3.

15. Shurtleff, *Records of New Plymouth,* 2:161–162.

16. *Second Report of the Record Commissioners of the City of Boston; Containing the Boston Records, 1634–1660, and the Book of Possessions* (Boston, 1881), 11.

17. Nathaniel B. Shurtleff, ed., *Records of the Governor and Company of the Massachusetts Bay in New England,* 5 vols. (Boston, 1853), 1:100, 102, 114; Wood, *New England's Prospect,* 60; Shurtleff, *Records of New Plymouth,* 1:131, 3:76; William B. Leavenworth, "The Changing Landscape of Maritime Resources in Seventeenth-Century New England," *International Journal of Maritime History* 20, no. 1 (June 2008), 33–62.

18. Charles S. Yentsch, Janet W. Campbell, and Spencer Apollonio, "The Garden in the Sea: Biological Oceanography," in *From Cape Cod to the Bay of Fundy: An Environmental Atlas of the Gulf of Maine,* ed. Philip W. Conkling (Cambridge, Mass., 1995), 61–76, quotation on 71.

19. John J. McCusker, "Measuring Colonial Gross Domestic Product: An Introduction," *William and Mary Quarterly,* 3d ser., 56 (January 1999), 3–8; McCusker and Russell R. Menard, *The Economy of British America, 1607–1789* (Chapel Hill, 1985), 5.

20. Shurtleff, *Records of New Plymouth,* 4:57, 4:66, 3:175.

21. Pulsifer, *Records of New Plymouth,* 10:251; Harry M. Ward, *The United Colonies of New England, 1643–1690* (New York, 1961); The Articles of Confederation of the United Colonies of New England, May 19, 1643, http://avalon.law.yale.edu/17th_century/art1613.asp.

22. Bigelow and Schroeder, *Fishes of the Gulf of Maine,* 317–333; Wood, *New England's Prospect,* 63.

23. J. W. Horwood and D. H. Cushing, "Spatial Distribution and Ecology of Pelagic Fish," in *Spatial Pattern in Plankton Communities,* ed. J. H. Steele (New York, 1978), 355–383; Emerson, *Letters from New England,* 33.

24. Pulsifer, *Records of New Plymouth,* 10:251.

25. Shurtleff, *Records of Massachusetts Bay,* 4 (pt. 2):450, 462; Shurtleff, *Records of New Plymouth,* 5:63; Pulsifer, *Records of New Plymouth,* 11:228.

26. Shurtleff, *Records of New Plymouth,* 6:139–140.

27. Shurtleff, *Records of Massachusetts Bay,* 4 (pt. 2):462; Shurtleff, *Records of New Plymouth,* 5:63, 5:107, 3:15–16.

28. Neill DePaoli, "Life on the Edge: Community and Trade on the Anglo-American Periphery, Pemaquid, Maine, 1610–1689" (Ph.D. diss., University of New Hampshire, 2001); Daniel Vickers, *Farmers and Fishermen: Two Centuries of Work in Essex County, Massachusetts, 1630–1850* (Chapel Hill, 1994), 85–100, quotation on 98; Christine Heyrman, *Commerce and Culture: The Maritime Communities of Colonial Massachusetts, 1690–1750* (New York, 1984), 31–35.

29. Shurtleff, *Records of Massachusetts Bay,* 1:158, 230, 256; Emerson, *Letters from New England,* 94; Leavenworth, "Changing Landscape of Maritime Resources"; Vickers, *Farmers and Fishermen,* 85–100.

30. Vickers, *Farmers and Fishermen,* 98. This section closely follows Vickers.

31. Ibid., 91–98.

32. Shurtleff, *Records of Massachusetts Bay,* 4 (pt. 2): 400.

33. Peter Pope, "Early Estimates: Assessment of Catches in the Newfoundland Cod Fishery, 1660–1690," in *Marine Resources and Human Societies in the North Atlantic since 1500: Papers Presented at the Conference Entitled "Marine Resources and Human Societies in the North Atlantic since 1500," October 20–22, 1995,* ed. Daniel Vickers (St. John's, Newf., 1997), 7–40, quotation on 12; Bernard Bailyn, *The New England Merchants in the Seventeenth Century* (Cambridge, Mass., 1955), 14; Levett, "A Voyage into New England," 180; *A Volume Relating to the Early History of Boston Containing the Aspinwall Notarial Records from 1644 to 1651* (Boston, 1903), 390–391.

34. Pope, "Early Estimates," 12; Petition of Samuel Knowles, Agent for the town of Eastham, to the House of Representatives of Massachusetts, October 25, 1748, Massachusetts Archives, 115:419–420, MSA; Petition of Grafton Gardner et al. of Nantucket to the House of Representatives of Massachusetts, June 1751, Massachusetts Archives, 116:127–129, MSA.

35. W. H. Lear, "History of Fisheries in the Northwest Atlantic: The 500-Year Perspective," *Journal of Northwest Atlantic Fisheries Science* 23 (1998), 41–73; Peter E. Pope, *Fish into Wine: The Newfoundland Plantation in the Seventeenth Century* (Chapel Hill, 2004), 33–37; George A. Rose, *Cod: The Ecological History of the North Atlantic Fisheries* (St. John's, Newf., 2007), 240–241, 286–387; Jeffrey A. Hutchings, "Spatial and Temporal Variation in the Exploitation of Northern Cod, *Gadus morhua:* A Historical Perspective from 1500 to the Present," in Vickers, *Marine Resources and Human Societies,* 43–68.

36. Leavenworth, "Changing Landscape of Maritime Resources," 36–37.

37. William Monson, *Naval Tracts* (1703), in *The Fish and Fisheries of Colonial North America: A Documentary History of Fishing Resources of the United States and Canada,* ed. John C. Pearson, *Part 1: The Canadian Atlantic Provinces,* NOAA Report No.

72040301 (Rockville, Md., 1972), 85–86; Montesquieu quoted in Clarence J. Glacken, *Traces on the Rhodian Shore: Nature and Culture in Western Thought from Ancient Times to the End of the Eighteenth Century* (Berkeley, 1967), 659; J. B. Lamarck, *Zoological Philosophy: An Exposition with Regard to the Natural History of Animals* (1809; reprint, Chicago, 1984), 45.

38. Petition of Henry Prescott, New Castle, New Hampshire, December 12, 1776, Petitions to the Governor, Council, and Legislature, New Hampshire Department of Archives and Records, Concord; Petition of George Frost Jr. on behalf of the town of New Castle, New Hampshire, December 1786, ibid.; William Hubbard, *A General History of New England from the Discovery to MDCLXXX* (Cambridge, Mass., 1815), 25; Lorenzo Sabine Papers, box 1, folder 10, "Fisheries as a Source of Wealth," October 7, 1832, New Hampshire Historical Society, Concord.

39. *Mourt's Relation or Journall of the beginning and proceeding of the English Plantation settled at Plimoth in New England* (London, 1622), 2. *Mourt's Relation* is considered to be the work of several authors, primarily William Bradford and Edward Winslow. John Braginton-Smith and Duncan Oliver, *Cape Cod Shore Whaling: America's First Whalemen* (Yarmouth Port, Mass., 2004), 148.

40. Bradford, *Plimouth Plantation*, 68.

41. Joe Roman and Stephen R. Palumbi, "Whales before Whaling in the North Atlantic," *Science* 301 (July 25, 2003), 508–510; C. Scott Baker and Phillip J. Clapham, "Modelling the Past and Future of Whales and Whaling," *Trends in Ecology and Evolution* 19, no. 7 (July 1, 2004), 365–371; Spencer Apollonio, *Hierarchical Perspectives on Marine Complexities: Searching for Systems in the Gulf of Maine* (New York, 2002), 59.

42. A. Rallo and Á. Borja, "Marine Research in the Basque Country: An Historical Perspective," in *Oceanography and Marine Environment of the Basque Country,* ed. Á. Borja and M. Collins (Amsterdam, 2004), 3–26, quotation on 5; Todd Gray, "Devon's Coastal and Overseas Fisheries and New England Migration" (Ph.D. diss., University of Exeter, 1988), 357–358; Alex Aguilar, "A Review of Old Basque Whaling and Its Effect on the Right Whales *(Eubalaena glacialis)* of the North Atlantic," *Reports of the International Whaling Commission* (special issue) 10 (1986), 191–199; Richard Mather, *Journal of Richard Mather* (Boston, 1850), quoted in Roman and Palumbi, "Whales before Whaling in the North Atlantic," 508–510. For an alternative but less convincing view that Basque whalemen probably did not diminish stocks in the Bay of Biscay, see Jean-Pierre Proulx, *Basque Whaling in Labrador in the 16th Century* (Ottawa, 1993), 12–13; Roger Collins, *The Basques* (Cambridge, Mass, 1986), 234–235.

43. Archaeologists point out that "the interpretation of data on . . . large whales [at Native sites is] poorly understood." See Arthur E. Spiess and Robert A. Lewis, *The Turner Farm Fauna: 5000 Years of Hunting and Fishing in Penobscot Bay, Maine* (Augusta, Maine, 2001), 141, 154, 157–159, quotation on 141. Russel Lawrence Barsh, *"Netukulimk* Past and Present: Mi'kmaw Ethics and the Atlantic Fishery," *Journal of Canadian Studies* 37, no. 1 (Spring 2002), 15–42; Hoffman, "Historical Ethnography of the

Micmac"; Elizabeth A. Little and J. Clinton Andrews, "Drift Whales at Nantucket: The Kindness of Moshup," *Man in the Northeast* 23 (Spring 1982), 19; Nicolas Denys, *The Description & Natural History of the Coasts of North America (Acadia),* trans. and ed. William F. Ganong (1672; reprint, Toronto, 1908), 403. During the seventeenth century Marc Lescarbot and Chrestian LeClerq referred in passing to Mi'kmaq whaling from seagoing canoes off eastern Canada. The only reference to Natives hunting whales off New England is found in James Rosier's *A True Relation,* describing Maine in 1605.

44. Little and Andrews, "Drift Whales at Nantucket," 33–35, 21, 29; John A. Strong, *The Montaukett Indians of Eastern Long Island* (Syracuse, N.Y., 2001), 25–26. Mather quoted in Glover M. Allen, "The Whalebone Whales of New England," *Memoirs of the Boston Society of Natural History* 8 (1916), 105–322, quotation on 154.

45. William Douglass, *A Summary, Historical and Political, of the First Planting, Progressive Improvements, and Present State of the British Settlements in North America,* 2 vols. (Boston, 1755), 1:58–62. Braginton-Smith and Oliver, *Cape Cod Shore Whaling,* 143, 145.

46. For conservative estimates of whale kills, see Randall R. Reeves, Jeffrey M. Breiwick, and Edward D. Mitchell, "History of Whaling and Estimated Kill of Right Whales, *Balaena glacialis,* in the Northeastern United States, 1620–1924," *Marine Fisheries Review* 61 (1999), 1–36. For more expansive estimates see Apollonio, *Hierarchical Perspectives,* 60–61. Mellen quotation in Donald G. Trayser, *Barnstable: Three Centuries of a Cape Cod Town* (Hyannis, Mass., 1939), 326–327.

47. Laurier Turgeon, "Fluctuations in Cod and Whale Stocks in the North Atlantic during the Eighteenth Century," in Vickers, *Marine Resources and Human Societies,* 87–122; John F. Richards, *The Unending Frontier: An Environmental History of the Early Modern World* (Berkeley, 2003), 584–589.

48. Braginton-Smith and Oliver, *Cape Cod Shore Whaling,* 145. Occasional references to shore whaling and whaleboats occur in Ipswich records as late as 1707, but not thereafter. Thomas Franklin Waters, *Ipswich in the Massachusetts Bay Colony: A History of the Town from 1700 to 1917,* 2 vols. (Ipswich, 1917), 2:235–236. For the abandonment of a Cape Cod whalers' tavern in Wellfleet, probably because of the failure of the inshore whale fishery, see Eric Ekholm and James Deetz, "Wellfleet Tavern," *Natural History* 80, no. 7 (August–September 1971), 48–56. On Indian whalemen, see Daniel Vickers, "The First Whalemen of Nantucket," *William and Mary Quarterly,* 3d ser., 40 (October 1983), 560–583; Vickers, "Nantucket Whalemen in the Deep-Sea Fishery: The Changing Anatomy of an Early American Labor Force," *Journal of American History* 72 (September 1985), 277–296.

49. On whales as constraints in ecosystems, see Apollonio, *Hierarchical Perspectives,* 14–15, 53–71. For a similar ripple effect from whaling in the Svalbard archipelago see Louwrens Hacquebord, "The Hunting of the Greenland Right Whale in Svalbard, Its Interaction with Climate and Its Impact on the Marine Ecosystem," *Polar Research* 18

(1999), 375–382; Hacquebord, "Three Centuries of Whaling and Walrus Hunting in Svalbard and Its Impact on the Arctic Ecosystem," *Environment and History* 7 (2001), 169–185.

50. Obed Macy, *The History of Nantucket: Being a Compendious Account of the First Settlement of the Island by the English, Together with the Rise and Progress of the Whale Fishery; And Other Historical Facts Relative to Said Island and Its Inhabitants* (Boston, 1835), 28; Paul Dudley, "An Essay upon the Natural History of Whales, with a Particular Account of the Ambergris Found in the *Sperma Ceti* Whale," *Philosophical Transactions (1683–1775)* 33 (1725), 256–269; James G. Mead and Edward D. Mitchell, "Atlantic Gray Whales," in *The Gray Whale,* ed. Mary Lou Jones, Steven L. Swartz, and Stephen Leatherwood (Orlando, 1984), 33–53; P. J. Bryant, "Dating Remains of Gray Whales from the Eastern North Atlantic," *Journal of Mammalogy* 76, no. 3 (1995), 857–861.

51. E. W. Born, I. Gjertz, and R. Reeves, *Population Assessment of Atlantic Walrus,* Meddelelser No. 138 (Oslo, 1995), 7–8, 31–32.

52. Molineux Shuldham, "Account of the Sea-Cow, and the Use Made of It," *Philosophical Transactions (1683–1775),* 65 (1775), 249–251; Joel Asaph Allen, *History of North American Pinnipeds: A Monograph of the Walruses, Sea-Lions, Sea-Bears, and Seals of North America* (Washington, D.C., 1880), 65–71.

53. John Winthrop, *History of New England, 1630–1649,* 2 vols., ed. James K. Hosmer (New York, 1908) 2:35–36; Born, Gjertz, and Reeves, *Population Assessment of Atlantic Walrus,* 10, 31–32.

54. Henry C. Kittredge, *Cape Cod: Its People and Their History* (Cambridge, Mass., 1930), 184.

55. Edward Chappell, *Voyage of H.M.S.* Rosamond *to Newfoundland and the Southern Coast of Labrador* (London, 1817), 197–198; George Cartwright, *A Journal of Transactions and Events during a Residence of Nearly Sixteen Years on the Coast of Labrador; Containing Many Interesting Particulars, both of the Country and Its Inhabitants, Not Hitherto Known,* 3 vols. (Newark, U.K., 1792), 1:xiv, 75, 186, and 2:48; Lorenzo Sabine, *The Principal Fisheries of the American Seas* (Washington, D.C., 1853), 58–60.

56. McCusker and Menard, *Economy of British North America,* 108, 115.

57. David B. Quinn and Alison M. Quinn, eds., *The English New England Voyages, 1602–1608* (London, 1983), 431; William Hammond to Sir Simonds D'Ewes (September 26, 1633), in Emerson, *Letters from New England,* 111; Spiess and Lewis, *Turner Farm Fauna,* 135–136, 155; Wood, *New England's Prospect,* 55, 107; Bigelow and Schroeder, *Fishes of the Gulf of Maine,* 82–83. Bigelow and Schroeder note that mature sturgeon up to twelve feet long and 600 pounds were landed occasionally in the Gulf of Maine during the early twentieth century, "but 18 feet, reported for New England many years ago, may not have been an exaggeration." For Natives' month names, see Hoffman, "Historical Ethnography of the Micmac," 243–246.

58. Paul J. Lindholdt, ed., *John Josselyn, Colonial Traveler: A Critical Edition of "Two Voyages to New England"* (Hanover, N.H., 1988), 140; *York Deeds,* 18 vols. (Portland,

Maine, 1887), 1: fol. 13; Thomas Morton, *New English Canaan* (Amsterdam, 1637), 88. For an identical mention of sturgeon as "regal," see Lindholdt, *John Josselyn, Colonial Traveler*, 76.

59. Richard C. Hoffmann, "Economic Development and Aquatic Ecosystems in Medieval Europe," *American Historical Review* 101, no. 3 (June 1996), 631–669, quotation on 649.

60. Smith, *Advertisements for the Unexperienced Planters of New England; Note-book Kept by Thomas Lechford, Esq., Lawyer, in Boston, Massachusetts Bay, from June 27, 1638 to July 29, 1641* (1885; reprint Camden, Maine, 1988), 377; *Aspinwall Notarial Records*, 423–424; Wood, *New England's Prospect*, 55. For the sturgeon fishery that began on the Pechipscut River (now the Androscoggin) in Brunswick, Maine, in 1628 and lasted until 1676, see George Augustus Wheeler and Henry Warren Wheeler, *History of Brunswick, Topsham and Harpswell, Maine* (1878; reprint, Somersworth, N.H., 1974), 552; Samuel Maverick, *A Briefe Description of New England and the Severall Towns Therein Together with the Present Government Thereof* (Boston, 1885), 11.

61. Lindholdt, *John Josselyn, Colonial Traveler*, 100.

62. Petition of William Thomas to the General Court, May 7, 1673, Massachusetts Archives, 61:3, MSA; John J. Currier, *History of Newbury, Mass., 1635–1902* (Boston, 1902), 282; Joshua Coffin, *A Sketch of the History of Newbury, Newburyport, and West Newbury* (Boston, 1845), 113–114; George W. Chase, *The History of Haverhill, Massachusetts* (Haverhill, 1861), 118–119; Jack Noon, *Fishing in New Hampshire: A History* (Warner, N.H., 2003), 61–64, 152–154; Matthew Patten, *The Diary of Matthew Patten of Bedford, N.H., from Seventeen Hundred Fifty-four to Seventeen Hundred Eighty-eight* (Concord, N.H., 1903), 96.

63. Currier, *History of Newbury, Mass.*, 283; Noon, *Fishing in New Hampshire*, 5–10, 61–64.

64. This is not to say that Atlantic sturgeon were extinct in New England's rivers, just that their populations had plummeted. Sturgeon were still being caught occasionally in rivers in Maine and New Brunswick at the end of the nineteenth century. See USCFF, *Report for the Year Ending June 30, 1898* (Washington, D.C., 1899), clxvi–clxvii; Theodore I. J. Smith, "The Fishery, Biology, and Management of Atlantic Sturgeon, *Acipenser oxrhynchus*, in North America," *Environmental Biology of Fishes* 14 (1985), 61–72; Inga Saffron, "Introduction: The Decline of the North American Species," in *Sturgeons and Paddlefish of North America*, ed. Greg T. O. LeBreton, F. William, H. Beamish, and R. Scott McKinley (Dordrecht, 2004), 1–21. E. O. Wilson, *The Creation: An Appeal to Save Life on Earth* (New York, 2006), 32; Merchant, *Ecological Revolutions*, 50–58.

65. Hubbard, *General History of New England*, 80; Shurtleff, *Records of Massachusetts Bay*, 1:258; Wood, *New England's Prospect*, 55; Lindholdt, *John Josselyn, Colonial Traveler*, 78.

66. For tension between Abenaki and settler fishers, see Bruce J. Bourque, *Twelve Thousand Years: American Indians in Maine* (Lincoln, Neb., 2001), 157.

67. *Laws of New Hampshire: including public and private acts and resolves and the Royal commissions and instructions with historical and descriptive notes,* 10 vols. (Manchester, N.H., 1904–1922), 3:537; Jeremy Belknap, *The History of New Hampshire,* 3 vols. (Boston, 1791–1792), 3:130–131; Currier, *History of Newbury, Mass.,* 283–284; Judge Benjamin Chadbourne, "A Description of the Town and Village" (ca. 1797), ms. transcription, Old Berwick Historical Society, South Berwick, Maine.

68. Daniel Vickers, "Those Dammed Shad: Would the River Fisheries of New England Have Survived in the Absence of Industrialization?" *William and Mary Quarterly,* 3d ser., 61 (October 2004), 685–712; Tony J. Pitcher, "Fisheries Managed to Rebuild Ecosystems? Reconstructing the Past to Salvage the Future," *Ecological Applications* 11, no. 2 (2001), 601–617, quotation on 604–605.

69. Vickers, "Those Dammed Shad"; *The Acts and Resolves, Public and Private, of the Province of the Massachusetts Bay,* 21 vols. (Boston, 1869–1922), 1:71, 102, 507–508, 644–645, 907.

70. Petition to Governor John Wentworth, the Council, and Assembly, May 1773, box 5, Old Congress Collection, Historical Society of Pennsylvania, Philadelphia; Petition of John Goffe to the Council and House of Representatives, March 16, 1776, Petitions to the Governor, Council and Legislature, New Hampshire Department of Archives and Records.

71. David Allen Sibley, *The Sibley Field Guide to Birds of Eastern North America* (New York, 2003); Apollonio, *Hierarchical Perspectives,* 71–77.

72. Marc Lescarbot, *The History of New France,* 3 vols. (1618; reprint, Toronto, 1908), 3:172, 231; Pierre Biard, *Relation de la Nouvelle France,* in *The Jesuit Relations and Allied Documents: Travels and Explorations of the Jesuit Missionaries in New France, 1610–1791,* ed. Reuben Gold Thwaites, 73 vols. (Cleveland, 1896–1901) 3:81; Ramsay Cook, ed., *The Voyages of Jacques Cartier* (Toronto, 1993), 4–5, 13–14, 40, quotation on 40; Richard Whitbourne, *A Discourse and Discovery of New-found-land* (London, 1620), 9.

73. Anthony Parkhurst, "A letter written to M. Richard Hakluyt of the middle Temple, conteining a report of the true state and commodities of Newfoundland, by M. Anthonie Parkhurst Gentleman, 1578," in Richard Hakluyt, *The Principal Navigations, Voyages, Traffiques & Discoveries of the English Nation,* 8 vols., ed. Ernest Rhys (London, 1907), 5:347; Jeremy Gaskell, *Who Killed the Great Auk?* (New York, 2000), 39, 52–53.

74. Gaskell, *Who Killed the Great Auk?,* 39, n. 6; Errol Fuller, *The Great Auk* (Southborough, Kent, 1999), 46; Capt. John Collings, mss. logbook, 1733–34, Portsmouth Athenaeum, Portsmouth, N.H.

75. John James Audubon, *The Complete Audubon: A Precise Replica of the Complete Works of John James Audubon Comprising the Birds of America (1840–44) and the Quadrupeds of North America (1851–54) in Their Entirety,* 5 vols. (Kent, 1979), 4:245; Fuller, *The Great Auk,* 60–77; Gaskell, *Who Killed the Great Auk?*

76. Anthony J. Gaston, *Seabirds: A Natural History* (New Haven, 2004), 143. Seabirds killed for bait included shearwaters, gannets, murres, gulls, puffins, terns, guillemots,

auks, cormorants, and others. While John James Audubon did not witness seabirds be-ing slaughtered for bait until the 1830s, his vivid accounts of a longstanding practice illu-minate its impact on the ecosystem. See Audubon, *The Complete Audubon*, 4:45–47, 156, 163–164, 176, 238–241; Maria R. Audubon, *Audubon and His Journals*, 2 vols. (New York, 1897), 1:361–362. On egging see ibid., 1:374, 1:383, 2:406–411, 2:423; Philip W. Conkling, *Islands in Time: A Natural and Cultural History of the Islands in the Gulf of Maine* (Rockland, Maine, 1999), 134. The quotation about killing petrels is from a nineteenth-century fisherman. See Captain J. W. Collins, "Notes on the habits and methods of cap-ture of various species of sea birds that occur on the fishing banks off the eastern coast of North America, and which are used as bait for catching codfish by New England fisher-men," in USCFF, *Report of the Commissioner for 1882* (Washington, D.C., 1884), 311–335, quotation on 334.

77. Morton, *New English Canaan*, 67–69; Wood, *New England's Prospect*, 48–53, quotation on 52–53; Bradford, *Plimouth Plantation*, 90; Pory to the Earl of Southamp-ton (January 16, 1622/1623), in James, *Three Visitors to Early Plymouth*, 10; Yasuhide Kawashima and Ruth Tone, "Environmental Policy in Early America: A Survey of Colo-nial Statutes," *Journal of Forest History* 27 (October 1983), 176; *Acts and Resolves, Public and Private, of the Province of the Massachusetts Bay*, 1:667–669, quoted in Kawashima and Tone, 176.

78. Samuel Penhallow, *The History of the Wars of New England, with the Eastern In-dians. Or, A Narrative of Their Continued Perfidy and Cruelty, from the 10th of August, 1703. To the Peace Renewed 13th of July, 1713. And from the 25th of July, 1722. To Their Submission 15th December, 1725. Which Was Ratified August 5th, 1726* (1726; reprint, Boston, 1924), 80–84; George L. Hosmer, *An Historical Sketch of the Town of Deer Isle, Maine, with Notices of Its Settlers and Early Inhabitants* (Boston, 1886), 16–18; Conkling, *Islands in Time*, 133–134. On Natives slaughtering molting eider ducks in the Bay of Fundy, see M. Audubon, *Audubon and His Journals*, 434–435.

79. Cartwright, *Journal of Transactions and Events*, 1:7; Rev. Jonathan Cogswell, "Topographical and Historical Sketch of Freeport, Maine," *Collections of the Massachu-setts Historical Society*, 2d ser., 4 (1816), 184–189. Looking for gulls, guillemots, cormo-rants, and other species in the Gulf of Maine in 1832, John James Audubon wrote de-spondently from Eastport, Maine, "*Birds* are very, very few and far between." See Alexander B. Adams, *John James Audubon: A Biography* (New York, 1966), 400.

80. Apollonio, *Hierarchical Perspectives*, 76–77. The impact of destroying seabird colonies on fish stocks is mentioned in Ernst Mayr, *This Is Biology: The Science of the Living World* (Cambridge, Mass., 1997), 225.

81. Edmund Burke, "Speech on Conciliation with America," in *The Beauties of the Late Right Hon. Edmund Burke, Selected from the Writings, &c. of That Extraordinary Man*, 2 vols. (London, 1798), 1:20.

82. Daniel Pauly, "Anecdotes and the Shifting Baseline Syndrome of Fisheries," *Trends in Ecology and Evolution* 10 (October 1995), 430; Petition of the subscribers,

February 7, 1778, Petitions to the Governor, Council, and Legislature, New Hampshire Department of Archives and Records.

3. The Sea Serpent and the Mackerel Jig

1. William Bentley, *The Diary of William Bentley, D.D., Pastor of the East Church, Salem, Massachusetts,* 10 vols. (Salem, Mass., 1914), 4:478; G. Brown Goode and J. W. Collins, "The Mackerel Fishery of the United States," in *FFIUS,* sec. V, 1:275–278.

2. Goode and Collins, "Mackerel Fishery," 278–287.

3. *Essex Register,* August 16, 1817, 3; Chandos Michael Brown, "A Natural History of the Gloucester Sea Serpent: Knowledge, Power, and the Culture of Science in Antebellum America," *American Quarterly* 42 (September 1990), 402–436.

4. The best treatment of contests over knowledge and authority regarding the living ocean in the early republic is D. Graham Burnett, *Trying Leviathan: The Nineteenth-Century New York Court Case That Put the Whale on Trial* and *Challenged the Order of Nature* (Princeton, 2007). For the period 1500–1800 see James Delbourgo and Nicholas Dew, eds., *Science and Empire in the Atlantic World* (New York, 2008). Joyce Chaplin, "Knowing the Ocean: Benjamin Franklin and the Circulation of Atlantic Knowledge," in ibid., 73–96; Louis Agassiz and Augustus A. Gould, *Principles of Zoölogy, Touching the Structure, Development, Distribution and Natural Arrangement of the Races of Animals, Living and Extinct: With Numerous Illustrations* (Boston, 1848), 10; Matthew Fontaine Maury, *The Physical Geography of the Sea. With Illustrated Charts and Diagrams* (London, 1855), 152–153.

5. John Lewis Russell, "An Address Delivered before the Essex County Natural History Society on Its Second Anniversary, June 15, 1836," in *Journals of the Essex County Natural History Society; Containing Various Communications to the Society* (Salem, Mass., 1852), 9. On the occupational prominence of seafaring, see Stanley Lebergott, *Manpower in Economic Growth: The American Record since 1800* (New York, 1964).

6. Percy G. Adams, *Travelers and Travel Liars, 1660–1800* (Berkeley, 1962); Hans Egede, *A Description of Greenland. By Hans Egede, Who Was a Missionary in That Country for Twenty-five Years* (London, 1818), 78–82.

7. Richard Judd, *Common Lands, Common People: The Origins of Conservation in Northern New England* (Cambridge, Mass., 1997).

8. Sara S. Gronim, *Everyday Nature: Knowledge of the Natural World in Colonial New York* (New Brunswick, N.J., 2007), 4–5.

9. *Salem Gazette,* August 1793, quoted in *Essex Register,* August 20, 1817, 3. For a similar account by Captain Joseph Brown, see ibid., August 30, 1817, 3.

10. Scholarship on sea monsters includes Bernard Heuvelmans, *In the Wake of the Sea-Serpents* (New York, 1968); Richard Ellis, *Monsters of the Sea* (New York, 1994). See also Anon., *Strange News from Gravesend and Greenwich, Being an Exact and More Full*

Relation of Two Miraculous and Monstrous Fishes (London, ca. 1680); Francis Searson, *A True and Perfect Relation of the Taking and Destroying of a Sea-Monster* (London, 1699).

11. Egede, *Description of Greenland*, 78–89, quotations on 86–89.

12. Thomas T. Bouvé, *Historical Sketch of the Boston Society of Natural History; with a Notice of the Linnæan Society, Which Preceded It* (Boston, 1880), 3; William D. Peck, "Description of Four Remarkable Fishes Taken near the Piscataqua in New Hampshire," *Memoirs of the American Academy of Arts and Sciences* 2 (1804), 46–57, quotation on 46; Augustus A. Gould, *Notice of the Origin, Progress and Present Condition of the Boston Society of Natural History* (n.p., 1842), 1–8.

13. Peck, "Description of Four Remarkable Fishes," 46, 51, 52, 55, 57.

14. John C. Greene, *American Science in the Age of Jefferson* (Ames, Iowa, 1984), 3; Harriet Ritvo, *The Platypus and the Mermaid and Other Figments of the Classifying Imagination* (Cambridge, Mass., 1997), 14. Ritvo's observation concerned the later nineteenth century, but it pertains to the earlier period as well.

15. Bentley, *Diary*, 4:471–472.

16. Greene, *American Science in the Age of Jefferson;* Burnett, *Trying Leviathan;* Charlotte M. Porter, *The Eagle's Nest: Natural History and American Ideas, 1812–1842* ([Tuscaloosa, Ala.], 1986); Delbourgo and Dew, *Science and Empire in the Atlantic World;* James E. McClellan III, *Colonialism and Science: Saint Domingue in the Old Regime* (Baltimore, 1992); Margaret Welch, *The Book of Nature: Natural History in the United States, 1825–1875* (Boston, 1998); Andrew J. Lewis, "A Democracy of Facts, and Empire of Reason: Swallow Submersion and Natural History in the Early Republic," *William and Mary Quarterly*, 3d ser., 62 (October 2005), 663–696; *Report of a Committee of the Linnæan Society of New England relative to a Large Marine Animal supposed to be a Serpent, Seen near Cape Ann, Massachusetts in August 1817* (Boston, 1817), 1–22.

17. This paragraph closely follows Brown, "Natural History of the Gloucester Sea Serpent," 409–414.

18. Bentley, *Diary*, 4:474–476.

19. Brown, "Natural History of the Gloucester Sea Serpent," 414–415.

20. Ibid., 408.

21. *Boston Weekly Messenger*, September 10, 1818.

22. Brown, "Natural History of the Gloucester Sea Serpent," 421–423.

23. Ibid., 425; *Essex Register*, September 9, 1820, 1.

24. *Essex Register*, August 12, 1820, 3; *Salem Gazette*, June 11, 1822, 2; *Essex Register*, June 12, 1822, 2; ibid., June 22, 1822, 2.

25. *Essex Register*, July 15, 1830; *Salem Gazette*, July 27, 1830, 1.

26. *Boston Gazette* story reprinted in *Portsmouth Journal of Literature and Politics*, July 31, 1830, 2; Samuel Clayton Kingman Journal (1847), Massachusetts Historical Society, Boston; Henry B. Bigelow and William C. Schroeder, *Fishes of the Gulf of Maine* (Washington, D.C., 1953), 20–44; D. Humphreys Storer, *Reports on the Fishes, Reptiles and Birds of Massachusetts* (Boston, 1839), 190.

27. Jerome V. C. Smith, *Natural History of the Fishes of Massachusetts, Embracing a Practical Essay on Angling* (Boston, 1833), 102; Storer, *Reports on the Fishes,* 47.

28. *Boston Weekly Messenger,* August 1817, quoted in Brown, "Natural History of the Gloucester Sea Serpent," 409; *Barnstable Patriot,* August 28, 1833.

29. William Douglass, *A Summary, Historical and Political, of the First Planting, Progressive Improvements, and Present State of the British Settlements in North America,* 2 vols. (Boston, 1755), 1:303; Daniel Vickers, *Farmers and Fishermen: Two Centuries of Work in Essex County, Massachusetts, 1630–1850* (Chapel Hill, 1994), 277; John J. Babson, *History of the Town of Gloucester, Cape Ann, Including the Town of Rockport* (Gloucester, Mass., 1860), 572; A. Howard Clark, "Statistics of the Inspection of Mackerel from 1804 to 1880," in MHMF, 280.

30. MHMF, 308–312; Gideon L. Davis, "The Old-Time Fishery at 'Squam," in *The Fishermen's Own Book, Comprising the List of Men and Vessels Lost from the Port of Gloucester, Mass., from 1874 to April 1, 1882* (Gloucester, 1882), 41–42.

31. Storer, *Reports on the Fishes,* 42; Samuel L. Mitchill, "The Fishes of New York, Described and Arranged," *Transactions of the Literary and Philosophical Society of New-York* 1 (1815), 355–492, 422–423.

32. MHMF, 207–208, 310.

33. Babson, *History of the Town of Gloucester,* 572; MHMF, 308–312; *Fishermen's Own Book,* 41–42.

34. *Fishermen's Own Book,* 41–42.

35. Babson, *History of the Town of Gloucester,* 572; Anon., "Mackerelling in the Bay," *Putnam's Monthly: A Magazine of Literature, Science and Art,* June 1857, 580; Samuel Clayton Kingman Journal (1847), Massachusetts Historical Society.

36. *Gloucester Telegraph,* July 12 and November 22, 1828; George H. Proctor, *The Fishermen's Memorial and Record Book* (Gloucester, Mass., 1873), 63.

37. Oscar E. Sette and A. W. H. Needler, *Statistics of the Mackerel Fishery off the East Coast of North America, 1804 to 1930,* U.S. Department of Commerce Bureau of Fisheries Investigational Report No. 19 (Washington, D.C., 1934), esp. 18–26. These figures were extrapolated from Massachusetts fish inspection records, estimated to be about 85 percent of the total New England catch. Given that some mackerel caught was marketed fresh, some canned, and some used for bait, the best estimates are that packed, salted mackerel—for which sound statistics exist—represented 69 percent of the total catch.

38. Kenneth F. Drinkwater et al., "The Response of Marine Ecosystems to Climate Variability Associated with the North Atlantic Oscillation," in *The North Atlantic Oscillation: Climatic Significance and Environmental Impact,* Geophysical Monograph 134 (Washington, D.C., American Geophysical Union, 2003), 211–234; Dietmar Straile and Nils Chr. Stenseth, "The North Atlantic Oscillation and Ecology: Links between Historical Time Series, and Lessons Regarding Future Climate Warming," *Climate Research* 34 (September 18, 2007), 259–262; *Barnstable Patriot* quoted in MHMF, 320; *Newburyport Herald* quoted in MHMF, 323.

39. MHMF, 320, 316.

40. MHMF, 318; Storer, *Reports on the Fishes*, 43; *Journal and Proceedings of the House of Assembly* [*Nova Scotia*], *1837*, (Halifax, 1837), app. 75 (April 10, 1837), 340, NSARM; *FFIUS*, sec. V, 1:279.

41. *Gloucester Telegraph*, August 7, 1839.

42. *Essex Register*, August 30, 1817, 3.

43. Ernest Ingersoll, *The Oyster Industry* (Washington, D.C., 1881), 19–21; Rev. Enoch Pratt, *A Comprehensive History, Ecclesiastical and Civil, of Eastham, Wellfleet and Orleans, County of Barnstable, Mass. from 1644 to 1844* (Yarmouth, Mass., 1844), 111, 135.

44. *Acts and Resolves, Public and Private, of the Province of the Massachusetts Bay* 21 vols. (Boston 1869–1922), 4:743; M. Lee et al., "Evaluation of Vibrio spp. and Microplankton Blooms as Causative Agents of Juvenile Oyster Disease in *Crassostrea virginica* (Gmelin)," *Journal of Shellfish Research* 15, no. 2 (June 1996), 319–329; Clyde L. McKenzie Jr., "History of Oystering in the United States and Canada, Featuring the Eight Greatest Oyster Estuaries," *Marine Fisheries Review* 58, no. 4 (1996), 1–78; Jeremy B. C. Jackson et al., "Historical Overfishing and the Recent Collapse of Coastal Ecosystems," *Science* 293 (July 27, 2001), 629–638.

45. Pratt, *Comprehensive History*, 82, 126–127; Frederick Freeman, *The History of Cape Cod: The Annals of the Thirteen Towns of Barnstable County*, 2 vols. (Boston, 1862), 2:112, 663.

46. John M. Kochiss, *Oystering from New York to Boston* (Middletown, Conn., 1974), 39–42.

47. Mitchill, "Fishes of New York," 399–400; Bigelow and Schroeder, *Fishes of the Gulf of Maine*, 479–484.

48. Storer, *Reports on the Fishes*, 38–39; Babson, *History of the Town of Gloucester*.

49. Bouvé, *Historical Sketch of the Boston Society of Natural History*, 20.

50. Report of the Committee on the Lobster Fishery (March 26, 1828), 23d article, record book 5, p. 196, Gloucester Archives, Gloucester, Mass.; Petition of Joseph Cammett et al. (1839) chap. 102, MSA; Remonstrance of Josiah Sampson et al., ibid.; *Fishermen's Own Book*, 248.

51. Petition of Zaccheus Howwaswee and 32 other Indians of the Gay Head Tribe (1839), chap. 85, MSA; Petition from the Town of Chatham Praying for Protection of the Fisheries, ibid.

52. Remonstrance of J. Baker et al., ibid.; Remonstrance of Samuel P. Bourne et al., citizens of Barnstable, ibid.; Petition of John Cook et al. (1850), chap. 6, MSA.

53. Petition of Joshua W. Norton et al. (1845), in Legislative Graveyard, box 174, folder 2, MeSA.

54. Bentley, *Diary*, 4:486–487; Storer, *Reports on the Fishes*, 111.

55. Storer, *Reports on the Fishes*, 3, 47–48, 410–416.

56. "Autobiography of Captain Nathaniel E. Atwood, of Provincetown, Mass.," in *FFIUS* sec. IV, 149–168, quotation on 150.

57. Ibid., 150, 163.

58. "Horatio Robinson Storer Papers, 1829–1943, Guide to the Collection," Massachusetts Historical Society; Bouvé, *Historical Sketch,* 51; Simeon L. Deyo, ed., *History of Barnstable County, Massachusetts* (New York, 1890), 995–997.

59. Bouvé, *Historical Sketch,* 44–45; Ellis, *Monsters of the Sea,* 54–57; Philip J. Pauly, *Biologists and the Promise of American Life: From Meriwether Lewis to Alfred Kinsey* (Princeton, 2000), 15–43.

60. "Autobiography of Captain Nathaniel E. Atwood," 165; Deyo, *History of Barnstable County,* 996.

61. Horatio Robinson Storer, "Observations on the Fishes of Nova Scotia and Labrador, with Descriptions of New Species," in *Boston Journal of Natural History, Containing Papers and Communications Read to the Boston Society of Natural History, 1850–1857,* vol. 6 (Boston, 1857), 266; MHMF, 342–360.

62. Deyo, *History of Barnstable County,* 996; Agassiz and Gould, *Principles of Zoölogy.*

63. "Autobiography of Captain Nathaniel E. Atwood," 166; MHMF, 114–115.

4. MAKING THE CASE FOR CAUTION

1. Petition of Jotham Johnson (1865), in Rejected Bills, box 463, folder 17, MeSA.

2. J. Reynolds, *Peter Gott, the Cape Ann Fisherman* (Boston, 1856), 60; James G. Bertram, *The Harvest of the Sea: A Contribution to the Natural and Economic History of the British Food Fishes* (London, 1865), 20.

3. A. D. Gordon to Chairman of the Committee on the Fisheries (February 1852), Petitions to the House of Assembly, RG 5, ser. P, vol. 53, no. 148, NSARM; M. H. Perley, *Reports on the Sea and River Fisheries of New Brunswick* (Fredericton, N.B., 1852), 7–8.

4. Affidavit of Joseph Cammett (February 25, 1856), chap. 214, MSA; Petition of Thomas Derry et al. (1859), Petitions to the House of Assembly, RG 5, ser. P, vol. 55, no. 8, NSARM.

5. George A. Rose, *Cod: The Ecological History of the North Atlantic Fisheries* (St. John's, Newf., 2007), 284–285; Sean Cadigan, "The Moral Economy of the Commons: Ecology and Equity in the Newfoundland Cod Fishery, 1815–1855," *Labour/Le Travail* 43 (March 1999), 9–42.

6. G. Brown Goode, *A History of the Menhaden* (New York, 1880), 162.

7. Ernest Ingersoll, "Around the Peconics," *Harper's New Monthly Magazine,* 57, October 1878, 719–723.

8. Bonnie J. McKay, "A Footnote to the History of New Jersey Fisheries: Menhaden as Food and Fertilizer," *New Jersey History* 98 (1980), 212–220; H. Bruce Franklin, *The Most Important Fish in the Sea: Menhaden and America* (Washington, D.C., 2007), 17–20, 50–55. The article in 1792 appeared in the first volume of *Transactions of the Society for the Promotion of Agriculture, Arts, and Manufactures, Instituted in the State of New York.*

9. Goode, *History of the Menhaden*, 71, 78–79; MHMF, 105; Capt. E. T. DeBlois, "The Origin of the Menhaden Industry," in *Bulletin of the United States Fish Commission Vol. I, for 1881* (Washington, D.C., 1882), 46–51; *FFIUS*, sec. V, 1:335.

10. *MeFCR for 1891–92* (Augusta, 1892), 29–30; MHMF, 105-111; Goode, *History of the Menhaden*, 109.

11. Franklin, *Most Important Fish*.

12. Petition of inhabitants of Southport, Boothbay, and vicinity (January 1852), in Legislative Laws, box 265, folder 125, MeSA.

13. Ibid.; Petition of inhabitants of Surry (January 27, 1853), in Legislative Graveyard, box 241, folder 9, MeSA; Petition of inhabitants of Ellsworth (January 25, 1853), ibid.; Petition of inhabitants of Sedgwick (March 9, 1854), ibid.; Petition of inhabitants of Gouldsboro (October 10, 1857), in Legislative Graveyard, box 256, folder 37, MeSA.

14. *FFIUS*, sec. II, 28; Francis Byron Greene, *History of Boothbay, Southport and Boothbay Harbor, Maine* (1906; reprint, Somersworth, N.H., 1984), 370–371.

15. Paul Crowell, "Report on the Fisheries," in *Appendix to the Journal of the House of Assembly of the Province of Nova Scotia for the Session Commencing the Twenty-ninth of January and Ending the Eighth of April, 1852*, app. 25, 169–170, NSARM.

16. Petition of inhabitants of Wells (February 8, 1855), in Legislative Laws, box 309, folder 104, MeSA; *Public Laws of the State of Maine, 1855* (Augusta, 1855), chap. 138.

17. Petition of inhabitants of Surry (March 1854), in Legislative Graveyard, box 241, folder 9, MeSA.

18. Remonstrance of Isaiah Baker et al. (1856), chap. 214, MSA.

19. Remonstrance of A. K. Chase et al. (1858), chap. 52, MSA; Remonstrance of the town of Dennis (1856), chap. 214, MSA; Remonstrance of Obed Baker et al., ibid.

20. MHMF, 212.

21. "An Act to Protect the Menhaden Fishery in the Towns of Duxbury, Plymouth, and Kingston" (1857), chap. 85, MSA.

22. Petition of Josiah Hardy et al. (1856), chap. 214, MSA.

23. Petition of the Selectmen of Mashpee, ibid.

24. *Journals and Proceedings of the House of Assembly of the Province of Nova Scotia, Session 1861* (Halifax, 1861), app. 32 [n.p.]; Henry Youle Hind, *The Effect of the Fishery Clauses of the Treaty of Washington on the Fisheries and Fishermen of British North America* (Halifax, 1877), xvi.

25. Larkin West, log of the schooner *Torpedo*, 1852, RG 36, box 88, folder 530a, NARA, Waltham, Mass.

26. Thomas Boden, log of the schooner *Iodine*, 1856, RG 36, box 71, folder 486b, NARA, Waltham, Mass.; "The Fishing Grounds," in USCFF, *Part XIV: Report of the Commissioner for 1886* (Washington, D.C., 1889), 85–102; Elijah Kellogg, *The Fisher Boys of Pleasant Cove* (Boston, 1874), 157.

27. The Beverly logs are in RG 36, boxes 56–91, NARA, Waltham, Mass.

28. Detailed analysis of these logbooks would have been impossible without a skilled team. I am indebted to the other members of the interdisciplinary University of New Hampshire Cod Project, and to our funders. Earlier versions of this work appeared as Andrew A. Rosenberg, W. Jeffrey Bolster, Karen E. Alexander, William B. Leavenworth, Andrew B. Cooper, and Matthew G. McKenzie, "The History of Ocean Resources: Modeling Cod Biomass Using Historical Records," *Frontiers in Ecology and the Environment* 3 (March 2005), 84–90; W. Jeffrey Bolster, Karen E. Alexander, and William B. Leavenworth, "The Historic Abundance of Cod on the Nova Scotian Shelf," in *Shifting Baselines: The Past and Future of Ocean Resources,* ed. Jeremy B. C. Jackson, Karen E. Alexander, and Enric Sala (Washington, D.C., 2011), 79–113.

29. Thomas Gayton, Log of the schooner *Susan Center,* 1857, RG 36, box 86, folders 526f and g, NARA, Waltham, Mass.

30. William Leavenworth, "Opening Pandora's Box: Tradition, Competition, and Technology on the Scotian Shelf, 1852–1860," in *The North Atlantic Fisheries: Supply, Marketing, and Consumption, 1560–1990,* ed. David J. Starkey and James E. Candow (Hull, U.K., 2006), 29–49.

31. Ibid.

32. Enos Hatfield, Log of the schooner *Franklin,* 1858, RG 36, box 67, folder 4740, NARA, Waltham, Mass.; Samuel Wilson, Log of the schooner *Lodi,* 1858, RG 36, box 74, folder 496g, ibid.; Solomon Woodbury, Log of the schooner *Prize Banner,* 1858, RG 36, box 82, folder 515b, ibid.

33. Spencer F. Baird, *Report on the Condition of the Sea Fisheries of the South Coast of New England in 1871 and 1872* (Washington, D.C., 1873), 119; *FFIUS,* sec. V, 1:159.

34. *Journals of the Assembly, Nova Scotia, 1861,* app. 32, NSARM; Joseph W. Collins and Richard Rathbun, "The Sea Fishing-Grounds of the Eastern Coast of North America From Greenland to Mexico," in Goode, *FFIUS,* sec. III, chart 4, opposite p. 67.

35. Thomas F. Knight, *Shore and Deep Sea Fisheries of Nova Scotia* (Halifax, 1867), 40–41, 106–107.

36. John Cleghorn, "On the Causes of the Fluctuations in the Herring Fishery," *Journal of the Statistical Society of London* 18 (September 1855), 240–242; Bertram, *Harvest of the Sea,* 232; Tim D. Smith, *Scaling Fisheries: The Science of Measuring the Effects of Fishing, 1855–1955* (Cambridge, 1994), 12.

37. "Resolve in Favor of Appointing a Fish Commissioner" (1859), in Laws of Maine, box 136, folder 53, MeSA; "Resolve . . . to report upon the present condition of the Sea Fisheries" (1861), in Legislative Graveyard, box 446, folder 3, MeSA; Smith, *Scaling Fisheries,* 1–14; *Report of the Commissioners* (1866), quoted in Callum Roberts, *The Unnatural History of the Sea* (Washington, D.C., 2007), 140.

38. *Report of the Commissioners* (1866), quoted in Roberts, *Unnatural History of the Sea,* 143–144.

39. Bertram, *Harvest of the Sea,* 475.

40. Stephen R. Palumbi et al., "Managing for Ocean Biodiversity to Sustain Marine Ecosystem Services," *Frontiers in Ecology and the Environment* 7, no. 4 (2009), 204–211.

41. *FFIUS*, sec. V, 1:127; Hind, *Effect of the Fishery Clauses*, 119–120.

42. George Brown Goode Collection, ser. 3, Collected Materials on Fish and Fisheries, box 14, folder "Misc. notes, mss, lists statistics" [n.d.], Record Unit 7050, Smithsonian Archives, Washington, D.C. Bait as a historical and ecological problem in nineteenth-century fisheries had been ignored by historians until Matthew McKenzie, *Clearing the Coastline: The Nineteenth-Century Ecological and Cultural Transformation of Cape Cod* (Hanover, N.H., 2010).

43. *FFIUS*, sec. V, 2:584.

44. Petition of inhabitants of Deer Isle (December 18, 1852), in Legislative Graveyard, box 241, folder 9, MeSA.

45. Ibid.; Petition of inhabitants of Deer Isle (January 10, 1853), in Legislative Graveyard, box 231, folder 12, MeSA.

46. Petition of inhabitants of Harpswell (January 1857), in Legislative Graveyard, box 248, folder 4, MeSA.

47. Remonstrance of inhabitants of Harpswell, ibid.

48. *Appendix to Journal of House of Assembly of Nova Scotia, 1852*, app. 13, 92–93, NSARM; *FFIUS*, sec. V, 1:280–281.

49. Goode, *History of the Menhaden*, 164–165.

50. Legislative Laws (1865), box 403, folder 140, MeSA; *Acts and Resolves as Passed by the Legislature of the State of Maine, 1865* (Augusta, 1865), chap. 313; Richard W. Judd, "Grass-Roots Conservation in Eastern Coastal Maine: Monopoly and the Moral Economy of Weir Fishing, 1893–1911," *Environmental Review* 12 (Summer 1988), 80–103.

51. *Public Laws of the State of Maine, 1866* (Augusta, 1866), chap. 30.

52. These petitions are in Legislative Graveyard (1867), box 470, MeSA.

53. *Journals of the House of Representatives Maine,* (Augusta, 1868), 115, 144, 168, 220, 228, 235, 372–373, MeSA.

54. "Rhode Island Fish Exhibit," *NYT,* March 10, 1893; *The Menhaden Fishery of Maine, with Statistical and Historical Details, Its Relation to Agriculture, and as a Direct Source of Human Food* (Portland, 1878), 16, 26.

55. *Menhaden Fishery of Maine*, 43–44.

56. USCFF, *Report of the Commissioner for 1872 and 1873* (Washington, D.C., 1874), xii, xiv; *MeFCR* (Augusta, 1874), 25; *Acts and Resolves as Passed by the Legislature of Maine, 1878* (Augusta, 1878), chap. 66, pp. 59–60; *Acts and Resolves as Passed by the Legislature of Maine, 1879* (Augusta, 1879), chap. 112, p. 124.

57. Goode, *History of the Menhaden,* 74–75, 78–80.

58. Ibid., 92–93; *Acts and Resolves as Passed by the Legislature of Maine, 1880* (Augusta, 1880), chap. 234, pp. 271–272.

59. Logbooks from schooners registered in the Frenchman's Bay Customs District are in RG 36, boxes 1–12, NARA, Waltham, Mass.

60. Karen E. Alexander, William B. Leavenworth, Jamie Cournane, Andrew B. Cooper, Stefan Claesson, Stephen Brennan, Gwynna Smith, Lesley Rains, Katherine Magness, Reneé Dunn, Tristan K. Law, Robert Gee, W. Jeffrey Bolster, and Andrew A. Rosenberg, "Gulf of Maine Cod in 1861: Historical Analysis of Fishery Logbooks, with Ecosystem Implications," *Fish and Fisheries* 10 (2009), 428–449.

61. I thank William B. Leavenworth for this insight.

62. *The Fishermen's Own Book, Comprising the List of Men and Vessels Lost from the Port of Gloucester, Mass., from 1874 to April 1, 1882* (Gloucester, 1882), 213.

63. David Humphreys Storer, *A History of the Fishes of Massachusetts* (Cambridge, Mass., 1867), 103, 138.

64. USCFF, *Report of Commissioner for 1872 and 1873*, xiv.

65. "A Bill Regulating the Taking of Fish on the Coast of Maine" (March 12, 1860), in Legislative Graveyard, box 443, folder 4, MeSA; *Journals of the House of Representatives (Maine)* (Augusta, 1860), 50–51, 73, 351, MeSA.

66. Committee on Fisheries (January 8, 1862), in Legislative Graveyard, box 447, folder 6, MeSA; Knight, *Shore and Deep Sea Fisheries of Nova Scotia*, 60; "Report of Committee on the Fisheries," in *Journals and Proceedings of House of Assembly of Nova Scotia, 1861*, app. 32 [n.p.].

67. "An Act to Prevent Trawl Fishing for the Purpose of Protecting the Cod Fishery on Our Sea Board" (1866), in Legislative Graveyard, box 468, MeSA.

68. Petition of Robert B. Hamer, *Journals of the House of Representatives (Maine)*, (Augusta, 1868), 235, MeSA; Petition of William H. Ryan et al. (February 20, 1865), Petitions to the House of Assembly, RG 5, ser. P, vol. 55, no. 45, NSARM; Baird, *Report on the Condition of the Sea Fisheries*, 119.

69. Richard A. Cooley, *Politics and Conservation: The Decline of the Alaska Salmon* (New York, 1963), 199–200; "An Act for the Protection of Their Rights in Catching Smelts in the Damariscotta River" (1866), in Rejected Bills, box 468, MeSA.

70. *MFCR* (Boston, 1870), 60–67.

71. *MeFCR* (Augusta, 1872), 7; *MeFCR* (Augusta, 1868), 12–13, 71; *MeFCR* (Augusta, 1869), 34–39; *MeFCR* (Augusta, 1870), 35; *MeFCR* (Augusta, 1870), 4, 8–12.

72. *MeFCR* (Augusta, 1869), 34–39.

73. Hind, *Effect of the Fishery Clauses*, xiv–xv.

74. Ibid., x, xi, xiv; "Hind, Henry Youle," in *Dictionary of Canadian Biography Online* (accessed January 25, 2011).

75. *Bulletin of the United States Fish Commission. Vol. VI, for 1886* (Washington, D.C., 1886), 75–76.

76. Hind, *Effect of the Fishery Clauses*, xv.

77. Alexander et al., "Gulf of Maine Cod in 1861," 428–449; USCFF, *Report of the Commissioner for 1904* (Washington, D.C., 1904), 247–305.

78. *Gloucester Telegraph*, March 23, 1870.

79. USCFF, *Report of the Commissioner for 1878* (Washington, D.C., 1880), 37.

80. USCFF, *Report of Commissioner for 1881*, xxiv–xxxvi; _____ to Spencer F. Baird, December 7, 1878, Records of the U.S. Fish Commission and Bureau of Fisheries, RG 22, Letters Received 1878–1881, General Records, box 1, folder A, NARA, College Park, Md.

81. USCFF, *Report of Commissioner for 1881*, xxxvi; American Net & Twine Company to Baird, March 29, 1878, Letters Received 1878–1881, Records of the U.S. Fish Commission and Bureau of Fisheries, RG 22, General Records, box 1, folder A, NARA, College Park, Md.

82. "Diary of Events for 1881 Report," Correspondence of Spencer F. Baird 1872–1876, Records of the Office of Commissioner of Fisheries, RG 22, box 1, folder 28849, NARA, College Park, Md.; USCFF, *Report of the Commissioner for 1883* (Washington, D.C., 1885), lxix–lxxi; J. W. Collins, "Gill-Nets in the Cod-Fishery," in *Bulletin of the United States Fish Commission. Vol. I, for 1881*, 1–16.

83. W. A. Wilcox, "New England Fisheries in May, 1885," *Bulletin of the United States Fish Commission Vol. V, for 1885* (Washington, D.C., 1885), 173; S. J. Martin, "Notes on the Fisheries of Gloucester, Mass.," ibid., 203–208; USCFF, *Report of the Commissioner for 1883*, lxix, lxxiv.

84. E. H. Haskell, "Second Annual Appearance of Young Cod Hatched by the United States Fish Commission in Gloucester Harbor in the Winter of 1879–80," *Bulletin of the United States Fish Commission Vol. II, for 1882* (Washington, D.C., 1883), 112.

85. Reynolds, *Peter Gott*, 89–92, 98–100, 105–108, 120–126, 164–165.

86. Charles Nordhoff, "Mehetabel Rogers's Cranberry Swamp," *Harper's New Monthly Magazine* 28, February 1864, 367–377.

87. "Destruction of Sea-Fisheries," ibid., 40, December 1869–May 1870, 307; Kellogg, *Fisher Boys of Pleasant Cove*, 277.

88. Samuel Adams Drake, *Nooks and Corners of the New England Coast* (New York, 1875), 88–89.

89. *MeFCR* (Augusta, 1874), 7.

90. Wayne M. O'Leary, *Maine Sea Fisheries: The Rise and Fall of a Native Industry, 1830–1890* (Boston, 1996), 161.

91. Richard Rathbun, "The Lobster Fishery," in *FFIUS*, sec. V, 2:658–794.

92. Howard Irving Chapelle, *The American Fishing Schooners, 1825–1935* (New York, 1973).

93. The best treatment of the rise and fall of the cod bounty is O'Leary, *Maine Sea Fisheries*, 40–77.

94. USCFF, *Report of Commissioner for 1872 and 1873*, vi.

95. George Perkins Marsh, *Man and Nature; or, Physical Geography as Modified by Human Action* (1864; reprint, Cambridge, Mass., 1965); Richard H. Grove, *Green Imperialism: Colonial Expansion, Tropical Island Edens and the Origins of Environmentalism, 1600–1860* (Cambridge, 1995).

5. Waves in a Troubled Sea

1. B. W. Counce, "Report of the Commissioner," in *MeFCR* (Augusta, 1888), 37.

2. "Mackerel from Ireland," *NYT*, December 7, 1888.

3. Occasional exceptions existed, notably for preserved specialty items such as sardines from France and Portugal.

4. Bruce Robertson, "Perils of the Sea," in *Picturing Old New England: Image and Memory*, ed. William H. Truettner and Roger B. Stein (New Haven, 1999), 143-170; Wayne M. O'Leary, *Maine Sea Fisheries: The Rise and Fall of a Native Industry, 1830-1890* (Boston, 1996).

5. *First Annual Report of the Bureau of Industrial and Labor Statistics for the State of Maine, 1887* (Augusta, 1888), 112-113.

6. Ibid., 111; Francis Byron Greene, *History of Boothbay, Southport and Southport Harbor, Maine* (1906; reprint, Somersworth, N.H., 1984), 370-371.

7. H. Bruce Franklin, *The Most Important Fish in the Sea: Menhaden and America* (Washington, D.C., 2007).

8. *FFIUS*, sec. V, 1:369; "The Way Menhaden Oil Is Made," *Scientific American,* September 27, 1862, 198.

9. Quotations from affidavit of Amos Rowe Jr. (1865), chap. 212, MSA. Numerous petitions, ibid.

10. Quotation from petition of citizens of Lakeville (1865), ibid. All of the petitions can be found in chap. 212, MSA.

11. Report by Mr. Lapham from the Committee on Fisheries re bill S. 155, *Senate Report No. 706*, 48th Cong., 1st. sess. (June 17, 1884), p. II; *The Menhaden Fishery of Maine, with Statistical and Historical Details, Its Relation to Agriculture, and as a Direct Source of Human Food* (Portland, 1878), 27; Douglas S. Vaughan and Joseph W. Smith, "Reconstructing Historical Commercial Landings of Atlantic Menhaden," SEDAR (Southeast Data Assessment and Review) 20-DW02 (North Charleston, S.C., June 2009), South Atlantic Fishery Management Council, NOAA.

12. Bruce B. Collette and Grace Klein-MacPhee, eds., *Bigelow and Schroeder's Fishes of the Gulf of Maine,* 3d ed. (Washington D.C., 2002), 133-135; Report by Mr. Lapham from the Committee on Fisheries, p. XII; *Menhaden Fishery of Maine,* 27.

13. Samuel Adams Drake, *Nooks and Corners of the New England Coast* (New York, 1875), 89; *MeFCR* (Augusta, 1878), 19.

14. *Menhaden Fishery of Maine,* 46-47, 26-27; O'Leary, *Maine Sea Fisheries,* 197-214; Depositions of Lewis Whitten, William Maddocks, and Jordan R. Blake (May 23, 1877), Testimony of Captains Involved in the North Atlantic Commercial Fishery, Mss. 375, box 1, folder 5, Peabody Essex Museum Library, Salem, Mass.

15. Report by Mr. Lapham from the Committee on Fisheries, pp. X-XII.

16. Collette and Klein-MacPhee, *Bigelow and Schroeder's Fishes of the Gulf of Maine,* 163-166; H. W. Small, *A History of Swans Island, Maine* (Ellsworth, Maine, 1898), 193-194.

17. "The Menhaden Industry," *NYT,* January 15, 1880, 8; Jianguo Liu et al., "Complexity of Coupled Human and Natural Systems," *Science* 317 (September 14, 2007), 1513–1516; Vaughan and Smith, "Reconstructing Historical Commercial Landings of Atlantic Menhaden," table 6. During the years 1878–1938, landings were less than those of 1878 for thirty-one years, and greater for eleven years. No data exist for the other years.

18. "The Menhaden Industry," *NYT,* January 15, 1880, 8; *Bulletin of the United States Fish Commission Vol. III for 1883* (Washington, D.C., 1883), 463.

19. Report by Mr. Lapham from the Committee on Fisheries, 20.

20. "Protecting the Food Fish," *NYT,* September 7, 1882, 2; "Questions of Food Fish," *NYT,* September 10, 1882, 8; "The Menhaden Fisheries," *NYT,* September 24, 1882, 3; Collette and Klein-MacPhee, *Bigelow and Schroeder's Fishes of the Gulf of Maine,* 134.

21. *FFIUS,* sec. V, 1:335, 355–356; Testimony taken under Senate Resolution of July 26, 1882, in Report by Mr. Lapham from the Committee on Fisheries, pp. 2, 13, 17–18.

22. Ray Hilborn and Carl J. Walters, *Quantitative Fisheries Stock Assessment: Choice, Dynamics and Uncertainty* (Boston, 2001).

23. Report by Mr. Lapham from the Committee on Fisheries, p. VI.

24. Ibid., pp. XX–XXI, 37.

25. Ibid, p. II.

26. Testimony taken under Senate Resolution of July 26, 1882, 19–21.

27. Report by Mr. Lapham from the Committee on Fisheries, pp. XXII–XXIII.

28. Ibid., pp. II–III, XIX.

29. MHMF, 104; Deposition of Peter Sinclair (September 3, 1877), Testimony of Captains Involved in the North Atlantic Commercial Fishery, Mss. 375, box 1, folder 4, Peabody Essex Museum; Deposition of James L. Anderson, September 3, 1877, ibid., folder 1; Shebnah Rich, *The Mackerel Fishery of North America: Its Perils and Its Rescue. A Lecture Read before the Massachusetts Fish and Game Commission of Boston* (Boston, 1879), 23; "Partial Failure of the Mackerel Fishery," *NYT,* October 28, 1872; R. E. Earll, "Statistics of the Mackerel Fishery," in *FFIUS,* sec. V, 1:304. The classic study linking ecology, economic production, and the law remains Arthur F. McEvoy, *The Fisherman's Problem: Ecology and Law in the California Fisheries, 1850–1980* (Cambridge, 1986).

30. G. Brown Goode and J. W. Collins, "The Mackerel Fishery of the United States," in *FFIUS,* sec. V, 1:247–304.

31. Goode and Collins, "Mackerel Fishery of the United States," 248; Rich, *Mackerel Fishery of North America,* 15; W. M. P. Dunne, *Thomas F. McManus and the American Fishing Schooners: An Irish-American Success Story* (Mystic, Conn., 1994).

32. *FFIUS,* sec. V, 1:265–266.

33. Ibid., 262.

34. Ibid., 274–275.

35. Ibid., 266.

36. Ibid., 303; MHMF, 212; Rich, *Mackerel Fishery of North America,* 20–21.

37. "Innovation in Mackerel Fishing," *NYT,* July 11, 1882, 2.

38. "The Destruction of Mackerel," *NYT,* October 22, 1882, 13.

39. "To Catch Mackerel Only," *NYT,* August 21, 1885, 1; "The Fisheries of Massachusetts," *Fishing Gazette* 20, no. 30 (July 25, 1903), 581.

40. J. W. Collins to Hon. Clifton R. Breckinridge (February 17, 1886), in *Statements to the Committee of Ways and Means on the Morrison Tariff Bill, and on the Hewitt Administrative Bill, the Hawaiian Treaty, Etc.,* 49th Cong., 1st. sess. (Washington, D.C., 1886), 51–54; Unpublished Hearings before the Senate Committee on Fisheries re bill HR 5538, An Act relating to the importing and landing of mackerel caught during the spawning season," *U.S. Congressional Record,* 49th Cong., 1st sess. (June 1 and June 29, 1886), 238.

41. Unpublished Hearings before the Senate Committee on Fisheries re bill HR 5538, 122–123, 132, 213, 218.

42. *Bulletin of the United States Fish Commission Vol. I for 1881* (Washington, D.C., 1882), 339; Unpublished Hearings before the Senate Committee on Fisheries re bill HR 5538, 185–187.

43. Unpublished Hearings before the Senate Committee on Fisheries re bill HR 5538, 193–195, 212.

44. Ibid., 4–9, 28–33; "Mackerel Catchers Alarmed," *NYT,* May 26, 1886, 2; "The Supply of Mackerel," *NYT,* May 28, 1886, 4.

45. *U.S. Congressional Record* 17, 49th Cong., 1st sess. (1886), 4779–4782; Unpublished Hearings before the U.S. Senate Committee on Fisheries re bill HR 5538, 244; "Food from the Waters," *NYT,* June 27, 1886, 10.

46. *U.S. Congressional Record* 17 (1886), 4779; James Grant, *Mr. Speaker! The Life and Times of Thomas B. Reed, the Man Who Broke the Filibuster* (New York, 2011).

47. *U.S. Congressional Record* 17 (1886), 4779–4780.

48. Unpublished Hearings before the U.S. Senate Committee on Fisheries re bill HR 5538, 85, 92, 97.

49. *U.S. Congressional Record* 17 (1886), 4783.

50. Ibid.

51. *Bulletin of the United States Fish Commission Vol. VI, for 1886* (Washington, D.C., 1887), 406–407.

52. *First Annual Report of Maine Bureau of Industrial and Labor Statistics, 1887,* 113–115; Small, *History of Swans Island,* 185–194.

53. Unpublished Hearings before the Senate Committee on Fisheries re bill HR 5538, 40.

54. *Congressional Serial Set,* vol. 2365, session vol. 11, Senate Report No. 1592, 49th Cong., 1st sess. (1886); "The Mackerel Bill," *NYT,* February 12, 1887, 4.

55. "Mackerel from Ireland," *NYT,* December 7, 1888, 3.

56. John Molloy, *The Irish Mackerel Fishery and the Making of an Industry* (Galway, 2004), 32–33.

57. Molloy, *Irish Mackerel Fishery,* 34–36; Séamus Fitzgerald, *Mackerel and the Making of Baltimore, County Cork,* Maynooth Studies in Local History No. 22 (Dublin, 1999), 10–13; *Regulation of the Fisheries Hearings before the U.S. House Committee on Merchant Marine and Fisheries,* 52nd. Cong., 1st. sess. (February 9, 17, 18, 24 and March 2, 16, 1892) (Washington, D.C., 1892), 92–93.

58. Fitzgerald, *Mackerel and the Making of Baltimore,* 13.

59. Ibid., 19, 22–23; "Mackerel from Ireland," *NYT,* December 7, 1888, 3.

60. Fitzgerald, *Mackerel and the Making of Baltimore,* 23–25, 54–55; "The Irish Mackerel Catch," *NYT,* August 25, 1891, 1; "Heavy Haul of Mackerel near Skull," *NYT,* September 23, 1894, 9.

61. "A Long Trip for Mackerel," *NYT,* September 28, 1889, 4; USCFF, *Part XVII. Report of the Commissioner for 1889 to 1891* (Washington, D.C., 1893), 203.

62. MHMF, 170–171, 324–325, 429–430.

63. MHMF, 242; Charles H. Stevenson, "A Review of the Foreign-Fishery Trade of the United States," in USCFF, *Part XX. Report of the Commissioner for the Year Ending June 30, 1894* (Washington, D.C., 1896), 431–571.

64. Stevenson, "Review of the Foreign-Fishery Trade," 436–447.

65. Ibid., 444–451, 464, 487.

66. "The African Mackerel," *NYT,* February 23, 1890, 8.

67. Henry B. Bigelow and William C. Schroeder, *Fishes of the Gulf of Maine* (Washington, D.C., 1953), 249–252; *FFIUS,* sec. V, 1:37.

68. Glenn M. Grasso, "What Appeared Limitless Plenty: The Rise and Fall of the Nineteenth Century Atlantic Halibut Fishery," *Environmental History* 13 (January 2008), 66–91.

69. *FFIUS,* sec. V, 1:30–37.

70. Grasso, "What Appeared Limitless Plenty," 71–72; *FFIUS,* sec. V, 1:37.

71. Grasso, "What Appeared Limitless Plenty," 72.

72. *FFIUS,* sec. V, 1:3–16.

73. Grasso, "What Appeared Limitless Plenty," 74; Edward A. Ackerman, *New England's Fishing Industry* (Chicago, 1941), 78, 214.

74. Grasso, "What Appeared Limitless Plenty," 77.

75. *FFIUS,* sec. V, 1:23; Mike Hagler, "Deforestation of the Deep: Fishing and the State of the Oceans," *The Ecologist* 25, no. 2/3 (March/April, May/June 1995), 74–79.

76. Grasso, "What Appeared Limitless Plenty," 77; *FFIUS,* sec. V, 1:32–34.

77. *FFIUS,* sec. V, 1:32–37; Grasso, "What Appeared Limitless Plenty," 66; Lorenzo Sabine, *Report on the Principal Fisheries of the American Seas: Prepared for the Treasury Department of the United States* (Washington, D.C., 1853), 197.

78. *FFIUS,* sec. V, 1:42–43, 58.

79. Ibid., 91–92.

80. A. Thorsteinson, "American Halibut Fisheries near Iceland," in *Bulletin of the U.S. Fish Commission Vol. V, for 1885* (Washington, D.C., 1885), 429; *FFIUS,* sec. V, 1:24, 33–34.

81. Thorsteinson, "American Halibut Fishers near Iceland," 429.

82. USCFF, *Part XIII. Report of the Commissioner for 1885* (Washington, D.C., 1887), xx–xxi, li–lii.

83. USCFF, *Part XVI. Report of the Commissioner for 1888* (Washington, D.C., 1892), 289–325; *FFIUS*, sec. V, 1:3; USCFF, *Part XXVII. Report of the Commissioner for the Year Ending June 30, 1902* (Washington, D.C., 1904), 149.

84. *FFIUS*, sec. V, 1:118.

85. Ibid., 90–91; Dean Conrad Allard Jr., *Spencer Fullerton Baird and the U.S. Fish Commission* (New York, 1978), 317–342.

86. Department of Commerce and Labor, *Report of the Bureau of Fisheries 1904* (Washington, D.C., 1905), 282; A. B. Alexander, "Notes on the Halibut Fishery of the Northwest Coast in 1895," in *Bulletin of the U.S. Fish Commission Vol. XVII, for 1897* (Washington, D.C., 1898), 141–144; Bureau of Fisheries, *Report of the U.S. Commissioner of Fisheries for the Fiscal Year 1918 with Appendixes* (Washington, D.C., 1920), 92–93.

87. *FFIUS*, sec. V, 1:5–6.

88. Ibid., 43–44, 60; Spencer F. Baird, *Report on the Condition of the Sea Fisheries of the South Coast of New England in 1871 and 1872* (Washington, D.C., 1873), 120.

89. Richard Hakluyt, *The Principal Navigations, Voyages, Traffiques & Discoveries of the English Nation,* 8 vols., ed. Ernest Rhys (London, 1907), 5:346; George Parker Winship, ed., *Sailors' Narratives of Voyages along the New England Coast, 1524–1624* (1905; reprint, New York, 1968), 182–183.

90. Kenneth R. Martin and Nathan R. Lipfert, *Lobstering and the Maine Coast* (Bath, Maine, 1985), provides the best overview of the American lobster fishery. See also John N. Cobb, "The Lobster Fishery of Maine," in *Bulletin of the United States Fish Commission Vol. XIX, for 1899* (Washington, D.C., 1900), 241–265.

91. Martin and Lipfert, *Lobstering and the Maine Coast,* 13–21; Richard W. Judd, *Common Lands, Common People: The Origins of Conservation in Northern New England* (Cambridge, Mass., 1997), 247.

92. Martin and Lipfert, *Lobstering and the Maine Coast,* 31–35.

93. Richard Rathbun, "The Lobster Fishery," in *FFIUS,* sec. V, 2:658–794, quotations on 669–678, 771.

94. Cobb, "Lobster Fishery of Maine," 241–265, quotation on 246–247.

95. *MFCR* (Boston, 1873), 29; *MFCR* (Boston, 1887), 20; *MFCR* (Boston, 1874), 46–47.

96. Judd, *Common Lands, Common People,* 247–262.

97. *Report on the Lobster Industry of Canada, 1892,* Supplement to *25th Annual Report of the Department of Marine and Fisheries* (Ottawa, 1893), 22–23.

98. Rathbun, "The Lobster Fishery," 725; *MFCR* (Boston, 1885), 21; *MFCR* (Boston, 1888), 18–21.

99. *Report on the Lobster Industry of Canada, 1892,* 5–8.

100. Ibid., 9; Rathbun, "The Lobster Fishery," 691; *MeFCR* (Augusta, 1886), 29.

101. "Historical Summary of the Maine Lobster Fishery," Maine Department of Marine Resources, www.maine.gov/dmr/rm/lobster/lobdata.htm (accessed July 29, 2011); *MeSSF* (Augusta, 1898), 7; *MeSSF* (Augusta, 1901), 17–18; Cobb, "Lobster Fishery of Maine."

102. *Report on the Lobster Industry of Canada, 1892*, 24–29; D. S. Pezzack, "A Review of Lobster *(Homarus americanus)* Landing Trends in the Northwest Atlantic, 1947–86," *Journal of Northwest Atlantic Fisheries Science* 14 (1992), 115–127.

103. *MeFCR* (Augusta, 1891), 29.

104. *Bulletin of the United States Fish Commission Vol. XVII, for 1897*, 217–224.

105. Rathbun, "The Lobster Fishery," 696–699.

106. "Mackerel Disappearing," *NYT*, July 6, 1889, 2: J. M. K. Southwick, "Our Ocean Fishes and the Effect of Legislation upon the Fisheries," in *Bulletin of the United States Fish Commission Vol. XIII, for 1893* (Washington, D.C., 1894), 40–41.

107. *MeFCR* (Augusta, 1892), 26, 31–33.

108. Charles F. Chamberlayne, *"State Rights in State Fisheries": An Argument by Charles F. Chamberlayne, Esq., of Boston, Mass., as Counsel for the Commission of Sea and Shore Fisheries of Maine, before the Committee on Merchant Marine and Fisheries February 24, 1892 in Opposition to the "Lapham Bill" to Permit Seining for Mackerel and Menhaden in State Waters Contrary to State Law* (Washington, D.C., 1892); *MeFCR* (Augusta, 1892), 41–43.

109. Chamberlayne, "State Rights in State Fisheries," 3, 35–36.

110. "Memorial of the Commission of Sea and Shore Fisheries of the State of Maine Remonstrating against the Lapham Bill," *Congressional Serial Set,* vol. 2904, session vol. 2, 52d Cong., 1st sess., Senate Misc. Doc. 96 (March 14, 1892), 4; "A Menhaden Trust," *NYT*, December 22, 1897, 1; "American Fisheries Company," *NYT*, January 9, 1898, 1.

111. "Memorial of the Commission of Sea and Shore Fisheries of the State of Maine Remonstrating against the Lapham Bill," 8, 23.

112. *MeFCR* (Augusta, 1892), 40–43; "Memorial of the Commission of Sea and Shore Fisheries of the State of Maine Remonstrating Against the Lapham Bill," 9, 11.

113. Robert F. Walsh, "Conservation of the Mackerel Supply," *Popular Science Monthly* 42 (April 1893), 821–827; John Z. Rogers, "Decline of our Fisheries," *NYT*, August 11, 1901.

6. An Avalanche of Cheap Fish

1. Principe DiGangi to Marshall McDonald, August 2, 1895, Records of the U.S. Fish and Wildlife Service, RG 22, Records of the U.S. Fish Commission and Bureau of Fisheries, Letters Received 1882–1910, box 244, folder 2248–2280 (1895), NARA, College Park, Md.

2. USCFF, *Part XXVII: Report of the Commissioner for the Year Ending June 30, 1901,* (Washington, D.C., 1902), 20; Bureau of Fisheries, *Report of the U.S. Commissioner of Fisheries for the Fiscal Year 1914 with Appendixes* (Washington, D.C., 1915), 79; Bureau of Fisheries, *Report of the Commissioner of Fisheries for the Fiscal Year 1908 and Special*

Papers (Washington, D.C., 1910), 8; USCFF, *Part XXVI: Report of the Commissioner for the Year Ending June 30, 1900* (Washington, D.C., 1901), 196.

3. *MFCR* (Boston, 1906), 24; "One Way of Increasing the Number of Fish in the Sea," *Fishing Gazette* 16, no. 16 (April 21, 1900), 241.

4. USCFF, *Report of the Commissioner for Year Ending June 30, 1900*, 7.

5. *MeSSF* (Augusta, 1907), 68; "One Way of Increasing the Number of Fish in the Sea," 241–242; Bureau of Fisheries, *Report of the Commissioner of Fisheries for the Fiscal Year 1906 and Special Papers* (Washington, D.C., 1906), 25.

6. *MFCR* (Boston, 1907), 5; *Bulletin of the Bureau of Fisheries Vol. XXVIII, for 1908* (Washington, D.C., 1910), 19, 189–192; "Now is the Time to Conserve Our Alaska Fisheries," *Fishing Gazette* 28, no. 41 (October 14, 1911), 1281. For a slightly different view on the cause of the problems, see Joseph William Collins, "Decadence of the New England Deep Sea Fisheries," *Harper's New Monthly Magazine,* 94, March 1897, 608–625.

7. Robert A. Widenmann, "Extermination Threatens American Sea Fishes," *NYT Sunday Magazine,* July 26, 1914, 4.

8. Ibid., 4.

9. Ibid., 4.

10. Ibid., 4.

11. Ibid.; "Decline of Our Fisheries," *NYT,* August 11, 1901; Bureau of Fisheries, *Report of the Commissioner of Fisheries for the Fiscal Year 1909 and Special Papers* (Washington, D.C., 1911), 21.

12. *The City of Gloucester Massachusetts, Its Interests and Industries. Compiled under the Auspices of the Publicity Committee of the Board of Trade* (Gloucester, 1916), 37, 40–41, 52–53; [advertisement], *Fishing Gazette* 24, no. 3 (January 19, 1907), 50; [advertisement], ibid., no. 5 (February 2, 1907), 99.

13. George H. Proctor, *The Fishermen's Memorial and Record Book, Containing a List of Vessels and Their Crews Lost from the Port of Gloucester from the Year 1830 to October 1, 1873* (Gloucester, Mass., 1873); *The Fishermen's Own Book, Comprising the List of Men and Vessels Lost from the Port of Gloucester, Mass., from 1874 to April 1, 1882* (Gloucester, 1882); Sir Walter Scott, *The Antiquary* (1816), chap. 11. For a compilation of Gloucester fishermen's mortality culled from the *Gloucester Telegraph,* the *Cape Ann Advertiser,* and the *Gloucester Daily Times,* see www.downtosea.com/list (accessed August 6, 2011). Gloucester's population in 1870 was 15,389.

14. Collins, "Decadence of the New England Deep Sea Fisheries," 609; W. M. P. Dunne, *Thomas F. McManus and the American Fishing Schooners: An Irish-American Success Story* (Mystic, Conn., 1994).

15. Gardner D. Hiscox, *Gas, Gasoline, and Oil Vapor Engines: A New Book Descriptive of Their Theory and Power. Illustrating Their Design, Construction, and Operation for Stationary, Marine, and Vehicle Motive Power* (New York, 1897), quotation from preface, n.p.; Stan Grayson, *Old Marine Engines: The World of the One-Lunger* (Camden,

Maine, 1982), 15–23; Grayson, *American Marine Engines, 1885–1950* (Marblehead, Mass., 2008), 4–18.

16. "Motorboating at Portland," *The Motorboat* 3, no. 14 (July 25, 1906), 28; [advertisement], ibid., no. 13 (July 10, 1906), 43; Grayson, *American Marine Engines*, 9, 51.

17. Clippings on Captain Solomon Jacobs from the *Cape Ann Weekly Advertiser* (1900) and the *Boston Globe* (1901), Cape Ann Historical Society, Gloucester, Mass.

18. Department of Commerce and Labor, *Report of the Bureau of Fisheries 1904* (Washington, D.C., 1905), 282, 288, 290; *MFCR* (Boston, 1902), 63; *MFCR* (Boston, 1905), 29; Bureau of Fisheries, *Report for Fiscal Year 1906*, 15, 42, 93.

19. *MFCR* (Boston, 1906), 10.

20. *Gloucester Master Mariners' Association, List of Vessels. The American Fisheries*, comp. J. H. Stapleton (Gloucester, 1917), lists 225 vessels of five tons or more registered in Gloucester, 95 in Boston, and 71 in Provincetown.

21. John Smith, *A Description of New England* (1616), in *The Complete Works of Captain John Smith (1580–1631)*, 3 vols., ed. Philip L. Barbour (Chapel Hill, 1986), 1:330, 333; Daniel Vickers, *Farmers and Fishermen: Two Centuries of Work in Essex County, Massachusetts, 1630–1850* (Chapel Hill, 1994).

22. George A. Rose, *Cod: The Ecological History of the North Atlantic Fisheries* (St. John's, Newf., 2007), 328–330.

23. Callum Roberts, *The Unnatural History of the Sea* (Washington, D.C., 2007), 131–132; John Dyson, *Business in Great Waters: The Story of British Fishermen* (London, 1977), 37–38, 73–81.

24. Roberts, *Unnatural History of the Sea*, 133–147; D. H. Cushing, *The Provident Sea* (Cambridge, 1988), 104–115.

25. Cushing, *Provident Sea*, 109; Dyson, *Business in Great Waters*, 245–248.

26. Baird wrote this in 1877 in *The Sea Fisheries of Eastern North America*, but it was not published until 1889. See USCFF, *Part XIV: Report of the Commissioner for 1886* (Washington, D.C., 1889), 121–123.

27. USCFF, *Part XVIII: Report of the Commissioner for the Year Ending June 30, 1892* (Washington, D.C., 1894), CLXXXI; Frank H. Wood, "Trawling and Dragging in New England Waters," *Atlantic Fisherman* 6 and 7, Parts 1 (January 1926), 10–23, and 2 (February 1926), 11–23, 1:10–11.

28. *Report of the Bureau of Fisheries 1904*, 291; Bureau of Fisheries, *Report of the Commissioner of Fisheries for the Fiscal Year 1911 and Special Papers* (Washington, D.C., 1913), 49–50.

29. Bruce B. Collette and Grace Klein-MacPhee, eds., *Bigelow and Schroeder's Fishes of the Gulf of Maine* (Washington, D.C., 2002), 545–586.

30. Wood, "Trawling and Dragging in New England Waters"; Anon., "Drudgin'," *New England Magazine* 41, no. 6 (February 1910), 665–671.

31. "The North Sea Fisheries," *Fishing Gazette* 20, no. 8 (February 21, 1903), 141.

32. *MFCR* (Boston, 1902), 66; "The North Sea Fisheries," 141–142; British statistics in *Hearings before the Committee on the Merchant Marine and Fisheries House of Representatives on H.R. 16457, Prohibiting the Importing and Landing of Fish Caught by Beam Trawlers* (Washington, D.C., 1913), 18.

33. Wood, "Trawling and Dragging in New England Waters," 1:11; "Jno. R. Neal and Co., T-Wharf, Boston," *Fishing Gazette* 24, no. 5 (February 2, 1907), 109; Andrew W. German, "Otter Trawling Comes to America: The Bay State Fishing Company, 1905–1938," *American Neptune* 44, no. 2 (Spring 1984), 114–131.

34. *Hearings on HR 16457, Prohibiting the Importing and Landing of Fish Caught by Beam Trawlers*, 8–9, 38.

35. *Fishing Gazette,* December 15, 1906; *Gloucester Daily Times,* January 6, 1909. These clippings in Records of the U.S. Fish Commission and Bureau of Fisheries, RG 22, vol. 10, entry 47, NARA, College Park, Md.

36. *Hearings on H.R. 16457, Prohibiting the Importing and Landing of Fish Caught by Beam Trawlers*, 12–14, 41, 60.

37. Ibid., 12–13.

38. Ibid., 19.

39. Ibid., 21–22.

40. Ibid., 44–52.

41. Ibid., 54–57.

42. Ibid., 67–72.

43. Ibid., 97–99.

44. Ibid., 77.

45. Ibid., 76–84; James Brendan Connolly, "Fishing in Arctic Seas," *Harper's Monthly Magazine,*110, April 1905, 659–668.

46. *Hearings before the Committee on H.R. 16457, Prohibiting the Importing and Landing of Fish Caught by Beam Trawlers,* 118, 124–125.

47. Ibid., 11, 94.

48. Ibid., 100–108, quotations on 93, 101.

49. *MFCR* (Boston, 1916), 83–92; "Boston Fish Bureau Report for 1913," *Fishing Gazette* 31, no. 10 (March 7, 1914), 289.

50. David Stradling, ed., *Conservation in the Progressive Era: Classic Texts* (Seattle, 2004); Kurkpatrick Dorsey, *The Dawn of Conservation Diplomacy: U.S.-Canadian Wildlife Protection Treaties in the Progressive Era* (Seattle, 1998).

51. *MeSSF* (Augusta, 1903), 40–43.

52. Ibid., 40–43.

53. *MeSSF* (Augusta, 1905), 51–52.

54. *MFCR* (Boston, 1902), 51–52.

55. *MeSSF* (Augusta, 1907), 46–55, quotations on 46, 49.

56. Ibid., 55.

57. *MFCR* (Boston, 1906), 32–34.

58. Ibid., 30–37.

59. Henry B. Bigelow and William C. Schroeder, *Fishes of the Gulf of Maine* (Washington, D.C., 1953), 47–51; Collette and Klein-MacPhee, *Bigelow and Schroeder's Fishes of the Gulf of Maine,* 54–57.

60. Bigelow and Schroeder, *Fishes of the Gulf of Maine,* 47; *New York Sun* quoted in *MFCR* (Boston, 1906), 167.

61. *MFCR* (Boston, 1906), 167.

62. Ibid., 98, 162–163; *MFCR* (Boston, 1905), 13.

63. *MFCR* (Boston, 1905), 97–169; Bureau of Fisheries, *Report for Fiscal Year 1906,* 22; *Fishing Gazette* 33, no. 10 (March 4, 1916), 302.

64. Michael J. Fogarty and Steven A. Murawski, "Large-Scale Disturbance and the Structure of Marine Ecosystems: Fishery Impacts on Georges Bank," *Ecological Applications* 8, no. 1, suppl. (1998), S6–S22.

65. Bureau of Fisheries, *Report of the U.S. Commissioner of Fisheries for the Fiscal Year 1915 with Appendixes* (Washington, D.C., 1917), 37–43.

66. *MeSSF* (Auburn, 1920), 14–15.

67. "Communication from the Commissioner of Fisheries to the Secretary of Commerce," January 20, 1915, in Bureau of Fisheries, *Report for the Fiscal Year 1914,* app. 6, "Otter-Trawl Fishery," 5; A. B. Alexander, H. F. Moore, and W. C. Kendall, "Report on the Otter-Trawl Fishery," ibid., 13–97, quotation 94. For contemporary European biologists' approach to the overfishing question, see Helen M. Rozwadowski, *The Sea Knows No Boundaries: A Century of Marine Science Under ICES* (Seattle and London, 2002), 50–56.

68. "Report on the Otter Trawl Fishery," 96.

69. Ibid., 95, 97.

70. Numerous advertisements for foreign fish include those in *Fishing Gazette* 24, no. 1 (January 5, 1907), 4.

71. Andrew W. German, *Down on T Wharf: The Boston Fisheries as Seen through the Photographs of Henry D. Fisher* (Mystic, Conn., 1982), 105–106; Bureau of Fisheries, *Report for Fiscal Year 1915,* 62.

72. German, *Down on T Wharf,* 124–137; "Report on the Otter Trawl Fishery," 13–97.

73. "Report on the Otter Trawl Fishery," 14.

74. Ibid., 58–59.

75. Ibid., 69.

76. "Communication from the Commissioner of Fisheries to the Secretary of Commerce" (January 20, 1915), 5–7.

77. "Report on the Otter Trawl Fishery," 27–28, 90.

78. Ibid., 90; National Research Council, Committee on Ecosystem Effects of Fishing, *Effects of Trawling and Dredging on Seafloor Habitat* (Washington, D.C., 2002); Les

Watling and Elliott A. Norse, "Disturbance of the Seabed by Mobile Fishing Gear: A Comparison to Forest Clearcutting," *Conservation Biology* 12 (December 1998), 1178–1197; Sue Robinson, "The Battle over Bottom Trawling," *National Fisherman*, August 1999, 24–25.

79. "Report on Otter Trawling," 91–93.

80. Ibid., 94–95.

81. Bureau of Fisheries, *Report for the Fiscal Year 1915*, 60–61; Records of Division of Scientific Inquiry, Records of U.S. Fish Commission and Bureau of Fisheries, RG 22, Draft Reports Concerning Trawl Fisheries and British Fisheries, 1912–1915, box 1, folder "Otter Trawl Charts," NARA, College Park, Md.

82. *Atlantic Fisherman*, March 1926, quoted in Michael Wayne Santos, *Caught in Irons: North Atlantic Fishermen in the Last Days of Sail* (Selinsgrove, Pa., 2002), 62.

Epilogue

1. Statement of Hon. John F. Fitzgerald, in *Hearings before the Committee on the Merchant Marine and Fisheries, House of Representatives on H.R. 16457, Prohibiting the Importing and Landing of Fish Caught by Beam Trawlers* (Washington, D.C., 1913), 21–22.

2. Sylvanus Smith, *Fisheries of Cape Ann: A Collection of Reminiscent Narratives of Fishing and Coasting Trips* (Gloucester, Mass., 1915), 86–95, quotations on 91–92.

3. Statement of Captain William G. Thompson, in *Hearings on H.R. 16457, Prohibiting the Importing and Landing of Fish Caught by Beam Trawlers*, 70–71.

4. Donald J. White, *The New England Fishing Industry: A Study in Price and Wage Setting* (Cambridge, Mass., 1954), 10–11.

5. *Report of the Joint Special Recess Committee to Continue the Investigation of the Fish Industry*, Mass. House Report No. 1725 (Boston, 1919), 18–38, 57–61; White, *New England Fishing Industry*, 19–27.

6. White, *New England Fishing Industry*, 42–49.

7. White, *New England Fishing Industry*, 8–15; Edward A. Ackerman, *New England's Fishing Industry* (Chicago, 1941), 226–231.

8. Ackerman, *New England's Fishing Industry*, 78–86; White, *New England Fishing Industry*, 103–105.

9. W. C. Herrington, "Decline in Haddock Abundance on Georges Bank and a Practical Remedy," *Fishery Circular No. 23* (U.S. Department of Commerce, Bureau of Fisheries), July 1936, 18; Edward A. Ackerman, "Depletion in New England Fisheries," *Economic Geography* 14 (July 1938), 233–238.

10. Herrington, "Decline in Haddock Abundance," 18; White, *New England Fishing Industry*, 21, 105.

11. White, *New England Fishing Industry*, 105.

12. *Atlantic Fisherman* was published monthly from 1919 to 1954, when it was re-named the *National Fisherman*. White, *New England Fishing Industry*, 4–5; David Boeri and James Gibson, *"Tell It Good-Bye, Kiddo"—The Decline of the New England Offshore Fishery* (Camden, Maine, 1976), 48–60.

13. William W. Warner, *Distant Water: The Fate of the North Atlantic Fisherman* (Boston, 1977), vii.

14. Ibid., 32–38; George A. Rose, *Cod: The Ecological History of the North Atlantic Fisheries* (St. John's, Newf., 2007), 383–388.

15. "Collapse of Atlantic cod stocks off the East Coast of Newfoundland in 1992," in *UNEP/GRID-Arendal Maps and Graphics Library,* http://maps.grida.no/go/graphic /collapse-of-atlantic-cod-stocks-off-the-east-coast-of-newfoundland-in-1992 (accessed January 29, 2012); Rose, *Cod,* 395–440.

16. Boeri and Gibson, *"Tell It Good-Bye, Kiddo";* Steven A. Murawski et al., "New England Groundfish," in *Our Living Oceans: Report on the Status of U.S. Living Marine Resources, 1999,* NOAA Technical Memorandum NMFS-F/SPO-41, June 1999, 71–80; New England Fisheries Science Center, "Status of Fishery Resources off the Northeastern U.S.," figs. 1.11 and 1.2, www.nefsc.noaa.gov/sos/spsyn/pg/cod (accessed January 29, 2012).

17. Sonja V. Fordham, *New England Groundfish: From Glory to Grief. A Portrait of America's Most Devastated Fishery* (Washington, D.C., 1996); Susan Hanna et al., *Fishing Grounds: Defining a New Era for American Fisheries Management* (Washington, D.C., 2000), 23–38.

18. Seth Macinko and Daniel W. Bromley, *Who Owns America's Fisheries?* (Covelo, Calif., 2002).

19. Fordham, *New England Groundfish;* Michael Harris, *Lament for an Ocean: The Collapse of the Atlantic Cod Fishery: A True Crime Story* (Toronto, 1998), 39–180; Rose, *Cod,* 434–477. The popular bumper-stickers were the brainchild of New England Marine and Industrial Supply, Portsmouth, N.H.

20. Peter Shelley, Jennifer Atkinson, Eleanor Dorsey, and Priscilla Brooks, "The New England Fisheries Crisis: What Have We Learned?" *Tulane Environmental Law Journal* 9 (Summer 1996), 221–244.

21. Scott Allen, "Tighter Fishing Limits Urged," *Boston Globe,* November 3, 1999, B1; Gareth Cook and Beth Daley, "Sea Change: The New England Fishing Crisis," *Boston Globe,* October 29, 2003, 1.

22. Recent developments can be followed in Carl Safina, *Song for the Blue Ocean: Encounters along the World's Coasts and beneath the Seas* (New York, 1998); David Helvarg, *Blue Frontier: Saving America's Living Seas* (New York, 2001); Colin Woodard, *Ocean's End: Travels through Endangered Seas* (New York, 2000); David Dobbs, *The Great Gulf: Fishermen, Scientists, and the Struggle to Revive the World's Greatest Fishery* (Washington, D.C., 2000); Daniel Pauly and Jay Maclean, *In a Perfect Ocean: The State of Fisheries and Ecosystems in the North Atlantic Ocean* (Washington, D.C., 2003); Rich-

ard Ellis, *The Empty Ocean: Plundering the World's Marine Life* (Washington, D.C., 2003); Paul Greenberg, *Four Fish: The Future of the Last Wild Food* (New York, 2010); Jeremy B. C. Jackson, Karen Alexander, Enric Sala, eds., *Shifting Baselines: The Past and the Future of Ocean Fisheries* (Washington, D.C., 2011).

23. "Fishery Management Plans, Northeast Multispecies—Sector Management," NOAA Fisheries Service, Northeast Regional Office, http://www.nero.noaa.gov/sfd /sfdmultisector.html (accessed January 31, 2012).

24. Sid Perkins, "A Sea of Plastics," *U.S. News and World Report* February 26, 2010, http://www.usnews.com/science/articles/2010/02/26/a-sea-of-plastics (accessed January 31, 2012); Miriam Goldstein, "Journey to the North Atlantic Gyre with Plastics at SEA," *Deep Sea News,* June 14, 2010, http://deepseanews.com/2010/06/journey-to-the-north-at-lantic-gyre-with-plastics-at-sea/ (accessed January 31, 2012).

25. Dean Travis Clark, "So Long, Oceans. Thanks for All the Fish," *Cruising World,* October 1998, 256.

GLOSSARY

alewife: *Alosa pseudoharengus*. An **anadromous herring**, also known as "river herring." Gregarious schooling fish, once as common in their spawning streams as the passenger pigeons that darkened American skies, alewives swim upstream from the sea to spawn in lakes and ponds in the spring. Easily caught from shore, alewives were used primarily for fertilizer and bait. Alewives grow to 15 inches, but adults average 10 to 11 inches. Grayish-green above, alewives are darkest on their backs, and paler and more silvery on their sides and belly. Historically alewives were distributed from Newfoundland to the St. Johns River in Florida.

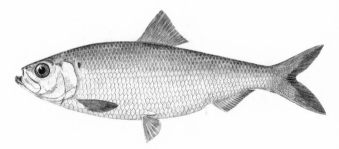

Alewife. *FFIUS*, sec. I: plate 208.

anadromous: Born in freshwater, anadromous fishes spend most of their lives in the ocean, but return to freshwater to spawn. Their life cycle takes advantage of ample food in the sea and relatively safe conditions for reproduction in rivers and streams. Examples include alewives, shad, sturgeon, and salmon. Each spring the return of vast numbers of these fish to human communities hungry for protein was a blessing—and a temptation to overfish.

basking shark: *Cetorhinus maximus.* The second-largest living fish, after the whale shark, the basking shark is a filter feeder with tiny teeth. It strains plankton through its oversize mouth with specially adapted gill rakers, which are so large they extend right around the neck. Harmless to humans, basking sharks were harvested for the oil in their livers. They can attain 40 feet, but generally average 20 to 26 feet, weighing about 5.2 tons. Basking sharks are grayish brown, slate gray, or nearly black, and often mottled. Found worldwide in boreal to warm-temperate seas, basking sharks follow concentrations of plankton.

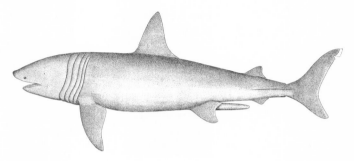

Basking shark. *FFIUS,* sec. I: plate 249.

beach seine: A seine net with floats on its upper edge and weights on its lower edge, operated from the shore. Beach seines were hauled by hand, or occasionally with the assistance of a horse. Sometimes beach seines were set with the aid of a small boat. Otherwise they were simply pulled through the water adjacent to the beach. Beach seines worked best for schooling fish such as **menhaden**.

Beach seine. *FFIUS,* sec. V: plate 98.

beam trawl: A cone-shaped net, dragged along the bottom, held open by a wooden beam. The beam, 10 feet to more than 40 feet long, had a metal runner attached at each end. Those runners kept the upper edge of the net several feet off the bottom. A bridle from the runners went to the towing line, and thence to the boat.

Beam trawl. *Bulletin of the United States Fish Commission. Vol. VII, for 1887* (Washington, D.C., 1887), plate XV.

benthic: Referring to the bottom of the sea or to the array of organisms living on the sea bottom. Benthic organisms include sea anemones, clams, oysters, sea cucumbers, and sea stars (also known as starfish).

bultow: A mid-nineteenth-century term for a **longline**, or tub-trawl. See **tub-trawl.**

capelin: *Mallotus villosus.* Slender forage fish in the **smelt** family, capelin feed on plankton, and in turn are eaten by seabirds, whales, seals, **cod**, squid, and **mackerel**, among other predators. Capelin are a key food of North Atlantic cod. Capelin spawn on sandy beaches and sandy bottoms in the spring. They have extremely high mortality after spawning, and harvesters historically scooped them up from beaches. Capelin rarely grow longer than 6½ to 7½ inches. Olive-green to dark green above, they have silvery sides below their lateral lines. Capelin are an Arctic and subarctic species regularly found in Labrador and Newfoundland, but only occasionally in the Gulf of Maine, the southern end of their range.

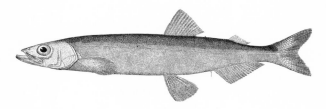

Capelin. *FFIUS,* sec. I: plate 201.

Chebacco boat: Named for Chebacco Parish, once part of Ipswich, Massachusetts, where they are said to have originated, Chebacco boats were common among the inshore fishing fleet near Essex, Ipswich, Gloucester, and Newburyport, Massachusetts, from before the American Revolution to about 1820. Simple, inexpensive boats, they had no bowsprits or jibs, and were rigged as cat schooners. Chebacco boats were flush decked, with two recessed well or cockpits in which the fishermen stood. Averaging about 30 feet in length, they rarely exceeded 40 feet. This image shows a Chebacco boat rigged with drails in pursuit of **mackerel.**

Chebacco boat. *FFIUS,* sec. V: plate 79.

clupeid: Clupeidae is the family including herrings, shads, sardines, and **menhaden**. Typically eating plankton, clupeids are among the most important forage fish in the North Atlantic because they serve as the link between the bottom of the food web (the plankton) and larger carnivores such as **cod**, tuna, and sharks.

cod: *Gadhus morhua.* Atlantic cod were once the most important fish caught by humans in the western Atlantic. Cod have flaky white flesh containing little fat. Their livers are rich in oil. Heavy-bodied fish with three dorsal fins and two anal fins, cod have a distinctive lateral line, a barbell dangling from their chins, and no spines on any of their fins. Cod could grow to enormous size. One more than 6 feet long and weighing 211¼ pounds was landed off Massachusetts in 1895. Cod of 50 to 60 pounds were not unusual. Cod vary widely in color, but all are in two main groups, the grayish-green and the reddish. In the western Atlantic cod ranged from the subarctic to the New York Bight off New York and New Jersey. In the eastern Atlantic cod ranged from northern Norway and the Barents Sea to the English Channel.

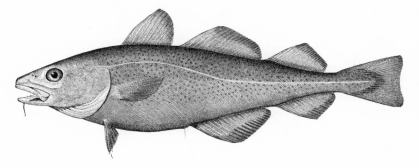

Cod. *FFIUS,* sec. I: plate 58A.

demersal: Referring to the part of the sea just above the seabed, and significantly affected by it. Demersal fishes are bottom feeders. They include flounder and **halibut**, which actually rest on the seafloor, as well as species such as **cod**, **haddock**, hake, and cusk, which cruise just above the seafloor.

dory: A small, shallow-draft boat, approximately 16 to 22 feet long, with relatively high sides, a flat bottom, and a sharp bow, dories were built of wide planks. Able to carry a heavy load for their size, they had high ultimate stability, yet were cheap to build. Banks dories had removable seats so they could be stacked on the deck of a fishing vessel. Other dories, such as Swampscott dories, were often used in beach-based fisheries for lobster, **cod**, and other species. This plate shows men lobstering from a dory.

Dory. *FFIUS*, sec. V: plate 247.

dory-trawling: Setting longlines from a **dory**. **Schooner** fishermen initially expanded the area they fished by deploying dories with men to handline at a distance from the schooner. During the 1860s and 1870s fishermen further multiplied their hook footprint by setting out longlines, which they called tub-trawls, from dories—thus leading to the term "dory-trawling." See also **tub-trawl**.

Dory-trawling. *FFIUS*, sec. V: plate 26.

drail: A short-lived form of fishing for **mackerel** using outrigger poles. See the entry for **Chebacco boat,** whose crew is fishing with drails.

fare: Another term for "trip," the span of time for fishermen between leaving port and returning. A fare could last several hours, several days, several weeks, or several months.

gadoids: The Gadidae are a large family of marine fishes important to humans, including **cod,** hake, **haddock,** cusk, ling, pollock, and whiting. They all resemble cod, a member of the family to which all the others are related.

gill net: A net suspended below the surface of the water at a set depth, and secured with anchors at its ends. Gill nets work at night. Fish cannot see them in the dark, and blunder into the mesh, becoming entangled (often near their gills) as they try to swim through the net. During the 1880s Massachusetts inshore fishermen took vast amounts of spawning **cod** with gill nets. Until that innovation, spawning fish had been relatively safe from capture, because cod did not eat while spawning, and thus rarely took baited hooks.

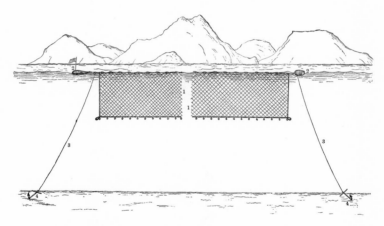

Gill-net. *FFIUS,* sec. V: plate 43.

haddock: *Melanogrammus aeglefinus.* Similar in many ways to **cod,** haddock have a black lateral line, and are smaller when mature. Haddock rarely reach 30 pounds, and most are less when landed, weighing 3 to 4 pounds. Haddock did not salt as well as cod, and during the heyday of the salt-cod fishery they were known derisively as the "white eye." With the advent of otter trawling and icing at sea, and later refrigeration, haddock became the Boston fleet's most actively sought bottom fish. Haddock prefer slightly warmer water than cod. They were rarely taken off Newfoundland or in the Gulf of St. Lawrence, but were numerous on Georges Bank.

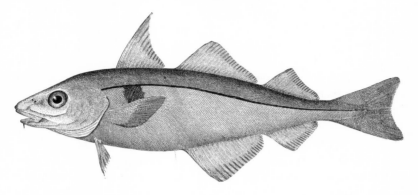

Haddock. *FFIUS*, sec. I: plate 59A.

halibut (Atlantic halibut): *Hippoglossus hippoglossus.* The largest of the flatfishes, Atlantic halibut are chocolate brown or slate brown on their eyed (upper) side, but white or blotched on their lower side. Halibut in unfished stocks could grow to 600 or 700 pounds. Halibut from 5 to 6 feet, ranging from 100 pounds to 200 pounds, were routinely taken. Halibut prefer sand, gravel, or clay bottoms, and were caught from Georges Bank or Nantucket Shoals to the Grand Banks of Newfoundland. Halibut are voracious feeders, preying mostly on fish (of many kinds), as well as on clams, lobsters, mussels, and occasionally even seabirds.

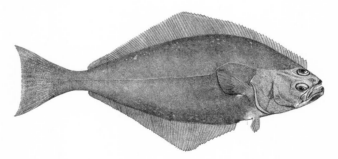

Halibut. *FFIUS*, sec. I: plate 54.

herring: *Clupea harengus.* The sea herring was the most commonly eaten fish in medieval Europe, but was not pursued on a similar scale in American or Canadian waters until the nineteenth century, when canning created a market for "sardines," as juvenile herring were called. Herring often were, and are, used for bait. Closely related to shad, hickory shad, alewives, and bluebacks, herring have prominent scales, silvery sides and bellies, and greenish-blue backs. A schooling fish, often congregating in huge schools, they are rarely seen individually. Herring grow to about 17 inches and weigh at most about 1½ pounds. They eat plankton.

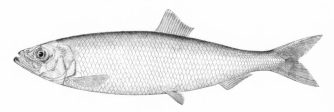

Herring. *FFIUS*, sec. I: plate 204.

jig: A hook with molten pewter or lead cast around its shank. **Mackerel** jigs were polished or shined to attract mackerel without bait. Fishermen made jigs in different sizes and weights so that they could select the best one for the conditions at hand. Jigs revolutionized the mackerel fishery circa 1815 to 1820. The illustration shows mackerel jigs and the molds used to cast them. **Cod** jigs were heavier and less elegant.

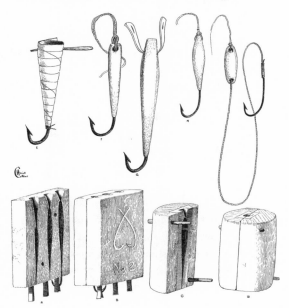

Jig. *FFIUS*, sec. V: plate 69.

jigging: A handline fishing technique in which the fisherman lowers the **jig** to the appropriate depth and twitches or jerks it up and down to attract fish. **Cod** fishermen lowered their jigs nearly to the bottom. **Mackerel** fishers kept theirs in the midst of the water column. The illustration shows mackerel jiggers in the mid-nineteenth century.

Jigging. *FFIUS*, sec. V: plate 70.

keystone species: A species playing a critical role in the structure of an ecological community; one with disproportionately large influence on its environment relative to its abundance. **Cod** was long a keystone species in the boreal North Atlantic.

longline: An apparatus for hookfishing consisting of a mainline to which shorter lines (called snoods) were attached at regular intervals. Each snood had one hook at its end. Longlines could be set on the bottom for fish such as **cod** or **halibut**. See also **bultow** and **tub-trawl.**

mackerel: *Scomber scombrus.* A fast, muscled, and predaceous **pelagic** fish, mackerel (like **herring** and bluefish) store fat in their muscles. Unlike **cod** and other **gadoids,** their flesh is relatively oily, so they could not be dried. Mackerel could, however, be preserved in a brine solution in barrels aboard a fishing boat or, if caught sufficiently close to port, be landed and sold fresh. Mackerel are beautiful fish, greenish-blue on their backs, with wavy tiger stripes on their upper bodies, silvery iridescence on their sides, and bellies of silvery white. Adult mackerel are generally 14 to 18 inches long and weigh about 1 to 1¼ pounds. Mackerel were typically encountered in dense schools. During the late nineteenth century they were American consumers' favorite fish.

Mackerel. *FFIUS*, sec. I: plate 91.

menhaden: *Brevoortia tyrannus*. Called "**pogy**" or "**porgy**" in Maine, but known by a host of nicknames farther south, including "bunker" and "mossbunker," menhaden are one of the most common fish in the North Atlantic. Members of the **herring** family, menhaden have huge, scaleless heads accounting for almost one-third of their length. Marked with a distinctive large spot on each side behind their gills, menhaden have other smaller spots contrasting with their blue-green or blue-gray upper coloring. Individual menhaden range from 12 to 15 inches. Like other herring, they always congregate in vast schools. Menhaden were valuable primarily for their oil and as bait, but not as food for humans. However, they are among the most important forage fish—for many predators—in the North Atlantic.

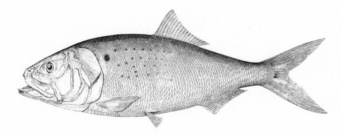

Menhaden. *FFIUS*, sec. I: plate 205.

Muscongus Bay boat: A small centerboard sloop, about 20 feet long, built in the area of Muscongus Bay and Penobscot Bay, Maine, during the middle of the nineteenth century. Later, as lobstering expanded to a year-round enterprise, the design was enlarged and built as a keelboat, becoming the familiar Friendship sloop.

Muscongus Bay boat. *FFIUS,* sec. V: plate 248.

otter trawl: A revolutionary form of fishing gear designed to be towed by a vessel and dragged along the bottom of the sea. Otter trawls had weighted footropes to keep them on the ground, and headropes with floats to keep the net open. They differed from beam trawls in that they were deployed from a bridle with offset doors on each end to spread the mouth of the net. Otter trawls were "active" gear: they scraped up everything in their path, in contrast to "passive" forms of gear, such as baited hooks, which relied on the fish coming to the gear. Otter trawls were difficult to fish, but extraordinarily productive. They created an avalanche of cheap fish in the early twentieth century, silencing several generations' concerns about depleted oceans.

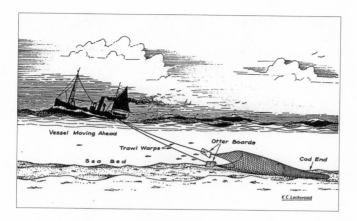

Otter trawl. John Dyson, *Business in Great Waters: The Story of British Fishermen* (London, 1977), 261.

peapod: A seaworthy double-ended boat, often 14 feet to 18 feet long, reminiscent of Viking ships. Peapods were rowed, and sometimes rigged with a simple sail. Penobscot Bay fishermen adopted them during the 1880s, and they became popular in the expanding lobster fishery.

Peapod. Detail from "Harbor, Round Pond, Maine," n.d., Eastern Collection, Penobscot Marine Museum, Searsport, Maine.

pelagic: Referring to the open sea, especially to water found neither near the shore nor close to the bottom, "pelagic" is often used as an adjective describing the conditions preferred by certain organisms. Pelagic birds include puffins, kittiwakes, and murres, which spend most of their lives at sea. Pelagic fish include **menhaden, mackerel,** and other species that live in the water column rather than on or near the seafloor.

pinkey: A simple **schooner**-rigged fishing boat, and the most common American fishing schooner during the first half of the nineteenth century. Fishermen joked that they were built with "a cod's head and a mackerel's tail," in other words, full forward and fine aft. Double-ended boats, they had a distinctive stern. This one has a **herring** net spread on the bowsprit.

Pinkey. *FFIUS*, sec. V: plate 117.

pogy, or **porgy:** Slang term for **menhaden.**

purse seine: An essentially rectangular net with floats on its headrope and weights on its footrope, the purse seine differed from other seines in that a rope passed through rings or blocks on its lower edge allowed a crew to gather the bottom edge of the net together, closing off escape for the encircled fish. The illustration here shows a bunched school of **mackerel** contained by the seine, which is being "pursed," or closed, by the men in the seine boat.

Purse seine. *FFIUS,* sec. V: plate 63.a

schooner: A sailing vessel with at least two masts, in which the mainmast is taller or both masts are of the same height. Typical American and Canadian fishing schooners had two masts and were gaff-rigged, as illustrated here.

Schooner. *FFIUS*, sec. V: plate 54.

sculpin: At least thirteen species of sculpins could be found in the Gulf of Maine. Sculpins have large spiny heads, numerous spiny fins, and a habit of grunting when molested. They range in size from 4 inches to 2 feet long. Most sculpins are omnivorous. Related to sea ravens, they had no commercial value except for occasional use as lobster bait, but were a commonly encountered spiny fish.

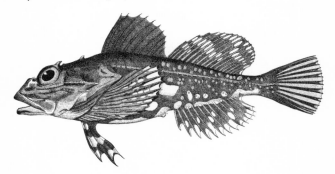

Sculpin. *FFIUS*, sec. I: plate 72B.

scup: *Stenotomus versicolor.* A schooling fish generally found no farther north than Cape Cod, scup typically were taken in traps or weirs along the cape, and as far south as Virginia or North Carolina. Individual adults are 12 to 14 inches, and 1 to 2 pounds.

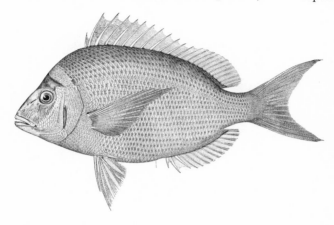

Scup. *FFIUS,* sec. I: plate 133.

smack: A generic term for a small fishing boat. Smacks could be rigged as sloops or schooners. By the early twentieth century, some smacks were motorized. Smacks could be used for transporting lobsters or fish or for catching them.

Smack. *Bulletin of the United States Fish Commission. Vol. XIX, for 1899* (Washington, D.C., 1901), plate 28.

smelt: *Osmerus mordax.* Smelt, close relatives of **capelin**, are another common forage fish in boreal North Atlantic ecosystems. Smelt are slender, about one foot long at their largest, but typically 7 to 9 inches. Schooling fish that live near shore, smelt spend all or most of their lives in estuaries. They live in saltwater but spawn in freshwater. Adult smelt congregate in harbors and estuaries in early autumn, where they are taken by hook. In places where tidal rivers freeze, they are often pursued by ice fishermen. Smelt range from eastern Labrador to New Jersey. Unlike some forage fish, such as **menhaden**, smelt are eagerly eaten by people.

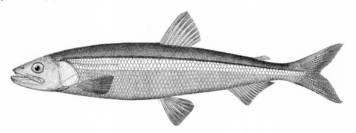

Smelt. *FFIUS*, sec. I: plate 199.

striped bass: *Roccus saxatilis.* Also known as "striper" and "rockfish," striped bass are a succulent and favorite eating fish. Bass can grow to more than 100 pounds. Usually, when landed, they range from 3 to 40 pounds. Governor William Bradford attributed the Pilgrims' survival to this fish, which arrives in the spring to spawn in freshwater. Known today primarily as a game fish or sport fish, striped bass were fished commercially so hard in New England and the mid-Atlantic region during the eighteenth century that they were almost exterminated. After imposition of diligent management and strict regulations, striped bass stocks rebounded very strongly at the end of the twentieth century.

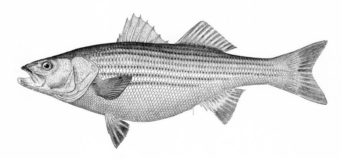

Striped bass. *FFIUS*, sec. I: plate 170.

tautog: *Tautoga onitis.* Known regionally as the "blackfish," tautog are stout dark fish ranging from blackish to chocolate gray. Their sides are irregularly blotched or mottled. Tautog rarely reach 3 feet; normally they are considerably shorter, and 2 to 4 pounds. A coastal-hugging fish, they feed primarily on invertebrates such as mussels. Found from Nova Scotia to South Carolina, they are most common between Cape Cod and Delaware Bay, but are relatively rare in the Gulf of Maine. Never numerous, but always delicious, they were eagerly sought when available.

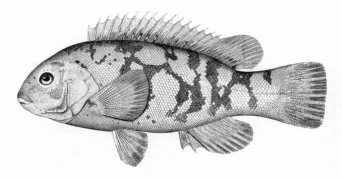

Tautog. *FFIUS*, sec. I: plate 85.

trawl (n.): A name used for several types of fishing gear, including the **beam trawl**, the **otter trawl**, the **tub-trawl** (also known as the **bultow** or **longline**), and a string of lobster pots.

trawl (v.): The action of catching fish with one of several types of gear. One could trawl for fish—as most nineteenth-century men understood it—by setting a **longline**. By the turn of the twentieth century, "trawling" increasingly came to mean towing a net across the bottom, using a **beam trawl** or an **otter trawl**. Nevertheless, the older meaning of the word (as in "tub-trawl" or "dory-trawl") continued to be used to refer to longline fishing until about 1940.

tub-trawl: A **longline** set on the bottom, with hooks at intervals of 10 or 12 feet. First introduced to the fishery in the mid-nineteenth century, fishermen called them "tub-trawls" because they were coiled in tubs. In the illustration, fishermen aboard a **schooner** are baiting their trawls (longlines) and coiling them in tubs prior to setting them from dories. A single tub-trawl, tended by two men in a **dory**, might have 400 to 600 hooks. See **dory-trawling**.

Tub-trawl. *FFIUS*, sec. V: plate 48.

weir: A kind of fish trap, or passive form of fishing gear, that depended on fish coming to it. Men built weirs by driving stakes or pilings into the bottom near the shore and stretching brush or netting between the stakes. In eastern Maine and New Brunswick, weirs were used primarily to catch **herring**. On Cape Cod, weir fishers caught many species, including **scup**, **tautog**, butterfish, squid, flounder, herring, and bluefish. Some weirs were very primitive; others, rather elaborate.

Weir. *FFIUS,* sec. V: plate 130.

well smack: This cutaway view of a well smack shows the wet well between the masts. Holes were drilled through the planking so seawater could circulate in the midships tank. In New England well smacks were used primarily to transport lobster, although other fisheries employed them when fishermen wished to bring live fish to market. The illustration shows a **halibut** well smack used on Georges Bank during the early 1840s.

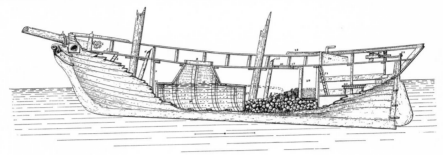

Well smack. *FFIUS*, sec. V: plate 4.

winter flounder: *Pseudopleuronectes americanus.* Also known as lemon sole, flounder, flatfish, and black flounder, the winter flounder is the darkest flatfish found in the Gulf of Maine. Common from the Straits of Belle Isle (between Labrador and Newfoundland) to the Chesapeake Bay, it is occasionally found as far south as Georgia, but generally in relatively shallow water. Rarely longer than 18 inches or heavier than 3 pounds, winter flounder have such weak mouths that they cannot be taken commercially by hooks. They became commercially important only after the development of beam trawls and otter trawls.

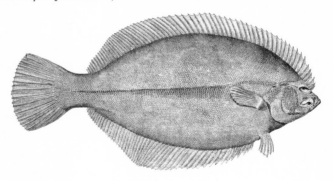

Winter flounder. *FFIUS*, sec. I: plate 44.

ACKNOWLEDGMENTS

It is a pleasure to thank the numerous people and institutions whose inspiration, encouragement, and assistance made this book possible. More than twenty years ago Richard C. Wheeler paddled his kayak on a solo voyage from Funk Island, Newfoundland, to Massachusetts, tracing the 1,500 mile route that great auks, the flightless North Atlantic "penguins," had paddled in their annual migrations. Auks have been extinct since 1844, a casualty of relentless overharvesting, but Wheeler felt their story might draw attention to the ongoing plight of North Atlantic ecosystems. As he later explained, fishermen in Newfoundland "led me farther than I expected. They had this intuitive sense that what they were doing was wrong and had been for a long time." *Time* magazine named Dick Wheeler a "hero of the planet" for his conservation work. He is an inspirational man who happens to be my father-in-law, and I have learned a lot from him over the years. As a historian, I was intrigued by his account of fishermen's sense of complicity, their notion that while they were bearing the brunt of the problem, they had actively contributed to it, and I wondered how deeply rooted a phenomenon that was.

I started teaching a course in marine environmental history at the University of New Hampshire. Shortly thereafter, by coincidence, the Alfred P. Sloan Foundation inaugurated the international Census of Marine Life, a visionary project to assess the diversity, distribution, and abundance of life in the oceans. One piece of that initiative concerned oceans past. Organized by Poul Holm, a Danish historian from the University of Southern Denmark, and Tim Smith, a fisheries scientist from NOAA's Northeast Fisheries Science Center, in Woods Hole, Massachusetts, the historical arm of the Census became known as the History of Marine Animal Populations (HMAP). Poul and Tim invited Andrew

A. Rosenberg, then Dean of Life Science and Agriculture at the University of New Hampshire (UNH), and me to establish an HMAP center. I am deeply indebted to the vision of the Census of Marine Life leaders, and feel fortunate to have played a role in both HMAP and the Census.

The interdisciplinary research group at UNH that Rosenberg and I formed became known as the Gulf of Maine Cod Project. Consisting of ecologists, statisticians, and historians—including faculty members, researchers, graduate students, and undergraduates—it evolved at the intersection of marine environmental history and historical marine ecology. I would not have been able to write this book without having been part of that extraordinary research group. Karen E. Alexander, a gifted researcher and writer who has degrees in both history and mathematics, and who had been one of my graduate students, became coordinator of the Gulf of Maine Cod Project. William B. Leavenworth, on whose doctoral dissertation committee I had served, became its chief researcher. I benefited immensely from their knowledge, insight, and hard work, as well as from grants and papers that our group wrote collaboratively. Leavenworth not only took the lead extracting data from nineteenth-century cod fishermen's logbooks, but also created electronic versions of historic fish commissioner reports from Maine and Massachusetts, thus assembling in one place an otherwise disparate set of records that were absolutely essential to my research. Other members of the Gulf of Maine Cod Project whose expertise contributed to my refashioning as an environmental historian include Andrew A. Rosenberg, Andrew B. Cooper (now at Simon Fraser University), Catherine Marzin (National Partnership Coordinator at NOAA's National Marine Sanctuary Program, and also a Ph.D. candidate at UNH), Matthew McKenzie (now at University of Connecticut, Avery Point), Stefan Claesson, Katherine Magness, and Emily Klein. A number of graduate students from the UNH History Department helped as research assistants. I want to thank Alison Mann, Jennifer Mandel, Lesley Rains, and Gwynna Smith. Joshua Minty, an undergraduate, also provided valuable research assistance.

The Gulf of Maine Cod Project received substantial funding from the Alfred P. Sloan Foundation; the National Science Foundation (HSD-0433497, 2004–2007); New Hampshire Sea Grant (four separate grants in 2002–2003, 2004–2006, 2006–2007, and 2010–2011); NOAA's Marine Sanctuary Program (Historical and Cultural Resources Grant 111814, 2004–2008); the Gordon and Betty Moore Foundation (2007); and the Richard Lounsbery Foundation (2009–2010). This study benefited from that generous support, as well as from the James H. Hayes and Claire Short Hayes Chair in the Humanities, which I held at UNH from 2002 to 2007, and from a UNH Center for the Humanities Senior Fellowship, which I received in 2008.

No researcher can thrive without the assistance of librarians and archivists. I thank the University of New Hampshire's Dimond Library staff, who helped time and time again: Louise Buckley and Peter Crosby from the reference desk; Bill Ross, head of Special Collections; and Linda Johnson and Thelma Thompson, who never were stumped by requests for obscure government documents. At the Massachusetts Historical Society, librarian Peter Drummey and his staff assisted me in numerous ways, as did Tom Hardiman and his staff at the Portsmouth Athenaeum, and Paul O'Pecko and his staff at Mystic Seaport's Blunt-White Library. Crucial research for this book was done at the Maine State Archives, the Maine Historical Society, the Maine State Library, the New Hampshire Historical Society, New Hampshire's Division of Archives and Records Management, the Massachusetts Archives, the Boston Athenaeum, the Northeast Fisheries Science Center Library in Woods Hole, Massachusetts, the Nova Scotia Archives, the Houghton Library and the Baker Business School Library at Harvard University, the Ernst Mayr Library at Harvard University's Museum of Comparative Zoology, the Peabody Essex Museum in Salem, Massachusetts, the Cape Ann Historical Society in Gloucester, Massachusetts, the libraries of the Smithsonian Institution, and the National Archives branches in College Park, Maryland, and Waltham, Massachusetts. Thanks to all.

As the book took shape, I benefited from the commitment and wise counsel of Molly Bolster, J. William Harris, Kurkpatrick Dorsey, James Sidbury, Jeremy B. C. Jackson, Daniel Vickers, Karen Alexander, and Bill Leavenworth, who critiqued the entire manuscript; and from members of the University of New Hampshire's History Department faculty seminar, who read sections of it. Ron Walters always has been available for advice. I hope he knows what that has meant to me. An article I published in the *American Historical Review* in 2008 elicited expert criticism from editors and reviewers. Sections of that article reappear in the Prologue and Chapters 1 and 2, and I thank Robert A. Schneider, editor of the *AHR,* for permission to reproduce them. Joyce Seltzer, who helped launch my first book years ago, has been an exemplary editor, and I feel fortunate to have been able to work with her again. I thank her capable assistant, Brian Distelberg, as well. He knows that the devil is in the details. A copy editor with an eagle eye, Ann Hawthorne saved me from myself in numerous places. I thank her and applaud her meticulousness. Melody Negron, the production editor, is overseeing the home stretch with thoroughness and professionalism. Thea Dickerman and Karen Alexander helped with the figures, and Philip Schwartzberg of Meridian Mapping created the wonderful maps. Many people helped with the illustrations, but I must single out Bill Bunting, expert nonpareil when it comes to nineteenth-century maritime photographs; and Elisabeth I. Ward (whom I have never met), from the University of California at Berkeley's Department of Scandinavian Studies. Elisabeth arranged use of the stunning photograph of the replica Viking ship *Íslendingur*. Thanks. As all of these friends and colleagues know, their assistance does not relieve me from full responsibility for errors of fact or interpretation.

Portsmouth, New Hampshire, where I live, was labeled "the old town by the sea" more than a century ago by a local author. It is a working seaport and fishing town, and an eminently walkable town. People here work hard on sustaining a sense of community, one nurtured by live music, great theatre, speakers' series, and community activism. I appreciate having been invited to speak about the issues at the heart of this book not just at academic conferences, but to my friends and neighbors in local land trusts, historical societies, neighborhood associations, libraries, and other organizations. Thanks for listening. Thanks, too, to the gang at Ceres Street Bakery, who have been making my lunch for years; to Breaking New Grounds, my favorite coffee shop; and to Win Rhoades and Claire Fleming, proprietors of South Street and Vine, the best wine shop in town.

I am lucky to have a family that has been my sheet anchor throughout this undertaking. My parents, Sally and Bill Bolster, to whom the book is dedicated, have remained my fans after all these years. My children, Ellie and Carl, have grown into remarkable young adults as I worked on this book. I am proud of them and their interests, and pleased that they had the opportunity over many summers to spend hundreds of days and nights sailing the Gulf of Maine with their mother and me. There is magic beyond the shore, beneath the sea, and throughout the island chain that defines the coast of Maine, and we have shared it together. The lion's share of my appreciation, however, goes to Molly, my wife and sounding board, and an activist who understands more than most the stewardship challenges we face. She has provided inspiration, encouragement, and assistance. Saying "thanks" simply cannot convey what I owe her, but it is a start. Thanks.

INDEX

Abenakis, 49–50, 79, 85

Acadia, 69–70

Account of Two Voyages to New England
(Josselyn), 93–94

Ada (schooner), 118

Advertisements, 228, 231, 270

Agassiz, Louis, 88, 117, 118, 119

Alcidae family of seabirds, 26, 83

Alewives: settlers' use of, 51–52; used
as fertilizer, 54; and fishing weirs,
56–57; conservation concerns,
58–59; depletion of, 81–82;
stocking of, 112

Alexander, A. B., 259

Alfonso XI, King, 32

Alice (schooner), 185, 194

Allerton, Isaac, 63

Alward, G. L., 236

American Academy of Arts and Sciences,
96, 98

American Fisheries Company, 219–220

"Americanization" of U.S. fishing fleet,
273–274

Anadromous fish: described, 23;
depletion of, 33–34, 80–82, 87;
alewives, 51–52, 54, 58, 81–82; Gulf
of Maine watershed and fishing
weirs, 57; Massachusetts Bay food

chains and cod fishery, 66–67;
sturgeon, 76–79; striped bass, 79–80

Archer, Gabriel, 40, 46

Aries (steam trawler), 237

Arrow worms, 19, 21

Artimon Bank, 133

Atkins, Charles G., 156

Atlantic Fisherman, 262, 270

Atlantic gray whales, 72

Atwood, Nathaniel, 104, 115–117, 118,
195, 206

Audubon, John James, 84

Auks: Norse harvest of, 26; Gulf of St.
Lawrence colonies, 36; great auks,
83, 84; used as bait, 83, 84; extinction of, 84, 109; nesting habits, 84

Baird, Spencer F., 149, 153, 155, 158, 160,
161, 167, 174, 180–181, 188, 191, 211, 237

Bait: auks used as bait, 83, 84; bait mills,
105; and mackerel fishery, 105, 145;
menhaden used as bait, 114, 126–128,
130, 131, 146–149; cod fishery and
tub-trawling, 137; seabirds used
as bait, 143; and criticism of U.S.
fishing regulations, 157–158;
expansion of bait fisheries, 165;
lobster fishery, 207